Mediated Intimacies

Social media platforms, characterized by user-generated content, interactivity, participation and community formation, have gained much research attention in recent years. At the same time, intimacy, affectivity and emotions are increasingly growing as fields of study. While these two areas are often interwoven, the actual interconnections are rarely studied in detail. This anthology explores how social media construct new types of intimacies, and how practices of intimacy shape the development and use of new media, offering empirical knowledge, theoretical insights and an international perspective on the flourishing field of digital intimacies.

Chapters present a range of research tools used, such as interviews, online ethnography, visual analysis, text analysis and video analysis. There is also rich variation in sources for the empirical material studied, including Tumblr, YouTube, dating sites, hook-up sites, Facebook, Snapchat, CouchSurfing, selfies, blogs and photographs, as well as smartphones, tablets and computers.

By focusing on the intersection between social media and intimacies, and their continuous co-constitution, this anthology offers new insights into the vast landscape of contemporary media reality. It will be a valuable resource for teachers, students and scholars with an interest in new media, communication, intimacy and affectivity.

Rikke Andreassen, PhD from University of Toronto, Canada (2005), Professor (mso) in Communication Studies at Roskilde University, Denmark. She is a researcher and teacher in the fields of media, gender, race and sexuality. She has recently published the book *Human Exhibitions: Race, Gender and Sexuality in Ethnic Displays* (2015), as well as co-edited the anthology *Race and Affectivity: Studies from a Nordic Context* (2015).

Michael Nebeling Petersen, PhD, Associate Professor, Department for the Study of Culture, University of Southern Denmark. His research centres on culture, power and identity, and he is interested in the intersections between gender, sexuality, kinship, race and nation. His recent publications include: 'Becoming Gay Fathers through Transnational Commercial Surrogacy' in *Journal of Family Studies* (2016) and 'Dad & daddy assemblages: Re-suturing the nation through transnational surrogacy, homosexuality, and Norwegian exceptionalism' in *GLQ* (with Kroløkke and Myong, 2016).

Katherine Harrison, postdoc at the Department of Media, Cognition and Communication, University of Copenhagen, Denmark, and a researcher at the Department of Gender Studies, Lund University, Sweden. Her areas of expertise include feminist cultural studies of technoscience with particular reference to digital technologies, science and technology studies and normcritical perspectives on gender and the body.

Tobias Raun, Associate Professor of Communication Studies, Roskilde University. He has published widely within the areas of visual culture, internet studies, cultural studies and gender studies, most recently the book *Out Online: Trans Self-Representation and Community Building on YouTube* (2016) and a forthcoming publication on transgender selfies in the edited collection *Sex in the Digital Age* (2017).

Routledge Studies in European Communication Research and Education

Edited by Claudia Alvares, Lusofona University, Portugal; Ilija Tomanić Trivundža, University of Ljubljana, Slovenia and Fausto Colombo, Università Cattolica del Sacro Cuore, Milan, Italy

Series Advisory Board: Nico Carpentier, François Heinderyckx, Denis McQuail, Robert Picard and Jan Servaes

ECREA

http://www.ecrea.eu

Published in association with the European Communication Research and Education Association (ECREA), books in the series make a major contribution to the theory, research, practice and/or policy literature. They are European in scope and represent a diversity of perspectives. Book proposals are refereed.

8. **Public Service Media in Europe**
A Comparative Approach
Edited by Karen Arriaza Ibarra, Eva Nowak and Raymond Kuhn

9. **European Media in Crisis**
Values, Risks and Policies
Edited by Josef Trappel, Jeanette Steemers and Barbara Thomass

10. **Digital Photography and Everyday Life**
Empirical studies on material visual practices
Edited by Edgar Gómez Cruz and Asko Lehmuskallio

11. **Gender Equality and the Media**
A Challenge for Europe
Edited by Karen Ross and Claudia Padovani

12. **Public Policies in Media and Information Literacy in Europe**
Cross Country Comparisons
Edited by Divina Frau-Meigs, Irma Velez and Julieta Flores-Michel

13. **Mediated Intimacies: Connectivities, Relationalities and Proximities**
Edited by Rikke Andreassen, Michael Nebeling Petersen, Katherine Harrison, Tobias Raun

https://www.routledge.com/Routledge-Studies-in-European-Communication-Research-and-Education/book-series/ECREA

Mediated Intimacies

Connectivities, Relationalities and Proximities

Edited by Rikke Andreassen,
Michael Nebeling Petersen,
Katherine Harrison and Tobias Raun

Routledge
Taylor & Francis Group
LONDON AND NEW YORK

First published 2018
by Routledge
2 Park Square, Milton Park, Abingdon, Oxon OX14 4RN

and by Routledge
711 Third Avenue, New York, NY 10017

Routledge is an imprint of the Taylor & Francis Group, an informa business

British Library Cataloguing-in-Publication Data
A catalogue record for this book is available from the British Library

Library of Congress Cataloging-in-Publication Data
A catalog record for this book has been requested

ISBN: 978-1-138-63186-1 (hbk)
ISBN: 978-1-138-63187-8 (pbk)
ISBN: 978-1-315-20858-9 (ebk)

Typeset in Sabon
by Saxon Graphics Ltd, Derby

Contents

Figures

Contributors

Rikke Andreassen, PhD from University of Toronto, Canada (2005), Professor (mso) in Communication Studies at Roskilde University, Denmark. She is a researcher and teacher in the fields of media, gender, race and sexuality. She has recently published the book *Human Exhibitions. Race, Gender and Sexuality in Ethnic Displays* (2015), as well as co-edited the anthology *Race and Affectivity. Studies from a Nordic Context* (2015).

Claire Balleys, PhD, Postdoctoral Researcher, Departement of Social and Public Communication, Université du Québec à Montréal, Canada. Claire Balleys is a sociologist who studies adolescence and digital social practices. She works on the relationship between social representations of intimacy and socialization, in particular between peers. Her research is on the observable links between teenagers' online practices, sociability, identity construction and gender expression. Her current research project is about gender performance on YouTube.

Christine Beasley, Professor in Politics, and from 2009–2013 Co-Director of the Fay Gale Centre for Research on Gender, at the University of Adelaide. Her books include, among others, *Heterosexuality in Theory and Practice* (with Heather Brook and Mary Holmes, 2012), *Gender & Sexuality: Critical Theories, Critical Thinkers* (2005), and *What is Feminism?* (1999). She is currently completing two co-authored books titled *The Cultural Politics of Popular Film: Power, Culture and Society* (forthcoming) and *Internet Dating* (2018).

Marco Bohr, Postgraduate Programme Director for the Arts at Loughborough University. In 2011 Bohr was awarded a PhD from the University of Westminster for a theoretical thesis that investigates contemporary Japanese photography. Before he joined Loughborough University in 2012, Bohr was Visiting Fellow at The Australian National University in Canberra where he taught photography theory and practice. In 2017 Marco was JSPS Postdoctoral Fellow at Ritsumeikan University in Kyoto. With Dr Basia Sliwinska he co-edited the forthcoming book *The Evolution of the Image: Political Action and the Digital Self*.

Rita Brito holds a degree in early childhood education, a PhD in educational technology and a post-doctoral research on the use of technologies by families and children up to 6 years old. She is a researcher at the Institute of Education, University of Lisbon, lecturing at the Lisbon College of Education, Polytechnic Institute of Lisbon in early childhood education Master and also supervises Master student internships in kindergarten. Her research focuses on the use of technology by children under 6 years old and elderly people. Rita has published several articles in national and international journals, as well as various book articles.

Sarah R. Davies, Associate Professor at the Department of Media, Cognition and Communication, University of Copenhagen. Her background is in Science and Technology Studies and her research focuses on the relationship between science and society, for instance within science communication, public engagement with science, and amateur science. Amongst other writing, she is the author of *Science Communication: Culture, Identity, Citizenship* (with Maja Horst, 2016) and *Hackerspaces: Making the Maker Movement* (2017).

Patrícia Dias, Assistant Professor of the Faculty of Human Sciences at the Catholic University of Portugal. She is also a postdoctoral researcher at the Research Centre for Communication and Culture, and coordinator of the post-graduate course on Communication and Social Media. Holding a PhD in Communication Sciences, her research interests are digital media, young children, mobile communication, marketing and public relations. Dias is author of *Living in the Digital Society* (2014) and *The Mobile Phone and Daily Life* (2008).

John Nguyet Erni, Chair Professor in Humanities and Head of the Department of Humanities & Creative Writing at Hong Kong Baptist University. Erni has published widely on international and Asia-based cultural studies, human rights legal criticism, Chinese consumption of transnational culture, gender and sexuality in media culture, youth consumption culture in Hong Kong and Asia, and critical public health. He is the author or editor of nine books, most recently *Visuality, Emotions, and Minority Culture: Feeling Ethnic* (2017); *(In)visible Colors: Images of Non-Chinese in Hong Kong Cinema – A Filmography, 1970s–2010s* (with Louis Ho, 2016); *Understanding South Asian Minorities in Hong Kong* (with Lisa Leung, 2014).

Debra Ferreday, Senior Lecturer in Sociology at Lancaster University. Her research centres on the affective cultural politics of digital and screen media, with a particular interest in questions of gender, sexuality and embodiment. She is the author of *Online Belongings* and co-editor of *Hope and Feminist Theory*. She is currently working on a research project entitled *Screening Rape*, which explores the complex relationship between media, mediation and sexual violence across a diverse range of platforms including film, television, internet and social media.

Florencia García-Rapp, MA., PhD Candidate, Department of Communication, Pompeu Fabra University, Barcelona, Spain. She holds a Master's Degree in Media Culture from Paderborn University in Germany and a Degree in Audiovisual Communication obtained in her homeland, Argentina. Her doctoral thesis examines YouTube's beauty community and the role of beauty gurus as online celebrities. Her broader research interests lie at the intersections of digital and celebrity culture with audience and fandom research.

Katherine Harrison, postdoc at the Department of Media, Cognition and Communication, University of Copenhagen, Denmark, and a researcher at the Department of Gender Studies, Lund University, Sweden. Her areas of expertise include feminist cultural studies of technoscience with particular reference to digital technologies, Science and Technology Studies and normcritical perspectives on gender and the body.

Larissa Hjorth, artist, digital ethnographer, Distinguished Professor and Director of the Design & Creative Practice ECP platform at RMIT University. Hjorth's books include *Screen Ecologies* (with Pink, Sharp & Williams, 2016), *Digital Ethnography* (Pink et al., 2016), *Mobile Media in the Asia-Pacific* (2009), *Games & Gaming* (2010), *Online@AsiaPacific* (with Arnold, 2013), *Understanding Social Media* (with Hinton, 2013), and *Gaming in Locative, Social and Mobile Media* (with Richardson, 2014).

Mary Holmes, Senior Lecturer in the Sociology Department at the University of Edinburgh. Her research is on emotions, intimacy and relationships and besides *Sociology for Optimists* (2016) her recent books include *Distance Relationships: Intimacy and Emotions Amongst Academics and their Partners In Dual-Locations* (2014) and *Heterosexuality in Theory and Practice* (with Chris Beasley and Heather Brook, 2014).

Jette Kofoed, PhD, Associate Professor, Department of Education, University of Aarhus, Denmark. Kofoed is originally trained within minority research and her research focuses on technologically mediated processes of inclusion and exclusion among children and young people in education. She is particularly interested in how social media intertwines with offline processes and how such processes are highly affective. Recent publications include: 'Suspended liminality: Vacillating affects in cyberbullying/ research', in *Theory and Psychology* (with P. Stenner, 2017) and 'A snap of intimacy. Photo-sharing practices among young people on social media', in *First Monday* (with M.C. Larsen, 2016).

Caroline Wamala Larsson, PhD, Senior Lecturer, Karlstad University, Sweden. Located in the Gender and Technology discipline, her research acknowledges the mutual construction of gender and technology, contributing a deeper understanding of the cultural embeddedness of technology. She also contributes to the practical development of

Information, Communication Technologies for Development as a Programme Manager with the Swedish Program for ICT in Developing Regions. Latest publications include: *Mobile Participation: Access, Interaction and Practices* (edited with Schraff and Hellström, 2015) and Mobile phones practices among market women in Kampala, in *Mobile Media & Communication* (2016).

Amparo Lasén, Professor of Sociology and member of the research group Sociología Ordinaria at the University Complutense de Madrid. Her research focuses on the social implications of the usages, practices and presence of ICTs especially in relationship with affectivity, the configuration of contemporary subjectivities and intimacies and everyday life. Prior to her current position, she was the Vodafone Surrey Scholar at the DWRC of Surrey University, where she conducted cross-cultural research on mobile phone uses and practices. She has been academic visitor at the Department of Sociology of the LSE and researcher of the Centre d'Études de l'Actuel et du Quotidien, Paris V-La Sorbonne.

Sun Sun Lim, Professor of Media and Communication and Head of Humanities, Arts and Social Sciences at the Singapore University of Technology and Design. She studies the social implications of technology domestication by young people and families, charting the ethnographies of their Internet and mobile phone use, publishing more than 50 books, articles and book chapters. Her latest books include *Mobile Communication and the Family – Asian Experiences in Technology Domestication* (2016) and *Asian Perspectives on Digital Culture: Emerging Phenomena, Enduring Concepts* (2016).

Maarten Michielse, PhD, works as a lecturer and researcher at Maastricht University, The Netherlands. He studies the interrelation between digital media, popular music and participatory cultures. He has done virtual ethnographic research on online remix, cover and mashup practices, with a special focus on the ways in which participants collectively develop and exchange musical and technical skills. His publications include: 'Musical chameleons: Fluency and flexibility in online remix contests', *M/C Journal* (2013) and 'Producing a meaningful difference: The significance of small creative acts in composing within online participatory remix practices', in *The International Journal of Community Music* (with Heidi Partti, 2015).

Cristina Miguel, PhD, Leeds Beckett University. Miguel has researched and published about issues related to intimacy practices, self-presentation, self-disclosure and privacy on social media. Her main research focuses on 'Intimacy in the age of social media'. She has also participated in the research project 'Social media monitoring and the social media industries' sponsored by HEIF V funding, where she co-authored the article 'On fairness: User perspectives on social media data mining', in *Convergence*. Another recent publication is 'Visual intimacy on social media: From selfies to the co-construction of intimacies through shared pictures', in *Social Media + Society.*

Kristian Møller, PhD, Part-time Lecturer at the Department of Communication and Arts, Roskilde University. His PhD thesis draws on critical mediatization and intimacy theory to conceptualize the ways in which hook-up apps transform gay men's social and sexual lives. Currently he is researching gay men's medicalized and mediatized sex practices, as both HIV-preventing medicine and new 'sex drugs' enter into sexual scenes. Recent works include: 'The media go-along: Researching mobilities with media at hand' (2016) and '"Boundary crossing, backstabbing opportunist": Practice based ethics as intimate boundary work' (2016, in Danish).

Michael Nebeling Petersen, PhD, Associate Professor, Department for the Study of Culture, University of Southern Denmark. His research centres on culture, power and identity, and he is interested in the intersections between gender, sexuality, kinship, race and nation. His recent publications include: 'Becoming gay fathers through transnational commercial surrogacy', in *Journal of Family Studies* (2016) and 'Dad & daddy assemblages: Re-suturing the nation through transnational surrogacy, homosexuality, and Norwegian exceptionalism', in *GLQ* (with Kroløkke and Myong, 2016).

Louise Yung Nielsen, Postdoc, University of Copenhagen. Yung Nielsen has a background in youth studies and media studies with a particular interest in media and bodies. Currently Yung Nielsen is studying gamers on YouTube with a particular interest in affective and cultural labour. Yung Nielsen is teaching within the broad field of media studies.

Susanna Paasonen, Professor of Media Studies at University of Turku, Finland. With an interest in studies of sexuality, popular culture, affect and media theory, she is currently co-authoring a volume on the uses of the hashtag #NSFW and exploring the dynamics of distraction, boredom and frustration connected to social media. She is most recently the author of *Carnal Resonance: Affect and Online Pornography* (2011) as well as co-editor of *Working with Affect in Feminist Readings: Disturbing Differences* (2010) and *Networked Affect* (2015).

Lin Prøitz, Researcher at Dept of Psychology, Uni of Oslo, holds a PhD on the topic of mobile telephone practices among youths in Gender and Media Science from Uni of Oslo (2007). Prøitz' publications include *Visual social media and affectivity* (2017); *Selvbilde: fra selvportrett til #selfie/ Self-image: from self-portrait to #selfie (2016)* and *Kids Code in a rural village in Norway* (with Corneliussen, 2016). Prøitz was originally educated as a photographer.

Tobias Raun, Associate Professor of Communication Studies, Roskilde University. He has published widely within the areas of Visual Culture,

Internet Studies, Cultural Studies and Gender Studies, most recently the book *Out Online: Trans Self-Representation and Community Building on YouTube* (2016) and a forthcoming publication on transgender selfies in the edited collection *Sex in the Digital Age* (2017).

Basia Sliwinska, PhD, Senior Lecturer in Cultural and Historical Studies at the University of the Arts in London. Her research is situated within feminist art history and critical theory and focuses on concepts of the body, activism, gender and citizenship within contemporary women's art practice. Recent publications include: *The Female Body in the Looking-Glass. Contemporary Art, Aesthetics and Genderland* (with I.B. Tauris, 2016).

Yang Wang, PhD Candidate at the Department of Communications and New Media, National University of Singapore. Her research interests focus on technology domestication by transnational households, digital media use and gender identity, as well as everyday politics of Chinese netizens. Her current research project delves into the domestication of information and communication technologies by Chinese 'study mothers' (peidu mama) in Singapore.

Eva Zekany, PhD in Gender Studies at Central European University, Budapest. Her research interests include biopolitics, philosophy of media and feminist game studies.

Yin Zhang, Research Assistant Professor in the School of Communication at Hong Kong Baptist University. His research focuses on social and psychological impacts of new media, with a special interest in social media and online network studies. He is currently working on a few projects related to social media uses by youth and social minority groups, social capital and poverty.

Introduction

Mediated intimacies

Michael Nebeling Petersen, Katherine Harrison, Tobias Raun and Rikke Andreassen

New media technologies and platforms are increasingly intersecting and intertwining with our daily lives, our bodily and intimate practices and our relationships. People find partners via hook-up and dating apps such as Tinder and Grindr, parents rely on digital media to educate their children, teenagers broadcast their intimate bedroom performances via YouTube, activists organise protests on Facebook and Tumblr facilitates new ways of connecting and shaping subcultural identities and communities. Politics, activism, family life, dating and other forms of intimacy are increasingly facilitated and moulded by digital media technologies and platforms, and it has become almost impossible to separate these forms of living and relating from their diverse forms of mediation.

This book deals with social media and technologies of digital socialities, with a particular emphasis on intimacies. We find that intimacy deserves particular attention with regards to social media because of the overwhelming presence of 'intimate moments shared for all to see' (Garde-Hansen and Gorton, 2013, p. 60). One might argue that social media is inherently designed to emphasise and facilitate intimate practices and connections – the nature of which affect the form and content of the media through which these practices are performed. Both the architecture of online spaces and the etiquette of behaving within these spaces tend to favour the dense proliferation of intimacies with others (Payne, 2014, p. 2). Furthermore, the commercialisation of social media sites and applications relies upon and has profited immensely from their ability to facilitate intimacy. As van Dijck states: 'While the first half decade gave rise to user communities embracing the web's potential for collaboration and connectedness, after 2006, the word "social" came to mean: technologically manageable and economically exploitable' (van Dijck, 2013, np.).

Media scholars Kember and Zylinska argue that 'our relationality and our entanglement with non-human entities continues to intensify with the ever more corporeal, ever more intimate dispersal of media and technologies into our biological and social lives' (Kember and Zylinska, 2015, p. xv). The chapters of this book illustrate that mediation is a fundamental part of the human condition and always has been; but the intensification identified by

Kember and Zylinska emphasises the particular importance of intimacy in our contemporary time. We continue to be increasingly related through and connected by media and technologies, which influence a greater part of our social and intimate lives. In light of this, attention to the co-constitution and connection of social media and intimacy seems more relevant and needed than ever before.

'Old' and 'new' media and mediation

While humans have always been intimately connected with media and technologies, the intensification of media in our intimate lives, combined with the development of online media platforms, has resulted in increased scholarly attention to the distinction between 'new' and 'old' media. This distinction has long been a trope in media theory, but recent scholarship shows a move away from a clear distinction towards an emphasis on the 'long standing social needs to account, reflect, communicate, and share with others using media of the times' (Humphreys et al., 2013, abstract). Instead of interpreting contemporary social media as completely new and different from former kinds of communication, one can argue that engagement with contemporary social media constitutes a continuation of previous uses of media. For example, online activism using hashtagging can be seen as a continuation of the use of media such as stickers and flyers to protest and connect in public spaces. Similarly, microblogging on Twitter or regular blogging can be understood as broadly similar to the practice of writing diaries and letters in the eighteenth and nineteenth centuries. These activities, and many others like them, can be interpreted as constituting a continuous need for and process of communicating about the self (Humphreys et al., 2013; van Dijck, 2007).

There are powerful reasons to investigate media objects as part of a longer process of mediation. Understanding digital media as part of a much bigger trajectory of mediation can facilitate nuanced analysis. Rather than studying media as isolated objects – which risks temporally categorising media as either 'old' or 'new', and thereby foreclosing the possibility of understanding continuing patterns of mediation – studying media through a historical perspective facilitates better understanding. Thus, in this anthology, we emphasise media uses and networks rather than media objects in and of themselves. We understand media objects to be situated within a broader pattern of human communication and interactions.

By titling this book *Mediated Intimacies*, we draw on the concept of mediation to conceptualise the ongoing entanglement of humans and media technologies. In using 'mediate' rather than 'media' in the title, we seek to align ourselves with a school of thought that sees mediation as an active process of doing and becoming, in and through media technologies (Deuze, 2012; Hillis et al., 2015; Kember and Zylinska, 2015; McGlotten, 2013; Paasonen, 2011). Indeed, social media 'are designed by, and entangled in, physical world social practices' (Tierney, 2013, p. 77). In other words, social media should not be understood as distinct from our lives or as passive, pre-existing channels through which we transmit ourselves and establish social connections; rather, social media are integrated parts of our lives. To paraphrase Deuze: we live *in* media, rather than *with* media (Deuze, 2011, p. 138). Or, as noted by Jose van Dijck, in the 'culture of connectivity', connections are determined as much by technology (through algorithms or platform architecture) as by users; thus, the meaning of 'social' in social media encompasses both human connectedness and automated connectivity (van Dijck, 2013, pp. 11–12).

In this volume, therefore, we use 'mediation' to conceptualise the process of co-constitution – or the mutual shaping of humans and media technologies – which implies that humans are always already performed through technologies. Elaborating on this, Kember and Zylinska state:

> we human users of technology are not entirely distinct from our tools. *They* are not a means to *our* ends; instead, they have become part of us, to an extent that the us/them distinction is no longer tenable. As we modify and extend 'our' technologies and 'our' media, we modify and extend ourselves and our environment.
>
> (2015, p. 13, emphasis in original)

Researching social media through the lens of mediation moves the analysis away from a focus on discrete media objects or media use, towards the ongoing entanglement of media and user as a fundamental part of the human condition. Although apparently stable media objects or coherent bodies of users emerge at particular times and places, they represent only temporary materialisations of this ongoing process of mediation (Kember and Zylinska, 2015, p. 21). Following this, the anthology shows how social media and intimacy function in a 'feedback loop': social media offer new ways to do intimacy, and, in turn, new practices of intimacy shape the development and uses of social media (Schofield, 2009). What is explored in many of the chapters is how practices and understandings of intimacy are both embedded in digitally mediated communication and generate innovative uses of new media.

Intimacy

Intimacy is a familiar concept. It rings a bell, though most people would find it difficult to define precisely. We instinctively know what intimacy is and feels like. Often connected with close relations between family members, partners and friends, intimacy is commonly considered to involve shared emotions, experiences and/or affective bodily proximities. It is typically viewed as a positive goal for a relationship, just as the 'value' of a relationship can be measured according to the level of intimacy achieved between participants. As noted in our opening paragraphs, it is perhaps no surprise, then, that intimacy is deeply interlinked and intertwined with social media, as the characteristics associated with intimacy seem inherent in the structure of social media: both intimacy and social media allow people to express and share what matters to them, and both encourage personalised connection and interactivity. Furthermore, intimacy has traditionally been understood in relation to a distinction between 'private' and 'public': practices of intimacy have been considered to belong within the 'private sphere', as have personal relationships associated with the family and the home (Chambers, 2013, pp. 41–42).

Throughout this anthology, intimacy is theorised and examined in relation to media. In the theorisations of intimacy, contributors are informed by two lines of thought, which are also present in the broader scholarship of intimacy. One strand stems from social science – especially sociology – while the other is connected to cultural studies and the humanities. In this section, we will elaborate on these two related yet different schools of intimacy theory.

The first line of thought, exemplified by Ken Plummer's (2003) work, investigates intimacy historically by examining the way in which relationships associated with intimacy have evolved, developing from traditional intimacies carried out in proximity to local communities and families to modern or late modern intimacies, characterised by relationships of choice (ibid., p. 9). Plummer attributes these changes to the societal developments of industrialisation. These developments were followed by urbanisation, which caused a number of individuals to break with former family traditions in relation to work and place of living, as well as the formation of partnerships, marriage and family. Most importantly, industrialisation led to increasing individualisation, which became mirrored in practices of intimacy and intimacy relations. Within this line of thought, the development of intimate relations is interpreted as a positive progression narrative. Contemporary intimacy is often analysed as an illustration of how an individual negotiates her/his close relations or investigates his/her self-reflection in relation to close relationships and narratives of identity (Plummer, 2003; Weeks, 1998).

The second line of thought, exemplified by the work of Lauren Berlant (1998, 2008), analyses intimacy as a normative and regulatory narrative. Departing from feminist deconstruction of the distinction between 'private' and 'public' (see, e.g., Yuval-Davis, 1997), Berlant argues that intimacy travels from 'public' institutions, ideologies and regulations to 'private' fantasies, desires and life goals, and vice versa (Berlant, 1998, pp. 3–4). To her, the public sphere is characterised by intimacy; that is, genres of intimacy (found in, e.g., self-help books or television talk shows) are consumed by individuals who, through their consumption, experience recognition and a sense of belonging (Berlant, 2008, p. viii). In this way, intimacy can be interpreted as a form of a script – one that does not emerge from the individual but is the result of the private and intimate negotiation of cultural norms and regulations.

Of the many volumes that examine social media, a handful attempt to think through media and intimacy. These can be loosely divided between those that follow the first line of thought on intimacy and those that follow the second. Amongst the authors who draw on Plummer's work is Deborah Chambers, who specifically addresses 'mediated intimacies'. Following Giddens (and Plummer), Chambers idealistically argues that intimacy has been de-traditionalised and democratised (Chambers, 2013, pp. 43–44). Intimacy is no longer perceived as restricted to heterosexual relationships and blood-related kinship, but has been diversified to include non-conventional partnerships as well as chosen ties and elected affinities (ibid., p. 48). In her reading, social media plays a significant role by offering greater possibilities for intimate contacts based on personal choice and individual control (ibid., p. 165). As she argues: 'The technological affordances of social media match aspirations towards the *pure relationship* by allowing a sense of control over the relationship, uncluttered by power and privilege' (ibid., p. 167). Self-disclosure has, in this regard, become an important marker of intimacy and trust, and hence the engine that drives new relationships (ibid., pp. 46–47). In this vein, Chambers underscores the importance and significance of social media as fora for the disclosure and display of emotions (ibid., p. 47). Intimacy, which has been traditionally based on exclusive access to events and information, has now been reconstructed as 'network intimacy', with friendship serving as both the common label and the privileged form of intimate relations (ibid., pp. 48, 165). Thus, Chambers argues that intimacy has been reframed 'beyond as well as within family and the private sphere to include friendships and the public spheres', thus challenging distinctions between former notions of 'public' and 'private' (ibid., p. 58).

Amongst those who follow the second line of thought, Shaka McGlotten is worth noting, particularly with respect to his 2013 volume, *Virtual Intimacies, Media, Affect, and Queer Sociality*. In line with the work of Berlant, McGlotten describes virtual intimacy as 'contacts and encounters, from the ephemeral to the enduring, made possible by digital and networked means', emphasising intimacy as 'a vast assemblage of ideologies, institutional sites, and diverse sets of material and semiotic practices that exerts normative pressures on large and small bodies, lives, and worlds' (McGlotten, 2013, pp. 7, 1). Hence, intimacy is emphasised (then and now) as scripted, supported by a range of discourses and practices (ibid., p. 9). Social media is here claimed to offer access to new kinds of pleasure and a certain level of freedom in relation to identity and sexuality, while at the same time maintaining some sociocultural norms and restrictions (ibid., p. 2). As McGlotten argues, both virtual intimacy and queer intimacy are often conceived of as failed or unsuccessful versions of 'real' or 'proper' intimacy, with virtual intimacies perceived of as 'failed intimacies that disrupt the flow of a good life lived right, a life that involves coupling and kids, or at least, coupling and consumption' and queer intimacies as 'pale imitations or ugly corruptions of the real deal – monogamously partnered, procreative, married, straight intimacy' (ibid., p. 7).

Turning now to this anthology, it is possible to organise some of the chapters according to the above distinction. The chapters that are informed by the first line of thought – that is, the sociological approach that associates contemporary intimacy with individual choice and progress (e.g. Balleys; García-Rapp; Miguel; Wang and Lim; Zhang and Erni) – typically investigate the way in which individuals disclose emotions and personal relations online, or how online self-expressions lead to and negotiate intimacies. In contrast, those chapters that take as inspiration the other line of thought – that is, the humanist approach to intimacy as a regulatory narrative (e.g. Beasley et al.; Ferreday; Kofoed; Møller and Nebeling Petersen; Raun) – analyse the way in which intimacies foster belongings and regulate identities and interactions, as well as how 'private' notions of intimacy circulate in and transform publics. Of course, the division between the two lines of thought is to some extent artificial, as exemplified by the chapters that draw on both sets of thinking (e.g. Andreassen; Michielse; Prøitz et al.). Furthermore, a number of chapters (e.g. Brito and Dias; Davies; Paasonen; Yung Nielsen) investigate the way in which users become intimately connected with the technology they use. Here, intimacy becomes a way of understanding the relations between subjectivity and technology; intimacy occurs at the intersection of bodies and technologies, where the subject becomes and takes form.

Traditionally, intimacies have been associated with physical proximity and have involved 'practices of close association, familiarity and privileged knowledge, strong positive emotional attachments, such as love, and a very particular form of "closeness" and being "special" to another person, associated with high levels of trust' (Jamieson, 2005, p. 189). This understanding is challenged in several of the chapters, which question the assumption that anonymity and physical distance hinder intimacy; these chapters, in diverse ways, illustrate constructions of intimacy in situations in which individuals who are not familiar with one another, and across distances, create feelings of intimacy and engage in intimate practices with one another. In some situations, it is precisely this distance and anonymity that enable these online practices of intimacy and mediated proximity. Despite the fact that the chapters in many ways rethink and refigure practices of intimacy, it is interesting to note that most of them turn to 'traditional' arenas of intimacy, such as dating, family and sex, when examining online intimacies. This suggests that intimacy is still strongly figured in relation to the home and the 'inner' self.

Contents of the anthology

This volume stems from a research project titled 'New Media – New Intimacies' (2015–2018), which investigates different forms of mediated intimacies, such as online dating sites, online communities, expressions of grief on digital platforms and the mediation of reproductive technologies.

The project is generously funded by the Danish Council of Independent Research and focuses empirically on Denmark and its mediated intimate global encounters. The anthology is part of the European Communication Research and Education Association (ECREA) book series, and the intention of the volume is to gather the most up-to-date European research within the field of mediated intimacy, representing scholars affiliated with institutions in the UK, Sweden, Denmark, Norway, Hungary, Portugal, Spain, the Netherlands and Finland. Although the volume is published within the framework of a European institution, ECREA, we are pleased to include chapters from an international group of scholars, including those based in Hong Kong, Singapore, Australia and Canada. The contributors also differ in academic representation; they vary from PhD candidates to full professors, and include independent scholars and artists.

Similarly, the anthology represents a variety of methodological approaches and empirical cases.

Methodologically, the chapters employ different analytical tools to assemble and approach the material, such as interviews, online ethnography, visual analysis, text analysis and video analysis. A large number of chapters employ mixed methods, drawing upon more than one method of analysis and questioning a strict division between online and offline. A similarly rich variation can be seen in the diversity of empirical material examined in the chapters, which includes Tumblr, YouTube, dating sites, hook-up sites, Facebook, Snapchat, CouchSurfing, selfies, blogs and photographs, as well as smartphones, tablets and computers.

The anthology is divided into four sections, each devoting special attention to different analytical perspectives and theoretical horizons: 1) 'Communities and activism'; 2) 'Relationship-making and maintenance'; 3) 'Integrating and domesticating'; and 4) 'Becoming and performing'.

Part I: Communities and activism

In the first section special attention is given to the way in which online media facilitate and enable new communities, counter-discourses and activism. It shows how online activism and communities can provide new intimate belongings and options for alternative voices and narratives.

Chapter 1, '"Something substantive enough to reach out and touch": The intimate politics of anti-rape activism', is written by Debra Ferreday. Departing from a critique of dominant narratives about rape survivors within contemporary rape culture, wherein rape is normalised and seen as a natural consequence of certain victim behaviours, the chapter analyses the way in which stories of sexual violence are told and retold. It shows how speaking out about rape in public is staged within a neoliberal recovery story, wherein the victim is discreetly blamed for the rape and expected to 'move on' – a form of cruel optimism. This narrative is contrasted with narratives enabled by the intimate community around Project Unbreakable, a Tumblr-based photography project that was founded in 2009. The images and narratives within this project demonstrate the normality of rape and refuse to simply accept it; rather, they 'embody and make visible the intimate work of survival that survivors must undertake in order to *be* survivors'. These digital counter-narratives thus mobilise the intimate and personal to political effect, forming 'islands of hope'.

Chapter 2, 'Intimate communities: Hackerspaces, digital engagement and affective relations', is written by Sarah R. Davies. The chapter investigates the way in which relational intimacies are carried out in contemporary society by carefully investigating the intimacies of the hackerspace community. Based on fieldwork in hackerspaces across the US as well as interviews with makers and hackers, the chapter shows how hackers form intimate relations within hackerspaces, to both technologies and one another. The spaces use digital tools and social media to connect hackers face-to-face, and although offline meetings are valued and given significance, they merge with online communication and meetings. Thus, the intimate relations seamlessly cross different forms of digitally mediated communication and face-to-face meetings. Though the hackers emphasise real world encounters, these encounters are seamlessly lived out online, and thus form a 'life-changing experience of local community but simultaneously, provide access to a worldwide "fraternity"'.

Chapter 3, 'Online community and new family scripts', is written by Rikke Andreassen. The chapter examines the way in which Scandinavian mothers with donor-conceived children connect with each other digitally through Facebook and form an intimate online community. Andreassen analyses how the mothers, who are single or living in lesbian couples, collectively challenge normative scripts in relation to family formations. The chapter explores how online communication, especially self-disclosure and knowledge-sharing among a closed group of women, can be interpreted as a continuation of women's consciousness-raising groups. As such, Facebook can be understood as a platform that enables older forms of communication and networks rather than a tool serving solely to create new forms of communities. Furthermore, the chapter illustrates – through its micro perspective on a specific community in which online media have proven important for forming intimacy – how features of social media sites, such as anonymity and distance across time, can dilute both communication and community creation, while simultaneously cultivating and upholding communication and community formation.

Chapter 4, 'Textures of intimacy: Witnessing embodied mobile loss, affect and heartbreak' is written by Lin Prøitz, Larissa Hjorth and Amparo Lasén. The chapter focuses on 'textures' that form in and around digital intimacy heartbreak, encompassing various forms of heartbreak and sadness, loss and mourning. The authors employ discursive analysis, online ethnography, qualitative interviews and workshops with regular users of visual mobile media to suggest how affective scripts around intimacy may be disrupted at moments of grief or mourning. Based on material from South Korea, Spain and Norway, the chapter is organised around two case studies: shame and sadness after a couple's break-up and analysis of selfie video footage of the South Korean ferry disaster of 2014 (the sinking of the *MV Sewol*). Using the notion of choreography, the authors aptly show how the practice of publicly sharing intimate moments of loss or grief using camera phones involves a (re)negotiation of public/private boundaries.

Chapter 5, 'Edge effect: New image formations and identity politics', is written by Marco Bohr and Basia Sliwinska. The chapter investigates visual activism by zooming into 'the formation of a new type of image that is perhaps less concerned with *representing* protest than with forming protest in its own right'. Analysing the case of the visual activism of Pussy Riot, the chapter argues that the band members' visual formations create and enable an intimacy between the digital and the analogue that forms a third shared space – what the chapter conceptualises as an 'edge effect' – which 're-energises images, making them political agents of resistance, and can produce and communicate new forms of identity, generating dialogue through intimate belonging across physical and virtual spheres'.

Part II: Relationship making and maintenance

The second section focuses on the way in which social media provide and facilitate intimate relations and connections. Importantly, this section investigates how users employ technologies to create, negotiate and maintain relationships.

Chapter 6, 'Innovations in intimacy: Internet dating in an international frame', is written by Christine Beasley, Mary Holmes, Katherine Harrison and Caroline Wamala Larsson. The chapter investigates new modes of developing intimate relationships that have risen from the growing use of internet dating sites across the world. Internet dating is a rapidly expanding and increasingly popular means of forming intimate social connections for a wide range of age groups and sexual preferences (Beasley and Holmes, forthcoming). However, research on internet dating is typically inattentive to its possibilities for social change, and most often geographically localised. The authors use qualitative content analysis to examine potential innovations in embodied intimate gender relations, practices and identities among men and women from four countries – Denmark, the UK, Australia and Uganda. The results of the study suggest that, despite the reproduction of gender norms, some possibilities for innovation appear in these practices of intimacy, such as 'mundane polyamory'. Furthermore, certain affordances of the digital medium, including the opportunity for both men and women to easily browse multiple potential partners, facilitate behaviour that may 'shift or even refuse gendered sexual frames and assumptions about their roles'.

Chapter 7, 'Infrastructures of intimacy', is written by Susanna Paasonen. The chapter analyses the network connectivity that is enabled through various online applications and devices, such as Tinder, Skype, text messaging and Facebook. Paasonen asked her undergraduate university students in Finland to write essays about their feelings when their phones, computers or other network connections broke down, and she used this empirical material to understand how young people feel about and experience networked connectivities, especially when these connectivities fail to perform as promised or expected. The chapter shows how network connectivity functions as an infrastructure of intimacy – an infrastructure that is important for creating and maintaining relations, such as friendships or sexual encounters. For Paasonen, intimacy does not simply refer to connections between individuals; rather, intimacy should be understood as the networked environments in which individuals' connections and relationships unfold. In other words, networked connections are sociotechnical affordances that modulate intimacy.

Chapter 8, 'Temporal ephemerality, persistent affectivity: Circulation of intimacies on Snapchat', is written by Jette Kofoed. The chapter examines how Snapchat co-forms intimacies among teenagers. Through fieldwork carried out among eighth graders in an ethnically diverse area of Copenhagen, Denmark, Kofoed analyses the ways in which the intimacy of Snapchat exchanges involves both 'feel-good' aspects of intimate belonging as well as the potential for betrayal via exposure of snaps to a wider public (when Snapchats are screenshot). Kofoed argues that a snap can be understood as a comment about how one is feeling; the exchange of pictures leaves affective trails ranging from the comfort of inclusion to the delight of maintaining emojis, to the fear of having unflattering or nude snaps shared with never-ending publics. While the snaps themselves can be seen as ephemeral, as the snaps self-destruct, the affective tenor of the exchanges persists.

Chapter 9, 'Beyond engineered intimacy: Navigating social media platforms to manage intimate relationships', is written by Cristina Miguel. The chapter examines the relationship between the architecture and politics of social media platforms and the emerging practices of intimacy that occur within them. Drawing on interviews of British and Spanish users of the dating and hook-up app Badoo, the hospitality service CouchSurfing, and Facebook, Miguel analyses the way in which these social media platforms function as intimacy mediators. Miguel shows how users adopt and adapt the technical affordances of these platforms to create and develop personal relationships. The chapter focuses particularly on the systems of the platforms' user verification and reputation, private features and privacy settings in order to understand how users apply these features to initiate and manage intimate relationships. Miguel's examination of 'privacy' engages with important questions of trust and safety, which have become central issues relating to mediated intimacy.

Chapter 10, 'In with expectations and out with disappointment: Gay-tailored social media and the redefinition of intimacy', is written by Yin Zhang and John Nguyet Erni. Based on an extensive literature review,

Zhang and Erni summarise some of the influential sociological roots and media affordances in gay-tailored social media in order to discuss the dilemmas of mediated intimacy. The chapter shows that gay men rely heavily on mediated methods of obtaining and managing relationships and fulfilling sexual needs. Social media is especially well suited for this purpose, as it is inexpensive and instant, and offers frequent and multiple relational targets. Zhang and Erni conclude, however, that many gay men have other notions of and hopes for intimacy than what they experience social media platforms as providing.

Part III: Integrating and domesticating

The third section examines the way in which new media are integrated and domesticated into intimate, emotional schemes. This section shows how users navigate and negotiate media and media affordances to practice habitual intimacies.

Chapter 11, 'Mediating intimacies through mobile communication: Chinese migrant mothers' digital "bridge of magpies"', is written by Yang Wang and Sun Sun Lim. The chapter presents the phenomenon of *peidu mama* (literally 'study mothers'), who accompany their young children as they pursue education abroad, leaving their husbands behind in China. As de facto 'single parents' in the host society, these Chinese 'study mothers' must overcome acculturation challenges and pave the way for their children to quickly thrive in an alien environment, while on the other hand maintaining affective bonds with their family and friends back home. The chapter presents narratives of three Chinese study mothers in Singapore, showing how they utilise mobile communication to manage their intimate relationships with their children and left-behind family and friends. The authors use an innovative combination of methods, weaving together a 'content-context diary' with observations and interviews to produce a 'transnational culturagram' model that maps the topographies of the mediated relationships. This approach allows the authors to identify three particular constraints – spatial, temporal and social – that shape the Chinese mothers' use of mobile technologies in their attempts to maintain and create intimacies.

Chapter 12, 'Young children and digital media in the intimacy of the home: Perceptions and mediation', is written by Rita Brito and Patrícia Dias. The chapter explores the relationship of young children to digital media devices. The authors argue that children are increasingly born into 'digital homes', where they are exposed to digital media from birth and where these devices play a role in the creation of family intimacies. The chapter presents an in-depth qualitative study of the engagement of children (younger than 8 years old) with digital media in the home. Using a set of interviews (with parents, children and families) and activities (a card game, a digital tour and a chart of digital use), the authors explore the dynamics between children, parents and devices, and also between practices and perceptions. Their findings show how rules are co-created, skills are co-developed with interchangeable roles of teacher and apprentice and playful and loving moments are shared around a game or a digital bedtime story. In this study, we see how digital media (particularly the tablet) are protagonists in family life, as they become intimate devices – personal, portable and affective – that, in a way, are extensions of the user.

Chapter 13, 'Connecting with the dead: Vernacular practices of mourning through photo-sharing on Facebook', is written by Tobias Raun. The chapter provides a virtual autoethnographic analysis of mourning through Facebook that stems from Raun's own photo-sharing, as well as his online fieldwork and interviews with grieving others. Raun zooms in on the practice of photographing a grave site and circulating it on Facebook – a practice that many of the users in his study engaged very actively in, and one that, in general, seems quite common on Facebook. The chapter identifies different tropes of representation and unfolds the significance of Facebook as a platform and photography as a performative practice, in relation to mourning. As argued, photography serves as a connecting force that can instantiate and create relational proximity by either gathering loved ones within the same picture or continuously pointing to a deceased loved one. The shared images thereby represent attempts to enfold a deceased relative's existence into an ongoing, everyday mediated life and to ensure a continued relationship with the deceased.

Chapter 14, 'Bleeding boundaries: Domesticating gay hook-up apps', is written by Kristian Møller and Michael Nebeling Petersen. Rooted in domestication theory, the chapter investigates the way in which gay men in non-monogamous relationships domesticate and integrate mobile hook-up apps into their intimate lives. Based on interviews with gay men using hook-up apps, the chapter pays close attention to the way in which intimacy is created by the affective work of keeping emotions *in place*. Intimacy is conceptualised as affective scripts of belonging that are formed in dominant and subcultural intimate publics. Thus, the chapter investigates two scripts of intimacy and demonstrates the way in which gay hook-up apps potentially disrupt 'old' senses of intimacy. The analysis shows how the men carefully domesticate the technologies by controlling the affordances of the apps and affectively and rhetorically keeping emotions in place, according to their different scripts of intimacy.

Part IV: Becoming and performing

The final section investigates the way in which individuals become subjects in, through and with technology. Drawing on various case studies, the section illustrates that technology and the body cannot be separated; rather, technology is necessary for building and creating identities and belonging.

Chapter 15, 'Teen boys on YouTube: Representations of gender and intimacy', is written by Claire Balleys. The chapter presents an online ethnographic study of amateur videos made by teen boys (aged 12 to 17) living in France, French-speaking Switzerland, Belgium and Québec. Drawing on the work of Judith Butler and Erving Goffman, Balleys analyses the gender performances and gender displays conveyed in these videos, regarding physical and relational intimacy. The analysis shows how the performed masculinity is deeply imprinted with a traditional form of heteronormativity. Humour is used as a genre and a vector of male confidence that enables the boys to talk about intimate matters.

Chapter 16, 'Technical intimacies and Otherkin becomings', is written by Eva Zekany. Framed within posthumanist theory, this chapter analyses the technological aspects of Otherkin becoming. Otherkin identify as partially or completely non-human, and Otherkin communities are often associated with blogging and social media platforms such as Tumblr and Reddit. By examining non-human intimacies and the way in which technological mediation through digital communication tools and internet media are used for making and maintaining Otherkin subjectivities and communities, the chapter discusses the relationship between technology and human becoming. The discussion moves between posthuman theories and the Otherkin case to argue that the human emerges in conjunction with technologies. The chapter argues that 'the human inhabits an ontological space that, at its core, is *non-human*'.

Chapter 17, 'Broadcasting the bedroom: Intimate musical practices and collapsing contexts on YouTube', is written by Maarten Michielse. Based on virtual ethnographic fieldwork in a community of bedroom musicians on YouTube, the chapter investigates how this form of musical practice and performance is staged and negotiated by the performers. The users seek to establish digital intimate relations with audiences and peers, and they seek to place their individual videos within a larger collective body of videos and to engage in a collective process of rehearsing. The chapter argues that individual videos are less important to the participants than the collective process, their experiences and their relations. Viewers outside the community often misunderstand these intentions, thus the videos collapse different contexts. The chapter shows how the participants carefully reflect on, stage and manage the videos to avoid context collapse.

Chapter 18, 'Fashion blogging as a technology of bodily becoming: The fluidity and firmness of digital bodies', is written by Louise Yung Nielsen. The chapter draws on theories of (posthumanist) performativity to analyse two Danish fashion blogs (Sidsel and Lasse; and Gina Jaqueline). The analysis revolves around the way in which clothing, fitness and plastic surgery – much as the blog as its own medium – become intimate technologies that produce new forms of embodiment. However, Yung Nielsen also identifies significant differences between the two bloggers in relation to notions and performances of identity, not least concerning the degree to which the body is staged as intimately connected to and intra-acting with these technologies.

Chapter 19, '"My friend Bubz": Building intimacy as a YouTube beauty guru', is written by Florencia García-Rapp. This final chapter investigates YouTube's beauty communities by examining the widely popular British-born Chinese 'beauty guru', Bubz. Drawing on studies of digital fandom and celebrity, García-Rapp argues that in order to nuance and understand the phenomenon of Bubz, one must examine the way in which she forges closeness and intimacy with her audience. The chapter shows how Bubz's YouTube videos – which differ between genres of information-rich tutorials; personal, humorous and entertaining vlogs; and motivational self-help videos – foster different types of connection and closeness with viewers, by analysing the way in which viewers consume, discuss, criticise and respond to the different styles of video content. Importantly, García-Rapp argues that viewers reciprocate by relating Bubz's content to their personal lives and engaging in self-disclosing narratives in their comments on Bubz's videos. Thus, the videos and viewers' responses to them function to disclose intimate and personal moments; this disclosure leads to the creation of a fan community built on feelings of closeness and connection between the viewers (followers) and the beauty guru.

Final remarks

When people mourn their dead, set out to find a new partner or friend or disclose their intimate stories of joy, pain and survival, they increasingly use digital and online communication tools. None of these intimacies is new – quite the opposite! Hence, the shift between different media – for example, finding a partner in a shady bar or through personal ads in magazines or online apps and dating sites – does not necessarily change the nature of the intimacies, as such. Rather, the ways in which the intimacies are enabled and performed – the ways in which we connect, relate and become close – change. Whether one wants to hook up at a shady bar or to do so online, one must learn the specific ways of dancing, talking and looking that are appropriate for the space; that is, one must learn how to mediate one's desires within a specific setting, place and culture. Hence, certain spaces and technologies offer specific affordances; however, these affordances are continually up for renegotiation. The etiquette of these spheres relates to context specificity rather than an all-encompassing change in traditional structures of intimacy.

This book's interest, therefore, in social and digital media does not assume that the technological developments within media disrupt feelings of intimacy; nor does it imply that digitally mediated intimacies are inherently different from other mediated intimacies. Rather, the book suggests that mediated intimacies can be fruitfully investigated by a close examination of *how* we connect, relate and become close, and particularly of the role of new media objects in connecting, relating and becoming close.

This focus is reflected in the subtitle of the book: *Connectivities, Relationalities and Proximities*. By highlighting these three associations of intimacy, we do not wish to suggest that intimacy is solely established by close connection to another person. Rather, we seek to suggest that intimacy is and always has been mediated. Practices of intimacy between people that draw on words or cultural signs of closeness or tenderness must be understood as mediations of intimacy, wherein the words or cultural signs mediate whatever feelings one wishes to transfer.

By highlighting the three words in the subtitle, we wish to suggest that mediated intimacy is best understood as a dynamic practice or a choreography. That what we, within the technological development of media, are witnessing is a new form of human-technological entanglement that does not radically change the dance, but rather where and how we move and are moved.

To summarise, this anthology provides a collection of texts that analyse various examples of mediated intimacy. By focusing on this intersection between social media and intimacies, and their continuous co-constitution, the anthology offers new insights into the vast landscape of contemporary media reality. In presenting a broad range of material, the book makes clear that attention to the specific limitations and affordances of apps and sites can contribute to building a rich, nuanced understanding of the intersection of social media and practices of intimacy. We hope that this focus and the many new perspectives and understandings contributed by this anthology will nuance the field of media and communication studies, as well as the field of intimacy studies, both inside Europe and outside the European countries.

References

Berlant, L. (1998). Intimacy: A special issue. *Critical Inquiry*, 24(2), pp. 281–288.

Berlant, L. (2008). *The Female Complaint: The Unfinished Business of Sentimentality in American Culture*. Durham, NC: Duke University Press.

Chambers, D. (2013). *Social Media and Personal Relationships: Online Intimacies and Networked Friendship*. Basingstoke and New York: Palgrave Macmillan.

Deuze, M. (2011). Media life. *Media, Culture & Society*, 33(1), pp. 137–148.

Deuze, M. (2012). *Media Life*. Cambridge and Malden: Polity Press.

Garde-Hansen, J. and Gorton, K. (2013). *Emotion Online, Theorizing Affect on the Internet*. Basingstoke and New York: Palgrave Macmillan.

Hillis, K., Paasonen, S. and Petit, M., eds. (2015). *Networked Affect*. Cambridge, MA and London: MIT Press.

Humphreys, L., Gill, P., Krishnamurthy, B. and Newbury, E. (2013). Historicizing new media: A content analysis of Twitter. *Journal of Communication*, 63, pp. 413–431.

Jamieson, L. (2005). Boundaries of intimacy. In: L. McKie and S. Cunningham-Burley, eds., *Families in Society: Boundaries and Relationships*. Bristol: Policy Press, pp. 189–206.

Kember, S. and Zylinska, J. (2015). *Life after New Media: Mediation as a Vital Process*. Cambridge, MA and London: MIT Press.
McGlotten, S. (2013). *Virtual Intimacies, Media, Affect, and Queer Sociality*. Albany, NY: State University of New York Press.
Paasonen, S. (2011). *Carnal Resonance, Affect and Online Pornography*. Cambridge, MA: MIT Press.
Payne, R. (2014). *Promiscuity of Network Culture*. New York: Taylor & Francis.
Plummer, K. (2003). *Intimate Citizenship: Private Decisions and Public Dialogues*. Seattle, WA and London: University of Washington Press.
Schofield Clark, L. (2009). Theories: Mediatization and media ecology. In: K. Lundby, ed., *Mediatization: Concept, Changes, Consequences*. New York: Peter Lang, pp. 85–100.
Tierney, T. (2013). *The Public Space of Social Media: Connected Cultures of the Network Society*. New York: Routledge.
van Dijck, J. (2007). *Mediated Memories in the Digital Age*. Stanford, CA: Stanford University Press.
van Dijck, J. (2013). *The Culture of Connectivity: A Critical History of Social Media*. New York: Oxford University Press.
Weeks, J. (1998). The sexual citizen. *Theory, Culture & Society*, 15(3), pp. 35–52.
Yuval-Davis, N. (1997). *Gender and Nation*. London: SAGE.

Part I

Communities and activism

1 'Something substantive enough to reach out and touch'

The intimate politics of digital anti-rape activism

Debra Ferreday

Introduction

On New Year's Eve 2016, a case of mass sexual assault attracted international attention. In cities throughout Germany, but mainly in Cologne, women were surrounded by groups of men who groped, assaulted, robbed and – in five cases – raped them. Media and police reports claimed that the men responsible were largely of non-German origin. In the context of the European refugee crisis, the case generated an international outcry focused on calls for tougher limits on migration. Rumours surfaced that the perpetrators had used social media to pre-arrange the attacks – rumours that are still widely repeated online, despite no evidence ever having surfaced. Media accounts emphasised the notion of mass sexual assault as a uniquely 'Arab' phenomenon, despite the fact that many reports estimated half the attackers to be white. In subsequent media reports, the image of violated white womanhood became central to calls for deportation and tougher limits on immigration. Most visibly, the Belgian journalist Esmerelda Labye, who was assaulted on camera while reporting on the festivities, became a focus of images of threatened white womanhood, despite the fact that the men seen attacking her in the clip are clearly white Germans – an anomaly pointed out by the British *Independent* newspaper.

Given the universal attribution of the Cologne assaults to racialised Others and the reliance on the figure of the innocent white victim, it might seem surprising that official responses continued the theme of victim blaming that has been characteristic of recent high-profile sexual violence cases, most famously that of the Canadian police officer and judge whose comments led to the inception of 'Slutwalk'. Yet the public response to the attacks was seen by many as a perfect example of victim blaming. In particular, the Mayor of Cologne, Henriette Reker, made a speech instructing women on how to avoid attack. The suggested measures included staying in groups, never walking alone, not smiling, not 'being in a celebratory mood' and always keeping an arm's length of distance between themselves and strangers (Hartley, 2016). In Britain, the right-wing *Telegraph* newspaper combined anti-German and anti-Islamic rhetoric to argue 'the EU referendum is about nothing less than the safety and security of British women – and that means we must get out of Europe' (Pearson, 2016). In Germany, pressure from the right and public outrage prompted Angela Merkel to state that she would consider tougher laws on sexual violence, but also increased powers to deport 'migrants', including those seeking asylum who had been convicted of crimes in Germany (Harris, 2016).

I outline this case in detail not because it is particularly unusual, but because it precisely illustrates the way in which the body of the rape victim is typically figured as a battleground for struggles over race, gender and national identity, while at the same time victim-survivors are made intimately responsible for the prevention of sexual violence. In these victim-blaming discourses, sexual violence survivors are either invisible or their suffering is made visible only in service of a wider argument about national identity. Further, the notion of a sudden wave of assault ignores the pervasiveness of everyday sexual and racial harassment in public spaces. Women are exhorted to engage in what Fiona Vera-Grey terms 'safety work': making deeply personal decisions about where to walk and what to wear, and minutely monitoring facial expression in order to, for example, look tough while not appearing serious enough to attract the opening gambit 'Cheer up' or 'Smile' (Vera-Grey, 2016). These forms of advice are still routinely dispensed by authorities, despite the fact that most assault happens in the home and despite the fact that the advised measures clearly do not work: Vera-Grey's study found that most women underestimate the amount of safety work they already perform (ibid.). The effect of this focus is to make women and minorities responsible for the violence they encounter, such that male violence is normalised as an everyday hazard – a normal part of urban life. The map of the city and the disposition of the body are simply different for those likely to become victims of sexual assault. In other words, public discourse about rape exemplifies Lauren Berlant's point that 'the inwardness of the intimate is met by a corresponding publicness' (1998, p. 281). Whatever the political stance taken by commentators on sexual violence, feminist activists and scholars have argued that they are united in perpetuating rape culture – 'a complex of beliefs that encourages male sexual aggression and supports violence against women' and a society in which 'violence is seen as sexy and sexuality as violent [...] [that] condones physical and emotional terrorism against women as the norm' – and repudiating the claim that this violence 'is neither biologically nor divinely ordained. Much of what we accept as inevitable is in fact the expression of values and attitudes *that can change*' (Buchwald et al., 1993, p. xi, emphasis added).

In rape culture, rape is imagined as a given – the natural and inevitable consequence of certain behaviours on the part of the victim. Such an account relies heavily on the normalisation of stranger rape, and especially on the figure of the bestial non-white male perpetrator: to 'get oneself raped' is the consequence of allowing oneself to come into contact with specific bodies and specific spaces. This recalls Berlant's (2011) notion of a 'cruel optimism', defined by 'compromised conditions of possibility' (2011, p. 24). She describes this condition as that of 'maintaining an attachment to a problematic object *in advance* of its loss' (2011, p. 21). The formula 'don't get (yourself) raped' requires women (as potential victims) to internalise and act out an attachment to cultural fantasies of the good life, wearing themselves out in the service of an imaginary fair and just society for whose subjects the only threat comes from outside (the abject foreign male attacker), even as it is implicitly imagined as stemming, intimately, from inside – from her own bodily movements and appurtenances. This intimate relation to the potentiality of violence thus embodies Berlant's account of cruel optimism as that which enables and reproduces deeply violent and destructive attachments under the banner of hope; or, as she puts it, 'the affective attachment to what we call the good life, which is for so many a bad life that wears out the subject who nonetheless, and at the same time, find their conditions of possibility within it' (2011, p. 27). Seen as inherently raped and rapeable, women are precisely exhorted to 'ride the wave of the system of attachment they are used to' (2011, p. 28), even as it continues to reproduce and extend the conditions through which they are victimised. The fantasy of the subject who is in control of whether or not she is raped thus not only operates to normalise rape, but further intersects with fantasies about nation, ethnicity, labour and justice that produce the capitalist state as essentially good, even as it massively reproduces the conditions that make violence almost inevitable and justice impossible. 'Don't get raped' discourse thus operates to revictimise survivors and, as extensive empirical research by Walby and colleagues has demonstrated, actively discourage survivors from reporting sexual assault (2013).

As the above cases show, mediation is central to struggles over rape culture: debates about rape figure into wider questions about the ways in which women's bodies are represented and objectified. In this context, the digital functions in multiple and complex ways as a space of intimate and affective community: a site of revictimisation and an activist space that offers users the potential to resist and speak back to dominant narratives. In this chapter, I examine the way in which digital spaces can rupture the intimate relations victim-survivors have to personal and public regimes of power and extend the possibilities for resistance in a way that continues what Deborah Withers calls feminism's 'already there' (2015, p. 1). I draw on Withers' concept to describe the strategies, ideas and practices that work to constitute affective and intimate relations between survivors and to disrupt public narratives that hold survivors responsible for sexual violence. In using this term, I aim at drawing attention to the ways in which digital activism draws on an archive of feminist resistance for its strategies. Current feminist research on digital feminism has precisely focused on the way that digital media has become integrated into the fabric of everyday life to construct new ways of continuing the feminist work of resistance. For example, Kember and Zylinska's argument that digital media offer the means to create 'unprecedented connections and unexpected events' (2012, p. 30) is taken up by feminist scholars such as Keller, Mendes and Ringrose (2016) as a way of thinking through responses to rape culture through what they term the 'increasingly mediated' nature of young women's lives. As they argue, girls and women are 'increasingly engaged with feminist critique and activism, often using digital media technologies to speak out against misogyny, rape culture and everyday sexism' (2016, p. 1). Focusing on 'the radical potential of digital culture to reanimate feminist politics online and off', Keller and colleagues argue that 'the affective nature of new forms of sharing, connection and solidarity' operate to make feminist activism more visible and accessible than ever before, enabling a 'previously impossible' means of speaking out about experiences of rape culture (2016, p. 13). While it is true that digital spaces enable the emergence of new attachments, it is crucial to note that feminism has always appropriated contemporary media technologies to speak back to hegemonic media discourses, using strategies ranging from culture-jamming in the form of feminist graffiti to producing alternative feminist films, performances, zines and music. Withers argues that, in understanding feminist resistance, we must dispense with the linear notion of past, present and future that, in our digital age, has been consumed by capitalism, and instead think in terms of heritage and emergence: to consider what heritages and histories feminism brings with it, and how they enable forms of activism and resistance to emerge (2015).

An important aspect of feminism's inheritance, then, is its critical engagement with the dominant imaginaries constructed by media; it is in this context, I argue, that contemporary digital activism must be understood. Historically, feminist work on media images of sexual violence has focused on rupturing public fantasies centred on the body of the victim in order to imagine alternative futures. As Tanya Horeck notes in her work on cinematic images of sexual violence, feminism's 'moral imperative' has been to shatter the fantasies produced by mainstream media 'in order to bring home the horror of rape to a culture that is either indifferent or hostile to stories of sexual violation' (2004, p. 4). Horeck's work draws attention to the ways in which images of rape function as fantasy; that is, as a site of both prurient spectatorship and objectification of the female body, and also the anxieties, repressions and conflicts that are at stake in pleasurable acts of looking. If, as she argues (following Elizabeth Cowie), psychoanalysis understands fantasy as 'arranging – or setting out – desire', then by analysing representations of rape it must be possible to see 'how rape is structured as a scene through which a multitude of conflicts are staged' (Horeck, 2004, p. 5). Importantly, spectatorship is not simply individual and private, but also public and social: in Elizabeth Cowie's terms, the stories we tell about rape can be understood as 'public fantasies' (1997, p. 137). What is often striking about these public fantasies is their sense of repetition and sameness. This leads Horeck to ask: 'Why do the same stories about rape get told and retold? What is the mythic status of rape in popular culture?' (2004, p. 7).

I shall turn in a moment to analyse the kinds of stories that get 'told and retold' about the survivor experience in mainstream media accounts of rape. Here, I want to note an important point about the politics of 'telling and retelling', which is that it mimics popular understandings of pathological trauma. The excessively traumatised victim-survivor is precisely imagined as a subject that is overly, unhealthily attached to its grief: the subject who commits the sin of 'allowing herself to be defined by victimhood' is a familiar figure in popular imaginaries of sexual violence and other forms of suffering. As Rebecca Coleman notes, questions of futurity have been of particular importance to feminism, since 'feminism as a political movement seeks to assess the material and imaginary conditions of women's pasts and presents and propose and progress towards different futures' (2008, p. 86). It is in this context that I seek to examine the intimate feminist encounters afforded by digital media and the ways in which digital space becomes a site for doing and undoing intimacies centred on the experience of sexual violence, in order to understand how the digital is becoming the most recent of many spaces in which the enforced intimacy of violation is transformed into what Jonathan Lear (2008) terms 'radical hope'. Below, I discuss how the figure of the 'good survivor' is taken up as a way of speaking for survivors, and how this figuration is complicated and questioned in spaces of digital survivor activism. First, though, I consider the terms on which victim-survivors have historically been granted access to the mediated public sphere. Echoing Spivak's original work on the subaltern, I ask: Can the 'rape victim' speak?

'It's good to talk': Public narratives of speaking out

In analysing the way in which survivor activism takes up the baton of feminist struggle, I turn to Nathan Rambukkana's work on intimate counter-publics, since debate over who gets to speak about sexual violence, and on what terms, is deeply entangled with questions of citizenship. Following critical work by Lauren Berlant (2007a, 2007b), Nancy Fraser (1992), Michael Warner (2002) and others, Rambukkana points out that much has been written about the limits of the Habermasian public sphere as a site of rational discourse between equals. Despite this, discussion about the democratic potential of digital media has tended to centre on technocentric assumptions about their capacity to produce spaces in which citizens might '[step] out of their private roles as interested individuals and into a public space where they become participants in disinterested discussion and debate' (2015). Following Nancy Fraser's work on the public sphere, resistance in the form of anti-rape hashtags and 'survivor selfies' can be seen to constitute what she terms a 'subaltern counterpublic', which functions, as she summarises, simultaneously as a needed 'space of withdrawal and regroupment' and a fertile ground for 'agitational activities directed towards wider publics' (1992, p. 68) in the shape of both victim-blaming discourse and wider racist and nationalist narratives concerning sexual violence. In contrast, Rambukkana argues for attention to a more intimate politics that is conducted in the digital sphere: in 'other publics: more-or-less subaltern, more-or-less rational, more-or-less critical, and almost certainly partial, affective, interested and loud'; and in 'the kinds of publics that do politics in a way that is rough and emergent, flawed and messy, and ones in which new forms of collective power are being forged on the fly, and in the shadow of loftier mainstream spheres' (2015). Following Nancy Baym's claim that digital technologies have sunk 'into the woodwork of everyday life' (2004, p. 21), he argues that 'digital intimacies are now [...] part of the new shape of human intimacy' (Rambukkana, 2015).

Below, I turn to these 'other publics' to understand how the politics of protest are taken up in survivor spaces. But first, in order to see how important this work of disruption is, we must consider the terms on which rape survivors are currently allowed to speak: If survivors are allowed access to the orthodox Habermasian public sphere, how and on whose terms might they speak?

It might seem paradoxical to claim that victim-survivors cannot speak, given the extent to which they are exhorted to do exactly that. This issue, which has been made central to questions of immigration and asylum, public health and Brexit, it might be argued, is hardly hidden from public view. Yet these very public debates, by producing rape as abhorrent, unusual and – crucially – something that comes from outside, only serve to screen the reality of rape culture and silence the lived experience of trauma. While feminist responses to rape culture have employed 'speak out' as a strategy since the second wave (Alcoff and Gray, 1993), in practice, this strategy is appropriated and fused with neoliberal narratives of the self – particularly the 'recovery journey' – that deprive it of its political force. It is worth turning to a historical example to see how the figure of the neoliberal good survivor becomes established in media accounts and takes on a monstrous life, obscuring the more fragmented and uncertain experiences that digital survivor movements often make visible.

In 2002, the *Oprah Winfrey Show* staged what was seen by many as a ground-breaking interview with the so-called 'Central Park Jogger', Trisha Meili. Meili was running in Central Park, New York, in 1988 when, according to the official record, she was set about by a gang of five men who gang-raped, tortured and beat her and left her for dead. Meili fell into a 12-day coma from which she emerged unable to read, speak or walk, minus one eye, with 75 to 80 per cent of her blood and a permanent inability to smell, and was so severely traumatised that she was unable to recall the attack. (The case would later become notorious for the police's mishandling of evidence, attributed to racism, which allowed probably the main assailant to go free: he later confessed to leading the attack.) Again, this case demonstrates the demonisation of men of colour that is at stake in so much media coverage of rape. Yet even in this 'perfect' media case, the white 'innocent victim' must be held responsible for her own violation, as interview transcripts demonstrate. In reply to the question: 'When I first heard about you, I thought, why were you running alone in Central Park at night?' Meili replies: 'You're not the first person to say that [...] I had this feeling that, hey, I have every right to run where I want, when I want. I'd been running in the park for two years,' but concludes that: 'It was not a smart thing to do.' Although she defends her actions saying: 'That is absolutely no justification for what happened to me,' Oprah responds: 'Believe me, I'm not sitting here trying to justify it. But the idea of running alone in Central Park is a foreign concept to me. You had to be the kind of person who either thought you were invincible *or who was just nuts* [emphasis added].'[1]

In subsequent years, this and other high-profile media cases arguably set the tone for discussions of sexual violence to this day: in contrast to the work that is expected of survivors, public discourse has not 'moved on'. Recently, a young British woman, Karina Vetrano, was raped and murdered while out running. Discussion of the case in the tabloid media and newspaper comments identically reproduced the same victim-blaming discourse. As social media comments collated by the tabloid *Sun* newspaper put it: 'It is your [women's] responsibility to be aware [...] stop jogging or going to the damn gym half naked, go back to where people wore sweat pants to sweat' (Celona and Hodge, 2016). Further comments extended this victim-blaming discourse:

> I always see attractive women running with their headphones on in secluded areas! How stupid can they be? It's unbelievable.
>
> Very unfortunate, but you have to be smart [...] Women forget that no matter how much equality they claim and obtain, they are still the weaker gender.
>
> (Celona and Hodge, 2016)

Again, even a victim who fits the profile of the tabloid 'ideal victim' – young, white, possibly attacked by a stranger – is held accountable for her own death by daring to go out alone in public. A woman using a public space for its intended purpose is either rendered insensible by privilege, or 'nuts'. Although Meili complained of her treatment in the Oprah interview, the theme of personal responsibility continued in the marketing of her *New York Times* bestselling memoir *I Am the Central Park Jogger*: the cover blurb, chosen by her publisher from a review in the *New York Times Book Review,* praises its absence of 'anger or resentment', claiming it will 'comfort and inspire anyone who has suffered a horrible trauma – and many who haven't' (Meili, 2003). The protesting woman is hence recuperated into the body politic through a politicised rhetoric of appropriate femininity: no longer nuts, selfish or a narcissistic yuppie, she has become a figure of 'inspiration'. The disruptive potential of her waiving of anonymity, which is the only right afforded to survivors, is hence neutralised and made safe.

'Something substantive enough to reach out and touch': Redefining rape culture

What, then, about survivors who do not 'comfort and inspire'? Recently, the equation of trauma with madness has become associated not only with the victim's silence, but also the silencing of others. The 'oversensitive victim' who refuses to engage with recovery is a shadowy figure that haunts media accounts of trauma. The woman who is insane enough to believe herself free is corrected – schooled by the hard knock meted out to her by her rapists. The desire to move freely in the world – or, more realistically, the realisation that one is in danger but to choose to hope for the best, as the alternative is a life of appalling constraint – becomes a kind of insanity. By producing the rape victim as not just culpable but also insane, 'we' (the audience) come to know our complicity with rape culture as sanity. As in neoliberal recovery narratives aimed at traumatised subjects and those categorised as disabled, the progression from victim to survivor is here imagined as linear and contingent on the assumption of personal responsibility for one's own recovery. This recalls JiJi Voronka's (2016) work on the victim-blaming that is implicit in mental health recovery discourse: as she reminds us, the subaltern cannot speak, since interpellation into language renders him/her complicit with the dominant culture. Similarly, in neoliberal recovery narratives, the 'rape victim' cannot speak, since the language of speaking out has been universally appropriated as the language of recovery. To speak as a victim is to become a not-victim, silencing the actual suffering occasioned by rape culture. Echoing Spivak's claim that 'the subaltern cannot speak', we might conclude that the victim-survivor cannot speak, since to speak is necessarily to take up the status of not-victim. While the women who are spoken for in the Cologne attacks must be imagined as permanently scarred victims for their stories to drive the racist and nationalist rhetoric of the right, 'to speak' is inherently to refuse such a positioning.

What is striking about the 'telling and retelling' of the survivor narrative of speaking is imagined in terms of a moving away: away from the moment of the rape, itself, and from the bodily violence that the rape inflicted. This moving away entails the hope of a better future that is achieved by taking personal responsibility. For all the graphic details that public and sensationalist media accounts incorporate, they are imagined as a point of origin from which one moves forward into a brighter and stronger future. To remain traumatised is to be stuck in the past; this 'stuckness' is attributed not to the actions of the rapist, but to the victim's own stubbornness, in allowing, as the popular therapy meme has it, the rapist to 'take up living space in one's head'. How, then, might digital activism enable another way of speaking about sexual violence – a way that does not necessarily place the onus on survivors to make the harm done by their abusers disappear?

Faced with the reality of an epidemic of private trauma that is both masked and invalidated by sensational media accounts of rape, feminist and survivor activists have responded by turning to feminism's 'already there' in order to re-animate second-wave analysis of rape culture. The notion of speaking the unspeakable that is at stake in digital feminist responses to rape culture is rooted in consciousness raising and in gender and women's studies as a pedagogic project of breaking silences. This fact is tacitly acknowledged in, for example, the recirculation of germinal texts such as Audre Lorde's 'The Transformation of Silence into Language and Action' as a popular meme. In online feminist and survivor spaces, Lorde's words travel precisely through the 'telling and retelling' facilitated by meme culture. The words 'I have come to believe over and over again that what is most important to me must be spoken, made verbal and shared, even at the risk of having it bruised or misunderstood. That the speaking profits me, beyond any other effect' (Lorde, 1980) become a call for a different kind of speaking out – one that entails the formation of arbitrary, shifting and fluid alliances that mobilise technology as a tool through which the bodily and intimate work of consciousness raising is carried out. One fourth-wave feminist blogger expresses eloquently how technology might provide an extension of feminist activist and caring work in response to rape culture. Writing on 'Rape Culture 101' for the feminist website Shakesville, Melissa McEwan reproduces the definition by Buchwald and colleagues cited above. But this academic definition of rape culture, she contends, is not enough. Instead, she argues that internet feminism must provide not simply an abstract definition, but something more visceral and affective: 'something substantive enough to reach out and touch, in all its ugly, heaving, menacing grotesquery' (McEwan, 2009). It is precisely the 'heaving, menacing, grotesque' reality of inhabiting a rape culture that Internet feminism acknowledges and makes visible, refusing the slick, linear narratives foregrounded by the mainstream media. However, this is not 'new' work enabled by technology; rather, it entails precisely the 'reaching out and touching' – the bodily and affective allegiances – that have always been integral to the work of feminism, as the adoption and adaption of Lorde's work makes visible.

Project Unbreakable[2] is a Tumblr-based photography project that was founded in 2009 by the photographer Grace Brown, which uses selfies to draw attention to the reality of rape and sexual abuse. Each of the thousands of entries follows the same format: an individual survivor holds up a placard on which the words used by their attacker at the time of the assault are written. As I have written elsewhere, the effect of these images is powerful, and it is impossible to illustrate their impact by including just one or two: the stories move us on an individual level, but, taken together, they are overwhelming, exposing the myth of rape as a rare occurrence that happens only to a few (Ferreday, 2017). Project Unbreakable not only constitutes an intimate community of victim-survivors, but it also exposes and refuses the intimacy imposed by rapists on their victims. As Lauren Berlant notes, intimacy 'involves an aspiration for a narrative about something shared, a story about both oneself and others that will turn out in a particular way' (1998, p. 281).

At stake in these images is a refusal of the enforced intimacy imposed by violence and a potential for creating new, intimate survivor networks that privilege self-care and galvanise resistance. Recent entries demonstrate the extent to which sexual abuse entails both physical and psychic trauma. One woman documents how she was told, at age 9: 'I could teach you how to have sex.' On telling her family three years later, they ask: 'Are you sure it wasn't a dream?' Another tells of the flashbacks she experienced after having been repeatedly raped by her friend's father between the ages of 4 and 5, her belief that she had imagined the whole thing and her continuing struggle with relationships, even after her attacker was jailed: 'I still look for him everywhere' (Project Unbreakable). For others, the rapist's words draw on cultural narratives of victim-blaming: a 13-year-old boy was beaten and raped by his best friend after coming out to him, and was told: 'You're gay, you should want this,' mobilising the cultural hypersexualisation of gay men to make the victim accountable for his own assault.

Overwhelmingly, these are stories of betrayals of trust: in family members, partners, teachers and friends; and in one's own right as a citizen to go about freely in the world without being considered 'a bit nuts'. What they reveal is how often our engagement with public space is constructed through private experiences of violence – how rape operates to produce forms of private suffering in the face of which advice on 'how not to get raped' offers the cruellest of cruel optimisms. Although stories of stranger rape pepper these accounts, the vast majority show that rape most often 'takes place within zones of familiarity and comfort: friendship, the couple, and the family form' (ibid.). What is at stake for the perpetrator is not an aspiration that all will 'turn out beautifully' (Berlant, 1998, p. 281), but that secrets will remain buried. Further, the images embody and make visible the intimate work of survival that survivors must undertake in order to *be* survivors. Many document depression, trauma or self-harm. You wonder whose stories are *not* being told, because the protagonists still do not feel able to speak or because they are no longer alive to tell them. Seeing these selfies, one realises how much of the bodily 'safety work' through which subjects manage their sense of their own rapeability is being done by an *already* abused and traumatised population (a population that includes all genders, denying the essentialist narrative of women as natural 'prey', which, as I have suggested, is the savage implication that underlies much bland media coverage of 'avoiding rape').

These images are savagely affecting: they do the opposite of 'comfort and inspire'. A more recent movement along similar lines is the Twitter hashtag campaign #beenrapedneverreported, through which women and men tweet their experience of sexual violence, often for the first time, breaking through the screen of complacency through which rape culture is accepted and reproduced. By making visible the private and intimate pain with which millions are forced to live on a daily basis, the tweets enable connections between violated subjects that are public enough to make sexual violence visible as a culturally pervasive phenomenon and simultaneously constitute an intimate proximity, enabling new affective communities to be forged and continuing the work of consciousness raising that has long been central to feminist activism. As Adi Kuntsman argues, they 'work by mobilising the intimate and personal to political effect' (Kuntsman, 2015).

Conclusion: Islands of hope

In this chapter, I have explored some of the strategies employed by survivor activists that mobilise social and digital media in order to challenge Western culture's endemic acceptance of sexual violence as inevitable. In enabling new relationalities and intimacies, social media have enabled the emergence of creative forms of dissent, consciousness raising and support. Campaigns such as Project Unbreakable adopt counter-hegemonic strategies to materialise victim-survivors' experiences, providing a space for the messy emotions that are invisible in everyday life to be felt and social media's own rape culture to be challenged. The counter-public they construct is messy: 'more-or-less subaltern, more-or-less rational, more-or-less critical, and almost certainly partial, affective, interested and loud' (Rambukkana, 2016) and, unlike the neat story of the 'journey to forgiveness' and/or horror stories of the bestial Other that the mainstream media allows, they offer no easy resolution. Instead, I would argue that digital survivor activism embodies what Back (2015) terms 'radical hope': it produces 'islands of hope' that enable 'attention to the present and the expectation that something will happen that will be unexpected and this will gift an unforeseen opportunity' (2015, p. 1).

Hope is not a destination; it is perhaps an improvisation towards a future not yet realised. It is not cruel optimism that hides behind a promise that is broken before it is even made. It is an empirical question, and the sociology of hope requires an attentiveness to the moments when 'islands of hope' are established and the social conditions that make their emergence possible.

In this context, survivor activism constitutes an extension of spaces of 'radical hope' to which social justice movements have always turned. Crucially, in making the reality of ongoing trauma visible (and hence risking the stigma of being named 'just nuts'), and in refusing to do the 'safety work' of reassurance that Western capitalism demands of its wounded, survivor activists constitute an intimate counter-public. Central to this organisation is a refusal of the cruel optimism that is inherent in 'don't get raped' discourse and what is revealed to be its inevitable counterpart: the neoliberal survivor/recovery narrative that ensues when 'don't get raped' inevitably fails. This work is made all the more necessary by the inevitability of pushback in digital spaces, which enable positive forms of connection but inevitably invoke revictimisation in the form of equally powerful digital assemblages of epistemic and actual violence.

By situating survivor selfies in the context of a long history of feminist struggle to name and transform rape culture, it is possible to see how they carry on a long history of resistance. Digital survivor activism embodies the gritty, bloody, embattled, sad, grief-stricken and haunted realities about which second-wave feminism encouraged the oppressed to speak: realities that disrupt the recuperative public fantasies that the mainstream media produce precisely through co-opting radical activist practices of speaking out and subjugating to the individualising and victim-blaming logics of capitalist neoliberal governance, and through the continual work of processing the violence of a vigorous online anti-feminism that, since the 2016 US presidential election, has only become more radicalised and confident. The radical hope that emerges through online activism is always a work in progress: at this historical moment, it is more contingent, more fragile and more urgently necessary than ever.

Note

1 Retrieved from http://cityroom.blogs.nytimes.com/2007/11/15/central-park-rape-victim-and-oprah-at-odds/?_r=0

References

Alcoff, L. and Gray, L. (1993). Survivor discourse: Transgression or recuperation? *Signs*, 18(2), pp. 260–290.

Alcoff, L. (2015). Rape and the question of experience. Public lecture given at the Australian Catholic University, 17 September 2015.

Back, L. (2015). Blind pessimism and the sociology of hope. Discover Society. Retrieved from http://discoversociety.org/2015/12/01/blind-pessimism-and-the-sociology-of-hope

Baym, N. (2010). *Personal Connections in the Digital Age*. Malden, MA: Polity.

Berlant, L. (2007a). Cruel optimism: On Marx, loss and the senses. *New Formations*, 63 (Winter), pp. 33–51.

Berlant, L. (2007b). *The Female Complaint: The Unfinished Business of Sentimentality in American Culture*. Durham, NC: Duke University Press.

Buchwald, E., Fletcher, P.R. and Roth, M. (1983). *Transforming a Rape Culture*. Minneapolis, MN: Milkweed Editions.

Celona, L. and Hodge, M. (2016). Social media users slammed for suggesting woman murdered while jogging brought attack on herself for wearing 'tight clothing'. *The Sun*, August 4.

Coleman, R. (2008). 'Things that stay': Feminist theory, duration and the future. *Time and Society*, 17(1), pp. 85–102.

Ferreday, D. (2017) 'Like a Stone in Your Stomach': articulating the unspeakable in rape victim-survivors' activist selfies. In: C. Kuntsman, ed., *Selfie Citizenship*. London: Palgrave MacMillan.

Fraser, N. (1992). Rethinking the public sphere: A contribution to the critique of actually existing democracy. In: C. Calhoun, ed., *Habermas and the Public Sphere*. Cambridge, MA: MIT Press, pp. 109–142.

Habermas, J. (1989 [1962]). *The Structural Transformation of the Public Sphere: An Inquiry into a Category of Bourgeois Society* (T. Burger and F. Lawrence, trans.). Cambridge, MA: MIT Press.

Haritaworn, J. (2013). Beyond 'hate': Queer metonymies of crime, pathology and anti/violence. *Jindal Global Law Review*, 4(2), pp. 44–78.

Harris, S. (2016). Angela Merkel says she'll consider making it easier to deport migrants who commit crimes in the wake of Cologne attacks. Huffington Post. Retrieved from www.huffingtonpost.co.uk/2016/01/09/angela-merkel-deport-migrants-crimes-cologne-attacks_n_8943508.html

Hartley, E. (2016). Mayor of Cologne, Henriette Reker, says women should adopt 'code of conduct' to prevent sexual assault. Huffington Post. Retrieved from www.huffingtonpost.co.uk/2016/01/06/mayor-of-cologne-response-to-sexual-assaults-is-code-of-conduct-for-women-_n_8920690.html

Hemmings, C. (2005). Telling feminist stories. *Feminist Theory*, 6(2), pp. 115–139.

Horeck, T. (2004). *Public Rape*. London and New York: Routledge.

Isin, Engin (2009). Citizenship in flux: The figure of the activist citizen. *Subjectivity*, 29, pp. 367–388.

Keller, J., Mendes, K. and Ringrose, J. (2016). Speaking 'unspeakable things': Documenting digital feminist responses to rape culture. *Journal of Gender Studies* (online). Retrieved from www.tandfonline.com/doi/full/10.1080/09589236.2016.1211511?src=recsys

Kember, S. and Zylinska, E. (2012). *Life After New Media: Mediation as a Vital Process*. Cambridge, MA: MIT Press.

Kuntsman, A. (2015). Acts of selfie citizenship. Presentation at Selfie Citizenship, Manchester, 16 April.

Lear, J. (2006). *Radical Hope: Ethic in the Face of Cultural Devastation*. Cambridge, MA: Harvard University Press.

Lear, J. (2006). *Radical Hope: Ethic in the Face of Cultural Devastation*. Cambridge, MA: Harvard University Press.

Lorde, A. (1980). *The Transformation of Silence into Language and Action. The Cancer Journals*. San Francisco, CA: Aunt Lute Books.

McEwan, M. (2009). Rape Culture 101. Shakesville. Retrieved from www.shakesville.com/2009/10/rape-culture-101.html

Pearson, A. (2016). Why the Brexit referendum will be swung by the horrific events in Cologne. Daily Telegraph. Retrieved from www.telegraph.co.uk/news/politics/12095265/Why-the-Brexit-referendum-will-be-swung-by-the-horrific-events-in-Cologne.html

Project Unbreakable. Retrieved from http://projectunbreakable.tumblr.com

Rambukkana, N. (2015). From #RaceFail to #Ferguson: The digital intimacies of race-activist hashtag publics. *The Fibreculture Journal* (26).

Spivak, G.C. (1988). Can the subaltern speak? In: C. Nelson and L. Grossberg, eds., *Marxism and the Interpretation of Culture*. Urbana, IL: University of Illinois Press, pp. 271–313.

Vera-Grey, F. (2016). Have you ever wondered how much energy you put in to avoid being assaulted? It may shock you. The Conversation. Retrieved from http://theconversation.com/have-you-ever-wondered-how-much-energy-you-put-in-to-avoid-being-assaulted-it-may-shock-you-65372

Voronka, J. (2016). Mapping mad studies in movements, knowledge, and praxis. Keynote presentation at the Disability Studies Conference, Lancaster University, 7 September.

Walby, S., Olive, P., Towers, J., Francis, B., Strid, S., Krizsán , A., Lombardo , E., May-Chahal, C., Franzway, S., Sugarman, D. and Agarwal, B. (2013). *Overview of the Worldwide Best Practices for Rape Prevention and for Assisting Women Victims of Rape*. London: European Parliament.

Warner, M. (2002). *Publics and Counterpublics*. New York: Zone Books.

2 Intimate communities

Hackerspaces, digital engagement and affective relations

*Sarah R. Davies**

Introduction

> It's just such a warm community. And I don't understand necessarily how a community made up of fairly antisocial basement dwellers can be so warm and welcoming, but they are. And, it's interesting to be, to be here and to be able to travel anywhere and be welcomed at any hackerspace.

The speaker of the above quote, Tiah, runs a hackerspace in the Bay Area, California.[1] As a relatively new mother, she spoke about how it was easy to feel isolated; how smart women with 'full careers' and rich sets of interests and experiences 'decide to have kids [...] and suddenly you're back in 1950'. Tiah's journey had been particularly tumultuous. When she was pregnant with her second child, her partner had been diagnosed with cancer, and in order to survive she had found that she had to do 'something that was kind of extraordinary'. What she did was to craft a community in the shape of a new hackerspace – a grassroots-led community workshop. She brought together a group of like-minded individuals, but in doing so, she also – as the quote above suggests – gained access to a wider community, one that was 'warm and welcoming' and spread around the world. The hackerspace, Tiah said, gave her 'energy to deal with the rest of my life'.

If intimacies are 'our closest relationships', which 'touch the personal world very deeply' (Plummer, 2003, p. 13), Tiah found herself within a deeply intimate community. Her personal world was rejuvenated through the new relationships she formed in her hackerspace. Through setting up her hackerspace and involvement in the wider hackerspace community she was able to share her most intense struggles and draw energy from the excitement

* As the methodology discussion describes, the fieldwork on which this analysis is based was carried out with a colleague at Arizona State University, Dr Dave Conz. Dr Conz was also involved in designing and planning the research, but, tragically, he died soon after the fieldwork was completed. It is important to me to acknowledge the central contribution he made to this work, and to express the hope that this writing can serve as a celebration of his research into making and hacking.

of sharing and developing her ideas. She and others involved – often similarly hard-pressed mothers – were able to 'be their best selves again'. In this respect, her experience is indicative of what I will argue in this chapter: that hackerspaces enable the performance of new kinds of affective relations – relations that are mediated through a combination of online and offline encounters. On their own, neither digital media nor face-to-face engagement are sufficient for developing these intimacies. Taken together, they enable a particular kind of intimate community. I thus view intimacy as, certainly, involving relationships that touch on the personal, but more importantly as involving particular affective valences. Intimacy is an affective entanglement that relates to personal meaning-making, identity and self-worth. It is elective and involves disclosure; it enables, then, the presentation and development of authentic selves (Chambers, 2013).

Context and method: Hackerspaces and the maker movement

Hackers are at pains to point out that hackerspaces are not spaces for hacking in the nefarious sense. Tiah told me that hacking is simply about 'changing something to suit your own needs'. As such it is a process, or mindset, that can be applied to anything from furniture to baking to computer operating systems. Hackerspaces are places that encourage or enable this mindset. '[T]he typical hackerspace is an organisation, like a club,' writes hacker John Baichtal, 'founded by its members for their mutual benefit [...] On a very basic level, hackerspaces are simply workshops that are available for rent' (2012, p. 3). Hackerspaces are thus public or semi-public spaces that provide access to a range of tools and equipment, from industrial sewing machines to wood lathes, laser cutters and 3D printers. Though the roots of hackerspaces go back to early 1960s computer hacks and the emergence of information technologies (Coleman, 2013; Levy, 1985), hackerspaces have exploded in number over the last decade, from 30 worldwide in 2007 to 1,233 active spaces in 2016 (Davies, 2017). They are viewed as one aspect of a broader 'maker movement': a wave of interest in, and tools and technologies for, diverse forms of making (Barba, 2015). 'Making has become a mainstream word,' argues Evan Barba, and 'discussions of its potential to alter industrial processes, consumer culture, and pedagogy are approaching critical mass' (2015, p. 639).

The maker movement is in many ways about a self-conscious return to engagement with the physical world. Though software, apps and digital products are also made in this movement, the emphasis is on a move 'from bits to atoms' (Gershenfeld, 2005) that takes advantage of new technologies for rapid prototyping and manufacturing.

The excitement that has arisen around hackerspaces and the maker movement – and there has been much – is frequently connected to their potential for fostering grassroots innovation and product development. For technology entrepreneur and writer Chris Anderson (a former editor of

Wired), for instance, the maker movement is ushering in a 'new industrial revolution' in which garage tinkerers are able to cheaply prototype and manufacture their ideas and, possibly, hit the big time (Anderson, 2012). In an age of cheap 3D printers and digital design, Anderson argues that inventors can now become entrepreneurs: 'The history of the past two decades online is one of an extraordinary explosion of innovation and entrepreneurship. It's now time to apply that to the real world' (p. 15). The movement thus emphasises the merging of the physical with the digital. The emphasis may be on 'atoms' rather than 'bits', but connectivities enabled by the internet and digital media remain a prerequisite for new manufacturing.

In 2012, I and a colleague visited 12 hackerspaces across the US, carrying out 30 interviews (some of which were with two or more people) and observing the dynamics of the spaces. Drawing on science and technology studies (STS), our research sought to describe emergent practices in hacker and makerspaces and to understand how these connect to wider dynamics around science, technology and democracy. We spoke to mundane users of hackerspaces, or 'ordinary hackers' (Schrock, in press), rather than high-profile leaders of the movement, such as Anderson, as we wanted to understand not so much the public excitement around making but the way that it was experienced by hackers and makers. We contacted hacker and makerspaces in four locations across the US and arranged visits to those spaces and interviews with individuals participating in them (usually carried out in the spaces). Given the emergent nature of the movement at that time, our research was exploratory and took an ethnographic orientation: we were interested in actors' terms and meanings (Hammersley and Atkinson, 1995) about hacking and making and the emerging movement around these activities. Recruitment was organised via convenience and snowball sampling (Cresswell, 2002). We used the website hackerspaces.org to identify hacker and makerspaces in four metro regions across the US (to ensure diversity in the spaces visited), contacted these spaces to arrange visits and recruit interview participants and, once on site, used snowball sampling to recruit further interviewees. Interviews were semi-structured, lasted approximately one hour and covered three main topics: participants' experiences of involvement in their space; their understanding of how this space was run and operated; and their connections with broader networks and organisations relating to hacking.

Analysis focused on the key themes that emerged from the interviews, as identified through iterative processes of interpretative coding (Silverman, 2001), and was shaped by STS traditions such as a focus on the interactions between material and social actors and a critical interest in the constitution of technoscience (Yearley, 2005). In addition, as the analysis developed, I mobilised notions of social capital (Putnam, 2001) and serious leisure (Stebbins, 2011) to better understand emergent themes. I was primarily concerned with the shared meanings that emerged from the interviews, rather than comparisons of spaces.[2] What common stories were being told by users of hacker and makerspaces about their practices?

In brief, while public proponents of the maker movement tend to emphasise the combination of digital technology with hands-on engagement with the physical world as a means of technological innovation, the hackers we spoke to largely saw such innovation as an interesting side-effect, if present at all. What they crafted in hackerspaces were new kinds of relations – to technology, but also to each other. They were making community, a community that was experienced as intimate in that it met deeply seated personal desires and needs. Just as Tiah's space 'gave her energy' and was 'something extraordinary', other hackers similarly talked about the life-changing effects of the intimacies that had developed through their hackerspace community. In what follows, I outline some of the key themes that emerged concerning hacking, community and intimacy as hackers and makers discussed their practices. I use illustrative quotes to represent widely shared concepts throughout.

New intimacies

Interviewees focused on two kinds of relations in their framing of the intimacies produced within hackerspaces. First, we were told that hacking, as a practice, enabled a new way of relating to technology. Rather than being constrained by devices or technologies, hackers were able to understand and participate in those technologies. They developed an intimacy with technology that reclaimed agency and empowerment. Second, they conveyed experiences of intimate interpersonal community. By participating in a hackerspace, hackers could 'find their people', experience a 'second lease of life' or find 'family' and 'home'. All of these forms of intimacy involved close relationships and deeply seated emotional commitments and experiences. They were constituted through in-depth knowledge of other actors (whether human or technological) and a range of strongly felt emotions, both positive and negative.

It is perhaps not surprising that hackers described themselves as having a special relationship with technology. The term 'hacker' retains connotations of computer hacking and of – as Tiah put it in the opening quote – 'anti-social basement dwellers' who are more adept at developing technology than honing their social skills. What is more striking is that this relation was emphatically not about expertise or skill. Being a hacker – an identity one could be encultured into through participation in a hackerspace – was about having a particular attitude towards technology, rather than knowing a lot about it. In addition, technology was itself understood in broad terms. Hackers might hack on very hi-tech things, such as software or 3D printers or drones, but they might also intervene in low-tech processes, such as beer brewing or carpentry, or even in the social technologies required to maintain a community. This is what New York-based hacker Nick had to say about the hacker 'approach'. He has been talking about a phone he had unlocked, contrary to the manufacturer's terms and conditions:

> That approach, I'm going to take this product and I'm going to do something with it. I'm going to bend it in a way that it wasn't intended, and

> it may not be permitted even in some cases. But I don't care because it's mine. I bought this; it's mine. [You can] take that attitude and you apply it to a large spectrum of things [...] I'll take my cleverness and skill to solve a problem, to deal with an issue, and create some workable situation.

Hacking, then, is not about a particular skillset so much as the attitude one takes to technology and, indeed, to the world at large. Other hackers spoke about taking control, reclaiming ownership or using technology to do what they wanted, rather than what it was designed for or how others thought it should be used. Of course, one also developed intimacies with specific technologies or tools. Hackers spoke about the pleasures of deep learning as they became intimate with problems, projects and objects. Building and maintaining a 3D printer, for instance, was both a relatively common hackerspace project and one that required you to become intensely familiar with its wood and metal components and the relevant software; more than this, however, and given that 3D printers were often temperamental and unstable, such projects required a deep sensitivity to and patience with the technology's moods and flaws and a degree of emotional investment (Bardzell et al., 2014). Beyond these specific intimacies, the broader point is that hackers are unafraid of technology. 'One of the cool things about hackerspaces,' Keith told us, 'is the shift from being someone who uses technology to someone who makes technology.' Being intimate with technology through hacking thereby involves a confident relation to it – its treatment as a close friend, whom one views with affection, rather than as something alien or intimidating.

This relation to technology – which was seen as distinct from mainstream societal attitudes – was itself intertwined with the development of new interpersonal relationships. As noted above, hackers frequently emphasised that use of their hackerspace was life-changing with regard to the access it granted them to a particular community. The hackerspace was both a venue for meeting like-minded people – others who shared the hacker attitude to life – and a petri dish for the formation of deep, messy, committed community. The relationships in this community were presented as a contrast to the superficial relationships, often mediated by social media, that were considered the norm in mainstream society. This is Arizonan hacker Kev talking about hackerspace community:

> Hackerspaces aren't clean and pretty and I don't want them to be clean and pretty. And by the way, community's not clean and pretty. The community's really fucking rough and ugly and dirty and is fighting about it and screaming at each other [...] I want to be clean insofar as we got our 501(c)(3) to prove that we're not like hackers who steal things. But other than that, I want to be a complicated pain in the ass, not a clean space, where decision-making isn't easy and you guys have to have an opinion.

Most people, Kev told us, are essentially passive. They go through life accepting the limitations and constraints that are presented to them and not needing to make much of an effort. But hackerspace community is more demanding, and requires the active participation and engagement of every person involved. This kind of community is 'dirty', requiring everyone to 'have an opinion', even if that involves 'fighting' and 'screaming'. The 501(c)(3) Kev mentions refers to the hackerspace's status as a non-profit organisation. They are, he says, 'clean' in that they are legal and not the kind of 'hackers who steal things', but dirty and messy otherwise. Performing community is thus hard, but reflects the 'real world' (Kev told us) and provides tangible benefits in terms of the satisfaction of committed relationships. As Keith, another hacker, told us: 'It's exciting for me to see people's time and energy going into productive products but also collaborating with each other.' Intimacy here is thus about closeness and commitment, even above positive affect. Intimate community is difficult, but for exactly this reason it is valued as a meaningful addition to one's personal life.

We can return to Tiah to see how profound this experience of community can be, and how it is used to meet deeply personal needs. Tiah's space was orientated towards mothers; based on her own experiences, she felt that parents needed a space to do more than simply 'talk about poopy diapers all the time'. This kind of community, which focused not on social roles (such as parenthood or profession) but on 'ideas', enables its members to be with 'their people' – to, in some way, be their genuine, authentic selves:

> So when a hacker mom comes in, immediately the conversation gets interesting. And we talk about – we kind of don't talk much about our kids. We don't talk about poopy diapers. We talk about ourselves and what we're interested in and what our projects are and, 'Oh, I know somebody who does this,' and, 'Do you need that?' [...] people are talking about ideas and the status of their project and their visions and stuff like that. It's so electric and inspiring.

For Tiah and many other hackers, the intimacy experienced within hackerspaces was a means of self-actualisation (Stebbins, 2011). The relationships in these communities were ones of recognition and affirmation, enabling the full expression of oneself and one's interests; they were intimate, then, in that they related to the personal and allowed its articulation in conditions of mutual support. Again, this doesn't necessarily imply straightforwardly positive emotions. Such authentic relationships could also involve the sharing of fears and failures. But, as with the difficulties of community described by Kev, this kind of intimacy was powerful exactly because it could be challenging. Some talked about the electrifying effects of finding this kind of community, and its importance to them. I have mentioned the metaphors of 'home' and a 'second lease of life' used by hackers; others spoke about 'loving and adoring the culture', having a permanent commitment to the maker movement no matter where they were in the world and their hackerspace being 'close to their heart'. Hackerspaces, it seems, met a need for a particular kind of community, and the performance of particular kinds of intimacies, that was not being met elsewhere.[3]

Merging digital media and face-to-face engagement

In contrast to much public discussion of the maker movement and hopes that hacking and making will stimulate innovation, these hackers told us that their involvement in hackerspaces met rather different needs. Rather than making products, they crafted new intimacies. The development of new kinds of relations with technology was intertwined with the satisfaction of a 'messy' but committed community and a 'camaraderie' or 'fraternity' that spoke to hackers' sense of identity. '[I]t's kind of like that brotherhood,' Kip told us, describing what it felt like to meet another hacker, 'and you kind of understand what they went through and what they do.' Hacker and makerspaces were viewed as spaces not for entrepreneurship, but for close emotional engagement with other actors, and the resulting intimacies were viewed as meeting important personal needs.

In some ways these intimacies were not dissimilar to those formed through other kinds of associations or hobby activities, which enable members to form close-knit social bonds and use membership to develop their sense of self (Stebbins, 2011). What is significant here, however, is the way in which such bonds were developed and maintained. Much has been made of the maker movement's potential for promoting physical manufacturing through the use of digital tools and connectivities (Anderson, 2012), and our interviews similarly indicated that hackerspaces were experienced and maintained through a merging of digital and social media with 'real world' engagement. This merging was, however, focused on interpersonal relationships and the crafting of community rather than on entrepreneurship or commercial manufacturing. The affordances of digital networks were valued because they enabled community and 'camaraderie' through their integration with face-to-face relationships, rather than for their economic potential.

Hackerspace intimacies were constituted through a number of flows across the digital and physical. First, and on the most pragmatic level, it simply would not have been possible to launch and recruit for many hackerspaces without new media. Most of the hackerspaces that we visited had started on social media platforms, such as a Reddit thread, message board community, Kickstarter project or other online community, before meeting in real life. Once these communities coalesced and – perhaps – found a permanent physical space, they often continued to rely on digital media to advertise and recruit. This reliance on social media led to a striking irony. Several people that we spoke to told us that they valued their hackerspace because it allowed them to meet like-minded people from their neighbourhood whom they would otherwise never talk to. 'There are people probably living next door to me that have great ideas and great skills,' said Simon, 'and I wouldn't know otherwise.' Hackerspaces were valued because they gave access to a local, real world community – a space to talk to one's (interesting) neighbours and discover shared interests in a way that was framed as unusual in contemporary urban and suburban America. But this very sense of locality was only possible because of digital networks such as Reddit, Meet-Up or Facebook, which spread the word to a neighbourhood and beyond without people having to *actually* talk to their neighbours or advertise through face-to-face means. Hackers presented themselves as hungry for real-life interaction; digital media, however, were fundamental for enabling this interaction.

Beyond this strictly utilitarian function of digital media, online engagement was also central to maintaining the *quality* of hackerspace intimacies. New media not only enabled face-to-face relationships, but were used to manage these intimacies in particular ways and to ensure that they took on a specific character. The hackers that we interviewed told us that online discussion and communication were central to the daily functioning of their space. In order to understand this, it is useful to know a little more about the online tools used by the hackerspaces we encountered. Hackerspaces generally had some social media presence, including a Facebook page, Twitter account and (perhaps) LinkedIn page, alongside a website and an associated wiki (easily updated by all members to show the status of particular projects or to advertise events). For the most part, however, these platforms were seen as 'output devices' – spaces to publish on rather than to perform community through. In contrast, email discussion lists, such as those hosted by Google Groups, were viewed as central to managing intimate community within a hackerspace.[4] Most spaces had several lists, some of which might be focused on specific aspects of the space (such as finances or events), alongside a general 'discuss' list; these discuss lists were often highly trafficked (with 10 to 15 emails a day). It was through the discuss list, in particular, that relations between hackers – who might only bump into each other in the space once a week, if that – were solidified and rendered capable of bearing the emotional weight that intimate community entailed.

It was clear, for instance, that email list discussions were framed as seamless extensions of the 'real life' conversation that took place in the hackerspace. This is Boston hacker Fee talking about how people used their discuss list:

> People write to the list a lot, you know, with kind of administrative complaints that you get running a shop like who left the band saw covered in dust, clean up after yourself [...] but the really interesting part of the list, and I think most of the traffic, is people discussing projects. People will send questions like where can I find this part or like I want to build this and I'm not sure how to do this part of it, [to get] advice.

Fee frames the email list as an overflow and extension of hackerspace interactions. It was used firstly for 'administrative complaints' (the virtual equivalent of someone yelling out: 'Who left the band saw covered in dust?'). Hackers placed a high priority on how one behaved in the space, with many noting that volunteer organisations such as theirs relied on people acting altruistically (by, for instance, leaving the space tidier than they found it). Email discussions therefore acted as a means for further normalising and policing this performance of community. Similarly, they extended another attitude that was seen as essential to hackerspace intimacies: openness and mutual learning (Davies, 2017). As Fee explained, much hackerspace communication, online or otherwise, was comprised of questions, requests for information or help and updates on projects. The use of online tools meant that intimacies with technologies and other hackers could be a focus without being confined to face-to-face engagement within the hackerspace. One might start by asking a question of others in the space, and continue by posting it to the mailing list. The wider community was thus always accessible as a pool of experience and expertise, and hacker principles such as 'learning from others' could be lived out continuously, rather than being limited to particular times or physical spaces.

Online discussion was seen as merging seamlessly with face-to-face community, with relatively little distinction made between interactions within the hackerspace and those mediated by the email list. But digital communication could also be used more strategically, as a way of ensuring that experiences of intimate community within the hackerspace were not marred by negatives such as bureaucracy or what was called 'drama' – interpersonal conflicts, arguments or unspoken tensions. It was thus used as a means of developing and maintaining the right kind of face-to-face intimacy – one that was cordial or constructive, rather than aggressive or bad-tempered. For instance, many hackerspaces used their email discussion lists to discuss potential decisions, ensuring that business meetings in the space were concise or at least that members were well prepared for them. Bay Area hacker Nicole told us that, in the past, they had saved up decisions relating to the shared organisation of the space for a single business meeting, but then 'everyone would want to talk about them, of course. That's fine. That makes sense. But then we're here until God knows when.' Their space therefore sought to reach consensus through online interactions before decisions were later ratified at a face-to-face meeting. Similarly, the mailing list was used to vent or express dissatisfaction in a way that, within the hackerspace, might have disturbed the experience of friendly, welcoming community that was viewed as essential. Hackers might not have necessarily felt comfortable yelling out: 'Who left the band saw covered in dust? Clean up after yourself!' or asking someone to move a large and unwieldy project that was taking up shared space. The mailing list was thus seen as something of an equaliser – a place where hackers could express 'drama' that, in person, would be considered aggressive or offensive, and a means of ensuring a (more) equal voice for different personalities or approaches. 'The mailing list works out very well for people having to actually express their interest or frustrations and stuff,' Dan told us, 'versus at a meeting where people will say something and the strongest personality wins out.'

Finally, digital tools enabled the ready extension of a local hackerspace community – intimacy with a local, tightly knit group – to an idea of wider fraternity. Tiah, as we saw in the opening quote, felt that she could 'travel anywhere and be welcomed at any hackerspace'. Despite the emphasis on the local and the face-to-face, hackers were also proud to be part of a 'brotherhood' that shared something 'universal'. The notion of community was thus mobilised in at least two ways. It was used to refer to a local community, one in which face-to-face engagement enabled life-changing intimacies; but it was also presented as a worldwide community, one in which hackers everywhere shared the same 'spirit'. Local intimacies were extended to a global hackerspace community in a slippage rendered possible by digital tools such as message boards and the map of hackerspaces maintained by the site hackerspaces.org. Hackers could thereby identify and find each other as they moved around the world, and could be confident of accessing the same kind of community they were already familiar with. 'A lot of times we'll have people that say, "I'm from this hackerspace, can I visit?"' Nick told us. 'And I will personally try to bend over backwards to try and be there.' Community was produced and managed in small, face-to-face groups, but social media enabled hackers to reproduce its intimacies as they moved around the world.

Conclusion: The 'exodus to the real world'

Why do people use hackerspaces? We were given a variety of reasons: hackers wanted access to tools, had a project they'd always meant to develop or wanted to participate in a course or workshop the space was running. Overwhelmingly, though, the reason most hackers became more seriously involved in their hackerspace was the experience of community it provided. 'The community,' we were told, 'is integral.' This community was described as one that relied on face-to-face interaction. One couldn't genuinely experience it by lurking on email lists (however important these lists were to hackerspace communication). As I've described, many hackers emphasised the value of engagement with other hackers in real life and the pleasures of interacting with both technologies and tools and other hackers in person. Hackerspaces were spaces for intimacy in that they enabled deep, committed and emotional relationships with other actors – relationships that were viewed as impinging on the personal. Importantly, this was an intimacy in which physical engagement was key, though it might be enabled by social media. Some hackers we spoke to referred to a kind of exhaustion with the digital, and a sense that too much of their life was lived via a screen. '[My hackerspace involvement] is sort of coming off of years of spending 14 hours a day working on a laptop,' Lou told us. Her priority was 'getting to work with my hands and sort of returning to the physical'. Similarly, Keith talked about the difference between a games night at his hackerspace and playing (the online game and app) Words with Friends online. It was great, he said, to see people collaborating in person and 'not just sitting at home' watching television or playing online games. Personally, this was an important move for him – he felt it was important, at this point in his life, to invest in real world relationships – but he also saw it as a broader positive development, something that was valuable for society as a whole.

In this respect, hackerspace involvement can be seen as part of what Shen and Cage call an 'exodus to the real world' (2015). In a study of meetups – real world get-togethers and events that spin out of online communities – they suggest that such encounters strengthen 'bonding' social capital (which solidifies ties within groups) but weaken 'bridging' social capital (which allows connections between diverse individuals and communities; Putnam, 2001), making it harder for newcomers to get involved in the community. The development of close-knit community is accelerated through face-to-face engagement; as such, members may find it most satisfying to combine online and real world encounters. People, they say:

> join an interest-based community to connect with like-minded others, they find the friends they seek, then strengthen these loose ties and tend to stay embedded within closed social groups. Meetups thus could be considered an accelerator of this process, converting interest-based and online-only ties among strangers to close connections that traverse online and offline boundaries.
>
> (Shen and Cage, 2015, p. 410)

Such 'close connections' are certainly provided by hackerspace involvement. What is striking in this context, however, is the degree to which these close ties continue to be enabled by online engagement. As I have argued, the intimacies of hackerspace community are supported by digital tools in multiple ways: social media are used to extend and prolong interpersonal interactions, to manage conflict and bureaucracy and to give a worldwide community the characteristics of a local one. However much hackers choose to emphasise the importance of face-to-face engagement, the character of that engagement was enabled and managed through online tools. Hackerspace intimacies therefore present us with a set of tensions. They emphasise real world encounters but are seamlessly lived out online. They are deeply personal but retain a public character (most hackerspace email discuss lists and other online materials are available to anyone). They offer a life-changing experience of local community but simultaneously provide access to a worldwide 'fraternity'. And, unlike the meetups that Shen and Cage studied, they seem to combine strong face-to-face ties with an online and offline community that newcomers can readily access. In these respects, hackerspaces may offer some clues about the complex ways in which intimacies are, and will be, performed in contemporary society, with its increasing dependence on the internet and social media. This data indicates, for instance, that intimacy can be experienced through the meshing of online and face-to-face encounters, and that it may even be deepened by this means of experiencing relationships. What this suggests is that any experience of community is unlikely to be straightforward, produced solely by a single kind of encounter. Rather, as with hackerspace intimacies, it will be made and managed via multiple platforms and in socially complex ways.

Notes

1 All names have been anonymised.
2 Further details about the research can be found in Davies 2017.
3 Whether hackerspace communities are actually distinct is another question. Those we spoke to said that hackerspaces met an important need in their lives, giving them access to a sense of community that they did not find elsewhere. But they also, at times, drew parallels between hackerspace communities and other kinds of social clubs or organisations (e.g. guerilla gardening, quilting circles, motorcycle co-ops). In practice, it seems likely that hackerspaces were experienced as important because they involved close-knit and committed community, not because they were the only places such community existed (see Davies 2017).
4 Some spaces also used instant messaging platforms or IRC (internet relay chat) channels for this kind of quick-fire discussion.

References

Anderson, C. (2012). *Makers: The New Industrial Revolution.* London: Crown Business.

Baichtal, J. (2012). *Hack This: 24 Incredible Hackerspace Projects from the DIY Movement.* Indianapolis, IN: Que.

Barba, E. (2015). Three reasons why the future is in the making. *Science, Technology & Human Values*, 40(4), pp. 638–650.

Bardzell, J., Bardzell, S. and Toombs, A. (2014). Now that's definitely a proper hack: Self-made tools in hackerspaces. In: *Proceedings of the SIGCHI Conference on Human Factors in Computing Systems, CHI '14.* New York: ACM, pp. 473–476.

Chambers, D. (2013). *Social Media and Personal Relationships.* London: Palgrave Macmillan.

Coleman, E.G. (2013). *Coding Freedom: The Ethics and Aesthetics of Hacking.* Princeton, NJ and Oxford: Princeton University Press.

Creswell, J.W. (2002). *Research Design: Qualitative, Quantitative, and Mixed Methods Approaches.* Thousand Oaks, CA: SAGE.

Davies, S.R. (2017). *Hackerspaces: Making the Maker Movement.* Cambridge: Polity.

Gershenfeld, N. (2005). *Fab: The Coming Revolution on Your Desktop – From Personal Computers to Personal Fabrication.* New York: Basic Books.

Hammersley, M. and Atkinson, P. (1995). *Ethnography.* London: Routledge.

Levy, S. (1985). *Hackers: Heroes of the Computer Revolution – 25th Anniversary Edition*. Sebastopol, CA: O'Reilly Media.

Maly, T. (n.d.). What we talk about when we talk about what we talk about when we talk about making. Quiet Babylon. Retrieved from http://quietbabylon.com/2014/what-we-talk-about-when-we-talk-about-what-we-talk-about-when-we-talk-about-making/ (August 17, 2016).

Nagbot, S. (2016). Feminist hacking/making: Exploring new gender horizons of possibility. *Journal of Peer Production* (8).

Plummer, K. (2003). *Intimate Citizenship: Private Decisions and Public Dialogues*. Montreal: McGill-Queen's University Press.

Putnam, R.D. (2001). *Bowling Alone*. New York: Simon & Schuster.

Schrock, A. (in press). Hackers are ordinary: Entanglement in hacker and maker spaces. In: J. Hunsinger and A. Schrock, eds., *Making Our World: The Hacker and Maker Movements in Context*. New York: Peter Lang.

Shen, C. and Cage, C. (2015). Exodus to the real world? Assessing the impact of offline meetups on community participation and social capital. *New Media & Society*, 17(3), pp. 394–414.

Silverman, D. (2001). *Interpreting Qualitative Data*. London: SAGE.

Stebbins, R.A. (2011). The semiotic self and serious leisure. *The American Sociologist*, 42(2-3), pp. 238–248.

Yearley, S. (2005). *Making Sense of Science: Understanding the Social Study of Science*. London: SAGE.

3 Online community and new family scripts

Rikke Andreassen

Introduction

This chapter describes how mothers with donor-conceived children from Denmark, Sweden and Norway connect with each other digitally through Facebook and form an intimate online community. Through analysis of a closed Facebook group connecting donor families with one another and interviews with members of this group, the chapter illustrates how characteristic features of social media sites (e.g. anonymity and distance across time) can ambivalently dilute communication while simultaneously cultivating and upholding it.

While some scholars, such as Frank, Clough and Seidman (2013, p. 5), argue that 'new cyber culture has encouraged public practices of self-exploration and identification that challenge the historic association of intimacy, self-disclosure and privacy', this chapter conversely shows that online culture does not necessarily challenge previous understandings of intimacy and self-disclosure; rather, it provides a platform for continuing historical forms of intimacy and self-disclosure.

While I have written elsewhere about the ways in which the online interactions of donor families can have a regulative function in maintaining normative understandings of family – that is, by upholding the nuclear family as an ideal (Andreassen, 2016, 2017) – I am here interested in the way in which an online community of donor families challenges pre-defined scripts of family formations. Thus, I am not interested in defining what intimacy *is*, but rather analysing what intimacy *does*.

In this chapter, I analyse the online Facebook donor community via contextualised perspectives and practices; in doing so, I do not claim to conclude anything general about Facebook, donor families or women and the internet. Rather, I seek to provide a micro perspective of a specific community in which online media have proven important for forming intimacy. This perspective is important for understanding (some of) the complexities of online interaction.

Theoretical framework

I draw upon Berlant's description of intimacy as a promise of belonging (Berlant, 2008, p. ix), but I define the term a bit differently, namely as an *experience of belonging*. I understand intimacy as relational: the experience of belonging and being connected, and the practices that accompany, lead to and negotiate belonging and connectedness. Berlant (1998) and McGlotten (2013) view intimacy as a normative and regulatory narrative. While I agree with this, I am also inspired by Frank, Clough and Seidman (2013), who argue in favour of adding a more subjective and interpersonal aspect to intimacy analysis. While they acknowledge that intimacy may function as a normative script, they also emphasise that the personal agency one employs when engaging in relations must be recognised in intimacy analysis (pp. 2–4). They promote a complex understanding of intimacy that employs perspectives of both individual agency and larger societal norms.

Thumin points out that online social networking and online self-representation are interlinked, as self-representation is often a condition for social network participation (Thumin, 2012, p. 137). This is especially true for the Facebook group analysed here, as its community is constructed via members' self-representations of personal family matters. While Thumin is mainly interested in self-representation, this chapter focuses on the way in which self-representations create community and intimate belonging.

In her article 'Let me tell you who I am', Nicholson (2013) describes how self-disclosure (which Thumin would term 'self-representation') has historically been a central means of establishing intimacy. Nicholson outlines the historical development of psychology, wherein self-disclosure evolved from a tool for understanding the inner self of deviant individuals at the turn of the twentieth century to a tool for developing more fulfilling relationships and, a hundred years later, a tool for achieving a successful life (Nicholson, 2013, pp. 34 ff.). Today, self-disclosure can both create and measure intimacy (ibid., p. 30). Nicholson argues that communication that entails self-disclosure has become a central aspect of contemporary relationships (ibid., p. 39). At the same time, structures of belonging (e.g. family) have changed from being fixed by law and customs to becoming more fluid and less defined by regulations (ibid.).

Another important development involving the self-disclosure of feelings has been the change from private self-disclosure (i.e. expressing feelings to one's intimate partner or doctor) to more public self-disclosure. During the 1960s and 1970s, self-disclosure changed from being a private affair to a more public affair (ibid., p. 41). The women's movement and women's consciousness-raising groups of the 1970s were important in this progression.

Over the previous decade, the development and expansion of public self-disclosure have been heavily fuelled by new media technologies, such as Facebook, Twitter and Instagram. Several media scholars have criticised the way in which these new media technologies invite self-disclosure and influence our interactions (McGlotten, 2013; Turkle, 2011). Turkle describes how, due to relationship fatigue, many people turn to artificial intelligence (AI) (e.g. robots) for companionship. She is critical towards the phenomenon that sees an increasing number of people drawn to 'easy' connections – connections that do not require demanding returns and can be interrupted or left as desired (Turkle, 2011, p. 10). Turkle's criticism of relationships between humans and AI creatures, as well as of online relations and communication, touches upon the 'old' question of authenticity. Authenticity was also at the centre of much early scholarship on online communities (Cooks, Paredes and Scharrer, 2003, p. 140), focusing on what constitutes a 'real' community and debating whether online meetings can count as equally 'real' and 'valuable' as physical meetings.

One alternative to the discussion of what is 'real' and 'authentic' is provided by Cooks, Paredes and Scharrer (2003), who explore the way in which online community is *experienced*, rather than focusing on what online community *is*. They describe the formation of an online community of women in their analysis of Oprah Winfrey's interactive website 'O Place', showing how the website functions as a vehicle for friendship and community: 'It is a place where women go to seek support from others, to give one another advice, to voice an opinion or describe an experience, and to come together as a community' (Cooks, Paredes and Scharrer, 2003, p. 140). Despite the obvious technological differences between a website from 2002 and a contemporary Facebook group, which involve important developments in the media landscape, I find their analysis very useful for understanding community formation. However, one central difference between their empirical material and mine should be highlighted: At the beginning of the twenty-first century, only a minority of US women had access to the internet; consequently, the members of the website analysed by Cooks, Paredes and Scharrer were middle- and upper-class women (p. 158). Today, internet penetration is much higher. In Denmark (where most members of the 'Donor group' live), Internet penetration is at 97 per cent (Internet World Stats). Furthermore, Facebook is very popular among Danes, with more than 3 million using the site (out of a population of 5.6 million) (ibid.). Members of the Donor group therefore constitute a much broader group of individuals, representing various social classes.

Analytically, Cooks, Paredes and Scharrer (2003) approach O Place as an imagined community that is already marked by everyday life practices (p. 143). Drawing upon Dietrich (1997), who argues that women participate online as 'subjects of culture' (Cooks, Paredes and Scharrer, 2003, p. 143) and hence engage in online communities as mothers, professionals and so forth, they see online practices as linked to everyday practices and the everyday subjectivity of culture(s). Similarly, Bennett (2015) points to the ways in which online media and media engagements are embedded in social structures and experiences; consequently, he suggests the contextualisation of participation and media in analyses of online engagement (Bennett, 2015, p. ix).

Methodology and empirical sources

The empirical sources for this chapter consist of analysis of the Donor Facebook group and in-depth interviews with 11 people who are active in this group. All interviewees are women, just as the majority of the Facebook group members are women. While there are a few male members in the group, none is active in the activities analysed here. The 11 qualitative interviews cannot claim to represent the views of the whole Donor group, but they provide insights for understanding group members' experiences. Interviewees were recruited via an advertisement placed on the Donor Facebook group, followed by the snowballing method (Russell, 2006, p. 192). All interviews were open-ended (Silverman, 2006, p. 110), lasting between one and two hours and carried out face-to-face (except for one, which took place over the phone). The interviews were recorded and transcribed in order to represent the interviewees' voices. Here, I approach the interviews qualitatively; I understand them as discursively constructed narratives that inform us of the interviewees' subject positions and experiences, rather than testimonies of 'truth' (Scott, 1991). This suits my aim of exploring the way in which online community is *experienced* (and what intimacy *does*), as opposed to documenting what online community (or intimacy) *is*.

In addition to conducting interviews, I also engaged in a qualitative analysis of the group's Facebook discussions. As the term 'community' was seldom mentioned in these discussions, I looked for posts and comments that expressed belonging, unity, familiarity and a sense of 'we-ness' (Cooks, Paredes and Scharrer, 2003, p. 148). I understand the posts, much like the interviews, as individual discursively constructed narratives that inform us of individual subject positions. However, I also see them as parts of a larger discourse, with each entry contributing to the formation of the online community. Mouffe and Laclau demonstrate that meanings are never fixed in discourses; there are ongoing antagonisms and different discourses competing for hegemony (Laclau and Mouffe, 1985). Informed by this perspective, but focusing less on struggles, I interpret the Facebook posts as negotiations: the posts and discussions constitute the online community, and its content and form continuously develop on the basis of the posts.

Analysis of a Facebook group raises ethical questions; Facebook posts differ from interviews, as they are not given in confidence (Kozinets, 2015, p. 140). I joined the Donor group three years ago, as I was interested in its discussions about alternative families. Since this time, I have participated in the group's discussions and knowledge sharing. My analysis of the group therefore builds on participatory observation (Emerson, Fretz and Shaw, 2001) and netnographic observation (Kozinets, 2015). When I decided to use the group as a case study, I posted a message on the wall of the group explaining my position; in doing this, I made my research interest public to the group. Although since that time I have received only positive comments about my research from members of the group, I am aware that members might feel differently at a later point. In order to protect the group and its members, I have chosen to secure anonymity for all. Thus, I call the group the 'Donor group' instead of listing its real name, and I replace the names of all members and interviewees with fictional names in order to render them anonymous. Furthermore, I only provide the month and year (not the date) of an uttered statement. In this chapter, I mainly give examples of one particular Facebook discussion (from December 2014). This discussion consists of one post that received 19 comments over two days. The discussion is typical of most group discussions, in both its quantitative size and its form of questions, answers and dialogue. The group is Nordic; most members are from Denmark but a large number are Swedish or Norwegian. The posts are multi-lingual, as most Scandinavians understand each other's languages. When citing interviews and Facebook posts, I translate from Danish/Swedish/Norwegian into English, while aiming at remaining as close to the original text as possible. I use the terms 'donor families' and 'donor children', as these are the terms that the majority of participants use to describe their families.

Self-disclosure and intimate community

Most activity in the Donor group is initiated by a post in the form of a question:

> Thank you so much for letting me be a member of this group. I am considering if this [conceiving via donor sperm] could be the way for a younger brother/sister to enter into our world. I am alone with a daughter who is 3. She was made the natural way. I am not in a relationship with her father, and he does not want any contact. I would like one more [child], and I think this might be the right way for me [to proceed]. But OMG, it is so hard to take the first step and call my doctor.
>
> (Karin Lund Hansen, December 2014)

This post, similar to most posts, asks other members for advice. Such posts are most often followed by a series of answers in which members offer advice based on their experiences. Below are examples of answers to Karin's post:

> It took me 1½ years to call my doctor. It was such a barrier-breaking transgressive act. Now I am sitting here laughing with my daughter who just turned 2. Just pick up the phone and call.
>
> (Lene Molberg Larsen, December 2014)

> I had a boy … who was 3, and who had a dad, when I made my decision. He is now 6 and older brother to the world's greatest Carla who will

> soon turn 2. So just get started. […] There are ups and downs, it is wonderful and tough but you will receive the greatest gift and it is worth it all. Good luck.
>
> (Leila Madsen, December 2014)

Both the question and the answers contain self-disclosure, wherein the women reveal their personal family situations, their concerns and their dreams. They honestly admit to their insecurities and the difficult aspects of parenting, especially as single mothers with donor-conceived children. Cooks, Paredes and Scharrer describe how much activity on O Place is constituted by members asking for and providing advice (2003, p. 149). They argue that this leads to a sense of 'we-ness' between the women (p. 148). A similar sense of we-ness – and hence belonging – surfaces in this discussion about having donor children. One member writes: 'I find such a post [Karin's question] really nice. Then one knows one is not alone with those thoughts/feelings' (Line Suzanne Dahl, December 2014). Here, sharing concerns that relate to one's family (or hopes about family) leads to belonging. The online community is intimate, as sharing concerns and knowledge creates understandings of we-ness and belonging. Similarly, another woman replies: 'I am in the same situation. I want it so much but it is also challenging to take the first step' (Lizy Mette Jørgensen, December 2014). By illustrating her ambivalent feelings about wanting a second child while simultaneously being concerned about having a donor child, she lets herself be vulnerable to the group. At the same time, she acknowledges Karin's vulnerability and turns it into a common denominator. They become united in their vulnerability and ambivalence, and they receive supportive advice from other members who have been in similar situations. One might argue that the intimacy created and cultivated within the Donor group takes Berlant's understanding of intimacy a step further. While Berlant describes cultural products as intimate, as they provide consumers with a promise of belonging (Berlant, 2008, p. ix), she also emphasises that such products are normative and regulatory. Conversely, the women in the Donor group are directly involved in constructions of intimacy by sharing their personal experiences and feelings. Thus, the Donor group's creation of intimacy may be understood as interactive and bottom-up, rather than Berlant's top-down and consumer-orientated construction of intimacy.

Consciousness-raising group

The members of the Donor group constitute an intimate online community that, in some ways, mirrors the women's consciousness-raising groups of the 1970s. In these groups, women would collectively discuss broad issues or problems through reference to personal stories and experiences, under the motto 'The personal is political'. Feminists have described such consciousness-raising groups as safe spaces 'to tell it like it is' (Hanisch, 1971). By sharing personal stories, the women realise that the issues they struggle with are not individual, personal problems, but larger, structural problems. While members of the Donor group would not necessarily ascribe to 'the personal is political', their group – and the intimate community it constitutes – functions very similarly to a consciousness-raising group. Technically, the group is closed: one must apply for membership, and members are screened by administrators before they are admitted. This procedure contributes to the feeling of the group as a safe space for sharing knowledge and personal testimonies. The group simultaneously constitutes a space of intimacy and a space where women can expose larger issues (relating to pregnancies, donor siblings, families, etc.) through shared personal experiences. It is not my intention to argue that a contemporary Facebook group is equivalent to historical consciousness-raising groups, but I do wish to underscore the similarities and suggest that online intimacy and Facebook communities should not be understood as completely new phenomena, but should rather be viewed from a historical perspective. Hence, one might argue that social media sites offer technological platforms that enable older forms of community and communication to continue in contemporary times (see also Nicholson, 2013, p. 33; Humphreys et al., 2013).

Dilution and cultivation of intimacy through online media

Cooks, Paredes and Scharrer explain that the technical conditions of online communities may dilute and disrupt communication while simultaneously cultivating it (2003, p. 152 f.). This observation holds true for the Donor group. The discussion about having a second (donor) child, referenced above, took place over two days, and its dialogue was therefore rather disrupted in time. Simultaneously, however, it is exactly this stretch over time that allows members to participate in the discussion. Many members post comments in the evening, often hours after a question has been asked. While this habit creates a long break between the time at which a question is asked and the time at which it is answered, it also allows single mothers to participate in the conversation (and hence the community). The majority of members in the Donor group are mothers, and a very large number of these mothers are single mothers. As a result, most members are only able to participate in the group in the evening, when their children are in bed. Turkle is critical of technological affordances that enable communication and connection whenever it is wished, as these lead to disruptions (Turkle, 2011, p. 13). However, it is precisely these affordances that suit single mothers. Despite the temporal disruption that is evident in the Donor group discussions, a dialogue clearly takes place. Members comment on each other's posts and answer each other; and the woman initiating the thread enters the conversation again, posting a reply to the many answers: 'It is so nice to hear your input' (Karin Lund Hansen, December 2014). One might even speculate that the community is made stronger by the contextual limitations imposed upon single mothers: because many of them are alone in the evening, they can gather online and feel a sense of belonging with women in similar situations.

There has been much discussion about whether the internet's options for anonymity dilute or strengthen the creation of community (Bromseth, 2006, pp. 145 ff.; Cooks, Paredes and Scharrer, 2003, p. 152). On the one hand, members might feel insecure about not knowing who the other members are, or they might fear that some Facebook profiles are fake. One interviewee is uneasy about the identity of other members: 'Sometimes, I wonder who is reading along? There are so many members, and anyone can create a profile [...]. It makes me uncomfortable not to know who is reading along' (Sanne, interview, February 2015). But at the same time, it might be exactly this lack of knowledge that allows members to open up and perform online self-disclosure. To individuals who have difficulty expressing themselves in the physical presence of people, the internet's lack of physicality and its potential for anonymity might provide comfort and a space to share concerns and knowledge.

The Donor group has many more members than the ones who actively participate by writing, discussing and posting photos on the site. boyd argues that social media are a 'stage for digital flâneurs' (boyd, 2007, p. 155), and many members of the group might be characterised as such. One interviewee explains how she uses the Donor group for advice and inspiration, but never contributes to the site: 'I follow the site a lot. [...] I am not active myself but I follow what is going on. I am almost like a voyeur' (Sanne, interview, February 2015). She spends quite a bit of time on the site and feels like a part of the group, yet, to other members, she might figure as a passive profile. This points to lurking as a form of participation: the Donor group can be seen as a community that allows members to be part of the community and to feel belonging to the community, despite a lack of actual contribution.

The technology of Facebook disrupts the Donor group's discussions in *time*, and this could potentially dilute the community; but the technology also cultivates the Donor group in *space*, and this strengthens the community. Members of the Donor group are geographically scattered: they live all over Denmark, in cities as well as rural areas, and several members live in Sweden and Norway. This scattered pattern prevents regular physical contact between members. In the early days of online community formations, several feminist scholars were critical about whether the internet and the changes it brought about would actually improve women's lives or empower them (e.g. Spender, 1995; van Zoonen, 1992). Conversely, Dietrich (1997) argued that the internet can provide affirmative spaces for women to engage in socially – despite geographical distance and time difference – and to explore relations and communities (Dietrich, 1997, p. 179). While it is not possible to draw a general conclusion about women and online communities on the basis of this case study, I argue that the technology of Facebook – and especially its ability to connect persons across time and space – is of central importance to the

Donor community. The many members living in small towns and rural areas are often isolated as single mothers and/or lesbian mothers; through the Donor group, they engage in a community that is not possible for them to engage in physically in their local area. As one member writes on the wall of the Donor group: 'Dear all. Thank you for a [...] relevant membership. I have found what I was looking for – a community around a certain donor' (Caroline Metz-Hansen, November 2014). Here, Caroline underscores that her needs can be fulfilled online, as opposed to offline.

Another technical feature of Facebook that both dilutes and cultivates community is the automatic ordering of posts, wherein the latest entry determines the order of posts on the wall. As a result of this, discussion threads move around (up and down), disrupting both the layout and the discussions. At the same time, interviewees explain how they use the wall as an archive: if they need advice or input related to a specific problem or concern, they scroll down the site and find older discussions about the theme in question (e.g. Jeanette, interview, March 2015). Thus, the wall functions as an archive, containing large amounts of advice and knowledge sharing that can be activated when needed, independent of the time at which it was written.

Co-constitution between media platform and users' practices

Van Dijck argues that it is a fallacy to think that social media platforms merely facilitate networking activities; rather, the platform and social practices are mutually constitutive (van Dijck, 2013, p. 16). Whereas Turkle is critical of technology engineering intimacy, as this reduces intimacy to connections (Turkle, 2011, p. 16), I would argue – with van Dijck – that technology never engineers networks or communities on its own. Rather, in the case of the Facebook group, it is the co-constitution between the technology (and its affordances) and the everyday practices used by the members to engage with the technology that forms the connections. Intimacy does not disappear, but rather – as an experience of belonging – fosters the community.[1] While Turkle tends to see technology as determining of our relations: 'We make our technologies, and they, in turn, shape us' (Turkle, 2011, p. 19), I see the relationship between users and media platforms (and hence between online media and intimacy) as continuously co-constitutive. The Facebook platform shapes the Donor group – for instance, through its technological disruptions – and the users shape the Facebook group. In order to understand this looping effect between users and media, the specific context and the specific situatedness of users must be taken into consideration. Cooks, Paredes and Scharrer argue that the 'imagined space of [online] community is perhaps already marked or shared through the mundane practices of everyday life' (2003, p. 143). In other words, existing social practices – for instance parenting – contribute to the formation of the online community. The members enter the Donor community as individuals who have already been shaped by identities (as mothers, single women, etc.), and their online practices are closely linked to their (offline) practices and subjectivities. Though some scholars have pointed to the internet's potential for creating subversive gender identities (Haraway, 1991; Braidotti, 1998), the Donor group illustrates the way in which everyday mundane practices and identities influence online activities. These specific conditions are constitutive for the Donor community and might explain part of its success in creating belonging: the women's contextual situation leads to their need for this online community, and their everyday practices of caring for children and creating alternative families lead them to uphold the community.

The Donor group can be interpreted as an affirmative group. As described above, members are supportive of each other. Furthermore, when there are discussion threads with topics upon which members disagree, there seems to be a pattern of members trying to 'restore harmony' by smoothing out potential conflicts. Often, such threads end with members posting statements such as the following: 'This is a topic on which we will NEVER agree, and there is simply not any correct answer. We all have to respect each other's different opinions. Have a nice weekend everyone' (Alexandra Arden Elg, November 2014). Castells argues that a network works via inclusion and exclusion; it maintains what is useful to it and excludes, ignores or eliminates what is not useful (Castells, 2000, p. 15). Interpreting the Donor group from Castells' perspective, one might argue that attempts to 'restore harmony' are examples of members trying to eliminate harsh debates, as these are not useful to the group. But another interpretation may be pursued – namely that networks such as the Donor group are not necessarily interested in eliminating elements (people or arguments) from their network; rather, they see the group as an intimate community where members should not be excluded but rather included in a way that maintain a 'proper tone' and harmony. While Castells is interested in larger systems and general rules for cyber networks, a context-specific analysis may provide a different interpretation. In their analysis of the women's community on O Place, Cooks, Paredes and Scharrer show how members use the site both to ask for affirmation from other members and to offer support to one another (Cooks, Paredes and Scharrer, 2003, p. 150). When members occasionally violate these (unwritten) affirmative rules for participation, other members interfere and reinstall the dominant format of (affirmative) participation (p. 151). Similarly, when debate within the Donor group becomes too aggressive, it is 'calmed down' by posts such as this: 'Everybody chooses a solution which is right in their life and according to their conviction [...] Remember to respect what each individual has chosen; the choices are made in love and with the best intentions ♥' (Camilla Vinter, November 2014).

Making a new script for creating families

Van Dijck is not the only person to point to the co-constitution between the media and the social; Clark (2009) argues that 'technology, human, and culture are all co-constructed, constituting and mediating each other in ways that open up new possibilities for thinking and acting' (Clark, 2009, p. 96). This opening of new possibilities might be one of the most important features of the Donor group. McGlotten shows that intimacy often becomes a regulatory and normative script: he describes intimacy as an 'assemblage of ideologies, institutional sites, and diverse sets of material and semiotic practices that exert normative pressures on large and small bodies, lives, and worlds' (McGlotten, 2013, p. 1). While I do not oppose the idea that intimacy can be regulatory and scripted in such a way, the Donor group illustrates that intimacy can also lead to new ways of thinking and acting, and hence new scripts. Self-disclosure within the Donor group creates intimacy and a sense of belonging, but self-closure is also important for the development of members as parents. Cooks, Paredes and Scharrer describe how the users of O Place 'attempt to both affirm and transform themselves and others' (Cooks, Paredes and Scharrer, 2003, p. 148). In a similar way, the women in the Donor group use the group to affirm each other ('one knows one is not alone with those thoughts/feelings', as Line Suzanne Dahl writes, cited above). But self-disclosure also leads to transformations, or new scripts for creating families. Several of the women describe how they initially felt very alone and isolated when they became single mothers with donor-conceived children. As one interviewee expresses: 'Honestly, I thought I was the only woman in the world having a child this way' (Jeanette, interview, March 2015). Another member relates how the Facebook group connected her to other mothers in similar situations: 'Facebook opened my horizons. There are, we are, so many different mothers with donor children out there' (Sanne, interview, February 2015).

Often, the disclosure of personal information online is connected with popularity; for instance, van Dijck writes: 'Popularity and disclosure are two sides of the same coin' (van Dijck, 2013, p. 51). But maybe the disclosure of information via self-exposure in the Donor group is not simply about popularity. Rather, it could perhaps be interpreted as a means of creating an intimate community through which new scripts for family formations can be formed. The many Facebook entries that affirm other members' donor families and offer supportive advice on how to construct a donor family can be seen as a series of small contributions to a larger discourse (Laclau and Mouffe, 1985). This discourse might cause the women to feel as if they are performing parenthood in the right way, despite their alternative life choice.

Nicholson argues that self-disclosure has become a means of creating intimacy and developing relationships and successful selves (Nicholson, 2013, pp. 30, 34 ff.). Within the Donor group, self-disclosure may be seen as a tool for not only creating intimacy (and thus establishing the community), but also narrating and building understandings of one's self (and one's position as a single mother of donor-conceived children) as acceptable and maybe even successful. Through self-disclosure, in the form of shared personal stories, feelings and experiences, the mothers create understandings of their parental choices as successful and collectively generate new scripts for the process of (successfully) establishing families. The online community becomes a means of ascribing new meanings to otherwise marginal positions as single mothers of donor-conceived children. Due to the geographical distance between members, this would not have been possible otherwise.

Concluding remarks

Turkle asks critically: 'Technology reshapes the landscape of our emotional lives, but it is offering us the lives we want to lead?' (Turkle, 2011, p. 17). Answering this from the perspective of the Donor group, one could argue that while technology alone might not provide the mothers with the lives they want to lead, it does facilitate community and intimacy – in the mothers' specific contexts – which allow for new narratives of families and lives. While online media might not be the preferred platform for organising social relations – van Dijck, for instance, criticises Facebook for 'becoming a centripetal force in organizing people's social lives' (van Dijck, 2013, p. 51) – geographical circumstances, combined with the situation of being a single mother in an alternative family, might make it a preferred choice. At the very least, it may be a choice that provides a community and facilitates belonging that cannot otherwise be found in the physical world.

By analysing the online donor community via contextualised perspectives, this chapter has shown how the mothers' self-disclosure fosters community and belonging. Rather than interpreting online communication as a phenomenon, which would challenge previous understandings of communication and intimacy, the chapter argues that Facebook offers a technological platform that enables an older form of communication and community to continue in contemporary times. Furthermore, the affordances of the media ambivalently dilute communication while simultaneously cultivating it. The chapter's micro perspective illustrates how everyday mundane practices of mothering influence online activities; this can be seen as an example of the way in which social practices and media practices are mutually co-constitutive. Most importantly, the chapter argues that the women's online knowledge sharing and self-revealing contribute to the narration of new family scripts and ascribe new meanings to otherwise marginal positions as single mothers of donor-conceived children. Throughout, the chapter has shown that specific situations and circumstances play important roles in the analysis of online communities. Thus, the chapter argues in favour of context-specific and context-sensitive analysis.

Note

1 Turkle's definition of intimacy might be different from mine. She does not define her use of the term specifically, but indicates that empathy, which leads to intimacy, develops best through face-to-face conversations.

References

Andreassen, R. (2016). Online kinship. Social media as a site for challenging notions of gender and family. *MedieKultur*, 32(61), pp. 76–92.

Andreassen, R. (2017). New kinships, new family formations and negotiations of intimacy via social media sites. *Journal of Gender Studies*, 26(3), pp. 361–371.

Bennett, L.W. (2015). Foreword. In: J. Uldam and A. Vestergaard, eds., *Civic Engagement and Social Media. Political Participation Beyond Protest*. New York: Palgrave, pp. viii–xiii.

Berlant, L. (1998). Intimacy: A special issue. *Critical Inquiry*, 24(2), pp. 281–288.

Berlant, L. (2008). *The Female Complaint*. Durham, NC: Duke University Press.

boyd, d. (2007). None of this is real: Identity and participation in Friendster. In: J. Karaganis, ed., *Structures of Participation in Digital Culture*. New York: Social Science Research Council, pp. 132–157.

Braidotti, R. (1998). Cyberfeminism with a Difference. Retrieved from www.let.uu.nl/womens_studies/rosi/cyberfem.htm.

Bromseth, J. (2006). *Genre Trouble and the Body that Mattered: Negotiations of Gender, Sexuality and Identity in a Scandinavian Mailing List Community*. PhD dissertation. Norwegian University of Science and Technology.

Castells, M. (2000). Materials for an exploratory theory of the network society. *British Journal of Sociology*, 51(1), pp. 5–24.

Clark, L.S. (2009). Theories: Mediatization and media ecology. In: K. Lundby, ed., *Mediatization: Concept, Changes, Consequences*. New York: Peter Lang, pp. 85–100.

Cooks, L., Paredes, M.C. and Scharrer, E. (2003). Creating a space for "every woman" at Oprah.com. *Electronic Journal of Communication*, 13(1).

Dietrich, D. (1997). Re-fashioning the techno-erotic women: Gender and textuality in the cybercultural matrix. In: S. Jones, ed., *Virtual Culture. Identity & Communication in Cybersociety*. London: SAGE, pp. 169–185.

Emerson, R.M., Fretz, R.I. and Shaw, L.L. (2001). Participant observation and fieldnotes. In: Atkinson et al., eds., *Handbook of Ethnography*. Thousand Oaks, CA: SAGE, pp. 356–357.

Frank, A., Clough, P. and Seidman, S., eds. (2013). *Intimacy: A New World of Relational Life*. New York: Routledge.

Hanisch, C. (1971). The personal is political. In: S. Firestone and A. Koedt, eds., *Notes from the Second Year: Women's Liberation*. New York: New York Radical Feminists.

Haraway, D. (1991). A cyborg manifesto: Science, technology, and socialist-feminism in the late twentieth century. In: D. Haraway, ed., *Simians, Cyborgs and Women: The Reinvention of Nature*. New York: Routledge, pp. 149–182.

Humphreys, L., Gill, P., Krishnamurthy, B. and Newbury, E. (2013). Twitter & historical diaries: A content analysis. *Journal of Communication*, 63(3), pp. 413–431.

Internet World Stats (2015). Retrieved from www.internetworldstats.com/stats4.htm#europe (May 16, 2016).

Kozinets, R.V. (2015). *Netnography. Redefined*. London: SAGE.

Laclau, E. and Mouffe, C. (1985). *Hegemony and Socialist Strategy. Towards a Radical Democratic Practice*. London: Verso.

McGlotten, S. (2013). *Virtual Intimacies. Media, Affect and Queer Sociality*. New York: SUNY Press.

Nicholson, L. (2013). Let me tell you who I am. Intimacy, privacy and self-disclosure. In: A. Frank, P. Clough and S. Seidman, eds., *Intimacy: A New World of Relational Life*. New York: Routledge, pp. 30–46.

Russell, B. (2006). *Research Methods in Anthropology. Qualitative and Quantitative Approaches*. Lanham: AltaMira Press.

Scott, J.W. (1991). The evidence of experience. *Critical Inquiry*, 17, pp. 773–797.

Silverman, D. (2006). *Interpreting Qualitative Data*. London: SAGE.

Spender, D. (1995). *Nattering on the Net: Women, Power and Cyberspace*. Melbourne: Spinifex.

Thumin, N. (2012). *Self-Representation and Digital Culture*. New York: Palgrave Macmillan.

Turkle, S. (2011). *Alone Together. Why We Expect More from Technology and Less from Each Other*. New York: Basic Books.

van Dijck, J. (2013). *The Culture of Connectivity*. Oxford: Oxford University Press.

Van Zoonen, L. (1992). Feminist theory and information technology. *Media, Culture and Society*, 14(1), pp. 9–13.

4 Textures of intimacy

Witnessing embodied mobile loss, affect and heartbreak

Lin Prøitz, Larissa Hjorth and Amparo Lasén

Introduction

Camera phone practices enact different meanings of the ordinary and mundane (Kindberg et al., 2005; Koskinen, 2007; Van House et al., 2005). As contemporary modes of vernacular photography, camera phones are integral to our everyday activities, relationships, senses, pleasures and ambivalent feelings. The photographic practices and performances that are conducted through these devices produce images of the banal and mundane that shape our contemporary visual culture and feed our online and offline conversations and interactions. These practices can be viewed as part of a normalisation of social orderings that feeds into a broader photographic history (Gye, 2007; Mørk Petersen, 2009; Palmer, 2012).

Camera phone and mobile media practices amplify inner subjectivities. While conforming to existing sociocultural rituals and practices, they also challenge and shift older rituals. As one of the most intimate devices in everyday life, the mobile phone is a vehicle used for haunting — that is, it is an evocative and affective tool that operates upon multiple material, symbolic and immaterial dimensions (Cumiskey and Hjorth, 2017). It is a vessel for – and of – our intimacies and emotions that shapes and is shaped by affective bonds. Thus, we can grasp and trace some of the normative aspects of everyday life and mundane intimacies by looking at *how* the production and sharing of digital images contributes to the modulation of presence and the modulation of intimacy beyond clear-cut divides between the private and public, closeness and distance (Lasén, 2015a). Camera phones have not only become a key aspect of our representation and experience of events, but they have also become – through their affective intimacy – entangled between witnessing and embodiment.

Intimate publics are increasingly shaped by new forms of 'mobile intimacy'; that is, the infusion of intimacy and various forms of mobility (across technological, geographic, psychological, physical and temporal differences) into public and private spaces (Hjorth and Arnold, 2013; Hjorth and Lim, 2012). These new forms of mobile intimacy underpin some of the ways in which life and death are represented – or, as Graham and colleagues note, 'how publics are formed and connected with through different technologies as much as which publics are created and networked' (2013, p. 135).

In this chapter, we bring together a variety of studies that have deployed online ethnography, qualitative interviews, fieldwork and workshops with regular users of visual communication and mobile media between 2013 and 2016 in South Korea, Spain and Norway (Hjorth, 2016; Hjorth and Arnold, 2013; Lasén, 2015a, 2015b; Lasén and García, 2015; Prøitz, 2014, 2016). Drawing on the insights gleaned from this fieldwork, we seek to bring a feminist analysis to the ways in which textures of intimacy, affective witnessing and structures of 'ugly feelings' play out across online and offline feelings of intimacy. Mobile media can be understood to facilitate an infrastructure around cultural practices of intimacy, whereby the infrastructure is only visible once it is broken (Star, 1999). Heartbreak and grief, as experienced in and through mobile media practice, heighten the broken aspects of this infrastructure, especially its social and tacit dimensions. These broken assemblages – what we call 'textures' – are important for negotiating mobile media in everyday life. In this chapter, these textures are illustrated through two cases: shame and sadness after a couple's break-up and analysis of selfie video footage of the South Korean ferry disaster of 2014 (the sinking of the MV Sewol).

Theoretically conceptualising digital intimacy

In a digital culture, networked camera phones and social media represent worlds within the world that can be organised in ways that challenge conventional ideas of time, space and presence, as well as feelings and intimacy. The boundaries between ourselves and others have become unclear, as Markham (2013) argues, and this blurred boundary is particularly acute in cases when shared information develops a social life of its own beyond one's immediate context. Changes in spatial, temporal and relational boundaries are central for understanding intimacy in a digital culture, wherein new conventions and expectations are continuously emerging (Lasén, 2015b). As Rettberg (2014) notes, technologies not only help us see ourselves but also shape *the way in which* we see ourselves.

Intimacy, according to Lynn Jamieson (2011), implies 'the quality of close connection between people and the process of building this quality'. Although there are cultural variations in the practice of intimacy, Jamieson defines intimate relationships as personal relationships that are subjectively experienced and may be socially recognised as close. In other words, intimacy is related to expectations of relations and a sense of belonging. The idea that forms of intimacy might be generated in public contexts is not new. In Berlant and Warner's (2002) debate on intimacy, they critically discuss the way in which intimacy is conceptualised as something preserved and individually limited – a form of intimacy they see as a public fantasy:

> Intimate life is the endlessly cited 'elsewhere' of political public discourse, a promised haven that distracts citizens from the unequal conditions of their political and economic lives, consoles them for the damaged humanity of mass society, and shames them for any divergence between their lives and the intimate sphere that is alleged to be simple personhood.
> (Ibid., p. 193)

A wider concept of intimacy is suggested, incorporating life-long to short-lived attachments and spontaneous 'emotional forms of communities between strangers [...] [in the pursuit of] recognition, acknowledgement or comfort in the public sphere' (Berlant, paraphrased in Lorentzen and Mühleisen, 2013, p. 16). In the second half of the 2000s, the introduction of social media and smartphones with front-facing cameras dramatically blurred the conventions and expectations of intimacy, privacy and the public sphere. In a digital material environment, intimate relations are not simply performed in pairs, bounded groups or cultural contexts; rather, they traverse the online and offline. This traversing sees physically public worlds entangled in electronic privacy, and an electronic public that is geographically private. Intimacy has taken on new geographies and forms of mobility, most notably as a kind of 'publicness' (Berlant, 1998, p. 281). As Marika Lüders (2008) highlights, what was previously considered private is no longer restricted to the private sphere.

Intimacy has various textures and dimensions. It is not just a relationality between individuals or objects. For Michael Herzfeld, cultural contexts inform the ways in which intimacy plays out in everyday practice. Herzfeld (1997, p. 44) notes that the 'intimate seeps into the public spheres that have themselves been magnified by the technologies of mass mediation'. Here, cultural intimacy takes three forms: historical, institutional and geographical. Through a notion of cultural intimacy, we can reconfigure intimate publics as they move in and out of digital practices.

Conceptualising the role of the digital in the wake of loss and death

Digital media are playing an increasingly key role in the representation, sharing and recollection of loss. Or, as Refslund Christensen and Gotved (2015, p. 1) note, digital media not only redefine death and its processes in terms of '*mediation* (the representation of something through media)' and '*remediation* (the representation of one medium in another)', but also through '*mediatisation* (the process through which core elements of a social or cultural activity assume media form)'. This process is heightened in the case of mobile media. Mobile media are exemplary of this phenomenon – they provide a continuum between older technologies and practices, while, at the same time, remediating rituals (Cumiskey and Hjorth, 2017). Thus, mobile media become progressively embedded within place-making and memorial culture.

From accessing Facebook during public tragedies to keeping digital traces of the deceased on a smartphone, mobile media practices both continue and depart from earlier memorial practices such as photography (Brubaker et al., 2012; Deger, 2008, 2006; Gibson, 2014; Graham et al., 2013; Leaver, 2003; Lingel, 2013; Nansen et al., 2015; Refslund Christensen and Gotved, 2015). Mobile media encompass a variety of platforms, techniques, textures and affordances that allow us to understand processes of continuity and discontinuity, mediation and remediation. Mobile media practices have taught us a lot about the fabric of contemporary life and, increasingly, they are providing us with new ways of negotiating, ritualising and reimagining death and the afterlife, especially within the everyday.

Digital data enable new ways of constructing life, death and the afterlife (Brubaker et al., 2013; Gotved, 2015; Graham et al., 2013). With online data affording new pathways for representing and experiencing these concepts, much of the literature has focused on online memorials (de Vries and Rutherford, 2004) and other forms of grieving online (Veale, 2004). Unlike Victorian rituals of death (Walter et al., 2011), which compartmentalised death to the grave and defined grief as something to 'get over' (Rosenblatt, 1996), the role of the digital in the relationship between life and death means that 'death and (after-) death are, once again, becoming more public and everyday' (Graham et al., 2013, p. 136). This quotidian placement of death is amplified in the rhythms of mobile media within everyday life.

Methods

This chapter deploys mixed methods to understand the complex ways in which affective textures of intimacy in and around mobile media might play out. Through interdisciplinary synthesis, the chapter explores online ethnography, workshops and fieldwork conducted in South Korea, Spain and Norway between 2013 and 2016. In order to analyse the data, an inductive and interpretative case study was undertaken. Coding techniques from grounded theory (Strauss and Corbin, 1990) were applied for the workshops and qualitative interviews, whereas discourse analysis was deployed for the ethnography.

In the South Korean case study, an online ethnography with discourse analysis was used. Given the nature of the material, the researcher did not contact families who were directly impacted, but instead conducted an ethnography with South Koreans to explore their responses to the event. The ethnography involved ten people and included follow-up discussions as well as an analysis of the discourse material and how this changed over time. For the Hangul components, a Korean research assistant served as a translator.

In Spain, a series of workshops about selfie practices were organised between December 2014 and May 2015, involving people of different age groups (18–25; 25–30; and 30–35) who were selected due to their ongoing interest in selfie practices and their willingness to participate. Different activities were carried out, such as selfie-taking and discussing and evaluating selfies and selfie practice. Finally, in small groups, the participants defined a set of rules about what makes a good and bad selfie, and what-to-do and what-not-to-do with selfies – rules that were later shared and discussed with the entire group.

The cases in Norway combine three focus groups, six semi-structured individual in-depth interviews and digital observations. All participants were actively engaged on social media in ongoing societal or political debates. The empirical study was carried out between 2013 and 2016 and involved 21 participants. Participants were recruited using the snowball method, both online and offline.

'Active now'

Meeting people through social media represents one form of encounter between individuals and social communities in the online public. Use of personal and social media has undoubtedly modified conventions and expectations of how to act in the public arena. For some research participants, forming relationships in a digital culture brings them more elastic relational aspects than offered by traditional discourses.

Let's take, for instance, Nina, a Norwegian therapist in her 50s. When reflecting upon her relations with people she has met online, Nina argues that it is easier to regulate a digital relation that is not qualified by tradition and history, but one that is preoccupied with *here and now*. First of all, she says, social media makes relations more distinct and less tied down: 'It doesn't need a long timeframe, but the value is being available, being present, being here now.' She continues to reflect upon the importance of having lengthy relations, or what she calls 'life witnesses', stating: 'For me, if the life witnesses don't give anything into the here-and-now relationship, it's like a bad marriage.'

The quality and the modulation of presence, or technology and time, is a thematic axis that runs as a thread through our analysis. Should we follow Markham's argument that a situation with contextual or timely proximity to an interaction reduces ambiguity to the context? For Nina, there is more to it. The 'active now' immediacy represents a relational currency – a sense of being here now, or, as Wolfgang Ernst (2013) points to, a tactile form of media-time in which the boundary between present and past (and between life and mediated life) dissolves and one that shapes the collective perception of time.

Through networked camera phone images and social media communities, one can constantly look at how other people have lived their lives over the last days or hours – and even check if they are active at that very moment. Nina elaborates on the idea of 'active now': 'When I see that she [her ex-partner] is "active now" it's like staring into the room, seeing a ghost. She is here, so close, but at the same time out of reach. The "active now", it's just awful.' When a message is published on Messenger, the message carves out a timely space for the mediated statement, with 'immediacy serving to create the illusion of a pseudo-co-presence' (Ernst, paraphrased in Lund, 2015, p. 104). When Nina receives a message or merely sees 'active now' on Messenger's header, a form of timely affect is produced. This, according to Ernst, implies that communication is not primarily about an exchange of meaning, but about 'sharing time, to be present simultaneously' (Ernst, paraphrased in Lund, 2016, p. 104).

Collective events, both online and offline

Social and personal media, video footage and camera phone images have expanded not only our bodily affordances, but also the spaces in which we are present. When, for example, a couple in love continuously uploads selfies with the hashtag #loveforever or when video footage from a tragedy as it is unfolding through selfie videos is shared online, these practices contribute to produce what Marie Løntoft calls 'dramaturgic traces offline'. The stories we tell online are performances of offline events and situations, as well as fantasies. These acts can, according to Løntoft (2014, p. 13), be seen as 'circular on- and offline performances that mutually interfere and affect each other' – not unlike Wolfgang Iser's (1972) notion of literary activation in text, arguing that: 'The virtual dimension is not the text itself, nor is it the imagination of the reader: it is the coming together of text and imagination' (Iser, paraphrased in Danove, 1993, p. 59).

One might argue that the dynamic interplay between those who 'act' and those who watch (though the positions alternate) collectively constitute the event (Fisher-Lichte, 2005). This mutual relationship suggests that the ways in which we experience intimacy and intimate relationships online affect the ways in which we act, see and experience intimacy *offline*. Intimacy, Lorentzen and Mühleisen (2013, p. 16) argue, is not a theme, but 'an affective economy, a structure of feeling and a culture which characterises different publics and spaces for interactions' [our translation]. Thus, media function as 'amplifiers and modulators of affect' (Gibbs et al., 2015, p. 6). Images, for example, work in an affective register, which, according to Zelizer (2010), has a language that exceeds what the image captures. One of the participants, 24 year old Morten, who has recently experienced a break-up, recaps one image that affected him strongly and made him create his own boundaries online:

> I remember having a strong emotional reaction to seeing a picture of a girl I had been seeing with her new boyfriend, with her partner [...] It was unpleasant, yeah, had very sharp stabbing pains, yeah [...] so what I eventually did was, firstly after having a conversation with her, which

> ended unpleasantly over Facebook, I then finally removed her from my Facebook so that I would no longer be tempted to talk to her, and secondly partly to do with that, but also more generally *I unfollowed everyone on Facebook*, so I stopped getting updates, so now when I log onto Facebook it's just a blank page and I use it to message people, but not to post or read statuses, and that is a relief.
>
> (Morten, 24 years old)

Morten's 'sharp stabbing pains' are expressions of an experience of what Sianne Ngai (2005) calls 'ugly feelings'. Similar feelings are described in the selfies workshop carried out in Madrid with youngsters aged 18 to 25. In previous research projects on couples and mobile phones in Madrid (Casado and Lasén, 2014), we found that after a couple breaks up, women delete their exes' numbers as a way of 'deleting' them from their lives: deleting their digital inscription in the mobile phone is both a physical gesture – materialising the separation – and a way of removing the temptation to contact them later. Nowadays, blocking an ex on social media platforms is a rite of passage – as if willing the affect of digital inscription gestures to become seamless with offline reality. This digital gesture ends the mutual accessibility, availability and transparency that characterised the former full-time intimacy.

In discussions in the selfie workshop hosted in Madrid, we come across instances of (mostly) women taking a hiatus from social media platforms (such as Facebook or Instagram) after a break-up in order to avoid the mutual affective witnessing and disclosure that shaped their full-time couple intimacy. In doing so, they intend to prevent the possibility of witnessing their exes' lives and likes and, vice versa, the possibility for their exes to watch their doings and likes. The temporary break of the social media routine is part of the grieving process following the break-up.

Camera phone practices in a culture of immediacy that is open 24 hours a day require new forms of self-regulation. This distanced closeness – the feeling of 'being here' physically and through a mental presence in real time, has produced a new, unregulated dimension. 'It used to be like bye-bye and then you left, secured the door with bolts and then you were done, right? But now in a way, it's no longer as simple as a clean-cut', the participant Nina says. Research on intimacy and mobile telephony (Casado and Lasén, 2014; Hjorth, 2007; Lasén, 2014; Lasén and Casado, 2012; Prøitz, 2007) has shown that technology invites new forms of presence and proximity. Bodily presence and emotions are not lessened, but they differ from their traditional forms.

It is significant that when particular emotions become connected and 'sticky', certain narratives and images accrue power through articulation and reiteration. 'Stickiness', in Ahmed's (2004, p. 90) work, refers to the 'effect of the histories of contact between bodies, objects and signs'. Ahmed connects emotions with past histories, narratives and potential experiences that merge into an affective encounter, resulting in sticky signs that circulate in the media, both online and offline (Ahmed, paraphrased in Nikunen, 2015, p. 23). According to Ahmed (2004), affect and emotions are not intrinsic to a subject; rather, they bind subjects together, as affect emerges both between bodies and within bodies, continually altering the subject's engagement with the world.

Although Nina argues that digital media have made us develop a higher pain threshold in order to endure performances of intimacy and pain in a limitless society, Sofie, a 26-year-old journalist, stresses the intensity and anxiety of being in a precarious, immediate culture in which one is able to 'know so much', and in which pain is without limit (Prøitz, 2016). Being lovesick or heartbroken in a culture without spatial or timely boundaries might, for some, be solved by blocking one's exes or, as Morten does, by drawing one's own boundaries by unfollowing everyone.

The role of mobile media – and especially the selfie – as a context for not only textures of intimacy but also affective witnessing processes, is particularly prevalent in the context of public disasters. In particular, we focus upon the selfie as a site for misrecognition as well as a vehicle for understanding trauma and grief. In the next section, we explore the textures of intimacy through the affective witnessing of the South Korean ferry disaster of 2014, whereby 246 high school children died.

Affective witnessing

In this case study, we argue that the selfie can be understood as a tool for and of digital intimate publics and affective witnessing. For Penelope Papailias (2016), witnessing in an age of the database is a viral process – one that creates particular assemblages of mourning and witnessing. Rather than recognising a divide between the mourner and witnesses, affective viral media shape new types of witnesses, who then become mourners. This is what Papailias calls 'affective witnessing' (2016). In the Sewol disaster we see the power of the selfie to remind us not only that media have always been social, but also that mobile media challenge the way in which the social is constituted by the political and the personal. Social media are not just tools for dissemination or publicity. They are part of the multiple seams that bind and unbind the personal to the political and the intimate to the public. While intimacy has always been mediated – if not by media then by language, gestures and memory – we see particular manifestations of continuities and discontinuities in and around mobile media practice. Within each culture, intimacy is shaped and experienced in different ways through the textures of language, gesture and memory.

On 16 April 2014, as soon as the ferry capsized, multiple mobile phones were on hand to capture the sheer terror of the events as they unfolded. After the ship sank, killing more than 300 passengers through either drowning or hypothermia, friends and family cradled the mobile media footage in disbelief. YouTube began to fill with hundreds of user-generated videos, consolidating public grief, anger and outcry. Many of the 246 high school children who died had filmed the event via selfies.

Through the selfies we feel the texture and colour of the trauma as the children drown. Some left eulogies of themselves for their family and friends. Others, who believed they would survive, mocked the severity of the situation with mundane selfie gestures such as the peace sign. Others cried uncontrollably. While a few of these stories were documented and disseminated in the global press after being translated from Hangul into English, dozens of stories of mobile media memorialisation processes were not translated and were only shared across vernacular Korean sites. While much of the literature around bereavement and online memorials has focused on the loss and experience of the mourner, the Sewol disaster provides examples of the role of mobile media – and especially camera phones – in memorialisation by the soon-to-be deceased. The quotidian, intimate and yet public dimension of mobile media undoubtedly created a different affect for and of grief.

In the Sewol disaster, many families received messages and videos from their children, unaware that these fragments would be the last moments captured of their children's lives. Here, the role of co-presence in mobile media's ability to traverse the intimate and the public, the mortal and the immortal, took new dimensions. While many YouTube clips remixed the deceased's mobile footage to consolidate grief globally, the videos also signified a relational bond – a cultural intimacy – that is specific to Korean culture. Here, the concept of *jeong* is significant as one of the most 'endearing and evocative' words of which there is no English equivalent (Kim, 1996). This is not to essentialise experience but rather to understand the specific cultural milieu from which the grief was formed. *Jeong* encompasses the meaning of a wide range of English terms: 'feeling, empathy, affection, closeness, tenderness, pathos, compassion, sentiment, trust, bonding and love ... Koreans consider jeong an essential element in human life, promoting the depth and richness of personal relations' (Kim, 1996, p. 14).

While a similar notion of *jeong* can be found in Chinese and Japanese culture (i.e. *jyo*), these related concepts have a far less significant role within cultural practice (Kim, 1996). The feeling of *jeong* is palpable in and through the tragic events and memorialisation of the disaster. *Jeong* binds the various selfies to multiple forms of digital intimate publics that move across macro and micro contexts. The mobile footage taken during the disaster leaves a lasting raw affect by capturing the pain, confusion and terror of the victims as they face their death. The role of mobile media in capturing this liminal stage is a testament to its specific digital intimate public affordances. Mobile media spectres haunt the dynamism of digital intimate publics in and through moments of life, death and the afterlife.

Going forward, we will see the role of mobile media in life, death and afterlife processes increase. For loved ones, mobile media will become a crucial embodied part of the passage from life to death and the afterlife. In all of the examples discussed in this chapter, we have explored entanglements between affective witnessing and embodied intimacy through camera phone practices. These textures of intimacy have taken various micro and macro forms that, in turn, have reshaped our representations and experiences of intimacy. The Sewol example provides what is perhaps the most extreme instance of the blurred boundary between witnessing and affect, whereby it is impossible as a viral witness to remain untouched. In the unevenness of power in and around bodies and mourning, the role of the camera phone is pivotal.

Conclusion

Camera phone practices are collective and choreographed performances, in the sense that they are highly relational and interactive, involving mutual attunement and resonance. They relate to affective labour, emotions and witnessing. As in dancing, when persons do not follow the right moves, they run the risk of stepping on other people's toes and suffering embarrassment or social punishment. The notion of choreography, instead of suggesting just a performance, highlights the existence of a score or script (Foster, 1998). Choreography is a set of conventions about what is appropriate (regarding how to pose, how to take snapshots, how to use filters, what to post, where to post, etc.); these conventions are collectively enacted and sustained in practices that also change over time.

Thus, camera phone images and performances are modes of collective resonance and atmospheric attunement (Stewart, 2011) that colour the mood of everyday moments and places, both online and offline. They contribute to the way in which we affect others and are affected. Furthermore, their contribution to our contemporary affective culture is a main aspect of their role in our sense-making of everyday subjectivities. The embarrassment, disquiets and vulnerability that are often elicited in these practices reveal the difficulty of managing these modulations and the normative complexity of photographic choreographies. In this chapter, through the flexible social fabric of the selfie, we have sought to demonstrate one of the many ways in which we might think through this phenomenon in terms of digital intimate publics and their relationship to cultural intimacy.

Acknowledgements

We would like to thank all of the participants involved in these studies; the research assistant Jung Moon for the South Korean study; and our co-researcher Antonio Garcia for his work in Spain.

References

Ahmed, S. (2004). *The Cultural Politics of Emotions*. Edinburgh: Edinburgh University Press.

Berlant, L. (1998). Intimacy: A special issue. *Critical Inquiry*, 24(2), pp. 281–286. Retrieved from www.jstor.org/stable/1344169.

Berlant, L. and Warner, M. (2002). Sex in public. In: M. Warner, ed., *Publics and Counterpublics*. New York: Zone Books, pp. 187–208.

Brubaker, J.R., Gillian R.H. and Dourish, P. (2013). Beyond the grave: Facebook as a site for the expansion of death and mourning. *Information Society: An International Journal*, 29(3), pp. 152–163. doi: 10.1080/01972243.2013.777300.

Casado, E. and Lasén, A. (2014). What is disturbing and why not to disturb: On mobile phones, gender and privacy within heterosexual intimacy. *Mobile Media and Communication*, 2(3), pp. 249–264.

Church, S.H. (2013). Digital gravescapes: Digital memorializing on Facebook. *Information Society: An International Journal*, 29(3), pp. 184–189. doi:10.1080/01972243.2013.777309.

Cumiskey, K. and Hjorth, L. (2017). *Haunting Hands*. Oxford: Oxford University Press.

Danove, P.L. (1993). *The End of Mark's Story: A Methodological Study*. Leiden, New York and Köln: EJ Brill.

Deger, J. (2008). Imprinting on the heart. *Visual Anthropology*, 21(4), pp. 292–309.

Deger, J. (2006). *Shimmering Screens*. Minneapolis, MN: Minnesota Univeresity Press.

Ernst, W. (2013). *Digital Memory and the Archive*. Minneapolis, MN: University of Minnesota Press.

Fischer-Lichte, E. (2005). *The Transformative Power of Performance*. London and New York: Routledge.

Foster, S.L. (1998). *Choreography and Narrative: Ballet's Staging of Story and Desire*. Indianapolis, IN: Indiana University Press.

Gibbs, M., Meese, J., Arnold, M., Nansen, B. and Carter, M. (2015). #Funeral and Instagram: Death, social media, and platform vernacular. *Information, Communication and Society*, 18(3), pp. 255–268. doi:10.1080/1369118X.2014.987152.

Gibson, M. (2014). Digital objects of the dead: Negotiating electronic remains. In: L. Van Brussel and Nico, eds., *The Social Construction of Death: Interdisciplinary Perspectives*.

Graham, C., Gibbs, M. and Aceti, L. (2013). Introduction to the special issue on the death, afterlife, and immortality of bodies and data. *Information Society*, 29(3), pp. 133–141. doi:10.1080/ 01972243.2013.777296.

Graham, C., Arnold, M., Kohn, T. and Gibbs, M.R. (2015). Gravesites and websites: A comparison of memorialisation. *Visual Studies*, 30(1), pp. 37–53. doi: 10.1080/1472586X.2015.996395.

Gye, L. (2007). Picture this: The impact of mobile camera phones on personal photographic practices. *Continuum: Journal of Media and Cultural Studies*, 21(2), pp. 279–288.

Herzfeld, M. (1997). *Cultural Intimacy: Social Poetics in the Nation-State*. New York: Routledge.

Hjorth, L. (2007). Snapshots of almost contact. *Continuum*, 21(2), pp. 227–238.

Hjorth, L. and Arnold, M. (2013). *Online@Asia-Pacific*. London: Routledge.

Hjorth, L. and Lim, S.S (2012). Mobile intimacy in an age of affective mobile media. *Feminist Media Studies*, 12(4), pp. 477–484.

Iser, W. (1978). *The Act of Reading*. Baltimore and London: John Hopkins University Press.

Jamieson, L. (2011). Intimacy as a concept: Explaining social change in the context of globalisation or another form of ethnocentricism? *Sociological Research*

Online, 16(4), p. 15. Retrieved from www.socresonline.org.uk/16/4/15.html 10.5153/sro.2497.

Kim, L. (1996). Korean ethos. *Journal of KAMA (Korean American Medical Association)*, 2, pp. 13–23.

Kindberg, T., Spasojevic, M., Fleck, R. and Sellen, A. (2005). The ubiquitous camera: An in-depth study of camera phone use. *IEEE Pervasive Computing*, 4(2), pp. 42–50.

Koskinen, I. (2007). Managing banality in mobile multimedia. In R. Pertierra, ed., *The Social Construction and Usage of Communication Technologies*. Singapore: Singapore University Press.

Lasén, A. (2014). Mobile sentimental education: Attachment, recognition and modulations of intimacy. In: G. Goggin and L. Hjorth, ed., *The Routledge Mobile Media Companion*. New York: Routledge, pp. 396–405.

Lasén, A. (2015a). Digital self-portraits, exposure and the modulation of intimacy. In J.R. Carvalheiro and A. Serrano, eds., *Mobile and Digital Communication: Approaches to Public and Private*. Covilha: LabCom Books, pp. 61–70.

Lasén, A. (2015b). Rhythms and flow: Timing and spacing the digitally mediated everyday. In: J. Wyn and H. Cahill, eds., *Handbook of Youth and Children Studies*. London: Springer, pp. 749–760.

Lasén, A. and Casado, E. (2012). Mobile telephony and the remediation of couple intimacy. *Feminist Media Studies*, 12(4), pp. 550–559.

Lasén, A. and García, A. (2015). '... But I haven't got a body to show': Self-pornification and male mixed-feelings in digitally mediated seduction practices. *Sexualities*, 18(5–6), pp. 714–730.

Lingel, J. (2013). The digital remains: Social media and practices of online grief. *Information Society: An International Journal*, 29(3), pp. 190–195.

Løntoft, M. (2014). Talk dirty to me! Sexblogging som performativ intervention og medieret tilblivelse. *Kvinder, Køn & Forskning* (Serie: Medier, offentligheder, køn, Årg), 23(3), pp. 8–21.

Lorentzen, J. and Mühleisen, W. (2013). Å være sammen: intimitetens nye kulturelle vilkår. Oslo: Akademika forlag.

Lüders, M. (2008). Conceptualizing personal media. *New Media and Society*, 10(5), pp. 683–702.

Lund, J. (2016). Samtidigheden æstetik: Teknik, tid og politik. *Agora*, 4(15), pp. 101–117.

Markham, A. (2013). Fieldwork in social media: What would Malinowski do? *Journal of Qualitative Communication Research*, 2(4), pp. 434–446. doi: 10.1525/qcr.2013.2.4.434.

Mørk Petersen, S. (2009). *Common Banality: The Affective Character of Photo Sharing, Everyday Life and Produsage Cultures*. PhD dissertation. ITU Copenhagen.

Nansen, B., Arnold, M., Gibbs, M. and Kohn, T. (2014). The restless dead in the digital cemetery. In: C.M. Moreman and A. David Lewis, eds., *Digital Death: Mortality and Beyond in the Online Age*. Santa Barbara, CA: ABC-CLIO, pp. 111–124.

Ngai, S. (2005). *Ugly Feelings*. Cambridge, MA: Harvard University Press.

Nikunen, K. (2015). Politics of irony as the emerging sensibility of the anti-immigrant debate. In: R. Andreassen and K. Vitus, eds., *Affectivity and race: Studies from Nordic contexts*, pp. 21–42. Farnham: Ashgate.

Palmer, D. (2012). iPhone photography: Mediating visions of social space. In L. Hjorth, J. Burgess and I. Richardson, eds., *Studying Mobile Media: Cultural Technologies, Mobile Communication, and the iPhone*. New York: Routledge, pp. 85–97.

Papailias, P. (2016). Witnessing in the age of the database: Viral memorials, affective publics, and the assemblage of mourning. *Memory Studies*, January 6, 20161750698015622058.

Prøitz, L. (2007). *The Mobile Phone Turn: A Study of Gender, Sexuality and Subjectivity in Young People's Mobile Phone Practices*. PhD dissertation. University of Oslo: Faculty of Humanities Unipub.

Prøitz, L. (2014). Male-stream móvil. Un estudio de la estética y los significados de los anuncios personales masculinos en deiligst.no. In: A. Lasén and E. Casado, eds., *Mediaciones Tecnológicas. Cuerpos, Afectos y Subjetividades*. Madrid: Centro de Investigaciones Sociologicas, pp. 87–98.

Prøitz, L. (2016). *Selvbilde: Fra selvportrett til #selfie* [Self-image: From self-portrait to #selfie]. Oslo: Universitetsforlaget.

Refslund Christensen, D. and Sandvik, K. (2014). *Mediating and Remediating Death*. London: Routledge.

Refslund Christensen, D. and Gotved, S. (2015). Online memorial culture: An introduction. *New Review of Hypermedia and Multimedia*, 21(1-2), pp. 1–9.

Rettberg, J.W. (2014). *Seeing Ourselves through Technology: How We Use Selfies, Blogs and Wearable Devices to See and Shape Ourselves*. Basingstoke: Palgrave Macmillan.

Rosenblatt, P. (1996). Grief does not end. In: D. Klass, P.R. Silverman and S.L. Nickman, eds., *Continuing Bonds*. Washington, DC: Taylor & Francis.

Star, S.L. (1999). The Ethnography of Infrastructure. *American Behavioral Scientist*, 43(3), 377–373.

Stewart, K. (2011). Atmospheric attunements. *Environment and Planning D: Society and Space*, 29(3), pp. 445–453.

Strauss, A.L. and Corbin, J.M. (1990). *Basics of Qualitative Research: Grounded Theory Procedures and Techniques*. Newbury Park, CA: SAGE.

Van House, N., Davis, M., Ames, M., Finn, M. and Viswanathan, V. (2005). The uses of personal networked digital imaging: An empirical study of cameraphone photos and sharing. Presentation at CHI 2005, 2–7 April, Portland, OR.

Veale, K. (2004). Online memorialisation: The Web as a collective memorial landscape for remembering the dead. *Fibreculture*, 3. Retrieved from http://three.fibreculturejournal.org/fcj-014-online-memorialisation-the-web-as-a-collective-memorial-landscape-for-remembering-the-dead/ (October 4, 2015).

de Vries, B. and Rutherford, J. (2004). Memorializing loved ones on the World Wide Web. *Omega: Journal of Death and Dying*, 49(1), pp. 5–26.

Walter, T., Hourizi, R., Moncur, W. and Pitsillides, S. (2011). Does the Internet change how we die and mourn? Overview and analysis. *Omega: Journal of Death and Dying*, 64(4), pp. 275–302.

Wendt, B. (2014). *The Allure of the Selfie: Instagram and the New Self Portrait*. Amsterdam: Institute of Networked Cultures.

Wolfgang, E. (ed.) (2013). Digital memory and the archive. *Electronic Mediations*, 39. Retrieved from http://melhogan.com/website/wp-content/uploads/2013/11/Ernst-Wolfgang-Digital-Memory-and-the-Archive.pdf (November 11, 2016).

Zelizer, B. (2010). *About to Die: How News Images Move the Public*. Oxford: Oxford University Press.

5 Edge effect

New image formations and identity politics

Marco Bohr and Basia Sliwinska

Introduction and theory

The digital age, as noted by Nancy Baym (2010), is marked by the evolution and expansion of new technologies. In this age, there is rapid growth in the number of ways we can communicate with one another and socially and culturally reorganise personal relationships and the means by and spaces in which messages are exchanged. The development of social media, as pointed out by Jeremy Hunsinger and Theresa Senft (2015, p. 1), enables and supports in-depth social interactions 'in ways that traverse the online and offline worlds'. The broad and plural landscape of the digital age offers opportunities for collaboration and the formation of communities that otherwise may not have come together. Hunsinger and Senft (ibid., p. 2), for instance, suggest that social media provide valuable spaces for existing communities to achieve better outreach. In this chapter, we reflect on the political and performative uses of social media, which form networked public and private spheres. Moreover, we argue that contemporary digital ecologies enable democratic action that might otherwise not be possible. Social media offer new opportunities to converse thanks to the wide range and multiple modes of communication resources. Here, we are interested in the communicative and transformative potential of images that are disseminated through social media. We closely analyse the images, their construction and their power and conclude that the images are political tools for constructing active and resilient identities. Images are often used by artists/activists or global political movements such as Black Lives Matter, and suggest a new generation of political activism that is disseminated through social media – and, more specifically, the sharing of photographs online – as spaces for critical political action.

Nicholas Mirzoeff names this form of political protest 'visual activism', which juxtaposes online presence with interventions aimed at creating social change. In this way, Mirzoeff creates a direct link between the representation of protest as a form of political action. Visual activism expresses an idea that is revealed visually to attract both attention and visual *and* critical thinking. It creates hope (Mirzoeff, 2015, p. 271). As Mirzoeff explains: 'For many artists, academics and others who see themselves as visual activists, visual culture is a way to create forms of change' (Mirzoeff, 2015, p. 289). Further:

> Today, we can actively use visual culture to create new self-images, new ways to see and be seen, and new ways to see the world. That is visual activism [...] Visual activism is the interaction of pixels and actions to make change. Pixels are the visible result of everything produced by a computer, from words created by a word processor to all forms of image, sound and video. Actions are things we do with those cultural forms to make changes, small or large, from a direct political action to a performance – whether in everyday life or in a theatre – a conversation or a work of art. Once we have learned how to see the world, we have taken only one of the required steps. The point is to change it.
>
> (Ibid., pp. 297–298)

Other scholars and artists, such as Trinh T. Minh-ha (2016), Zanele Muholi (2010, 2016), Burak Arikan (2014) and Terry Kurgan (2013), among others, discuss the visual forms that art can take when engaging in political and social activism.

In this chapter, we take this notion of 'visual activism' as a starting point to describe the formation of a new type of image that is perhaps less concerned with *representing* protest than with forming protest in its own right. The chapter explores how this new type of image – one that actively engages with political protest – primarily hinges on the relationship between the digital and the analog. Through analysis of two images taken in 2014 by Nadya Tolokonnikova and Masha Alyokhina of Pussy Riot, we explore a new type of image that is enabled by contemporary digital ecologies – one that is produced, shared and consumed via digital technology yet also alludes to the analog attributes that have historically been associated with the medium of photography. We investigate the intimacies between the digital and the analog as co-existing spheres or habitats that, once crossed, create a third shared space. Borrowing from the field of biology, we call this crossing the 'edge effect'. The combined realm negotiates new forms of meaning that inform the evolution of the visual in digital communities. The edge effect thus re-energises images, making them political agents of resistance, and can produce and communicate new forms of identity, generating dialogue through intimate belonging across physical and virtual spheres. The destabilised space leads to greater biodiversity and enables images to become active visual tools for use in digital communities and within cultural ecologies.

Pussy Riot and images from a police van

In February 2014, Nadya Tolokonnikova and Masha Alyokhina – members of the feminist punk group Pussy Riot, which was founded in Russia in 2011

– were arrested in Sochi, Russia, together with other activists, for an alleged theft of a woman's handbag from the hotel in which they were staying. At the time of detention, they were walking on the streets of Sochi, where they had arrived to perform a song entitled 'Putin will teach you to love the motherland', which called for the freedom of political protesters. The song showed support for prisoners and, particularly, Evgeny Vitishko – a Russian activist on hunger strike serving a three-year sentence for using spray paint to demonstrate the environmental damage caused by the 2014 Winter Olympics in Sochi. While Tolokonnikova and Alyokhina were detained in a police van, they took and tweeted two images, one of which was a selfie. One of the photographs portrays their faces, with Tolokonnikova's closer to the camera, behind the metal cage of the police van. Only their eyes and noses are visible in the dark space of the car. The other photograph shows only Alyokhina's face and the palm of her hand, which rests on one of the bars. Later, in 2015, Tolokonnikova was arrested with artist Katya Nenasheva at Bolotnaya Square, where they had staged a protest over prison conditions for women. Again, images were tweeted from behind bars.

Pussy Riot became well known and recognised after three members of the group were imprisoned for their guerilla performance of 'Punk prayer' in Moscow's Cathedral of Christ the Saviour in 2012. Tolokonnikova and Alyokhina served two-year jail terms for hooliganism motivated by religious hatred, as their performed protest song was considered to be laced with profanity and critical of Russian President Vladimir Putin. The members of Pussy Riot are political activists who follow the route of female activism that addresses the role performed by individual and collective identity in motivating political action – particularly with respect to the intersection of minority statuses such as gender, class, sexuality and race. Women's contributions to social change began in the activist women's movements that were organised in the late nineteenth and early twentieth centuries. Pussy Riot pursues the legacy of punk aesthetic and feminist politics adopted by Riot Grrrl, an underground feminist hardcore movement that emerged in the United States in the early 1990s. Similar to other bands associated with Riot Grrrl – such as Bikini Kill, Bratmobile, Emily's Sassy Lime and The Third Sex, and groups such as Guerilla Girst, who perform artistic activism – Pussy Riot explores the way in which female identity shapes women's involvement in social justice. The band's performances and social media visibility strategically attack patriarchal structures of the state, religious orthodoxies and post-Soviet kleptocracy.

The members of Pussy Riot fight for the freedom of individuals by activating their bodies as tools to enact change. Their bodies become political constructs and sites of identification and construction of the self; the band members express themselves *with* and *through* their bodies. Since the seventeenth century, when Cartesian dualism separated the mind from the body and, in extension, male from female, women have been enmeshed in corporeal experiences. With the early nineteenth century women's movements and suffrage campaigns, women began to challenge such assumptions and confronted the body in order to subvert constructions of sexed difference. The disciplining and appropriate gendering of the body became a major theme in 1970s feminist writing by, for example, Dworkin (1974). In the 1990s, attention was refocused on policing one's body (Bordo, 1993; Braidotti, 1994, Gatens, 1996; Grosz, 1994; Weiss, 1999). Subsequently, the body became a battleground for many artists and activists who used it to fight against patriarchal repression. Since the late 1960s, the body has become a medium of expression for women to both claim control over their bodies and question social and political issues. In this sense, the body has become an active tool for resisting the state's efforts to 'normalise' it. Being mindful of Michel Foucault's application of Bentham's concept of the Panopticon, which is referenced below, the body can be understood to function as a metaphor for the state, which exercises control over society through continuous surveillance via institutions (e.g. the police) and physical means (e.g. CCTV). The state's aim is to tame the body and behaviour, creating docile social beings rather than inquisitive and curious members of society. Pussy Riot's activism goes beyond representational strategies and becomes a form of visual protest.

The members of Pussy Riot directly engage with politics through their bodies. Their photographs from the police van are literal and physical signifiers of their beliefs. The band uses images alongside protests to inspire critical political action. Thus, their musical performances in the public sphere are accompanied by another set of performances in the digital realm. Members of Pussy Riot wear balaclavas (when arrested for their performance in Moscow's Cathedral of Christ the Saviour in 2012, their faces were obscured), which goes against the current cult of personality that focuses on displaying one's face as a sign of individualism and often self-promotion. Another activist artistic group that uses a similar strategy of wearing masks to remain anonymous is the Guerilla Girls. On the group's website, the band members explain: 'We're feminist masked avengers in the tradition of anonymous do-gooders like Robin Hood, Wonder Woman and Batman.' (Guerilla Girls, 2016). Hiding their identities enables them to focus 'on the issues rather than their personalities' (ibid.). This strategy also demonstrates that, in fact, as Slavoj Žižek (2012) remarks, Pussy Riot is an idea, not a band of individuals, and it does not matter which band member gets arrested, as the members choose to be anonymous. However, in the trial following the arrest of two of the band members, their identities became scrutinised. The photographs distributed over cyberspace also show their faces and activate identity. The theorist and activist Maria Chehonadskih observes, in her article in *Radical Philosophy* (2012) that balaclavas worn by the Pussy Riot differ from:

> the Guy Fawkes masks of people crowded in the square in V for Vendetta. [...] The old Soviet dissident logic recognises only 'personality'

in the revolt against the authorities. As a result, the faces and personal stories of the members of Pussy Riot have become of central importance.

The 'naked' faces in the images show victims. According to Judith Butler, the narrative of a victim begins from a first person point of view. In *Precarious Life* (2004), Butler analyses media technologies of victims' images and notes that our Western understanding of violence is framed by the narratives that have been circulated since 9/11. This framing contributes to an ill-informed conception of agency. The focus on the first person explains where an individual makes a mistake. A focus on the second or third person, however, would enable us to move away from the 'I' and the face. Butler (2004, p. 5) argues that this kind of discourse 'works as a plausible and engaging narrative in part because it resituates agency in terms of a subject'. Here, she follows the conception of agency she introduced in *Gender Trouble* (1990). Individual agents and conditions do not act in the same way, but agents do not act without conditions. This understanding of agency brings forth the notion of responsibility. Moving away from the first person narrative of US unilateralism means that individual responsibility for acts of violence is embedded within collective responsibility for normative violence (Butler, 2004). The unmasked faces of Pussy Riot members, as seen in these photographs, emphasise this second or third person point of view. As we will explore in a more detailed image analysis, the photographs show individualised yet collective 'I's resisting patriarchy and tyranny, fighting for human rights and challenging authoritarianism. They activate solidarity across borders and across the analog and the digital. After the photographs were taken, the internet buzzed with responses from fans and followers. The image of Alyokhina that was tweeted by Tolokonnikova was almost instantly retweeted 297 times; people commented on the image and spread it further. First, Alyokhina tweeted a photograph of her view from the police van, then her image appeared on Tolokonnikova's account. Shortly afterwards, Tolokonnikova posted her mobile phone number so that journalists could reach her. She answered their calls and reporters were able to hear what was happening inside the van. The online community commented on short texts published by internet news outlets and user-generated content sites. Thus, Pussy Riot's action enacted the participation of an online audience. It might be argued that their activism is an ongoing networked performance that functions in the real and the virtual through images that verge on the analog and the digital.

It is not the scope of this chapter to analyse the activity of Pussy Riot; however, it is important to note that the group's actions are open-ended provocations that depend on the response of authorities, the mass media and the public. The members of Pussy Riot reclaim space and fight for democracy. It matters that the images they generate fall on the verge of the analog and the virtual. The group's online presence invites the audience to participate in their activities – to view them, to share them and to comment on them. Their actions are invested with social capital, and their protest is reciprocal. (Tolokonnikova said in an interview for an Australian Broadcasting Corporation broadcast on 1 September 2014 that: 'If you put on a balaclava, you could make a statement like that as well and it would be completely legit and credible because we still have the same opinion that anyone can be Pussy Riot and we want people, we want anyone to be Pussy Riot.')

The politics of looking

With the emergence of social media, looking at images has become more complex than ever. The rate at which images are produced, uploaded, shared, linked and liked (or disliked) is increasing with each passing year. Mirzoeff (2015, p. 6) reminds us that Americans take more photographs every two minutes than the total number of photographs taken in the nineteenth century. In 2014, the global photography archives increased by approximately 25 per cent relative to the number of photographs that existed worldwide in 2011. In light of this development, the production and consumption of images has unveiled a new type of political subjectivity that emphasises identity and engagement with and understanding of the world. Eliciting political action through art is not a novel way of raising, responding to and critiquing world events and pertinent ethical, social or cultural issues. Through socially engaged artistic practice or critical opposition, artists intervene to question normative politics. Often, this form of critique is representational and does not result in direct action. The Western cultural system anticipates critique, as discussed by Slavoj Žižek. In *The Sublime Object of Ideology*, Žižek (2008) argues that everyone now practices ideological critique, which results in the reflective cynicism present in our political and cultural systems that marks the distance between reality and ideological masks. He also discusses protests that acknowledge their reactionary impulses against global capitalism (Žižek, 2013). Such protests reveal discontent with issues that are economic and, as in the case of Pussy Riot's images, politico-ideological matters demanding democracy and freedom. The inconsistency of the system presents opportunity for action. Such active resilience, achieved through representational strategies, allows for intervention into hegemonic ideology.

We demonstrate that because of the slippage between the analog and the digital, some images become effective activist tools that are not assimilated into the ideological mainstream but instead lead towards social transformation. We argue that the rise of social media has enabled a new type of image and given artists a new platform for not only raising awareness but also enacting change. This platform is used to act *through* images, which tactically intervene in the social order of consumer capitalism. The images act and activate new spaces for action, changing the historic status quo of the image.

In his essay entitled 'The right to look', Nicolas Mirzoeff (2011, p. 472) connects the act of looking with political subjectivity:

> I want to claim the right to look. This claim is, neither for the first nor the last time, for a right to the real. It might seem an odd request after all that we have seen in the first decade of the twenty-first century on old media and new, from the falling of the towers, to the drowning of cities, and to violence without end. The right to look is not about merely seeing. It begins at a personal level with the look into someone else's eyes to express friendship, solidarity, or love. That look must be mutual, each inventing the other, or it fails. As such, it is unrepresentable. The right to look claims autonomy, not individualism or voyeurism, but the claim to a political subjectivity and collectivity.

'The right to look,' argues Mirzoeff (ibid., p. 474), is 'the claim to a subjectivity'; its opposite is visuality, not censorship. It is our right to see when we are told there is nothing to see. As aforementioned, political engagement in art is not a new phenomenon. However, social media gives artists an opportunity for perhaps more spontaneous and intimate action and public involvement. Social media are also universal media, given that every second Google processes more than 40,000 search queries; this means that there are more than 3.5 billion searches per day and 1.2 trillion searches per year, worldwide (Internet Live Stats, 2016a). There are almost 3.5 billion internet users in the world, which is just below half the world population (estimated at 7.4 billion). In comparison, in 1995, less than 1 per cent of the world population had an internet connection; now, it is around 40 per cent (Internet Live Statistics, 2016b). Shared images activate the right to look and enable political subjects to negotiate – through physical and virtual reality – events in a responsible and response-able manner. Artistic activism uses aesthetics beyond its representational capacity.

The edge effect

Today, images that are of interest are not primarily those that mark human achievements, endeavours or experiences, but are quite literally introverted images, depicting people looking at themselves through a reflection in a mirror via the photographic apparatus, and hence marking an exaggerated or even extreme interest in the self. This is clearly evident from the rising number of self-taken self-portraits, commonly known as 'selfies'. Apparently, more than one million selfies are taken daily by 18- to 24-year-olds (Infogram, 2016). In many ways, the camera has become a digital mirror; indeed, a number of smartphone apps provide a mirror function. In this technological context, the boundary between looking at oneself in the mirror and photographing oneself is blurred. However, this comparison is incomplete, because it does not adequately address the fact that representations of the self via the selfie are primarily produced for the purpose of being looked at. Indeed, one could argue that it is the *sharing* and *distribution* of such images on social media that constitute the main characteristics of the selfie (Baym, 2010; Rettberg, 2014; Senft and Baym, 2015).

In other words, photographs that are shared online are more than just mirror images; they are mirror images that are reliant on being seen by persons outside the mirror. Here, we evoke Michel Foucault's thoughts on the Panopticon, as explored in his classic book *Discipline and Punish* (1977): the selfie dissociates the see/being seen dyad. The subject in the selfie is always seen without having the ability to see beyond the moment of being photographed. In this context, it is important to stress that the selfie is synonymous with digital visual culture – or, more specifically, an image shared on the World Wide Web. Once the photograph is uploaded, the subject loses a sense of control that might have otherwise been retained when sharing an analog photographic print. As various celebrity scandals over the past few years have illustrated, images that are shared online take their own journey and can be used in ways that were unintended by their original makers. This dynamic evokes notions about gaze as a form of control over a subject. In this context, the image is subject to a quasi mob culture, wherein the 'right' to comment on and to share images that have been taken by others is tested, contested and at times abused. In her analysis on selfie culture, Burns argues that by 'being discursively constructed as both problematic and feminine, the selfie enables the targeted discipline of young women by perpetuating stereotypes, maintaining hierarchies, and normalizing the punishment and correction of subjects perceived to be abnormal' (Burns, 2015, p. 1730).

It is easy to dismiss the ever-growing image economy of today as superficial, self-centred or vacuous because of its preoccupation with the self. The rapid speed at which such images are produced, disseminated and consumed online can also contribute to this judgment. However, we believe that the formation of new image economies primarily hinges on the relationship between the digital and the analog. Yet the notion of formation presupposes a certain fixity between one and the other. Thus, we propose a more fluid relationship that feeds off both aspects and, quite literally, evolves.

In this context of evolutionary images, we address the resonance between the analog and the virtual and the opportunities enabled by contemporary digital ecologies. Seemingly, these two habitats exclude each other. However, this 'evolution' can also be seen in the many ways in which image economies are described: they become viral and they grow and diminish in popularity, much like living organisms. In some ways, their growth cannot be entirely controlled: they react to each other and are connected to each other like veins in a body. Ernst Haeckel (1866), who coined the term 'biology', defined the field as the relationship between organisms and their environment. He argued that it included the material effects of environmental media (e.g. air or water) and other factors (e.g. temperature) that impact upon morphological articulation, adaptation and the survival of organisms. Thus, he emphasised the element of transformation, which enabled going beyond the biological limitations embedded in the genetic level of the genome, following Darwinian thought. Haeckel's understanding of ecological evolution offered a variable matrix within which transfigurations between ecologies or networks and intimate biotic communities were possible. The boundary between ecosystems or realities might, in fact, be considered a transitory space that enables greater biodiversity. These biological constructs may be applied to describe how the physical and the virtual cross and how what seems like a native habitat (analog) both affects and resonates with processes and communities in the fragmented habitat of the virtual (and digital). We propose the biological concept of the 'edge effect' to test the transformations occurring at the boundaries of contrasting habitats. When calculating habitat suitability while observing, for example, the behaviour of birds in the Atlantic forest,[1] the edge effect impacts on the reformulation of communities *in* and *across* environments. This demonstrates the permeability of the seemingly contrasting matrix and enables connectivity in the *in between*. We argue that this destabilised space leads to greater biodiversity and, consequently, enables images to become active visual tools for use in digital communities and within cultural ecologies to communicate identity.

The edge effect and a new type of image formation

The edge effect and its relation to a new type of image formation can be illustrated by two aforementioned images taken by Pussy Riot and distributed via Twitter in 2014. The first image depicts Masha as she looks through the metal bars of the police van towards the lens. The device used to create the image was most likely a smartphone with a built-in flash, which slightly overexposed the metal bar at the top of the image. The crudeness of the metal surface is visually reinforced by the harsh shadows, which cut across Masha's face. A visually literate person will automatically understand that the image was taken in a dark space: this is not only suggested by the strength of the flash but also by the red eye effect that hauntingly emanates from Masha's eyes. The subject's freedom, as is clearly visible in the image, is curtailed. We, the viewer, look at someone 'behind bars'. The subject thus becomes an Other. Masha's right hand, which holds on to the bar, signifies an attempt to clutch on to a degree of freedom. The vantage point from which the image has been taken is crucial in this context because it emphasises the political struggle for which Pussy Riot has been known since their infamous arrest at the Cathedral of Christ the Saviour in 2012. Part of their visual identity is their (ongoing) confrontation with authority and, more specifically, what Althusser calls the 'repressive state apparatus' (Althusser, 2014). To that extent, two apparatuses merge in this image: first, the photographic apparatus facilitated by the mobile phone technology and second, the state apparatus, as signified by the metal bars. Pussy Riot do not show us a photograph of an interior of a police van. Rather, they show us themselves, behind metal bars, in a specific situation after a specific event.

The image is shared instantly and Masha's telephone number is provided for people to respond to what they see on their Twitter feeds. Pussy Riot make the space of the image real. In this sense, the act of seeing is expanded and involves the politics of being seen. The point here is that Pussy Riot actively use the photographic apparatus not just to confront, but also to subvert the authority of the state. The image becomes a form of visual protest – a protest described by Žižek and referred to above – that presents an opportunity for intervention. Paraphrasing the words of Mirzoeff, as quoted at the beginning of this chapter, Pussy Riot show us the world. They make us see, through the juxtaposition of pixels and actions, the need to change the world.

This dynamic between the freedom to photograph and the state's attempt to curtail the subject's freedom is also visible in the second image, which was also taken from the interior of the police van. Here, both Masha and Nadya look through the metal bars into the lens. Taken at an angle, the photograph captures the back of the police van, with daylight coming through. The automatic sensor of the camera did not trigger the flash and, overall, the image looks more composed. The contrast between the light through the window (100 per cent whiteness) and the dark space behind the bars (100 per cent darkness) references a classic convention for black and white prints connected with American photographers such as Ansel Adams. The formal aspects of the image, such as the vanishing point or a vague implementation of the rule of thirds, are further accentuated by the depiction of the subject through the metal bars. The image represents at least three visual planes: the space behind the bars, signifying incarceration; the space in front of the bars, signifying freedom; and the space between the two (e.g. the metal bars), signifying the repressive state apparatus. This visual trope has been applied by photographers since the very birth of the photographic medium. It is usually assumed that the subject is standing 'behind bars' – not just figuratively but also literally. This trope therefore suggests that the vantage point of the photographic apparatus is somehow free: not just free to look but also free to photograph and document the subject behind bars. This is precisely the dialectic explored in these images.

The Pussy Riot photos are particularly relevant to current discourse on new image formation because they were taken and shared by the subjects, themselves.[2] In other words, the subjects in the images and the persons who took and disseminated the images were the same. Following the trope explained above, the subjects are both incarcerated and free at the same time. By being freely switching between these modes, Pussy Riot subvert, make visible and ridicule the action of the state. Crucially for this chapter, however, the photographic and discursive understanding of the photographic apparatus is strategically applied to counter the action of the repressive state apparatus and make it real to those looking at the image on their Twitter feed (and responding to it by sharing, retweeting and calling the number displayed). In that way, the members of Pussy Riot are political activists who use photography as a method of political subversion.

But the case study goes further than this, because – as these images were shared on Twitter and other social media platforms – the members of Pussy Riot were able to further undermine the authority of the state by sharing the images with their followers. This suggests, as we argue in this chapter, the merging of two habitats: the physicality of photography as a form of political protest and the subsequent sharing of photographs as a means of further undermining the authority of the state and responding to the political protest. The online image sharing during the subjects' physical arrest in the back of the police van also raises questions about the notion of 'freedom' in this context: while the subjects might not be physically free, they are apparently free to conduct a visual form of protest and share it widely on the internet.

The implications of this newfound freedom – the new type of visual activism and the new type of image formation we describe here as the 'edge effect' – has vast implications for political action across the globe. Whether it is Black Lives Matter, the Occupy Movement, the UK-based organisation Object, SlutWalk, the Arab Spring, the Green Revolution or another social/ political movement, the new generation of image makers strategically apply the power of online networks for social and political causes. Thus, we classify this edge effect in biological terms: a coming together of two habitats to create an entirely new space with new opportunities and challenges.

Conclusion

Pussy Riot's selfies show the edge effect in action. In these images, we see how two spheres essentially cross to create a totally new type of image. On the one hand, the images are a type of digital protest, transcending cultures, languages and time zones. On the other hand, the images allude to a physical reality, as represented by the crude barriers in the police van. The subjects are, to use a photographic term, quite literally fixed to their environment. In the past, these two spheres would rarely collide or even come close to each other. Cameras would have been too big to hide and film would have been confiscated, and even if the camera and the film were to have made it past the authorities, the resulting images would have been subjected to censorship. The edge effect supersedes these structures via the immediacy of the internet and the mobility of camera technology. Yet the true power of the edge effect does not relate to a technological determinism; rather, it relates to the determinism of a new generation of political activism. Indeed, one could make comparisons to a variety of other global political movements, such as Black Lives Matter, the Occupy Movement, the Arab Spring, global anti-austerity protests or SlutWalk. This shows the true potential of the edge effect: from the local to the global, from the micro to the macro or from the invisible to the visible.

Jean Baudrillard (2005) starts the final section of his text entitled 'Violence of the virtual and integral reality' with the words 'I dream of an image'. He goes on to write: 'I believe that images affect us immediately [...] In that sense, an image is always absolutely surprising.' Baudrillard laments on contemporary photographic images, which often lack the power of genuineness and represent nothing. We propose that imagery such as the photographs taken by Pussy Riot, demonstrating the edge effect in action, might make Baudrillard's dream come true after all.

Notes

1 See, e.g., Zurita, G., Pe'er, G., Bellocq, I.M. and Hansbauer, M.M. (2012). Edge effects and their influence on habitat suitability calculations: A continuous approach applied to birds of the Atlantic forest. *Journal of Applied Ecology*, 49(2), pp. 503–512.
2 The first image, whilst not strictly speaking a selfie, was taken by Nadya.

References

Althusser, L. (2014 [1971]). *On the Reproduction of Capitalism: Ideology and Ideological State Apparatuses* (G.M. Goshgarian, trans. and ed.). London: Verso.

Arikan, B. (2014). Collective Networking. Burak Arıkan in Conversation with Basak Senova. Retrieved from www.ibraaz.org/interviews/127 (7 September 2015).

Baudrillard, J. (2005). Violence of the virtual and integral reality. *International Journal of Baudrillard Studies*, 2(2). Retrieved from www.ubishops.ca/baudrillardstudies/vol2_2/baudrillardpf.htm (7 September 2015).

Baym, N.K. (2010). *Personal Connections in the Digital Age*. Cambridge: Polity.

Bordo, S. (1993). *Unbearable Weight: Feminism, Western Culture and the Body*. Berkeley, CA: University of California Press.

Braidotti, R. (1994). *Nomadic Subjects: Embodiment and Sexual Difference in Contemporary Feminist Theory*. New York: Columbia University Press.

Burns, A. (2015). Self(ie)-discipline: Social regulation as enacted through the discussion of photographic practice. *International Journal of Communication*, 9(Feature), pp. 1716–1733.

Butler, J. (1990). *Gender Trouble, Feminism and the Subversion of Identity*. London: Routledge.

Butler, J. (2004). *Precarious Life: The Power of Mourning and Violence*. London: Verso.

Chehonadskih, M. (2012). What is Pussy Riot's 'Idea'? Retrieved from www.radicalphilosophy.com/commentary/what-is-pussy-riots-idea (19 May 2014).

Dworkin, A. (1974). *Women Hating*. New York: Dutton.

Foucault, M. (1977). *Discipline and Punish: The Birth of the Prison*. New York: Pantheon Books.

Gatens, M. (1996). *Imaginary Bodies: Ethics, Power and Corporeality*. London and New York: Routledge.

Grosz, E. (1994). *Volatile Bodies: Towards a Corporeal Feminism*. London: Routledge.

Guerilla Girls (2016). Guerrilla Girls Reinventing the 'F' Word: Feminism. Retrieved from www.guerrillagirls.com/#open (accessed 13 November 2016).

Haeckel, E. (1866). Generelle Morphologie der Organismen [General Morphology of Organisms]. Retrieved from https://archive.org/details/generellemorphol01haec (7 September 2015).
Hunsinger, J. and Senft, T. (eds.) (2015). *The Social Media Handbook*. New York: Routledge.
Infogram (2016). Selfie Statistics. Retrieved from https://infogr.am/selfie-statistics (21 June 2016).
Internet Live Stats (2016a). Google Search Statistics. Retrieved from www.internetlivestats.com/google-search-statistics (28 September 2016).
Internet Live Stats (2016b). Internet Live Statistics. Retrieved from www.internetlivestats.com/internet-users (28 September 2016).
Kurgan, T. (2013). Public art, private lives. *Cultural Studies Journal* (special issue): *Private Lives and Public Cultures in South Africa*, 27(3), pp. 462–481.
Minh-ha, T.T. (2016). The image and the void. *Journal of Visual Culture*, 15(1), pp. 131–140.
Mirzoeff, N. (2015). *How to See the World*. London: Penguin Books.
Mirzoeff, N. (2011). The right to look. *Critical Inquiry*, 37(3; Spring 2011), pp. 473–496.
Muholi, Z. (2010). *Faces and Phases*. New York: Prestel.
Muholi, Z., Mannya, S. and Thomas, V. (2016), In conversation with Dominic Willsdon. *Journal of Visual Culture*, 15(1), pp. 162–171.
Rettberg, J.W. (2014). *Seeing Ourselves through Technology: How We Use Selfies, Blogs and Wearable Devices to See and Shape Ourselves*. Basingstoke: Palgrave Macmillan.
Schafter, M. (2014). Interview with Pussy Riot. Australian Broadcasting Corporation. Retrieved from www.abc.net.au/7.30/content/2014/s4078785.htm (June 21, 2016).
Senft, T.M. and Baym, N. (2015). What does the selfie say? Investigating a global phenomenon. *International Journal of Communication*, 9(Feature), pp. 1588–1606.
Weiss, G. (1999). *Body Images: Embodiment as Intercorporeality*. New York and London: Routledge.
Žižek, S. (2008). *The Sublime Object of Ideology*. London: Verso.
Žižek, S. (2012). The True Blasphemy. Retrieved from http://chtodelat.wordpress.com/2012/08/07/the-true-blasphemy-slavoj-zizek-on-pussy-riot (19 May 2014).
Žižek, S. (2013). Trouble in paradise. *London Review of Books*, 35(14). Retrieved from www.lrb.co.uk/v35/n14/slavoj-zizek/trouble-in-paradise (12 September 2016).
Zurita, G., Pe'er, G., Bellocq, I.M. and Hansbauer, M.M. (2012). Edge effects and their influence on habitat suitability calculations: A continuous approach applied to birds of the Atlantic forest. *Journal of Applied Ecology*, 49(2), pp. 503–512.

Part II

Relationship making and maintenance

Is anything Changing

- concieved normal is everyon is straight
- new possibilities with online dating
- studying social media and intimacy
  you can draw conclussians about the society where the user(s) are from

- Do you think certain societies emphasize certain things?
- what do you think someone would write in their profile?

6 Innovations in intimacy

Internet dating in an international frame

Christine Beasley, Mary Holmes, Katherine Harrison and Caroline Wamala Larsson

Introduction: Innovative intimacies

Research focused on internet dating (ID) and innovation has revealed gaps in the existing literature around analyses of and directions for social change, particularly with regard to 'older' people and developmental contexts. In this chapter, we consider ID and heterosexual intimacies through the particular lens of heterodox (non-normative) heterosexualities. Rather than simply looking at the question of whether people undertaking ID are engaged in 'new' or supposedly more individually advantageous activities (in technological or social terms), we are interested in whether innovations in social interconnection and power relations are occurring and whether the emergence of ID has produced directions for progressive social change around heterogendered sexualities.

We draw on our previous work concerning innovations in heterosexuality and heteromasculinity (Beasley et al., 2012). This work suggests that it is necessary to challenge the orthodoxy that heterosexuality is homogeneous and synonymous with heteronormativity (the institutionalised and dominant idea that heterosexuality is the natural, normal and best form of sexuality; see Warner, 1999). If heterosexuality is simply equated with heteronormativity, the hegemonic coherence of heteronormativity is ironically upheld and social change is conceived of as arising only at the margins. In contrast, we are here concerned with 'undoing' the illusory homogeneity and authority of the heteronorm, in a similar fashion to Butler's 'undoing' or 'troubling' of gender (Butler, 1990), in order to open a space for considering social change. In this context, we also draw on Lauren Berlant's conceptualisation of intimacy as a

> narrative about something shared, a story about both oneself and others that will turn out in a particular way. Usually, this story is set within zones of familiarity and comfort: friendship, the couple, and the family form, animated by expressive and emancipating kinds of love.
>
> (Berlant, 2000, p. 1)

Our work examines a familiar kind of intimacy – dating – but is focused on the possibilities offered by ID to open up a wider field for desire and love.

We consider it important to theorise the nuances of innovative intimacies and their transformative potential in terms of gender equality. Since ID has become an ever more significant method for developing intimate relationships, it is important to investigate its possibilities in terms of social change.

Study aim

Existing studies of ID have paid little attention to social innovation. There has been some focus on online representations (Gibbs, Ellisson and Heino, 2006), the impact of gender on online self-presentation for dating purposes (Whitty, 2008) and the way in which online identities are recreated and have a direct bearing on offline behaviour (Yurchisin et al., 2005; see also Chambers, 2013; McGlotten, 2013). In order to address the gap relating to novel practices, a pilot study of ID sites in four countries (Australia, Denmark, the United Kingdom and Uganda) was conducted (from 15 December 2015 to 15 January 2016), with attention to diverse cultural and technological contexts beyond North America (the dominant context of the existing literature).

In this chapter, we consider the extent to which the growing use of ID sites across the world offers transformative potential for heterosexual intimate relationships. Our guiding research questions are:

- Is there any transformative potential in new technologies of intimacy?
- Is there anything that looks new, different and non-normative?

Theoretical framing of innovative intimacies

It is important to theorise the nuances of innovative intimacies and their transformative potential in terms of gender equality. Thus, we place our analysis within a feminist frame that gives a distinctive flavour to our discussion.

First, feminist scholarship (including scholarship in critical men/masculinity studies) is impelled by a specific rationale that eschews claims of gender neutrality and foregrounds the ongoing impact of gendered power relations. It offers a sociopolitical rationale that is centrally concerned with resisting the inequities of the present while being, as Rosi Braidotti puts it, 'worthy of our times' – 'engag[ing] with the present in a productively oppositional yet affirmative manner' (Braidotti, 2010, pp. 42–46).

Second, in developing this rationale, feminist scholarship takes a different approach that is generated 'in relations, in connections', in practices and in a 'radical relationality' (Braidotti, 2010, p. 45). This approach is profoundly critical of perspectives proclaiming atomistic individualism. In this context, feminist commentaries have long argued for a vision of social life favouring engagement with social connection and recognition of the ongoing significance of relationality (even while acknowledging the importance of autonomy) (Anderson and Christman, 2005; Mackenzie and Stoljar, 2000; Westlund, 2009).

Third, a feminist approach offers an alternative methodology involving attention to the micro politics of social life, including the everyday, embodied, emotional, libidinal and personal aspects of private conduct. This means that feminist work has theoretical, empirical and strategic advantages associated with enabling attention to both macro *and* micro politics, as well as their interconnection and interaction.

Feminist foregrounding of the significance of power relations, relationality and the micro politics of social life enables a conception of modern sociality in which changes in social life cannot be assumed to be only top-down. This concern with micro politics makes looking at practices of intimacy (such as dating) a means of understanding developments and innovations in social life. In particular, social media sites that depend on user-generated content and are, by their very nature, designed for relationality offer highly charged social spaces where gendered power relations are potentially challenged.

written by users!

Since ID is becoming an ever more significant method for developing intimate relationships, it is a matter of some urgency for feminists to investigate its possibilities for social change.

Methods and material

The study offers a comparative analysis of gendered dimensions of ID across three continents. As noted earlier, it is a pilot study with the intention of refining theoretical frameworks and methodological tools regarding multinational analyses of intimacy and social change and the multinational coding strategies associated with these analyses. This preliminary research draws on a qualitative content analysis of ID sites. Content analysis encompasses varied stances towards and means of analysing textual materials, including visual texts (Cavanagh, 1997). These stances range from impressionistic to strictly calculable, from those placing a qualitative stress upon the complexity of language, context and meaning to those with a quantitative focus on manifest content and word frequencies (Rosengren, 1981). This method may be 'prescriptive' and attentive to a closed set of parameters, or 'open' and intent on bringing to light dominant, reiterated and innovative themes (McKeone, 1995). It may involve coding arising from the textual data ('conventional' coding), from pre-existing theoretical frameworks or research findings ('directed' coding) or from key words (or themes) that are interpreted through the lens of the context ('summative' coding) (Hsieh and Shannon, 2005). The preliminary status of this research and the contextual variability of our multinational scope necessarily situates our use towards the impressionistic and interpretive end of the content analysis continuum. Our research and theoretical interests lead to an 'open' emphasis on themes (both dominant and innovative), in keeping with a qualitative concern with meaning and intentionality rather than a strict, closed concern with specific, frequently repeated words. The overall shape of the study is framed by pre-existing theoretical research around possibilities for heterodox innovation (taking a 'directed' approach), but we also make efforts to allow for a high degree of contextual sensitivity associated with cultural/national variation (reflecting a 'summative' approach).

Context impacts on the nature of the material collected due to the differing ease of internet access in the countries under study. For example, material from Uganda is limited to a small elite group of internet users. Less than 10 per cent of the population has access to mobile internet and less than 1 per cent have fixed internet subscriptions. These figures largely describe a very young, economically privileged group of individuals who may turn to the internet for building intimate relationships. By contrast, Denmark, the UK and Australia have broadly similar and much higher usage levels, with around 80 per cent of households having access to the internet. Nevertheless, the similar levels of usage in these countries should not blind us to possible cultural/national differences around intimacy, gender relations and social change concerning gender equity. Men and women in all four countries are roughly equally likely to use the internet and ID sites, and – with the exception of Uganda – older people are the fastest growing group of users.

The contexts chosen for analysis are those that the authors are either currently working in or originally from; some of the authors work in their country of origin. Hence, the choice of the four countries was strongly informed by our knowledge of the context and our ongoing research on ID sites. We sought to uncover significant differences in the four sites that might be relevant when comparing the findings. This meant that we specifically did not require researchers to code in exactly the same way, as rigid requirements for inter-coder 'reliability' (see, for example, Weber, 1990, p. 12) were thought to potentially limit responsiveness to context.

Instead, we posed an overarching theoretically informed question to users (or referred to existing online accounts of their experiences) about whether they found anything new or different in meeting people through ID sites. We assumed in advance that we might receive contextually varied responses to this question.

We undertook an analysis of 80 'profiles' (of 40 men and 40 women) across the four designated countries to discern any presentations of self, attitudes and practices that might suggest new non-normative developments in gendered intimacy. Each team member purposively selected 20 profiles from their chosen site to cover a variety of ages and a mix of male and female users. Profile analysis focused on meta-level patterns in, for example, popular descriptors, and was thus completely anonymised. We posted a question to chat sections or Facebook groups that were related to some of the sites, asking if users could identify new or different experiences of ID compared with traditional experiences of dating. On these platforms, the study and the researcher's purpose for joining the group were introduced before the question was posed. Group members were therefore able to opt out of the research. With some sites we were able to analyse online accounts of users' experiences that were already publicly available through blogs that were attached to the sites. These variations were adopted to ensure that each researcher complied with the ethical approvals obtained for their research.

Results

Plenty of Fish and a large paid site, UK

When loading Plenty of Fish (PoF), about five profiles appear at a time. These profiles were selected on the basis outlined above until 20 profiles (10 men and 10 women) had been analysed. Creating a personal profile is necessary for users to contact people via the site, but basic profiles can be viewed by anyone. Most profiles belong to users in their 20s and 30s, with fewer belonging to persons over 40. For this study, profiles were selected from four age groups (20s, 30s, 40s and 50s). Eighteen users identified as white and two identified as black. Limited information was available about level of education and employment.

Clicking on a profile leads to an in-depth page providing basic details: name, description, city, gender, height, religion, ethnicity, intent (e.g. wants to date but nothing serious), education, personality (e.g. 'daredevil') and profession. There is a large image on the left-hand side and a text-based section with short responses to statements indicating the type of relationship the user is seeking, their marital status, their level of ambition, their number of pets and so on. Following this is a paragraph that the person has written about themselves and what they are seeking.

In addition to analysis of Plenty of Fish, a content analysis was conducted between September and December 2014 on a large UK ID site that charges for message exchange. However, users can register on the site and view profiles without paying. A profile named 'Researcher' was temporarily put up and men were searched for in the age range of 25 to 45. One hundred and twenty profiles were analysed.

There is evidence of the reproduction of normative ideals of 'emphasised femininity' (Connell, 1987, pp. 183–190) in this sample of profiles, and only small innovations in the presentation of masculinity. On PoF, women's main profile photos were mostly headshots, of which several showed the women pouting suggestively. All of the women wore makeup and most had long hair. The women described themselves as 'divas', fashionistas or princesses, and one or two as loyal or honest. Research has found that the visual markers men use when presenting themselves online emphasise beautiful bodies (Siibak, 2010), but this was not especially evident in this sample. Men's photographs on the paid site were mostly headshots, with an even balance of those taken indoors and those taken outside; only a handful featured men doing active, sporty, 'manly' things (Connell, 1987). Very few men were pictured with cars. The men's main profile photos were predominantly torso shots and only one or two of these men were topless – one with two surfboards. Thus, active, sporty portrayals appeared on this ID site, with many men in the sample wearing sunglasses – perhaps another marker of outdoor activeness. Yet many poorly taken selfies were also featured, showing a certain disregard for concern with one's appearance, something that has previously been associated with some forms of hegemonic masculinity (Connell, 1987; Ricciardelli et al., 2010, p. 65). Some resistance to heteronormative ideals of gendered relationships was evident in the words people used to describe themselves. For example, a few of the women's profiles challenged normative understandings of women as dependent on men (Kittay, 2013). These women described themselves as 'independent' and/or mentioned that they worked and owned their own home. Such women were mostly older (in their late 30s and 40s). It is striking that, across both sites, the descriptor 'easy-going' was frequently used for men. Adventurous and funny were the second most frequently used adjectives, although 'fun' was commonly used in the PoF profiles. Men also made more references to athleticism or a fondness for sports or the gym. Several men said they were not looking for commitment or anything serious, and two included no description. These profiles seem to conform to the stereotypical trope of men looking for casual sex online. Nevertheless, further research is needed to determine what men intend to communicate with the term 'easy going', and whether it is meant to imply that they are simply not aggressive or hyper heteromasculine.

Some gender innovation is evident in the way in which some women used the ID site to signal their intolerance for heteromasculinity and to filter out or screen men who were sexually aggressive, inappropriate or sexist (Beasley and Holmes, 2018, forthcoming). A few of the women's profiles, for instance, contained pleas for men to only contact them if they were seriously interested in a relationship and asked them not to send 'knob shots' (photos of their penises), to propose casual sex or an affair or to call the women 'luv' or in other ways 'waste' their time.

'Nothing to lose and everything to gain' – Mingle2, Uganda

In Uganda, ID must be understood within the context of national internet access and use. Uganda has a population of almost 40 million (worldmeters.info), of which 1.6 million reside in the Kampala district,[1] which houses the nation's capital and has the largest share of the country's broadband (Freedom on the Net, 2012). Subsequently, this is where the majority of internet users live. More than 70 per cent of Uganda's population are 'youth' under 35 (Wamala, 2013), with the majority residing outside this connected metropolis (Freedom on the Net, 2012). Most of the nation's internet users are young people in Kampala (Wamala, 2013); thus, access and use of the internet for romantic pursuits is typically characteristic of a very restricted and small population.

The analysis of Mingle2 – the Ugandan version of the dating site – was augmented with offline conversational interviews and analyses of dating profiles in local newspapers and television dating shows, in order to fully understand the potential for innovation in ID. Like PoF in the UK, Mingle2 is partially free, inviting online chatting and email options with potential matches. Eighteen of the profiles were of users younger than 35, fitting the demographic described above. All 20 profiles used English as the language of communication. English is the medium of instruction at all educational levels in Uganda, meaning that language is not a barrier to internet use.

English also allows access to partners beyond the geographical boundaries of Uganda. Four of the 10 women were very frank in communicating their desire to meet white partners outside Uganda. Three women aged 30 and over were also candid in their hopes that their online profile would yield 'a long-term committed relationship', and one stated that she was 'not here for internet games'. Among the male profiles analysed, a 49- and a 56-year-old were 'looking for serious women to marry'. Age is likely to be a factor here, because the other male profiles and two of the female profiles in their early 20s were more casual, even coy.

In Uganda, social maturity for men and women is aligned with marriage, and the older one gets before settling down and marrying the more elusive his or her maturity appears (Nannyonga-Tamusuza, 2005, pp. 134–135). For women, regardless of marital status, the passage to womanhood is aligned with motherhood. The women on Mingle2 expressed a keen interest in having children, and although not mentioned explicitly, bearing children was considered more urgent than long-term commitment. This is because a woman who has never given birth, irrespective of her age, is seen as 'lazy ... useless' (Nannyonga-Tamusuza, 2009, p. 375). The question of whether the women on ID sites have children or not is especially sensitive for the women, for whom the 'useless' label casts a shadow on their status as 'proper women' in Ugandan society. This adds to their desire to find a man, especially for women over 30. However, going online is not always seen as the best way of achieving this:

> putting oneself out there through the newspapers or television is somewhat less embarrassing, than going online. Women who go online they are thought to be easy.
>
> (Fiona, 33)

> girls in the past have not been the aggressor in the pursuit. Technology helps them to be able to approach [...] even the shy ones. Those who go on *Bukedde*[2] and *Abanonya*[3], majority of them are women.
>
> (Tendo, 72)

> Girls who go online, are most likely to come from upper-middle-class educated backgrounds, one would not expect them to struggle finding someone, but those who go to the newspapers have nothing to lose and everything to gain, they are not from the same social background as those going online, even though five or so years ago, it was also demeaning to put one's image in the lonely newspaper columns.
>
> (Paul, 35 and Fiona, 33)

As mentioned in the interviews, a woman taking on the aggressor role is different and innovative within the Ugandan context. Online dating allows women to engage with what Judy Wajcman calls a 'technofeminist approach' (2007), emphasising the fluidity and flexibility of gender relations through technology. Aware of the social stigma that goes with putting oneself online, closed Facebook pages and other social media platforms such as WhatsApp groups are escalating. Nevertheless, Ugandan women and 'older' men are populating cyberspace and embracing technological change (see Wajcman, 2007). This is allowing their search prospects to extend beyond their immediate vicinity, which is also innovative for a country with such a strong ethnic awareness.

Extramarital intimacy, Victoria Milan – Denmark

Whilst online dating sites have long been used as a covert way of finding additional partners or extramarital intimacy, recent years have seen an increase in the variety of social media services explicitly targeting unfaithful partners. Victoria Milan is an international dating site that specialises in connecting people who are already in relationships and wish to have an affair. Norwegian entrepreneur Sigurd Vedal founded the site in 2010. It offers approximately 30 different country versions and its print and radio advertisements have been particularly visible in the Nordic region. For this study, the Danish site was analysed.

In order to access profiles one must register and create a profile. For this study, a 'basic' profile was created free of charge, which allowed us to browse profiles but not interact with others on the site. Following the creation of this profile, a search was performed for men within 10km of Copenhagen aged 18 to 50, whose profiles included pictures. This produced well over 1,000 results. A similar search for women produced approximately 800 hits. For both men and women, most profiles belonged to users in their 30s and 40s. No users were aged under 20 and there were significantly fewer profiles in the 20s and 50s age brackets. The majority of users identified as white Danes.

Clicking on a profile from a selection of thumbnail images leads to an in-depth profile page with a large image on the left-hand side and three text-based sections on the right hand side. Each profile page has a 'headline' providing the user name, age and location, with a subheadline that summarises the user's situation – whether they are married, the kind of relationship they are looking for (e.g. an online flirt or a full-on relationship) and their reason for being on the site (e.g. feeling neglected by their partner). The first of the text-based sections is titled 'About Me' and comprises 24 categories focused on physical appearance/lifestyle (e.g. height, weight and sex drive). The second section is organised as a series of responses to a set of prompts: 'I am a ...', 'I am turned on by ...' (this includes characteristics, body types and sexual practices) and 'I am interested in ...' (this is used mostly for hobbies). Responses to both sections are selected from a long list provided by the site, and display a wide variety. The third section is titled 'My Ideal Match' and comprises 10 'basic' categories specified by the site, including height, weight, age, location, body art, smoking habits, drinking habits, sex drive and sexual orientation.

The design of the site carefully controls the profiles by relying heavily on lists of pre-defined categories to describe appearance, personality and sexual preferences. For example, there are 25 possible responses to the statement 'I am a …' in the second section of the profile. For the men's profiles analysed, the most popular responses to this prompt were as follows (starting with the most popular): good sense of humour, flirty, active, empathetic, sporty, honest and confident. In contrast, for women's profiles, the most popular responses were (in order of popularity): honest, passionate, open, good sense of humour, spontaneous and empathetic. Whilst some overlap can be seen between the genders, there is a clear distinction in what is considered attractive for men compared to women. For example, the men's profiles (similar to the UK profiles) show a much stronger emphasis on physical activity and sport.

Sites such as Victoria Milan attempt to change negative stereotypes around non-consensual non-monogamy, whilst the affordances of the digital medium (Baym, 2010) make it easy for customers to access their services. These are important innovations in both the practice and public presentation of extramarital dating. However, the sites also reproduce certain norms around bodies, genders and sexual practices. This is in part due to the format of the site, wherein reliance on pre-defined lists restricts the way in which people can describe themselves. These 'tick-box' selections mean that users must stick to 'known pathways and rarely venture into the unknown' (Garde-Hansen and Gorton, 2013, p. 7). The result is that, through a combination of presented content and structural features of the site, certain bodily and practice norms may be reproduced. The qualities selected by men and women in the analysed profiles, for example, demonstrate how existing heteronormative ideals about gender performance are reproduced in this particular space.

RSVP and OkCupid, Australia

The material in this section is focused on profiles of heterosexual members on the RSVP and OkCupid Australian websites. However, some attention is given to information guides and published research on these sites. The section also draws on blogs/guides and popular media articles that are specifically focused on ID in Australia (e.g. http://forums.whirlpool.net.au/archive/744310 and www.freedatingaustralia.com.au/blog, among others).[4] However, this is exploratory data and requires further empirical study. Profiles from RSVP were chosen on the basis of the 20 profiles that came into view as the site loaded. Most profiles belonged to users in their 40s, with significantly fewer under or over this age range. An even number of male and female profiles were chosen from this selection (two in their 20s, three in their 30s, 10 in their 40s, one in their 50s, three in their 60s and one in their 70s). These RSVP members did not mention their ethnic/racial identities, though superficially all but one appeared to be white. Educational backgrounds were roughly balanced in terms of tertiary education. The site does not charge users to view profiles, but requires payment for establishing contact.

The RSVP profiles are set up with a profile photo and a short snappy lead, followed by basic information about the person that is coupled with how the person sees their ideal partner in terms of that information. For example, the person's age is coupled with the preferred age range of their imagined ideal partner. Finally, short statements describe what the person is looking for in a partner and their own interests in music, books, sports and other entertainment activities. Overall, the most evident feature of the narratives is that men in the sample wrote comparatively less than women and regularly mentioned their relaxed temperament and activity and fitness levels; women, in contrast, were more likely to mention their upbeat and fun temperament and sociability. These differences in the vocabularies employed in the profiles indicate intransigent patterns around gender relations; nevertheless they offer signs of non-normative opportunities.

The heterosexual men, as opposed to the heterosexual women, were much more likely in these profile pictures – which were presumably intended to portray themselves as desirable – to locate themselves in relation to markers of traditional gender roles such as cars, motorcycles and boats. Such tropes in the ID profiles might seem to suggest that the heterosexual men, and perhaps particularly the heterosexual men over 40, were attempting to uphold/recuperate quite traditional conceptions of masculinity, appearing to remain concerned about maintaining authority over women and resisting/shutting out change.

There are also signs that traditional conceptions of romantic 'meeting up' may still be in play (see, e.g., Whitty, 2008). In one of the blogs analysed, a heterosexual woman commented that:

> You might think online dating would create some much-needed 'fairness' between the sexes. [BUT] In the realm of hetero courtship, tradition still reigns supreme [...] every day, when I log into the dating site of my choice, I play the passive role, the receiver of attention, the awaiter of messages.
>
> (Moss, 2013)

Furthermore, it would appear that the heterosexual women were most likely – by a large margin – to refuse sex on a first date. When asked about their ideal sexual encounter, they were considerably less likely to find taking control appealing.[5] More clearly, investigating Australian ID websites such as RSVP and forums such as Whirlpool[6] revealed an alarmingly noticeable gender difference around age that could be observed in the ideal partner age range. The heterosexual men were looking for younger women (frequently much younger), and the heterosexual women were looking for men of around their own age.

However, despite the reproduction of traditional gender roles in the profile content, there were some clear indications of innovative behaviour, often facilitated by the technology itself, as the concluding section suggests.

In conclusion: Looking for innovation across four countries

When we bring to the fore our research agenda of attending to heterodox (non-normative) practices within ID, there are some possible signs in favour of innovation.

One evident practice that arises in ID is 'mundane polyamory'. Dating several people at once is common and comparatively easy in ID, whereas it is much more difficult in offline contexts. Comments by ID users indicate that they can and do talk and meet with several potential partners for varying periods of time, as they 'sort' through their options. Indeed, ID sites are precisely set up for such episodic multiple connections to arise. In the Australian-based RSVP research, 54 per cent of the heterosexual men surveyed were accommodating of mundane polyamory, but intriguingly, women were also more willing to engage with this innovation (RSVP, 2015).[7] Sites such as Victoria Milan take this one step further by explicitly using the technical affordances of ID to facilitate extramarital relationships and by aiming their advertising campaigns at decreasing the stigma associated with this practice. However, the preponderance of men on these sites suggests this 'innovation' is at least equivocal in terms of gender equity.

Second, while older people (and older women in particular) tend to be normatively viewed in desexualised ways and are often perceived as self-evidently undesirable, some ID research has challenged these perceptions. Certain studies, for example, have reported greater opportunities for older heterosexual women to undertake casual sex and to do so with a wide variety of age groups (see, e.g., Malta, 2007).

Third, the shared knowledge by ID website users that both men and women can peruse possible partners has, to some extent, the potential to counter traditional conceptions of masculinity as active, in control and/or sexually predatory. We note, in this context, that in the case of Uganda, which has a gender structure that leans towards these conceptions of masculinity, the female online engagements – even when conforming to this ideal – still managed to challenge it.

Such cross-national indications of innovations in intimacy suggest that women users have more opportunities to shift or even refuse gendered sexual frames and assumptions about their roles and capacities. For example, research by the Australian-based OkCupid in March 2016 suggests that heterosexual women have a greater likelihood of getting dates if they initiate the first move.[8] Within ID, it seems, heterosexual men must also deal with mundane polyamory and women taking the initiative.

Finally, given that ID website users are likely able to contact a wide variety of people, this can enable them to undertake social connections with and experience desire/intimacy in response to a greater array of gender/sexual diversity. The softening of parochial borders around intimacies opens up space for change that is much less possible when gendered heterosexualities are restricted to homogamous options bounded by geography and existing social networks (see Yancy, 2007).

The feminist frame, in our case, enabled scrutiny of gender and gender relations, allowing us to glimpse the transformative potential of ID as a site for social change. In Uganda, as in Australia, ID opens up a wider field for desire and love that is perhaps particularly advantageous to those whose space for action has been typically constrained by culture, nation, age and gender.

Notes

1 National Population and Housing Census 2014. Uganda Bureau of Statistics.
2 Local newspaper.
3 Local television dating show.
4 See, e.g., Horin, A. (2013). Online Dating After 60. Retrieved from http://adelehorin.com.au/2013/07/08/online-dating-after-60-liars-cads-and-bores/ (August 2015); SlinkyDating. Dating Blog. Retrieved from www.slinkydating.com/ (July 2016); Dating 101 Sydney's Blog – A Dating Guide for Sydney-Siders. Retrieved from https://dating101sydney.wordpress.com/ (August 2016); Arndt, B. Getting On and Still Getting it On. Retrieved from www.bettinaarndt.com.au/online-dating (July 2016).
5 OkCupid (2016). The Deep End – A Digital Decade: Sex. Retrieved from https://www.okcupid.com/deep-end/digital-decade-sex?cf=email (July 2016).
6 Whirlpool. ID Sites: Scam or Score. Retrieved from http://forums.whirlpool.net.au/archive/744310 (August 2016).
7 This material stems from five dating tips that arose from members' comments to a survey conducted by RSVP of more than 2,400 members in 2015. The tips were posted by the RSVP team on 15 January 2016.
8 OkCupid. The Deep End – A Woman's Advantage. Retrieved from https://www.okcupid.com/deep-end/a-womans-advantage?cf=email (August 2016).

References

Anderson, J. and Christman, J. (eds.) (2005). *Autonomy and the Challenges of Liberalism: New Essays*. Cambridge: Cambridge University Press.

Baym, N.K. (2010). *Personal Connections in the Digital Age*. London: Polity.

Beasley, C. and Holmes, M. (2018, forthcoming). *Internet Dating*. London and New York: Routledge.

Beasley, C., Brook, H. & Holmes, M. (2012). *Heterosexuality in Theory and Practice*. London: Routledge.

Berlant, L. (2000). Intimacy: A special issue. In: L. Berlant, ed., *Intimacy*. London and Chicago: University of Chicago Press, pp. 1–8.

Braidotti, R. (2010). On putting the active back into activism. *New Formations: A Journal of Culture/Theory/Politics*, 68(June), pp. 42–57.
Butler, J. (1990). *Gender Trouble and the Subversion of Identity*. New York and London: Routledge.
Cavanagh, S. (1997). Content analysis: Concepts, methods and applications. *Nurse Researcher*, 4(3), pp. 5–16.
Chambers, D. (2013). *Social Media and Personal Relationships: Online Intimacies and Networked Friendship*. Basingstoke: Palgrave Macmillan.
Connell, R. (1987). *Gender and Power: Society, the Person and Sexual Politics*. Cambridge: Polity and Blackwells.
Garde-Hansen, J. & Gorton, K. (2013). *Emotion Online: Theorizing Affect on the Internet*. Basingstoke: Palgrave Macmillan.
Gibbs, J.L., Ellison, N.B. & Heino, R.D. (2006). Self-presentation in online personals: The role of anticipated future interaction, self-disclosure, and perceived success in ID. *Communication Research*, 33(2), pp. 152–177.
Hsieh, H.-F. & Shannon, S. (2005). Three approaches to qualitative content analysis. *Qualitative Health Research*, 15(9 November), pp. 1277–1288.
Kelly, S., Cook, S. and Truong, M. (eds.) (2012). *FREEDOM ON THE INTERNET 2012. A Global Assessment of Internet and Digital Media*. Freedomhouse.org. https://freedomhouse.org/sites/default/files/FOTN%202012%20FINAL.pdf (accessed 31st Aug. 2017).
Kittay, E.F. (2013). *Love's Labor: Essays on Women, Equality and Dependency*. London and New York: Routledge.
Mackenzie, C. and Stoljar, N. (eds.) (2000). *Relational Autonomy: Feminist Perspectives on Autonomy, Agency, and the Social Self*. New York: Oxford University Press.
Malta, S. (2007). Love actually! Older adults and their romantic Internet relationships. *Australian Journal of Emerging Technologies & Society*, 5(2), pp. 84–102.
McGlotten, S. (2013). *Virtual Intimacies: Media, Affect, and Queer Sociality*. New York: SUNY Press.
McKeone, D.H. (1995). *Measuring Your Media-Profile: A General Introduction to Media Analysis and PR Evaluation for the Communications Industry*. Hampshire: Gower Press.
Moss, E.H. (2013). Online Dating Sucks for Men Because of Women Like Me. Mamamia. Retrieved from www.mamamia.com.au/relationships/online-dating (June 2013).
Nannyonga-Tamusuza, S. (2009). Female-men, male-women, and others: Constructing and negotiating gender among the Baganda of Uganda. *Journal of Eastern African Studies*, 3(2), pp. 367–380.
Nannyonga-Tamusuza, A. & Baakisimba, S. (2005). *Gender in the Music and Dance of the Baganda People of Uganda*. New York and London: Routledge.
Ricciardelli, R., Clow, K.A. & White, P. (2010). Investigating hegemonic masculinity: Portrayals of masculinity in men's lifestyle magazines. *Sex Roles*, 63(1–2), pp. 64–78.
Rosengren, K.E. (1981). Advances in Scandinavia content analysis: An Introduction. In: K.E. Rosengren, ed., *Advances in Content Analysis*. Beverly Hills, CA: SAGE, pp. 9–19.

Siibak, A. (2010). Constructing masculinity on a social networking site: The case-study of visual self-presentations of young men on the profile images of SNS Rate. *Young*, 18(4), pp. 403–425.

Wajcman, J. (2007). From women and technology to gendered technoscience. *Information, Community and Society*, 10(3), pp. 287–298.

Wajcman, J. (2013). *TechnoFeminism*. Cambridge: John Wiley & Sons.

Wamala, C.V. (2013). I have to give an 'I can' attitude. *SAGE Open*, 3(1).

Warner, M. (1999). *The Trouble with Normal: Sex, Politics and the Ethics of Queer Life*. Cambridge, MA: Harvard University Press.

Weber, R.P. (1990). *Basic Content Analysis* (2nd ed.). Newbury Park, CA: SAGE.

Westlund, A. (2009). Rethinking relational autonomy. *Hypatia*, 24, pp. 26–49.

Whitty, M.T. (2008). Revealing the 'real' me, searching for the 'actual' you: Presentations of self on an ID site. *Computers in Human Behavior*, 24(4), pp. 1707–1723.

Yancy, G. (2007). Homogamy over the net: Using Internet advertisements to discover who interracially dates. *Journal of Social and Personal Relationships*, 24(6), p. 913–930.

Yurchisin, J., Watchravesringkan, K. & McCabe, D.B. (2005). An exploration of identity recreation in the context of ID. *Social Behavior and Personality: An International Journal*, 33(8), pp. 735–750.

7 Infrastructures of intimacy

Susanna Paasonen

Introduction

What was two decades ago a special, knowing and ultimately rare added layer of communication in the form of mundane social arrangements made through email, webcam sessions, newsgroup exchanges or internet relay chat (IRC), exchanges in and through networked media have, especially with the ubiquity of social media services and the mobile internet, become elementary components of social communication. Connections are constantly made, maintained and severed in Tinder matches, flirtatious Facebook interactions, sexual Snapchat sessions, Skype conversations, vitriolic Twitter exchanges and confessional WhatsApp messages.

This chapter argues that network connectivity is not merely an instrumental factor – or 'channel' – for mediated belongings, but a sociotechnical affordance that supports and modulates them. Everyday lives are lived and intimacies surface and wither in networks composed of human and non-human actors. These networks facilitate and condition the myriad forms that individual agency, intimacy and other attachments take. Following Lauren Berlant, intimacy is a matter of 'connections that *impact* on people, and on which they depend for living' (2000, p. 4, emphasis in the original). Describing sensations and relations of closeness, trust and desire, intimacy cuts across all divides between the online and offline, which, in the era of constant connectivity, are increasingly ephemeral to begin with. Network connectivity functions as an affordance and resource without which individual and collective lives would no longer function in quite the same way. In fact, connectivity has grown into a matter of infrastructure that is reminiscent of electricity, gas or water supply, or heating.

All kinds of mundane routines and connections with partners, friends and family are paced and facilitated by networked communications (e.g. Lasén and Casado, 2012; Macgregor Wise, 2015). Network connectivity functions as an *infrastructure of intimacy* that plays a key role in the creation and maintenance of friendships, sexual arrangements and affairs of the heart, as well as in the forging of their shapes and intensities. Intimacy, as discussed here, therefore refers not only to connections between people but to the networked environments in which these connections unfold and the connections that are formed through devices, apps and platforms: each of these aspects impacts on people, and people depend on them to live.

In order to examine the role that network connectivity plays as an infrastructure of intimacy, I draw on a body of 70 essays written by Finnish undergraduate media studies students between 2013 and 2015, describing the sensations evoked by the failure or breakdown of mobile phones, computers and network connections. By asking the students to write about how such instances of technological failure felt, I wanted the class to tackle the elusive yet tangible affective underpinnings of ubiquitous connectivity with the premise that these most readily manifest in moments of rupture (for more detail, see Paasonen, 2015). While some students focused on the immediate irritances of failure, others addressed ruptures of network connectivity as broader modulators of their sense of agency and intimacy attachments. It is the latter set of essays that this chapter builds on.

Written in response to a given theme as a class assignment, with the authors having granted permission for their work to be used as research material, some of the essays are knowingly hyperbolic in their stylistic choices, flourish and expressions of frustration and rage. Written as they are by media studies majors, they include more allusions to Marshall McLuhan's thoughts on the novel 'extensions of man' than one might otherwise anticipate. The students who composed the essays, aged 21 to 44 at the time, are undoubtedly privileged in their access to media and communication technology. They are all residents of a fairly wealthy Nordic country that has 100 per cent net connectivity in the population under 35; also in this population, mobile phone penetration and smartphone use have long been high (Statistics Finland, 2015). I propose that the intimate connections and disconnections the essays address nevertheless resonate across generations as 'structures of feeling' (Williams, 1977, pp. 133–134) in societies where the mobile internet has come to be taken for granted (Ling, 2015; also Richardson, 2007).

As particular as the essays are in their format, scope and purpose, they offer insightful vignettes into the affective dynamics of living with and through network technologies. Cutting through the essays is a tension between the desire for technology to function and to instrumentally improve the quality of life, and the recurrent experiences of failures, lags and dysfunctions that fuel fundamentally suspicious outlooks toward the devices and applications and the kinds of connections and attachments they facilitate or fuel. Arguing against the ideal of frictionless technological operation, the essays depict prosthetic cohabitation with apps and devices as generative of both joy and anxiety, and as persistently haunted by the shadow of disconnection that disrupts not only intimate arrangements but also possible ways of being in the world, more generally.

Always at hand

The degree to which the operability of everyday lives is dependent on network access tends to become viscerally evident when there is none: 'Without internet connection it feels like living in darkness. As if anything can happen and I have no means of finding out about it' (female, born 1983). This is particularly the case with smartphones: 'When it's taken away, one no longer knows what to do' (female, born 1990). The lack of connectivity involves being cut off from the multiple networks that give rise to individual agency as providing modes of engaging with the world, the people, objects and spaces within it (see Latour, 2011; Gomart and Hennion, 1999). These networks are technological as well as social, and connected to the obligations of study and work and the thrills of entertainment and romance, alike. Device use is premised on human control – even human control over the world, more generally (Macgregor Wise, 2015). When lack of connectivity renders such control inaccessible, the limitations of one's capacity to act become palpable, to the degree that one may feel 'completely cut off from the world' (female, born 1990).

Smart devices afford both emotional and social relational presence (Hjorth and Lim, 2012) that may be cumbersome to construct through other means. The 'salient and transitory modes of intimacy' (ibid., 2012, p. 477) afforded by mobile technology have been broadly explored in relation to their affective nuances and ambiguities. Networked communications help to keep intimate relations together and bind them with more force, while extending their spaces, shapes and rhythms (see Ito and Okabe, 2005; Schofield Clark and Sywyj, 2012). By doing so, they blur the lines of the private and the public – as compromised, convoluted and murky as these arenas are to start with.

For the older students, networked connections were not always part of mundane routines but had long since grown into their elementary constituents: 'Computer and mobile phone are as self-evident as breathing – until they fail' (female, born 1970). Students born in the 1990s had grown up with mobile phones and may have had smart phones since their early teens. Members of this generation described mobile phones as their body parts as early already in the 2000s, well before the rise of app culture (see Oksman and Rautiainen, 2003; also Schofield Clark, 2013). Having navigated different generations of devices with varying communication and entertainment functions, the students were highly aware of their current attachments to the devices:

> Before my phone broke down, I hadn't thought how dependent one can be on one small gadget and in this case on one of the gadget's single functions [SMS]. Little like a body part, the performance of which is always so much taken for granted that one gets all confused when it's damaged.
>
> (Female, born 1988)

> Different communication and media technologies have been moulded into extensions of the senses. They attach to us as solidly as our limbs and if problems occur in their use it feels like someone amputating our hands – or at least momentarily tying them with cable ties so that we wouldn't be able to use them without great pain. One can consider them as third legs of sorts, without which we feel castrated. We constantly stick our hand into our pants just to check if it's still there: we glimpse Facebook and WhatsApp on our phones, waiting for something, checking that the connection still works, that it's still there.
>
> (Female, born 1993)

In these accounts, attachments concern devices and – predominantly – their overall functionality. The perpetual use of smart devices has, as in the sarcastic account cited just above, become incorporated into bodily schema through gestures and motions that are repeated both purposefully and routinely. Writing of bodily schema, Ingrid Richardson (2005, n.p.) defines technologies and bodies as covalent participants in mapping out meaning and environment, which constantly intermesh as forms of 'techno-soma'. Not only are smart devices central nodes for managing everyday lives, but they are also carried physically close to the body, operated via touch and occasionally even slept with. Examining accounts of intimate attachments to technological objects, Jaakko Suominen (2011, p. 18) identifies them as 'technological romances' of longing and fascination, spanning the era of modern computing. Devices are used as tools for connecting with romantic interests, yet human-technology relations, themselves, follow romantic patterns in their highlights, frustrations and disappointments (Suominen, 2011). Care is given to our cohabitation with devices, precisely because they afford 'connections that *impact* on people, and on which they depend for living' (Berlant, 2000, p. 4, emphasis in the original).

Mobile devices have become crucial to our ways of feeling out the world. Yet somatic and haptic intimacies of this kind ultimately seem to have an instrumental edge connected to operability. In the student essays, devices come across as elementary in their affordances, but also as easily replaceable material objects. They are seldom loved as such, or held on to for sentimental reasons alone.

> Problems related to cell phones are particularly irksome since one has grown somewhat dependent on one's phone and the possibility of constant communication [...] The thought that I cannot be reached or that I cannot reach others at the moment of my own choosing felt and still feels difficult and even odious.
>
> (Female, born 1991)

Above, the student describes the simultaneous desire and obligation to maintain constant reachability in ways that resonate with discussions of mobile phones engendering 'intimacy and a feeling of being permanently tethered to loved ones' (Vincent, 2006, p. 39) through perpetual compulsory connection (also Gardner and Davis, 2013). The desire and obligation for reachability is galvanised by a sense of potential – an orientation towards that which is possibly within reach or possible to occur. These potentialities, as described in the essays, are centrally about contact and the risk of missing out, as well as the fear of missing out on the events that are unfolding in the world more broadly. Defined as 'a pervasive apprehension that others might be having rewarding experiences from which one is absent', fear of missing out (FoMo) associated with social media involves a 'desire to stay continually connected with what others are doing', even when it is inconvenient (Przybylski et al., 2013, p. 1841; also Fox and Moreland, 2014).

If one goes offline, a message from a lover or friend may go unnoticed, and one may miss out on social engagements and new connections. This virtual sense of the possible involves an investment in things that are soon to come. Thus, it orients and motivates the use of smart devices (cf. Deleuze, 2002). Without network access, the virtual remains separate from and inaccessible to the actual, resulting in an experience of isolation and a diminished capacity to act:

> The user is violently cut off from all the legal commodities belonging to him and forced to plan his actions entirely anew. The situation feels a little like losing a mobile phone; I've been cut off from all my social networks, I'm truly alone. Internet represents at least for me also some kind of electronic presence, constant reachability. Being separated from that against one's will comes as a bit of a shock.
>
> (Male, born 1991)

> When the mobile phone is left at home or breaks down, reachability ceases. It feels like being isolated from the whole world. Often in moments just like this I imagine that of course everyone is missing me right now when I don't have my phone with me. And when I finally get hold of the phone again I notice that nobody has tried to reach me all day.
>
> (Female, born 1992)

> Of course there are also days when it would be nice if nobody could get in contact and I even long for some isolation from people. Then the mobile phone not working can feel like a relief. Fairly soon after such positive sensations however fear hits of for example missing an important call or for example my parents getting worried since they don't happen to get in contact for a minute [...] I wouldn't think of leaving anywhere without the phone really.
>
> (Female, born 1994)

This mood of constant expectation is simultaneously one of obligation and concern, involving social ties as well as the very operability of everyday life. Going offline means cutting people off and possibly causing worry to intimate others by mere unreachability. Thus, breaching the expectation of constant mediated presence may be experienced as stressful (see Fox and Moreland, 2014). Escapes from connectivity may have their allure, but they are less sustainable in practice:

> Inability to access the Net may occasionally cause certain experiences of disappointment if for example you've waited for messages from friends or want to follow up on the news on things important to you. One may imagine being left out of something and fear isolation from the online world but also from society on some level. These days full membership in society seems to also involve a certain requirement of participation facilitated by the internet in particular.
>
> (Female, born 1990)

The mood of expectation is tied in with the rhythm of devices' notifications of new messages, posts and updates. As these punctuate and puncture everyday life, one's focus constantly shifts, moves and re-emerges as distracted attention (Paasonen, 2016). The steady flow of notifications can be experienced as disruptive and disturbing (Gardner and Davis, 2013), yet the mood of expectation is also one of possibility, and hence steeped in degrees of hopefulness.

Forced slowness

If there is one default aspect of technology, it is its imminent failure: devices eventually break down and applications are haunted by glitches. Even if these are expected, abrupt instances of technological failure can evoke sharp sensations of irritation and helplessness. Yet they may also involve degrees of joy over the lack of access. The following excerpts, in which students describe their smartphones breaking down and their momentary resort to older devices, address the pleasure involved in transformed routines of communication:

> As a smart phone user I'm used to browsing the Net even several times an hour but the shell [shaped phone] made it only possible to call, send SMS and play Snake. Against all expectation, using a device several years old felt very liberating rather than frustrating as it was completely unnecessary to constantly fiddle with the mobile.
>
> (Female, born 1993)

> It was fascinating to notice that during those two days I actually felt quite liberated. Instead of WhatsApp I needed to call or send traditional

> text messages, I didn't check Facebook every 15 minutes and when I wanted to know what the weather was like, I had to look out the window instead of just staring at the forecasts on the phone's weather app.
>
> (Female, born 1993)

While describing their fears of missing out, these students also write of shifting from phatic Facebook communication – that is, communication for communication's sake – to more substantial messaging. This was experienced as liberating for the time it took them to get their smartphones back from repair: a week and two days, respectively. The moment of failure facilitated a reflexive reversion to earlier communication habits, as dictated by the concrete limitations of older generation devices. This break from regular rhythms of network use was experienced as enjoyable, due to its impermanence: it did not involve a permanent detachment from platforms through which sociability was organised.

The 'aesthetic of attachment' (Berlant, 2000, p. 5), through which intimacy spreads and lives, involves connectivity routines that are particular to applications and platforms. In addition to abrupt gaps in operability, there are a plethora of ways in which mediated intimacies can lag, from momentary glitches to congested networks and the frustrations of asynchronous communication. Slow connections irritate due to the default assumption of immediacy: 'I consider myself a pretty patient person but when the Net is both extremely slow and cuts off, it's hard to remain calm' (female, born 1992). The expectation of immediacy that is associated with smartphones entails the instant availability of information, goods, services and people (Gardner and Davis, 2013). Lags interfere with this by forcing a slower tempo or discontinuous rhythm on one's interactions.

> Waiting doesn't go with contemporary high tempo, information-glutted life, neither does 'slowing down' as a concept for that matter. Even philosophers and yoga teachers talking about slowing down want technology to work without fault and fast.
>
> (Female, born 1990).

While a different speed of use would have been not only tolerable but even expected a few years ago, high-speed connectivity has since become ingrained in sensory schema as a matter of habit. As we are increasingly attuned to immediacy, forced disconnection gives rise to unsavoury affective dissonance. The experience is one of speed and potentiality coming to a halt – indeed, of one's very life being at the risk of lessening (Anderson, 2004) – as one falls out of sync with the surrounding world. Many scholars have theorised about the stress and cost of lives speeding up, particularly in connection with networked media (e.g. Hassan, 2012; Stiegler, 2012; Wajcman, 2015). Such analyses have addressed the toll of accelerated lives, wherein time seems to rush by as well as to run out, and there is all too much numbing stimulus for sustained attention. The student essays foreground the incompatibility of the stress and toll of forced slowness with the overall rhythm of life. It is therefore not the speed that is framed as an issue, but speed slowing down against one's will, and the limited options for social engagement that this engenders.

Intimate connections and disconnections

Intimacy is about gradations of proximity and, as such, is always relational to detachment. Connections that are made and maintained through networked media can be equally considered disconnections, as Tero Karppi's (2014) and Ben Light's (2014) studies of social media render evident. Karppi notes how '[d]isconnection interferes with daily routines and operations of connective social media'. More than a passing irritation, the lack of connectivity basically reconfigures available ways of being in the world. Karppi uses disconnection as an analytical prism for understanding the ambivalent appeal of social media services and the difficulty of fully detaching from them. For his part, Light (2014) is interested in the social and spatial disconnections that people plan and execute in social media through acts of friending, liking, unfriending, blocking and limiting the accessibility of updates.

Disconnection can, from both of these perspectives, be seen as the default effect of connectivity that is not simply negative in its resonances. This is crucial to keep in mind, given the evident appeal of narratives of loss connected with networked communications. According to these narratives, relationships are becoming shallow and people are feeling increasingly lonely as they isolate themselves behind screens rather than engage in direct interaction (see Gardner and Davis, 2013). Sherry Turkle opens her widely read *Alone Together* by arguing that 'technology proposes itself as the architect of our intimacies', yet 'networked life allows us to hide from each other, even as we are tethered to one another' (Turkle, 2011, p. 1). According to this line of argumentation, the navigation of emotional lives through smart devices leaves us lonely and lacking in the kinds of intimacies that physical proximity and face-to-face communication allow. A similar perspective emerges in studies exploring the 'dark side' of social media, according to which the high use of SNS correlates with a lower quality of life, lower self-esteem and feelings of distress (Fox and Moreland, 2014, p. 169). When setting out to explore the so-called dark side, one is likely to discover it – just as studies examining the sunnier side tend to find something of the sort. Ambiguities fit poorly with such binary framings.

This line of argumentation is familiar to a media historical perspective. Television, for example, has been diagnosed as both a medium that isolates family members from one another and one that facilitates new forms of togetherness (see Tichi, 1991). Broad narratives of lost sociability connected to media see devices as taking over the role of human partners, and see media content as replacing human-to-human communication. In practice, this involves much more complex assemblages of human and non-human actors, routines, social roles and obligations, aims and interests, as well as times and spaces of communication.

Following Light (2014), relationships and intimacies that are managed in social media are always part of a broader nexus of social proximities and distances, mediated presences and absences. Some intimacies are publicly communicated in relationship status updates and manifestations of love and affection that are shared with social media friends and followers. Other intimacies, particularly those that fail to fit the normative intimate patterns of monogamous partnership, kinship and friendship (Berlant, 2000), may be kept under wraps. Networked exchanges are stored and accumulated in personal archives (as on Facebook), or may disappear with little trace from the users' sight (as in Snapchat). Yet all such attachments are visible to the services used, through the massive user data archives they compile, store and mine. While users may experience their data as private, the data is actually corporate property that is impossible for the users to manage or delete (e.g. Gehl, 2011; van Dijck, 2014). Intimacies that are managed through social media depend on the ever-increasing performance of server farms, the capacity of underwater cables and the usability of material devices, alike.

Devices and applications are also incorporated into our corporeal organisation as externalised memory archives of people, moments and places (Gehl, 2011; Pybus, 2015). The student essays describe the involuntary effacement of such archives as particularly unnerving. The loss of digital photographs was equated with an effacement of one's actual past (female, born 1970; female, born 1989), while the destruction of a SIM card was compared with letters and photographs having been thrown into a fire (female, born 1989): 'Photographs, music and text messages disappear with devices, which feels as if memories themselves disappear when they are no longer concretely visible' (female, born 1991). These are not accounts of technology amputating intimacy, à la Turkle. On the contrary, they point to the importance of technology in supporting intimate connections of the past, present and future:

> Early in the summer I worked in Stockholm for a couple of months and I mainly kept in touch with my girlfriend through Skype. We both had sufficiently fast internet connections and well functioning computers so everything was supposed to be okay. But when we did talk with the video image on, sound turned to mush or got cut up so that it was impossible to make it out. It was absolutely infuriating that we couldn't keep in contact in ways intended. Especially since one was used to seeing the other 'live' daily before leaving for Stockholm.
>
> (Male, born 1989)

Planning and setting up a session using the video call service Skype with a significant – yet geographically distant – other may result in absolute joy in seeing that person's face, hearing their voice and sharing a moment. These connections are nevertheless routinely marred by glitches as the video image freezes, the sound grows patchy and incomprehensible and connections get lost. Lagging connections, frozen exchanges and the fading of mediated presence into snippets of out of sync sound may fuel frustration that can, in retrospect, seem disproportionate. Moments of failure involve the loss of immediate contact as well as a more visceral sense of aborted or deferred intimacy. There is a violent edge to the feeling of having been cut off against one's desire – and against human agency, more broadly construed. When an expectedly routine form of exchange fails, the uneasy precariousness of network media connections becomes manifest: on the network, intimate contact can be easily lost in instances when it matters so very much.

Like all applications, Skype emerges from an assemblage of human actors, network technologies, services and representations as immediate and intensely mediated, as intimately proximate and persistently distant. Looking into the eyes of the person on the screen involves simultaneously looking at the camera, the screen, the image and the person, with all these dimensions intermeshing in the hybrid yet ever so human figure available to us. The mirror images displayed by webcams add a further layer of mediation, as the sight of the other person's face is always subtly different from that which is witnessed in person. Amplified through loudspeakers, the grain of another's voice is similarly altered, resulting in a sound that is simultaneously familiar and a little strange.

The reliance on the visual and the auditory in webcam communication cuts off elementary parts of human sensoria, such as the sense of touch. Yet the webcam image viewed on screen, accompanied by a familiar voice and animated by a sense of immediacy, involves a particular sense – or texture – of presence of the kind that Ken Hillis (2009, p. 263) conceptualises as 'affective materiality specific to online exchanges'. Similar to Jenny Sundén, who studied the embodied underpinnings of textual online exchanges (2003), Hillis explores the dynamics of absence and presence facilitated by networked connectivity, seeing it as laced with desire for 'someone so near yet still so far because just out of material reach' (Hillis, 2009, pp. 14, 210). In other words, mediated contact – on Skype, or elsewhere – does not do away with physical distance or a sense of absence. It may, in fact, heighten these things.

Conclusion: Re-emergences and transformations

Online communication is driven by the dynamic and imperative of immediacy, yet it also entails a panoply of asynchronicity, relating to users' different time zones and varying personal rhythms of checking apps and logging in and out. In this way, connection and disconnection, attachment and detachment are routinely – even inextricably – fused in ways that are both comfortable and not. The question is not only what might be lost in the course of networked communication, but also what might emerge – as in structures of feeling. In Raymond Williams' (1977, pp. 133–134) classic definition, structures of feeling are emergent formations and social experiences 'in solution' – matters of 'particular linkages, particular emphases and suppressions [...] starting-points and conclusions'. Structures of feeling are qualities and experiences of life that are common to specific generations, contexts and locations. They are ephemeral in the sense that they are still emergent, and hence difficult to quite pin down.

The structures of feeling that emerge from the student essays are those of constant connectivity marred by perpetual lags and fuelled by expectations of imminent experiences. While a sense of anticipation folds into the future, it also entails a sense of the past, connected with memories that are stored and shared as digital data. The notion of structure implies degrees of fixity and sameness, yet these can, following Brian Massumi (2015, p. 87), be seen as 'dynamic, open-ended, composed of ongoing variations on itself' – processes that make it possible to see 'how are certain regularities enabled to *re-emerge*, across the variations, in always new forms'. Framed in this vein as re-emergence, the memory reserves stored on Facebook or a memory card reverberate with the more physical archives of print photos while the glitches of Skype can be considered in relation to the noise and interference of long-distance phone calls.

In past decades and centuries, mediated intimacies – and mediated interpersonal communication, more generally – depended largely on the postal system and telephone network. These were both, and remain, infrastructures of intimacy with their own speeds and tempos. Letter exchange involves a rotation of days – and, historically, that of weeks – during which one can do little else but wait. The synchronicity of telephony, since the late nineteenth century, did away with the need for such anticipation, while also tying communication to specific devices that were, before the era of mobile telephony, bound to particular physical locations (e.g. Fischer, 1994). As horizons of possibility, technologies open up forms of connection and exchange while framing others out. In doing so, they build on previous solutions and routines of communication – as in the shift from paper mail to email – while also fundamentally transforming them (Bolter and Grusin, 1999). As novel forms, rhythms and avenues of mediated connection emerge, they feed into patterns and structures of feeling that provide everyday lives with a particular tempo and feel.

At the same time, much of the intimacies and lags addressed above involve novel forms of emergence that do not follow the patterns of telephone communication or letter exchange. The contemporary media landscape involves distinct affective intensities. Sensory attunement to the presence and functionality of personal devices – and the information networks they are connected to – structures everyday lives in ways that are uncharacteristic of the telephony or much of the computing culture that preceded the 1990s. Both the expectancy of things to occur and the perpetual engagement with platforms, resources and applications orient the present and provide it with a particular tenor, as uneasily as this may sometimes reverberate. In moments of failure, some of this routine unravels, momentarily disrupting forms of contact and accessibility. The inaccessibility of infrastructures of intimacy generates patterns of restlessness and frustration that render palpable the degree to which current re-emergences of mediated connection and disconnection differ in their qualities from those previously exercised, felt and lived.

References

Anderson, B. (2004). Time-stilled space-slowed: How boredom matters. *Geoforum*, 35, pp. 739–754.

Berlant, L. (2000). Intimacy: A special issue. In: L. Berlant, ed., *Intimacy*. Chicago, IL: University of Chicago Press, pp. 1–8.

Bolter, J.D. and Grusin, R. (1999). *Remediation: Understanding New Media*. Cambridge, MA: MIT Press.

Deleuze, G. (2002). The actual and the virtual. In: C. Parnet, ed., E. Ross Albert, trans., *Dialogues II*. New York: Columbia University Press, pp. 148–152.

Fischer, C.S. (1994). *Calling America: A Social History of the Telephone to 1940*. Berkeley, CA: University of California Press.

Fox, J. and Moreland, J.J. (2015). The dark side of social networking sites: An exploration of the relational and psychological stressors associated with Facebook use and affordances. *Computers in Human Behavior*, 45, pp. 168–176.

Gardner, H. and Davis, K. (2013). *The App Generation: How Today's Youth Navigate Identity, Intimacy, and Imagination in a Digital World*. New Haven, CT: Yale University Press.

Gehl, R.W. (2011). The archive and processor: The internal logic of Web 2.0. *New Media & Society*, 13(8), pp. 1228–1244.

Gomart, E. and Hennion, A (1999). A sociology of attachment: Music amateurs, drug users. In: J. Law and J. Hassard, eds., *Actor-Network Theory and After*. Oxford: Blackwell, pp. 220–248.

Hassan, R. (2012). *The Age of Distraction: Reading, Writing, and Politics in a High-Speed Networked Economy*. New Brunswick: Transaction Publishers.

Hillis, K. (2009). *Online a Lot of the Time: Ritual, Fetish, Sign*. Durham, NC: Duke University Press.

Hjorth, L. and Lim, S.S. (2012). Mobile intimacy in the age of affective mobile media. *Feminist Media Studies*, 12(4), pp. 477–484.

Ito, M. and Okabe, D. (2005). Intimate connections: Contextualizing Japanese youth and mobile messaging. In: R. Harper, L. Palen and A. Taylor, eds., *Inside the Text: Social Perspectives on SMS in the Mobile Age*. Dordrecht: Springer, pp. 127–145.

Karppi, T. (2014). *Disconnect.me: User Engagement and Facebook*. Turku: University of Turku.

Lasén, A. and Casado, E. (2012). Mobile telephony and the remediation of couple intimacy. *Feminist Media Studies*, 12(4), pp. 550–559.

Latour, B. (2011). Reflections of an actor-network theorist. *International Journal of Communication*, 5, pp. 796–810.

Light, B. (2014). *Disconnecting with Social Networking Sites*. Basingstoke: Palgrave Macmillan.

Ling, R. (2015). The mobile phone (and texts) as taken-for-granted mediation. In: A. Herman, J. Hadlaw and T. Swiss, eds., *Theories of the Mobile Internet: Materialities and Imageries*. New York: Routledge, pp. 171–186.

Macgregor Wise, J. (2015). A hole in the hand: Assemblages of attention and mobile screens. In A. Herman, J. Hadlaw and T. Swiss, eds., *Theories of the Mobile Internet: Materialities and Imageries*. New York: Routledge, pp. 212–231.

Massumi, B. (2015). *The Politics of Affect*. Cambridge: Polity.

Oksman, V. and Rautiainen, P. (2003). "Perhaps it is a body part": How the mobile phone became an organic part of the everyday lives of Finnish children and teenagers. In: J. E. Katz, ed., *Machines that Become Us: The Social Context of Personal Communication Technology*. New Brunswick: Transaction Publishers, pp. 293–308

Paasonen, S. (2015). As networks fail: Affect, technology, and the notion of the user. *Television & New Media*, 16(8), pp. 701–716.

Paasonen, S. (2016). Fickle focus: Distraction, affect and the production of value in social media. *First Monday*, 21(10). Retrieved from http://firstmonday.org/ojs/index.php/fm/article/view/6949/5629.

Przybylski, A.K., Murayama, K., DeHaan, C.R. and Gladwell, V. (2013). Motivational, emotional, and behavioral correlates of fear of missing out. *Computers in Human Behavior*, 29(4), pp. 1841–1848.

Pybus, J. (2015). Accumulating affect: Social networks and their archives of feelings. In: K.K. Hillis, S. Paasonen and M. Petit, eds., *Networked Affect*. Cambridge: MIT Press, pp. 235–249.

Richardson, I. (2005). Mobile technosoma: Some phenomenological reflections on itinerant media devices. *Fibreculture*, 6. Retrieved from http://six.fibreculturejournal.org/fcj-032-mobile-technosoma-some-phenomenological-reflections-on-itinerant-media-devices/.

Richardson, I. (2007). Pocket technospaces: The bodily incorporation of mobile media. *Continuum: The Australian Journal of Media and Culture*, 21(2), pp. 205–215.

Schofield Clark, L. and Sywyj, L. (2012). Mobile intimacies in the USA among refugee and recent immigrant teens and their parents. *Feminist Media Studies*, 12(4), pp. 538–549.

Schofield Clark, L. (2013). *The Parent App: Understanding Families in the Digital Age*. Oxford: Oxford University Press.

Statistics Finland (2015). More mobile Internet use, more personal devices. Retrieved from www.stat.fi/til/sutivi/2015/sutivi_2015_2015-11-26_tie_001_en.html

Stiegler, B. (2012). *Uncontrollable Societies and Disaffected Individuals*. Cambridge: Polity.

Sundén, J. (2003). Material virtualities: Approaching online textual embodiment. New York: Peter Lang.

Suominen, J. (2011a). Hurma, himo, häpeä ja hylkääminen. Kaarroksia konesuhteissa. [From fascination to rejection: The life-cycle of techno affairs]. In: P. Saarikoski, U. Heinonen and R. Turtiainen, eds., *Digirakkaus II* [Digi Love II]. Pori: University of Turku, pp. 17–32.

Tichi, C. (1991). *Electronic Hearth: Creating an American Television Culture*. Oxford: Oxford University Press.

Turkle, S. (2011). *Alone Together: Why We Expect More from Technology and Less from Each Other*. New York: Basic Books.

van Dijck, J. (2013). *The Culture of Connectivity: A Critical History of Social Media*. Oxford: Oxford University Press.

Vincent, J. (2006). Emotional attachment and mobile phones. *Knowledge, Technology & Policy*, 19(1), pp. 39–44.

Wajcman, J. (2015). *Pressed for Time: The Acceleration of Life in Digital Capitalism*. Chicago, IL: Chicago University Press.

Williams, R. (1977). *Marxism and Literature*. Oxford: Oxford University Press.

8 Temporal ephemerality, persistent affectivity

Circulation of intimacies on Snapchat

Jette Kofoed

Introduction

Snapchat is a photo-sharing app that is currently popular amongst young people. The app is characterised by user-generated content, relationality between users, the destruction of content after up to 10 seconds and, above all, its ephemeral nature (Kofoed and Larsen, 2016, Bayer et al., 2016, Christensen et al., 2015, Katz and Crocker, 2015). The label of 'ephemerality' refers to the app's lack of information feeds, which prevents users from organising, using and remembering in ways that enable documentation and sharing (Bayer et al., 2016), which have come to be understood as core characteristics of social media (boyd, 2010, Rettberg, 2016, May 22). The affordances we have come to take for granted in social media are absent in Snapchat. However, this is beginning to change. Instagram has recently added a new feature, 'Instagram Stories', which resembles 'MyStory'. Furthermore, Snapchat has added the 'memories' feature, which allows users to share 'snaps' or photos that they have saved on to their phone. In this way, the lines of demarcation that made Snapchat unique during the first three years of its life are now becoming blurred.

Based on fieldwork in three eighth grade classes in Copenhagen, this chapter investigates how the ephemerality of Snapchat entangles with intimate practices of youth life; that is, how the practices and affects of snapping, sharing and taking screenshots are deeply enmeshed with this particular affordance. The basic tenet of this chapter is that the interfacial affordances of Snapchat are not innocent. Lack of innocence here refers to the fact that the particular affordances have agency in the way in which intimacies are lived. The affordances of Snapchat thus provide different agential spaces from those of, say, Facebook and Instagram.

In this chapter, I examine the way in which Snapchat seems to co-form intimacies among teenagers that are both inwardly lived among friends and exposed to a broader public. The chapter unpacks the way in which the intimacy of snap-exchanges involves all of the feel-good aspects of intimate belonging but also carries the potential for betrayal via the threat of exposure to an unending public. This fear of betrayal stems from instrumental betrayal, which occurs when snaps are screenshot. Fear also feeds from witnessing the way in which snaps and affects travel beyond the demarcated space of the class to greater Copenhagen, and how some snaps travel even further, to revenge porn sites and tens of thousands of viewers.

Setting the scene: Going viral – or not

Anna Munster talks of 'virals going viral' and quotes Bilton, who 'draws our attention to three characteristics of networked things going viral' (Bilton, quoted in Munster, 2013: 100): speed of spread, quantity of views or users and unpredictability of what will spread. Munster uses these characteristics to discuss the sharing of content. With respect to Snapchat and the self-destruction of content, one could say that the app itself (rather than its content) has gone viral. But since Snapchat content self-destructs, it only goes viral if the affordance of self-destruction is bypassed.

Daniel Miller contextualises his study of Snapchat within the ethnographic study of photography. His 'take' is 'the photograph' and how the existence of social media alters the consumption of photographs (Miller, 2015). Miller notes that 'the vast majority of contemporary photographs are now social-media photographs' (Miller, 2015: 4). Indeed, this is an important change. As he puts it: 'It is probably Snapchat that has bludgeoned to death our conventional view of photography [...]. A ten-second lifespan cannot possibly be associated with memorialization or the materiality of the photo' (Miller, 2015: 10). The fact that a snap consists of a photo, a short piece of text and possibly added features or an emoji suggests that 'a snap' is more than a photo, more than a text message and more than icons. Snapchat challenges conventional views of photography, Miller argues, before adding that 'often a Snapchat constitutes a comment about how one is feeling' (Miller, 2015: 11). It is precisely this issue of 'how one is feeling' when entangled with the viral nature of Snapchat that this chapter investigates.

A methodology of entering and of courage

In studying 'how one is feeling' among a group of teenagers in and through Snapchat, the terminology of 'social media use' lends itself willingly as appropriate. This terminology, however, implies that 'use' of social media lies outside of so-called 'users'. As all aspects of my fieldwork suggested that 'they', their bodies and their everyday lives are enmeshed with social media, I developed a terminology that allowed me to bypass the distinction between 'user' and 'technology'. Throughout the analysis, I thus make use of a hyphenated collocation of words (e.g. teenagers-temporality-affect-social media) to indicate that the body, the technology of the smartphone, the affordances of the Snapchat app and the affectivities and temporalities of its communications cannot be untangled.

Such terminology is embedded in a methodology of 'entering'. In a recent interview, Gayatri Spivak argued for what she terms 'critical intimacy'.[1] Spivak uses this term to refer to the fact that researchers do not criticise from the outside. She points to Derrida and deconstruction, claiming:

> it was an engagement with that part of deconstruction, which looked at what is excluded when we construct systems. That part of deconstruction which said the best way to proceed is a very robust self-critique. And that part of deconstruction which said that you do not accuse what you are deconstructing. *You enter it.*
>
> (Spivak, 2016, my emphasis)

The process of not-accusing becomes acutely relevant when studying highly normative topics such as cyberbullying, 'sexting' or sharing of nude photographs. The empirical material scrutinised in this chapter stems from fieldwork on cyberbullying and picture sharing. As I have argued elsewhere (Kofoed and Staunæs, 2015), these fields of research are embedded within normativities of shame, moral panic and the desire to do good. Strategies are needed to navigate such normativities and to avoid writing the obvious stories about 'ephemeral and superficial young people' or the 'shaming of young people who share nude photos', which currently seem to reign. The strategy I took in this fieldwork was one of *intimacy*. Intimacy in methodology (as well as in analysis) refers to Spivak's idea of 'entering'. In this fieldwork, entering entailed entering the school, Snapchat, the affective sphere of young people sharing snaps and the multiple temporalities of this sphere. Entering also referred to entering into the phenomenon intimately; that is, with the intention of grasping and understanding what was at stake for the teenagers-temporality-affect-social media involved. To this end, the hyphenated terminology was needed. The methodology of entering and intimacy involved processes of including and excluding the researcher. Some participants exercised their right to refuse me; others allowed the researcher in. For those who did not refuse my presence, courage was required.

It is by no coincidence that I highlight the tearing open of ephemerality of Snapchat as a matter of courage and heroism. In some respects, the social media lives of the young people I met was lived within an interpretative framework of adults 'who did not understand'. Through this framework, some teenagers presented what I came to think of as the 'standard presentation of youth life entanglements', which accounted for the apps used, the number of snaps sent and an estimate of the superficiality of the app. I came to understand this as an account that was customised for the anticipated adult assumption that young people on social media lack digital *Bildung*, and that social media allows for only superficial attachment to others. I do not suggest that these teenagers were superficial, and I am sure that they had good reasons for meeting me in ways that adhere to standard interpretations. However, I also met teenagers who, after their initial presentation, willingly tore their entanglement with social media open. It is these young people I think of as courageous, as they allowed myself and others to sense, affect and co-live their social media lives for a short while. They dug into the perplexities of sending and receiving snaps so regularly that they each had several friends 'on fire' (referring to the emoji that indicates a frequent exchange of snaps). These teenagers paved the way for a scholarly understanding of new media and intimacies around Snapchat and youth life. They showed courage by 'tearing open' bits and pieces of their lives, which on the one hand were continuously shared, and on the other hand were affectively private. Exposing the embarrassing affects of intimacies – including intimacies that were threatened or unknown – and savouring the unknown became the core activities of these interviews, when *entering*.

A visual matrix interview

The students and I ventured into the unknown together. Tearing open and coaxing is part of what Lisa Blackman and Couze Venn talk of as the need 'to develop new ways of being attentive to empirical material and develop other ways of 'noticing' and attending within our research endeavours' (Blackman and Venn, 2010: 9). The development of 'new ways' was, in this case, inspired by the so-called 'visual matrix methods' developed by Lynn Froggett and Julian Manley (Froggett et al., 2015). The visual matrix method was developed for 'understanding a shared imaginary through an image-led process. The matrix facilitates associative thinking among participants by asking not what they *think* about the object of inquiry, but what they *feel* and *visualise*' (Liveng et al., 2016: 10). The aim of the approach is to set the stage for reverie and associative thinking, using visual stimuli.

The set-up of this particular interview was deeply inspired and informed by the visual matrix method as laid out by Froggett and colleagues (Froggett et al., 2015). The basic tenets of allowing the interview to be guided by visual stimuli, sitting in a snowflake formation and creating shared associative thinking based on visuals, was followed. However, my interview did not qualify entirely as a visual matrix method interview as it differed from the approach in two important respects: it stood alone (i.e. it was not followed up by subsequent group analyses) and the interview did not create the sort of reverie that is the overall aim of the method.

The interview was conducted as part of a larger fieldwork among eighth graders in an ethnically diverse area of Copenhagen. The fieldwork lasted for approximately six weeks in the early summer of 2016. In the fieldwork, I focused on cyberbullying. While research has shown that cyberbullying is very affective (Kofoed, 2014, Kofoed and Ringrose, 2012, Ringrose and Harvey, 2015, Ringrose and Rawlings, 2015), far less is known about photo-sharing practices in cyberbullying. The intention of the current research project was to upgrade our scientific insight into this practice.

Hence, the fieldwork had two foci: cyberbullying practices and, more broadly, use of photo elicitation apps such as Snapchat and Instagram. The research project was funded by the Danish National Research Council and was part of a larger project titled 'Affects, Interfaces, Events' (2015–2019). Within this fieldwork, one interview was conducted, inspired by the visual matrix method. This interview is the focus of the core analysis in this chapter. Five girls, aged 14 and 15, took part in the interview. To contextualise the girls' narratives, observations from the broader fieldwork are included when relevant in the following analysis.

The visual stimuli comprised a collection of photos that had been shared on social media. The photos were selected after a month of fieldwork, based on knowledge of the kinds of photos that were shared amongst this group of teenagers. The selection comprised selfies and photographs of double chins, brutal cyberbullying messages drawn from other parts of my research (for instance, a message exclaiming: 'You are too fat, you ought to die'), semi-nude images of six packs, underwear and breasts, pictures of food (lunches or brunches) and photographs of miniskirts and slim, tanned legs. This selection covered more or less the full range of pictures that these teenagers shared.

A concept of intimacy

The narratives of this interview were scrutinised from a Lauren Berlant-inspired 'take' on intimacy, drawing on both the normativities of closeness and the betrayal and dramas that relate to it (Berlant, 1998). Berlant, from the outset, pinpoints how the 'inwardness of the intimate is met by a corresponding publicness' (Berlant, 1998: 281). Her basic point about intimacy is that all of its positive and desirable sides inevitably meet with instability, drama and betrayal. Closeness and drama are at the core of Snapchat youth life, which is lived in and between an unending public and a 'twosome-ness'. Intimacy in Snapchat embeds strong ambivalences that are explained – read through Berlant – by the latent vulnerability it carries, alongside the potential for closeness (Berlant, 1998, p. 282). This is a pivotal starting point, as it articulates the way in which intimacy carries both strong normative ideas of positivism – or what Berlant calls 'utopian, optimism-sustaining versions of intimacy' (Berlant, 1998, p. 282) – and aspects that are usually perceived of as dangerous. Berlant takes the view that 'contradictory desires mark the intimacy of daily life: people want to be both overwhelmed and omnipotent, caring and aggressive, known and incognito' (Berlant, 1998, p. 285). Such contractions seem to be at the core of Snapchat. Berlant stresses not only the publicness of intimacy but also the 'unavoidable troubles' and 'disruptions that make things turn out in unpredicted scenarios' (Berlant, 1998: 281). She understands 'moral dramas of estrangement and betrayal, along with terrible spectacles of neglect and violence' as inevitable aspects of romance and friendship (Berlant, 1998: 281).

This theoretical perspective allows the analysis to go beyond what, at first sight, might appear as breaches of intimacy but which – on closer examination – consist of the foundation of intimacy as it is lived in the perplexities of inclusion and potential betrayal. The teenagers share intimate details of their mundane everyday life with selected others. This sharing entails a potential publicness, but it also entails the potential drama of misunderstanding, or what the teenagers refer to as 'bitchfights'. In and through Snapchat exchanges, many pictures are snapped, screenshot, archived and possibly made public.

The intimacies of Snapchat seem to exist in a web of affects that are not limited to joy or connectivity, but include all the difficulties of not-knowing, feeling exposed and negotiating with the self and others about what to share and how to save face. The analytical promise held in Berlant's notion of intimacy in relation to Snapchat is captured in the refusal to view the normativities of intimacy as purely good and the acknowledged contradictions of Snapchat's temporal ephemerality and circulation of affects.

A mandatory crafting of 'uglies'

> How do I feel when receiving such a snap [a double chin]? I get happy. When you have exchanged snaps of double chins then you are officially friends. The first double chin in a friendship is really important.

When browsing through the fieldwork material an immediate pattern surfaces, revealing the way in which photo elicitation practices via Snapchat are highly mundane and performed through the ordinariness of the snaps. 'Ugly' selfies are exchanged at high speed on an everyday basis, and these exchanges are embedded in a hub of affectivity. The affects are multiple: delight in being snapped, excitement in having 'fire' (the emoji indicating a continuous conversation), desire not to lose the 'fire', disgust in receiving unsolicited dick pics and fear of losing face, friendship and closeness. Whereas Instagram invites glamorous and sexy images (Larsen and Kofoed, 2015, Miller, 2015), Snapchat seems to invite pictures that are ordinary, familiar and confidential.

However, Snapchat also requires, if not invites, a sense of whom such ordinary photos should be shared with. As Emily explains: 'of course there are people with whom you would never share a double chin'.

The young people talk of Snapchat as their preferred app, and in their everyday life in school they regularly snap each other, both within the peer framework of the school and beyond. The exchange of snaps seems to cross school life.

> It is the fact that we have a conversation that is important. What we say is less important. If we need to make some real dates we use Messenger, because we forget what we have agreed upon on Snapchat.

On the basis of Emily's description, it seems that the content of the snap is not considered vital. Rather, the *exchange* of snaps is of the utmost significance in maintaining or splitting up friendships (Kofoed and Larsen, 2016). Snaps and their claimed insignificance are at the core of the exchange. Hence, the (claimed) lack of significance is, in itself, affectively significant – the girls do not share 'uglies' and foolish selfies with just anybody. On Instagram, they share 'with just about everybody', as Emily explains, and these pictures are often carefully crafted as high performing and beautiful (i.e. worthy of being liked and followed by 'everybody'). The pictures shared on Snapchat, however, do not gain significance through the obvious crafting of beauty. Quite the contrary: the snaps are crafted along other lines of normativity (showing ugliness, everyday life and dull moments), and the intimacy and significance is crafted through the paradox of the insignificance, in itself, elevating the importance of the exchange.

The crafting of images of double chins – or 'uglies', as Miller suggests and as also pointed out by Handyside and Ringrose (Miller, 2015, Handyside and Ringrose, forthcoming) – has been supported by other studies. Double chins, ugly faces and snaps of everyday moments are some of the most regular snaps shared on Snapchat. This finding was substantiated by a Danish qualitative survey conducted from 2015 to 2016 with 230 primary school students aged 12 to 17. The study found that 'uglies' and foolish selfies are the most frequently shared images (Kofoed and Larsen, 2016). Mundane everyday selfies are often taken from below to expose double chins or outstretched tongues. These snaps are unique in their exhibition of chins from below and ugliness, and they possess what Munster refers to as 'singularity' (Munster, 2013). It is worth noting, though, that these singularities add up to a pattern of shared content. On the one hand, the pictures expose singularity, as they depict different chins and different tongues; on the other hand, these singularities create a pattern of what could be termed a 'mandatory crafting of uglies'.

On Snapchat, the 'fire' emoji plays a particular role. 'Fire' indicates that a person has been exchanging snaps daily. Next to the fire emoji, a number is displayed to indicate the number of days of a continuous exchange. If the people involved in the exchange do not snap for an entire day, the fire emoji disappears. Amongst the 14-year-olds in this study, the fire emoji is an important signifier of closeness and intimacy. Keeping the emoji alive and increasing the number of days attached to it is an important signifier of intimacy and closeness, as witnessed on the screen. As Emily explains:

> It becomes kind of an obsession to keep the fire alive. I don't want it to disappear. It is merely the sense of being connected every day [...] it is a way of reassuring that we exist.

Snapchat thus seems to tangle delightful encounters of small moments with the ugliness of ordinariness.

Living with unflattering snaps

Silvie touches upon an important feature of the Snapchat app: the ability to save and exchange unflattering photos. A person who takes care of these saved photos is seemingly affirmed as a friend. Thus, such unflattering photos – be they taken by oneself or others – play a key role in the maintenance of intimacy and friendship.

> Anna has soooo many bad pics of me, so that if we one day fall out, she can do just about anything she wants with them …

Silvie describes how sharing uglies is experienced as compulsory for a desired and cherished friendship. The fact that uglies are saved constitutes a potential threat, but by *not* forwarding the pictures, a person can create a cherished bond. In this way, Snapchat is an important daily – and nightly – player in maintaining friendships, as friends must navigate the possibility of their photos being shared. Silvie continues:

> The odds that you have shared a really bad pic in a long friendship are high […] It might be that she uploads some of them for my birthday. I need to trust her …
>
> Double chins […] You only share those with good friends. With your friends you can be ugly, you have seen each other in the morning, when you look like dead dogs, we have seen each other without makeup […] I look like a troll […] We can send ugly pictures and we can send the really hot ones. They know that I can be hot and really ugly. They have seen both sides and they don't judge me.

Trust that one will not be judged is essential in the continuous sharing of snaps. The absence of judgment between friends becomes proof of closeness and affective bonding, creating a sense that the two friends *know each other*. An additional player in the entanglements of teenagers-temporality-affect-social media thus seems to be knowledge of which snaps to share. Hannah elaborates on this and explains that some snaps need to be ugly:

> It is really annoying when someone only shares the really nice pics. A friend of mine does not know how to send an ugly. She sends only the nice pics.

Hannah goes on to explain that the practice of sharing pictures that are too nice (instead of uglies) prevents a friendship from becoming close. Hannah's friend does not play by the rules of Snapchat and seems to mistake the app for Instagram or Facebook, as Hannah explains:

> The things you send on Snapchat [...] People would think it really weird if I posted something like that on Facebook or Instagram.

The friend Hannah is referring to does not grasp the particularity of teenagers-temporality-affect-social media when she sends Instagram-like pictures on the 'wrong' app. The lack of delicate, fine-tuned knowledge of Snapchat seemingly detaches this particular friend from Hannah. Hannah explains that sharing photos within the specific affective interfacial affordances of Snapchat requires reciprocity and trust. Her friend does not, in Hannah's view, grasp this code of conduct and thus bypasses the chance of a (Snapchat-mediated) friendship. Such trust involves uncertainty over whether the snap will stay within the comfort zone of Snapchat and within its intended recipients. Hannah's narrative of uploading the wrong pictures to the wrong app points not only to the importance of a code of conduct but also to the balance of trust relating to the potential sharing of unwanted pics. This trust is at the core of Snapchat's entanglement with teenagers, temporality and affect. The crude point that the content is of less importance cannot, however, stand alone. Sometimes the content is of the utmost importance, such as when the 'wrong' content (e.g. a glamorous, Instagram-like picture) is shared or when the content is not meant for the eyes of third parties. This is particularly true when the snap is saved and the affordance of self-destruction is bypassed. The teenagers adjust to the fact that snaps disappear. This adjustment requires moving to another platform when specific arrangements need to be remembered (e.g. events on Facebook) and taking fights off Snapchat because one cannot keep track of who said what. The potential for judgment and misunderstanding carve out the likelihood of betrayal, which, following Berlant, is part and parcel of intimacy. When pictures are screenshot and forwarded beyond the network in which they were initially shared, a lack of judgment is exchanged with public evaluation and exhibited betrayal.

Nausea

A breadth of affectivities is thus opened by the temporal ephemerality of Snapchat. These affectivities provide fertile ground for intimate bonding in teenage friendships but also carry the potential for extreme exclusion when intimate snaps are screenshot and spread to other social media. This often occurs in cases of cyberbullying and the unconsented sharing of nudes. Nora explains what it feels like when the exchange of snaps is no longer delightful but becomes a trail of blatant and gross messages:

> I feel powerless. You think about it all the time. I feel sick and nauseous. Why can't they leave me alone [...] You want to see the other snaps, the nice ones, from other friends, but you cannot bypass the rude ones. You cannot control it. You feel totally out of control.

Nausea occurs in the everyday interpretation of pictures and text. The teenagers explain how they must stop themselves getting cross by deliberately preventing themselves from misreading a snap. Emily explains:

> You feel sick. Physically sick [...] your stomach aches and you get nausea because you don't know, you cannot figure out how to react, because you are just sitting at home with your phone or your computer on your lap and you cannot figure out whether to climb or descend the conflict ladder.

Nausea is a strong bodily affect of discomfort and disorientation. Nora explains it to be sickening; similarly, Emily describes incidents of social media exchanges that travel directly to her stomach. Brøgger and Staunæs (in an analysis of nausea in higher education) remind us – via Sara Ahmed – that: 'Disgust [...] does not come from within the body, but evolves in *contact zones* and involves a relationship of touch and sensuous proximity between surfaces of bodies and objects' (Ahmed 2004, p. 84, quoted in (Brøgger and Staunæs, 2016: 237). Nora and Emily's nausea is experienced in their bodies, yet it is not limited to their individual bodies. When Nora feels nausea the sensation surfaces in a context – or, as Brøgger and Staunæs point out, in a contact zone in which bodies and objects are in sensuous proximity. The nausea described by Nora and Emily is lived through their individual bodies but intermingled with content on the screen and content that has been left off the screen and resides in the sender and potential audiences and the pace and persistence of the circulation of affects. Many of the ingredients that cause nausea are invisible. However, they are imaginable, and the potential of what *might happen* is an effective trigger for this feeling.

But there is more to Nora's nausea. The affective signifier in Nora's stomach might be tangled with a potential new horizon of the spread of her snaps. Let me, for a moment, dwell on the potentiality of how snaps might travel as a trigger for nausea. Nora knows that a core player in this particular class, Sophia, has recently moved out of the immediate zone of the 'class' and entered a larger group of peers, spanning multiple neighbourhoods. Sophia is a 'first mover' in this regard, as she has moved on and beyond the school class in her social media profiles. Sophia prefers to use Instagram, on which she has 4,500 followers; in contrast, her peers report to have 100 to 200 followers. Sophia thus reaches far beyond her peers and the friendships provided in her school and interacts with many more teenagers throughout wider Copenhagen. She uses Instagram far more than she uses Snapchat. She disturbs the assumed normativities of her class by gaining far more followers than anyone else and by receiving offers to advertise (and hence earn money) on Instagram, and she celebrates her success, which alienates her from her peers. Nora and her peers no longer feel safe with Sophia, as they fear that she will spread their snaps to a much larger audience. Nora's nausea is thus not without reason. She knows what she has shared with her intimate friends, she knows the risks and she knows the circles to which her snaps might travel. In addition, she knows the story of a particular girl whose nudes were recently shared. Tens of thousands of viewers saw them, everybody was talking about them and the story hit the media. Recently, the girl uploaded a YouTube video to explain what happened, pleading people to stop sharing what she considered her private pictures.[2] Even though this girl lives in a different city, she – and the potential for others to feel exposed in the same way – intersects with teenagers-temporality-affect-social media in ways that lead to Nora's nausea. Nora talks of it, as do her peers.

Conclusion

Hannah explains:

> The thing is [...] You cannot see all the emotions in a message. Yeah, you can insert a smiley or emoji but it does not reveal anything about how this person feels. The feelings below the message are a lot more complicated than the feelings visible on the screen.

Hannah pinpoints Miller's core argument that snaps constitute a comment about how one is feeling. The snap itself contains intensity, irrespective of whether the captured feeling is obvious. The exchange of pictures leaves affective trails, though they are hardly visible, as Hannah explains above. These affective trails range from the comfort of inclusion and belonging to the delight of maintaining the fire emoji to the fear of having unflattering or nude snaps shared with never-ending publics (ranging from neighbouring classes to porn sites to parents).

In the above analysis, the teenagers unpacked how snapchatting is a highly affective affair in which ephemerality and persistency entangle. While Snapchat might be perceived as an ephemeral social media because snaps self-destruct, the affective tenor of the exchanges seems highly persistent. Bypassing the ephemeral interfacial affordance seems to pose what Berlant calls potential 'moral dramas of estrangement and betrayal' (Berlant, 1998: 281). Persistence in affectivity does not refer to temporal or spatial persistence, but to the continuous circulation of affects and the way in which this circulation is registered by the teenagers. Intensity and temporality seem to create a specific dynamic when they meet the interfacial affordance of disappearance. This dynamic sets the stage for certain affects, ranging from the joy of inclusion to the fear of exposure and betrayal.

To conclude, Snapchat involves the sharing of uglies, the daily negotiation of having unflattering snaps floating within the comfort zone of friends and nausea at the prospect of having unflattering snaps float further. Nausea is triggered by everyday experiences of friendship misunderstandings, even when these are easily resolved; it is also triggered by worry about having photos of double chins and nudes shared widely and by (known) incidents of revenge porn originating in Snapchat exchanges. The teenagers in this study allegedly had no experience with or exposure to personally sexualised pictures. However, stories of those who did have this experience travelled quickly through their network. Such knowledge comprises the affective landscape in which Snapchat lives out its daily entanglements with teenagers-affects-temporality. Within this scene, their sense of comfort is challenged and nausea rises when intimacy threatens to dissolve and be betrayed. Disagreements and potential betrayals are lived within what Bilton describes as the core characteristics of viral media: speed of spread, quantity of views and unpredictability of what will spread. While seemingly nothing much happens, significant affectivity occurs when living the social media life in and between safe inclusion and potential betrayal. While Snapchat is indeed an ephemeral mode of communication, affects nonetheless seem to persistently circulate.

Notes

1 https://lareviewofbooks.org/article/critical-intimacy-interview-gayatri-chakravorty-spivak

2 This girl, of course, has a name and is presently well known amongst Danish teenagers. She has suffered from having pictures shared without her consent and there is no need to further mention of her name.

References

Bayer, J.B., Ellison, N.B., Schoenebeck, S.Y. & Falk, E.B. (2016). Sharing the small moments: ephemeral social interaction on Snapchat. *Information, Communication & Society,* 19, 956–977.

Berlant, L. (1998). Intimacy: A Special Issue. *Critical Inquiry,* 24, 281–288.

Blackman, L. & Venn, C. (2010). Affect. *Body & Society,* 16, 7–28.

boyd, d. (2010). Social Network Sites as Networked Publics: Affordances, Dynamics, and Implications. *In:* Papacharissi, Z. (ed.) *Networked Self: Identity, Community, and Culture on Social Network Sites.* New York: Routledge.

Brøgger, K. & Staunæs, D. (2016). Standards and (self)implosion: How the circulation of affects accelerates the spread of standards and intensifies the embodiment of colliding, temporal ontologies. *Theory & Psychology,* 26, 223–242.

Christensen, J.R., Hansen, J.C., Larsen, F.H. & Nielsen, J.S. (2015). From Snapshot to Snapchat: Panopticon or Synopticon?. *Akademisk kvarter,* 11, 69–84.

Froggett, L., Manley, J. & Roy, A. (2015). The Visual Matrix Method: Imagery and Affect in a Group-Based Research Setting. *Forum: Qualitative Social Research,* 16.

Handyside, S. & Ringrose, J. (forthcoming). Snapchat Memory and Youth Digital Sexual Cultures: Mediated temporality, duration, and affect. *Journal of Gender Studies.*

Katz, J. & Crocker, E. (2015). Selfies and Photo Messaging as Visual Conversation: Reports from the United States, United Kingdom and China. *International Journal Of Communication,* 9.

Kofoed, J. (2014). Non-simultaneity in cyberbullying. *In:* Schott, R.M. & Søndergaard, D.M. (eds.) *School Bullying. New Theories in Context.* Cambridge: Cambridge University Press.

Kofoed, J. & Larsen, M.C. (2016). A Snap of Intimacy. Photo-sharing practices among young people on social media. *First Monday,* 21.

Kofoed, J. & Ringrose, J. (2012). Travelling and sticky affects: Exploring teens and sexualized cyberbullying through a Butlerian-Deleuzian-Guattarian lens. *Discourse: Studies in the Cultural Politics of Education,* 33, 5–20.

Kofoed, J. & Staunæs, D. (2015). Hesitancy as ethics. *Reconceptualizing Educational Research Methodology,* 6.

Larsen, M.C. & Kofoed, J. (2015). Snip snap snude – dobbelthagerne er ude: Analyse: Hvorfor hitter Snapchat? *Kommunikationsforum* [Online].

Liveng, A., Lading, Å., Gripsrud, B.H., Manley, J., Froggett, L., Hollway, W. & Ramvi, E. (2016). Imagining transitions in old age through the Visual Matrix method: thinking about what is hard to bear.

Miller, D. (2015). Photography in the age of Snapchat. *Anthropology & Photography,* 1, 1–17.

Munster, A. (2013). Going Viral: Contagion as Networked Affect, Networked Refrain. *In:* Munster, A. (ed.) *An Aesthesia of Networks: Conjunctive Experience in Art and Technology.* Cambridge; MA: MIT Press.

Rettberg, J.W. (2016), May 22. *What if the web is almost over?* [Online]. http://jilltxt.net/?p=4492. [Accessed 2016].

Ringrose, J. & Harvey, L. (2015). Boobs, back-off, six packs and bits: Mediated body parts, gendered reward, and sexual shame in teens' sexting images. *Continuum,* 29, 205–217.

Ringrose, J. & Rawlings, V. (2015). Posthuman performativity, gender and 'school bullying': Exploring the material-discursive intra-actions of skirts, hair, sluts, and poofs. *Confero: Essays on Education, Philosophy and Politics,* 3, 1–37.

Spivak, G.C. (2016). Critical Intimacy. An Interview with Gayatri Chakravorty Spivak. *In:* Paulson, S. (ed.). Los Angeles Review of Books.

9 Beyond engineered intimacy

Navigating social media platforms to manage intimate relationships

Cristina Miguel

Introduction and methodological approaches

The main objective of this chapter is to answer the question: What is the relationship between the architecture and politics of social media platforms and the emergent intimacy practices that take place within them? To explore this topic, I use a multi-sited case study composed of three distinct social media platforms: Badoo, CouchSurfing and Facebook. Badoo is a hook-up/dating platform on which users interact one-to-one, mainly through chat. CouchSurfing provides free hospitality exchange for its members, and its users organise regular social meetings in major cities. Facebook is the mainstream social media platform *par excellence*, and it is mainly used to communicate with existing relationships. The study included 30 participants (aged 25–49) from Leeds (UK) and Barcelona (Spain), whose identity was protected with pseudonyms. Here, I combine user profile analysis with analysis of users' feature choices, which some scholars denominate 'ethnography of affordances' (see Race, 2015). In this process, I take a twofold approach: I look at the role of social media platforms as intimacy mediators and explore the way in which adults adopt and adapt the technical affordances of these platforms to create and develop personal relationships. In particular, I focus on verification and reputation systems, private features (e.g. the chat feature and the inbox) and privacy settings. I analyse the workings of these features and examine the relationship of users with them when managing their intimate relationships: whether they choose to verify their accounts and which options they choose to do so; whether they leave and receive references and what kind of information they disclose in references; and what kinds of privacy settings they apply to their profiles (e.g. private pictures on Badoo). The discussion covers issues of privacy, trust and safety, which were identified as important topics relating to intimacy on social media.

In this study, most participants referred to the concept of intimacy as a 'sense of closeness within personal relationships, achieved by sharing inner thoughts and feelings'. Intimacy was often located within privacy and, as a result, some participants identified both concepts and considered it inappropriate to disclose intimacy in public, as doing so was often seen as an act of exhibitionism. Most participants' perceptions of privacy were in line with Schoeman's (1984) definition, wherein privacy includes the norms that protect personal and intimate information and also serves as the gated space in which people can develop meaningful relationships beyond the watch of outsiders. Participants often used the word 'sharing' to describe the conveyance of intimate information about the self through social media; this is significant because sharing one's emotions is the constitutive activity of intimate relationships. The activity of sharing entails specific interpersonal dynamics such as trust, reciprocity and openness, and most participants identified these dynamics within their intimacy practices on social media. On the other hand, a few participants identified intimacy only with sexual relationships and love. Nevertheless, bearing in mind that it is not possible to experience physical intimacy when interacting through social media, intimate interactions on these platforms should be understood to be based on sharing/exchanging text and pictures. Therefore, one question arises: How do people navigate social media platforms to manage their intimate relationships?

Engineered intimacy – theoretical perspectives

Social media platforms do not exist outside the physical world; on the contrary, as observed by Tierney (2013, p. 77), 'they are designed by, and entangled in, physical world social practices'. The pervasive use of social media platforms in everyday life leads Langlois (2013, p. 125) to affirm that, rather than referring to social media platforms as tools for sociability, we should talk about 'platforms through which we live our lives', which is in line with Deuze's (2012) observations that we live *in* media rather than *with* media. Drawing on Ira Wagman (2010), Lomborg (2013) explains that the use of social media has become an everyday activity, opening space for intimacy practices. This pervasive integration of techno-sociality in our everyday lives renders the architecture of social media platforms invisible. Thus, scholars (e.g. Langlois, 2013; Papacharissi, 2011; van Dijck, 2013) claim that social media platforms engineer sociality in an invisible way, and users thus lose agency over the management of their personal relationships. They argue that technology is not neutral, but fosters particular kinds of interactions; the design of technology facilitates some actions and complicates others. Papacharissi (2011, p. 306) observes how social media architecture and their networked structure shape the way in which users interact: 'A model of networked sociality emerges on online spaces, the architectural affordances of which inform human activity, by suggesting possibilities for interaction.' By the same token, Lievrouw (2014, p. 49) points to the theory of *affordances* of communication technology, developed by Hutchby (2001), as a possible model for approaching the study of the power relations that are inherent in the design of social media platforms, insofar as the affordances of the platforms 'create and regulate social knowledge and power'. Nevertheless, as Rybas and Gajjala (2007) observe, users are not just 'rule followers', but they make choices and are creative in their relationships with technology.

I find it useful to draw together boyd's (2010) concept of 'networked publics' (2010, p. 39) and Papacharissi's (2010) notion of the 'networked self' (2010, p. 307), in order to conceptualise 'networked intimacy': intimacy in the context of social media. Indeed, the concept of networked publics (boyd, 2010, p. 39) is helpful in conceptualising the notion of networked intimacy because it considers the ways in which the affordances (persistency, replicability, searchability and scalability) of social media platforms generate a particular kind of environment in which users interact. Furthermore, boyd (2010) uses the concept of networked publics to refer to the collections of people connected by different social media platforms, such as MySpace or Facebook, who negotiate their self-(re)presentations and public lives through these platforms in a way that allows them to experience different levels of publicity. This is useful when considering the concept of networked intimacy because it reframes notions of public and private – boundaries considered central to intimacy – for a digital world. A further consideration relates to Papacharissi's (2010) notion of the networked self (2010, p. 307), which asks us to consider both the interaction between people on social media and the conceptualisation of the self in the digital age. Indeed, within the context of networked sociality, a networked self arises as a result of the convergence of different practices (political, intimate, professional and economic) that occur on the social media stage. Hinton and Hjorth (2013, p. 19) suggest that activities that can be considered banal in the social media environment generate 'new forms of affective sharing', and that users negotiate their level of intimacy by carefully selecting the publics they share particular information with: 'Choosing what to share and who to share with allows people to control the privacy or publicness of their information that goes beyond the relatively clumsy tools provided by social networks.' As intimacies are increasingly performed and managed on social media, Papacharissi (2010) stresses how important it is for a social media platform's architecture to allow users to control the levels of privacy and publicness in their online communications. Attempting to control the access of different publics to personal information disclosed on a user's profile, most popular social media platforms incorporate privacy settings that range from simple public/private options, to more sophisticated features, such as the friends list, in the case of Facebook. In this sense, Trepte and Reinecke (2011, p. 67) affirm that privacy helps to build trusting relationships online: 'By creating intimate social interactions and enhancing confidentiality and trust among interaction partners, privacy is very likely to increase the willingness for openness, sincerity, and truthfulness in close relationships.'

In addition, Marar (2014, p. 77) argues that intimacy requires a degree of trust, that 'we are confident enough to confide our confidences to a confidant: "for your eyes only"'. Trust fosters intimate self-disclosure and therefore involves positive and negative implications for the trustors. As Chambers (2013, p. 47) puts it: 'In this online framework intimacy as *disclosure* becomes a marker of authentic, *bona fide* intimacy in a broad sense. It performs a symbolic role as an indicator of closeness and trust.' In the context of online interaction between strangers, as scholars have argued (e.g. Ess, 2014; Vincent and Fortunati, 2009; Wessels, 2012), the lack of co-presence makes establishing trust challenging; hence, social media platforms constitute a difficult environment for intimacy to flourish in. In response to the general mistrust of the authenticity of identities and disclosures displayed through social media interaction, some social media companies have incorporated verification and reputation systems to overcome deceptive practices, foster the creation of new relationships and enhance safety. These verification and reputation systems help to warrant users' identities. Through ratings and evaluations, reputation systems provide histories of members and give visibility to their previous actions. Future interactions can be set on the basis of these reports. In addition, most social media platforms require users to use their real name and to disclose their preferences; this is not only required for their behavioural data to be mined, but also because authenticity fosters the creation of new relationships. Andrew McNicol (2013) highlights that although it may be true that the disclosure of an authentic self is beneficial for personal relationships, social media companies also profit from this enforced authenticity.

Verification and reputation systems

Verification systems allow identities to be checked by connecting other social media accounts or a phone number to user profiles. Badoo and CouchSurfing offer optional verification systems to validate users' identities in order to generate trust and safety among users. Verification systems are useful for controlling fake profiles, and they also serve as a security measure, as they can identify users in the event of a crime. For example, some Badoo participants reported that they had been contacted by unverified users they thought to be robots. These 'users' asked them to click on certain links or to call premium numbers. Preventing the presence of robots is one of the reasons why Badoo (2015) claims to employ a verification system, as explained in its privacy policy. It is actually very easy to verify one's Badoo account with a Facebook, Instagram, LinkedIn, Google+ or Twitter account, or a telephone number. However, only a few Badoo users had had their accounts verified, mainly through connection to their mobile numbers, Google+ or Facebook accounts. As Bechmann (2014) observes, users do not connect data across platforms unless they are forced to do so to optimise the service. On Badoo, verified users have the option of only allowing contact from people who are verified. Raquel (35, Spain) explained that she chose this option not for security reasons, but because she was tired of receiving a large number of messages; the setting worked as a filter, cutting down on the messages she received. In relation to the level of safety provided by this verification system, Viel (37, Spain), who works in IT, highlighted the ease with which one can trick these verification systems, and he pointed to the possibility of creating a network of fake social media accounts on several sites. Another way of verifying an account on Badoo is to buy 'superpowers' (premium services that enable more visibility on the platform), which work in a similar way to CouchSurfing's verification system: when users purchase superpowers their identity is verified through their credit card details.

CouchSurfing's verification system involves verification of the user's identity, telephone number and location. In this case, the verification of location is important because of the hospitality exchange objective of the platform. Although the company claims that the verification system helps users find a host quickly because they feel safer, most participants did not see it in this way, and most were not verified members, themselves. The feature that was considered more useful in generating trust and safety among users was the 'references'. References are a key component of reputation systems, enabling users to rate one another within a network in order to generate trust and safety among strangers. In the case of CouchSurfing, experiences with other users are rated as positive, neutral or negative. These references cannot be deleted, and they are reciprocated most of the time. On one level, the references help to create a safe environment insofar as they reflect past interactions among members. Robert (43, UK) observes that it is very unlikely that a user with a lot of positive references is a bad person. As Gibbs and colleagues (2011) note, the verification of users' identities through third party comments is an important aspect in the process of warranting trust. CouchSurfing participants often collaborated on this system by writing references about people they had met offline, and they also carefully read the references when deciding whom to host or be hosted by. The participants used Badoo and CouchSurfing to meet new people and enrich their social and intimate life, especially when they did not know many people in the area. CouchSurfing appeared to be more effective for finding a partner or dating than Badoo, although dating is not the purpose for which the service was designed. The fact that a traveller (surfer) must be accepted by a host following a request for accommodation, combined with the fact that the traveller must have first evaluated the profile of the potential host (which usually includes references that other users have left), means that the relationship starts from an initial mutual liking. From this starting point, friendship or a romantic or casual sexual relationship may develop.

Moreover, when analysing CouchSurfing profiles, I noticed that through some references, one could infer that a certain kind of intimacy had been developed between the users during meetings or host-guest experiences. References might contribute to building the online identity of the referred user through the storytelling of (intimate) shared moments, as some participants put it:

> It is more about CouchSurfing, because on CouchSurfing when you put the reference, you actually know some information, like private

> information, like we've been there and there, or he took me there and there. So you put more information about the person and it could be more private than on Facebook for me, because you do share more than normally would, just to present the person in a really good way or in a bad way as well.
>
> (Noelia, 25, UK)

> A little blink towards that person. I have a couple of references that I'm reading them and I perfectly understand what this person is trying to tell me but I don't know if other people understand what this person is trying to tell me with that reference ... I feel that intimacy, but I don't know if other people would understand it, but I perceive it because I know about our relationship.
>
> (Gemma, 43, Spain)

The way participants negotiate references on CouchSurfing is a good example of how they prefer not to talk about their intimate experiences with other users in public. For instance, when participants who had had a casual sexual relationship left references for each other implying a certain level of intimacy, they did so in a concealed way – through what boyd and Marwick (2011) label 'social steganography' (2011, p. 22) – so that other users would not fully understand what had happened between them.

In the same vein, at the beginning of 2015, Badoo incorporated the feature of 'secret comments' – a reputation system based on private feedback between users. Badoo users cannot read the feedback that other users have left about them through this channel, and only verified users can leave and receive comments in this way. This reputation system allows users to publish comments about other users without their awareness. The system tries to prevent abusers from damaging other users by posting warning comments about that particular user. The secret comments feature was not available when I conducted my fieldwork, and therefore I was not able to collect participants' opinions on this feature. However, some participants suggested that a similar private reference system should be put in place on CouchSurfing. Reputation is very important on CouchSurfing in order for users to secure a host; therefore, most users explained that they did not want to leave bad references, in order to avoid receiving them in return. This viewpoint echoes the view found by Teng and colleagues (2009), who concluded that ratings are more accurate when they are more private. In response to these demands, CouchSurfing changed the reference system as of October 2015. In the new system, CouchSurfing users have 14 days to write a review after the hospitality exchange; these references cannot be changed later on, and it is possible to leave 'private' feedback.

Despite these reputation and verification features, most Badoo participants affirmed that they did not trust the people they met through the site, mainly due to the abundance of fake or deceptive profiles and the ease with which the verification system could be manipulated. In the case of CouchSurfing, most participants claimed that they generally trusted the platform and other users. Reputation systems were deemed more useful for developing trust than were verification systems. Thus, the public display of connections and references seemed to help build trust among users and to facilitate the creation of intimate relationships. This may be why Badoo has recently incorporated the 'common Facebook friends' tool for users who have verified their profile with their Facebook account, and the 'secret comments' feature, which allows users to leave a public reference about other Badoo users without them seeing it.

Private features and privacy configuration

In this section, I examine the way in which Badoo, CouchSurfing and Facebook provide different features and privacy configurations to allow users to communicate in private, and how users employ these features to develop intimate relationships through these platforms. In the study, all users had their Facebook accounts set to private, while Badoo and CouchSurfing were more often set to public. In general, all users expressed their preference for the chat feature when communicating intimate topics.

The chat feature and message system are the most private forms of communication on Badoo, CouchSurfing and Facebook. In reference to Badoo, Ana explained that she considered the chat feature more intimate because it allowed for private interaction:

> It's a bit more intimate, because the conversation is between you and the other person, it's not published what you talk to the other person about, I think there is privacy there. Everybody can see the profile pictures, but the conversations are private.
>
> (Ana, 35, UK)

On Badoo, the chat feature works very similarly to the chat feature on Facebook, through which users can access recorded conversations at any time. Some participants pointed out that they did not disclose intimate information through social media because the information would be there forever and it might be leaked. This concern is linked to the concept of persistency, discussed by boyd (2010). On the other hand, other participants were not concerned about their conversations being recorded. For example, Isaac expressed his preference for the change in Facebook's chat to create permanent records, because it allowed him to access past conversations. He did not believe that the permanency of information on Facebook would prevent him from being intimate with people through the chat feature. On the contrary, he found it useful for conversations to be recorded, because this helped him manage his personal relationships by removing the need for him to rely solely on memory. He illustrated this point by sharing an anecdote about an intimate moment he had had with a close friend through the Facebook chat feature:

> One of my very close friends she told me that she was pregnant. But it was one of those days, I'd just had an accident and I was confused and I did not remember anything for a few days. During that time I was chatting with her, but I did not remember that conversation. One month later, when she mentioned it, I did not remember I had that conversation with her. So she said: 'No, go and look! We actually spoke about it, and I told you I'm pregnant.' I actually went back and looked, and it was the case: she did tell me that she was pregnant. So that was very helpful.
>
> (Isaac, 26, UK)

On the other hand, there are some public features through which users can communicate to anyone visiting their profile; these include 'about me' sections, the Facebook 'wall' (which is also accessible through the news feed), 'references' on CouchSurfing (which I discussed in the previous section) and 'comments' in pictures on Badoo (which are hardly ever used). Most participants agreed that they did not negotiate their private lives through social media in public very often; for instance: 'No, I'm not publishing anything connected with my private life' (Noelia, 25, UK). Some participants explained that they used to publish more intimate information on Facebook, but had stopped doing so since they no longer considered it appropriate. After an initial phase of experimentation with social media and the various levels of publicity they allow, participants seem to have learned and internalised the social norms governing different social media platforms, wherein users generally do not reveal intimate information.

In order to control the audience that can access one's profile, social media platforms provide privacy settings to help users manage the publicity level of the content they share. On Badoo, privacy settings allow users to show their profile to members only and to control who can see their email address and who can comment on their pictures, among other options (e.g. users can also set pictures as private). In the case of CouchSurfing, the platform only provides two privacy options: public or members only. Facebook includes three main privacy options: public, 'friends of friends' and 'only friends'. It also provides more sophisticated privacy settings, which include the ability to create a number of 'friends lists' to categorise different kinds of relationships (e.g. best friends, friends, work colleagues, etc.) that can be applied to photo albums and posts. Other privacy options allow users to control tags on pictures and the visualisation of the friends list.

A few participants expressed some confusion over how such privacy settings worked, though they did not seem overly concerned about privacy, as they had not investigated privacy options further. Marc (39, Spain), for example, reported that his Facebook account was public, although it was actually set to private. He claimed that he had configured his Facebook account as public because he did not publish anything he deemed intimate and because he did not apply a friends list to the content he published; thus, he considered it public in the sense that all of his 319 friends could see the content he uploaded. He also thought that his Badoo profile was private, when it was actually public. There were a few other participants who believed that their profiles were private on Badoo or CouchSurfing, when they were actually public. Also, some participants were not aware that they could change their profiles to private; thus, their profiles were set to public (as this was the default setting). In the case of Vanessa (29, Spain), she was not sure about her privacy configuration on CouchSurfing because she had shared passwords with her boyfriend and thought that he might have changed their account settings. The act of sharing one's passwords and devices with a partner is a symbol of trust and intimacy within personal relationships, as Lenhart and Duggan (2014) found: '67% of internet users in a marriage or committed relationship have shared the password to one or more of their online accounts with their spouse or partner.'

On Badoo and CouchSurfing, some people chose a public configuration either because they wanted to achieve more visibility or because they had no concerns about privacy, since they claimed they did not disclose any intimate information on those platforms. Nevertheless, most participants claimed that they uploaded more content to Facebook than to other platforms, and hence were more concerned about who could access their Facebook content. For instance, Robert did not want some 'Facebook friends' to interact with the content he uploaded, so he created a personalised list of friends: 'I've changed the settings because there are some people that are always commenting, commenting, commenting and you don't really want that' (Robert, 43, UK). Robert highlighted that he wanted to choose who could participate in his shared memories because they were not meant for everybody – only for certain people. In this sense, he created circles of intimacy by restricting access to his profile to people he did not consider part of his inner group. Likewise, Ana (35, UK) explained that she used friends list to curate the privacy settings on Facebook depending on the different publics she was interacting with. Exclusive access to private content creates a sense of intimacy among users. Online intimacy here is mainly understood as self-disclosure to an exclusive group of significant others. As commented earlier, it is 'an indicator of closeness and trust' (Chambers, 2013, p. 47).

In fact, many participants made particular reference to pictures when defining online intimacy. For example, Esteban (35, Spain) explained that it was possible to experience intimacy with a specific group of friends on Facebook by creating a private album. Badoo also allows users to set some pictures to private, but no participants had private pictures on their Badoo profile. On Badoo, private pictures are often erotic pictures, and users must give permission for other users to view them. Petro (29, Spain) provided an interesting anecdote in reference to a different use of private pictures on Badoo. He was talking to a girl who he thought had really ugly pictures on her profile, and he could not believe that she was actually the girl in the pictures, because he was used to seeing 'more or less' sexy pictures on female Badoo profiles. After talking to her for a while, she allowed him to see her 'private pictures' and he could see that she was actually pretty. In this case, she was using fake pictures as a filter to discourage shallow men from contacting her. When allowing Petro to access her real pictures, she created a circle of intimacy between them. On the other hand, Badoo requires users to upload pictures from Facebook if they want to see Facebook pictures from other users. Petro also mentioned that he had tried, by mistake, to upload pictures from Facebook to Badoo, but he was very uncomfortable when he saw all his Facebook pictures on Badoo. He immediately proceeded to delete all of these pictures, because he did not want his spheres of Badoo and Facebook to collide. In order to avoid context collapse (boyd, 2010), Badoo participants rarely add other Badoo users on Facebook. They prefer to move the interaction to WhatsApp, because there is less information there. Other participants explained that they set their profile to private because they did not want to appear in public searches. Luis (30, Spain) reported that he chose a private configuration for his Badoo account because he did not want his Badoo profile to show up if someone were to search for a picture of him on Google. He expressed concern about using dating sites because he believed there was a certain social stigma around using social media to meet new people – a statement that other Badoo users agreed with.

At the other end of the spectrum, some participants had all of their accounts set to private. The most extreme case of privacy protection was shown by Mateo (47, UK), who did not even allow people to write on his Facebook wall and had to approve tags in pictures, as well. His Facebook account was more professional, which might have been the reason why he sought to prevent users from adding content he deemed irrelevant or too intimate. In relation to her work, Caroline (26, UK) commented that her Facebook account was very private because she was a teacher and did not want her students to find her or add her as a friend. Thus, she did not want to mix her personal life with her professional life. Caroline is a lesbian, and it is easy to find out about her sexual orientation by looking at her Facebook profile. During the interview, she expressed her concern that some of her family members (who did not know about her sexual orientation) would guess that she was a lesbian by her posts or pictures. Nevertheless, she disclosed her sexual orientation on CouchSurfing, where her profile was public, through her membership in lesbian groups. Since her interaction on CouchSurfing was with strangers, she did not find it problematic to disclose her sexual orientation on this platform.

Despite a few of the participants' unawareness of the workings of privacy settings on Badoo and CouchSurfing, most of them knew how privacy settings worked. Thus, in opposition to moral panics about oversharing due to a lack of digital literacy or due to the contemporary turn to a more public intimacy, it is clear that participants were learning how the social media platforms they used operated and how to manage their privacy on those sites. Although on occasion the participants may have engaged in public intimacy practices through the disclosure of intimate moments – in references or through pictures – most of the time they preferred to discuss intimate topics through private features (e.g. chat), as they considered the explicit negotiation of intimacy in public anti-normative. As I have discussed elsewhere, most participants chose not to publish intimate information on social media in order 'to protect their privacy and because they considered that intimacy loses its status when it is advertised' (Miguel, 2016, p. 8).

Conclusion

Trust is a prerequisite for revealing personal information and, hence, building intimacy through social media. In the context of online interactions between strangers, the lack of co-presence complicates the development of trust, as some scholars have argued (e.g. Vincent and Fortunati, 2009; Wessels, 2012; Ess, 2014). Participants mainly used Badoo and CouchSurfing to create new friendships and to find (sexual) partners. Social media platforms on which interaction is among strangers have increasingly incorporated reputation and verification systems and implemented 'real name policies' to try to verify users' identities and provide a trustworthy and safe environment for the creation of new relationships. Participants had many different privacy configurations, and their use of verification and reputation systems was diverse. It is clear that although social media platforms provide tools for generating trust and safety among users, users may operate on these platforms in many different ways; that is, users are creative in their choices (Rybas and Gajjala, 2007), as my study also shows.

Despite growing debates over a more public disclosure of intimacy, in my study, participants preferred to communicate privately in order to negotiate intimate relationships or disclose intimate topics. In fact, most participants considered public intimacy anti-normative, since they believed that intimacy should remain in the private realm. Thus, participants preferred to use the chat feature rather than public means of communication (e.g. references or the 'wall') to talk about intimate issues. They also tended to have private configurations on most of their social media platforms, especially Facebook, since this was the platform they used most often and the one on which they disclosed more intimate information (e.g. pictures of family and lovers). On Facebook, participants increasingly negotiated the level of intimacy within their personal relationships by controlling access to private pictures or posts through friends' lists. Nevertheless, although Badoo also allows the configuration of private pictures, participants did not use this feature in their profiles due to a lack of trust in other users.

These tensions between trust, privacy and self-disclosure when negotiating intimacy through social media platforms remind us that intimacy is both reconceptualised in a digital age and long standing – embedded within existing practices and social norms. Indeed, the digital age is not leading to a radical transformation of the notion of intimacy, but an adaptation of intimate interaction to social media environments, which possess particular affordances labelled 'networked intimacy'. As Byam (2010, p. 59) acknowledges, 'people appropriate media characteristics as resources to pursue social and relational goals'. For me, the extent to which the intimacy that exists on social media is different from that which occurs offline touches the heart of these debates, not least because it directly addresses the presumptions surrounding intimacy as a concept, as well as the digital environment in which that concept is currently contested.

References

Baym, N.K. (2010). *Personal Connection in the Digital Age*. Cambridge: Polity Press.

Bechmann, A. (2014). Managing the interoperable self. In: A. Bechmann and S. Lomborg, eds., *The Ubiquitous Internet: User and Industry Perspectives*. London: Routledge, pp. 54–73.

boyd, d. (2010). Social network sites as networked publics: Affordances, dynamics, and implications. In: Z. Papacharissi, ed., *A Networked Self: Identity, Community, and Culture on Social Network Sites*. London: Routledge, pp. 39–58.

boyd, d. and Marwick, A. (2011). Social steganography: Privacy in networked publics. In: *61st Annual International Communication Association Conference, 26–30 May 2011, Boston, MA*.

Chambers, D. (2013). *Social Media and Personal Relationships: Online Intimacies and Networked Friendship*. Basingstoke: Palgrave Macmillan.

Deuze, M. (2012). *Media Life*. Cambridge: Polity.

Ess, C. (2014). Trust, social identity, and computation. In: R. Harper, ed., *Trust, Computing, and Society*. New York: Cambridge University Press, pp. 199–228.

Gibbs, J.L., Ellison, N.B. and Heino, R.D. (2006). Self-presentation in online personals: The role of anticipated future interaction, self-disclosure, and perceived success in Internet dating. *Communication Research*, 33(2), pp. 1–26.

Hinton, S. and Hjorth, L. (2013). *Understanding Social Media*. London: SAGE.

Hutchby, I. (2001). *Conversation and Technology: From the Telephone to the Internet*. Oxford: John Wiley & Sons.

Langlois, G. (2013). Social media, or towards a political economy of psychic life. In: G. Lovink and M. Rasch, eds., *Unlike Us Reader: Social Media Monopolies and their Alternatives*. Amsterdam: Institute of Network Cultures.

Lenhart, A. and Duggan, M. (2014). Couples, the Internet, and social media. Pew Internet & American Life Project. Retrieved from www.pewinternet.org/2014/02/11/couples-the-internet-and-social-media.

Lievrouw, L. (2014). Materiality and media in communication and technology studies: An unfinished project. In: T. Gillespie and P. Boczkowski, eds., *Media Technologies: Essays on Communication, Materiality, and Society*, pp. 21–51.

Lomborg, S. 2013. *Social media, social genres: Making sense of the ordinary*. New York, NY: Routledge.

McNicol, A. (2013). None of your business? Analyzing the legitimacy and effects of gendering social spaces through system design. In: G. Lovink and M. Rasch, eds., *Unlike Us Reader: Social Media Monopolies and their Alternatives*. Amsterdam: Institute of Network Cultures, pp. 200–219.

Marar, Z. (2014). *Intimacy*. London: Routledge.

Miguel, C. (2016). Visual intimacy on social media: From selfies to the co-construction of intimacies through shared pictures. *Social Media+Society*, 2(2), pp. 1–10.

Papacharissi, Z. (2011). Conclusions. In: Z. Papacharissi, ed., *A Networked Self: Identity, Community, and Culture on Social Network Sites*, pp. 304–317.

Race, K. (2015). Speculative pragmatism and intimate arrangements: Online hook-up devices in gay life. *Culture, Health & Sexuality*, 17(4), pp. 496–511.

Rybas, N. and Gajjala, R. (2007). Developing cyberethnographic research methods for understanding digitally mediated identities. *Forum: Qualitative Social Research/Sozialforschung*, 8(3). Retrieved from www.qualitative-research.net/index.php/fqs/article/view/282/620.

Schoeman, F. (1984). Privacy and intimate information. In: F. Schoeman, ed., *Philosophical Dimensions of Privacy: An Anthology*. Cambridge, MA: Cambridge University Press, pp. 1–33.

Teng, C., Lauterbach, D. and Adamic, L.A. (2010). "I rate you. You rate me": Should we do so publicly? In: *3rd workshop on online social networks, 22/25 June*, Boston. Retrieved from www.usenix.org/legacy/event/wosn10/tech/full_papers/Teng.pdf

Tierney, T. (2013). *The Public Space of Social Media: Connected Cultures of the Network Society*. New York: Routledge.

Trepte, S. and Reinecke, L. (2011). The social web as a shelter for privacy and authentic living. In: S. Trepte and L. Reinecke, eds., *Privacy Online: Perspective on Privacy and Self-Disclosure on the Social Web*. New York: Springer.

van Dijck, J. (2013). *The Culture of Connectivity: A Critical History of Social Media*. Oxford: Oxford University Press.

Vincent, J. and Fortunati, L. (2009). *Electronic Emotion: The Mediation of Emotion via Information and Communication Technologies*. Oxford: Peter Lang.

Wagman, I. (2010). Log on, goof off, and look up: Facebook and the rhythms of canadian Internet use. In: Beaty, B., Briton, D., Filax, G. and Sullivan, R. eds. *How canadians communicate: Contexts of canadian popular culture*. Athabasca: Athabasca University Press, pp.55–77.

Wessels, B. (2012). Identification and the practices of identity and privacy in everyday digital communication. *New Media & Society*, online publication Jul, 23 2010. doi: 1461444812450679.

10 In with expectations and out with disappointment

Gay-tailored social media and the redefinition of intimacy

Yin Zhang and John Nguyet Erni

Introduction and methodological approach

The term 'intimacy' suggests a strongly perceived need for values and comforts that a family unit, romantic partnership or even friendship is supposed to embody in our daily lives. According to Sternberg (1986), intimacy is one of three components of love, with the other two being passion and commitment/decision. In this chapter, we employ a broader definition of intimacy that encompasses emotional or sexual closeness with another person, as this definition allows for more flexibility in interpreting the relationships formed on gay-tailored social media. In other words, intimacy can be casual, stable (long term) or a combination of both.

Furthermore, in the context of LGBT relationships, we believe that intimacy is not only perceived closeness between individuals but also a human experience of the communicative interactions that tangibly embody relationships. Nowadays, the adoption of social media has made significant changes to the ways in which we imagine and form intimacy. It has increased our opportunities to flexibly redefine the meaning of intimate relationships, allowing these to stretch across the conventional heterosexual-homosexual divide. Regarding sexual minorities, for whom relationships tend to be disembedded from traditional and morally preferred social structures, few guidelines have existed. Considering the differences in their romantic patterns, it is worthwhile to investigate the subjective and socially derived elements of intimacy among LGBT individuals.

Based on an extensive literature review, the current study serves as a cultural criticism piece for future research and attempts to summarise the process of reinventing intimate life. In particular, the study traces the relationship between social media technologies and intimacy in the formation and fading-out processes experienced by gay individuals. We hope to contribute to the field with both summaries of the influential sociological roots and media affordances of communication over gay-tailored social media and discussion of the dilemma of the mediated intimacy, in order to develop a better understanding of the dynamics between cultural norms, social practices and individual well-being. We also discuss the way in which media technologies interact with and construct intimacy.

Subjective and socially derived elements of intimacy

Beck (1992) and others (Beck and Beck-Gernsheim, 1995) note various transformations in people's intimate lives that suggest a period of 'reflexive modernisation' in the development of Western societies. But this pattern is not only seen in the Western world; Asian societies have also been massively shaped by the rise of an individualist ideology – the idea that we are autonomous beings who are able to choose whom to marry, when to divorce, how many children to have, whether or not to have an abortion, whether or not to conceive children through artificial means, what kind of sex to have, what kind of relationships to have – be they homosexual, heterosexual, bisexual or even multi-sexual – and how to behave as a man, a woman or along a range of points on the gender continuum. A number of sociological works are orientated towards understanding this changing social environment in which 'a world of choices' has been taken for granted, and the right to choose has been recognised as a default by an increasing number of scholars.

Giddens (1991) points out that the freedom brought about by modernity – the disembedding from traditional society and the challenge to older sources of authority – has important implications for intimate relationships. For people whose ultimate goal is to control their own lives, the freedom to choose lifestyles and particular kinds of partnerships on a democratic and egalitarian basis is crucial. Building upon emotional and sexual equality, an intimate relationship, in the form of a 'pure relationship', is solely supported by the rewards it generates and is sustained by the gratifications derived from each party (Giddens, 1992). Giddens (1992, pp. 15, 58) suggests that gay and lesbian relationships are more likely to approximate pure relationships, not least because they are believed to be free from the constraining effects of relationship norms. Intimacy has effectively become a matter of emotional communication 'with others and with the self, in a context of interpersonal equality' (p. 130).

Bauman (2003) describes the era of 'liquid love', in which intimacy is commodified and committed relationships have been replaced by fleeting connections. Online dating typically embodies the relational manifestation of the social condition of 'liquid modernity' (Bauman, 2000). It offers the opportunity for people to have 'fast and furious' sexual relationships in which commitment is absent yet quantity and frequency are consistently calculated, allowing for risk avoidance and an instant termination of contact without emotional loss or regret (Bauman, 2003, p. 65). Meanwhile, consumption logic, as extended to relationship building, is also criticised. People tend to apply a set of consumption criteria to evaluate relationships, such as instantaneity, efficiency, attractiveness, novelty, disposability and so on.

Expert systems' reallocation of risk to individual responsibility has been described as the 'privatisation' of risk, wherein individuals subsequently bear the anxieties of risk decision-making because 'the awareness of dangers comes together with the intimation of the individuals' blame for continuing risk-exposure and individual responsibility for risk-avoidance' (Bauman, 1993, p. 202). Both 'love' and 'trust' may be envisaged as alternatives to doubt and solutions to risk or uncertainty in social relationships (Beck and Beck-Gernsheim, 1995; Giddens, 1992; Joffe, 1997; Luhmann, 1986). Barraket and Henry-Waring (2006) point out that Giddens' and Bauman's respective ideas about 'pure relationships' and 'liquid love' present conflicting perspectives on the possibilities of intimacy and relationship formation online. They argue that online dating epitomises liquid love because it is a highly commercially mediated activity (Fiore and Donath, 2004), which constructs relationship formation as an individualistic activity based on rational choice.

Plummer (2003) uses the term 'intimate citizenship' to capture the plurality of public discourses about how to live a personal and intimate life in a late modern and global world, where individuals are often confronted with an escalating series of choices and have difficulty forming intimacy. The term suggests appropriate ways of sharing lives with others and fostering the civilizing of relations at a time when some people see only breakdown, 'dumbing down' and a general lack of civility in social life (Anderson, 1992; Himmelfarb, 1999). Issues surrounding 'intimate citizenship' differ from those surrounding the citizenship of old, for intimate citizenship recognises: a) the constant skirmish between insiders and outsiders; b) traditional tribalism struggling against multicultural diversity; c) the need for dialogues across these seemingly impossible differences; and d) the need to try to establish – against all fragmentations of postmodern social theory – some emerging sense of a differentiated universalism. Life in the future world of intimacy will not be any easier than it has been in the past.

In response to the social, political, economic and cultural changes caused by the spread of networked digital information and communication technologies, some theorists have applied the expression 'network society' to describe the world embodied by communication networks (Castells, 2000; van Dijck, 1999). Rainie and Wellman (2012) call the project of the self in a network society 'networked individualism'. They argue that individuals are detached from traditional communities and organisations – similar to Giddens' argument – and that individuals are re-embedded in multiple networks of relations. Networked individuals rely heavily on their diverse social networks and use communication technologies to manage these diverse relationships.

It is important to consider these groundbreaking thoughts mentioned above when considering the transition from an old social condition to a new social condition and how such changes reshape the nature of intimacy. Living in a heterosexual world, sexual minorities often experience confusion and loneliness during their identity formation process. Hence, it is necessary to consider the individualistic social environment that may largely affect intimacy in today's mediated world.

Characteristics of relational patterns over gay-tailored social media

The rise of the internet, smartphones and social media opens up a larger space for identities (including sexual identities) and relationship patterns. In the past decade, a boom in social media (e.g. online forums and social networking services) targeting both heterosexual and homosexual networking has emerged. In this section, we examine related studies on gay-tailored social media and discuss the relations between communication and intimacy. Generally, 'social media' is used here to refer to the diverse media platforms through which individuals and communities share, co-create, discuss and modify user-generated content.

From the uses and gratifications (U&G) perspective (Katz, Blumler and Gurevitch, 1974), several empirical studies have explored various social media used by gay men and their purposes for doing so. Specifically, popular gay-tailored social media in Asia include social networking sites (e.g. Fridae.com and m2.com), discussion forums (e.g. TT1069.com), SMS groups (e.g. WhatsApp and Line) and dating applications (e.g. Grindr, Jack'd and Hornet) (Chong et al., 2015). Findings have shown that various motivations and perceived benefits drive gay men to choose different media for different social purposes and relational agendas (Gudelunas, 2012). As convenient tools for maintaining and establishing social ties, these social media facilitate community information exchange, identity development, emotional support and even risk management for HIV transmission (Chong et al., 2015; David et al., 2006). Chan and Lee (2016, p. 20) summarise the features of six popular gay-tailored dating apps, suggesting that different functional features fulfil different needs relating to social media usage.

Among all motivations for social media use, seeking intimacy is frequently mentioned by non-heterosexual individuals. Essentially, finding similarly sexually orientated individuals and staying connected with them is a consistent need of sexual minorities. It is suggested that the LGBT population is routinely disembedded from traditions and morally preferred social structures. Often, online environments and virtual networks are safe and comfortable spaces for exploring sexual identities (Bargh and McKenna, 2004). Existing findings reveal that online tools facilitate the search for intimate relationships and change the way in which individuals connect and communicate with friends and romantic/sexual partners (David et al., 2006; Gudelunas, 2005; Hardey, 2004). To summarise, communication over gay-tailored social media includes a few common features:

Low cost

Except for the cost of basic devices and ICT settings (e.g. internet access on smartphones, tablets or computers), little economic cost is required on online platforms. Besides, the devices remove the need for physical presence, which is required of the old means of finding each other (e.g. by visiting a bar or fitness centre). According to Bargh and McKenna (2004, p. 586), the internet has 'unique, even transformational qualities as a communication channel, including relative anonymity and the ability to easily link with others who have similar interests, values, and beliefs'. Today, nearly all social media are able to be launched on smartphones. Whenever mobile devices are connected to the internet, users can easily engage in intimacy-seeking activities.

Location proximity

The mobile versions of social media on smartphones are usually enabled with a global positioning system (GPS) function. A sense of mutual presence was found to be effective in social interaction and self-presentation on social media (Blackwell, Birnholtz and Abbott, 2014). Users can identify and search for people with the same sexual orientation or similar relational goals within a proximate area. This means that communicative action, as well as intimacy-seeking activity, can now be carried out in geographical proximity. Schwartz (2011) found that, rather than enabling local, in-person interactions, the absence of location proximity limited the ability of young users to develop a sense of the local gay community and create autonomous actions to promote local gay identity work.

Instantaneousness

Online matching and dating include immediate interaction. Many gay-tailored social media are designed for easy adoption, giving users almost immediate access to a cascade of profiles. Because of the large number of potential partners, the process of selecting interactive objects usually takes a very short time. Such an instant decision-making process primarily relies on the incomplete information provided on the object's profile, including ambiguous relationship goals, which the user modifies based on his mood and circumstances.

Orientation towards appearance

The goal of most gay-tailored social media use is often face-to-face interaction. Therefore, physical appearance, which is reflected in profiles, is more important than it would be in other contexts. Chan and Lee (2016) found that a user's main profile picture and certain physical attributes (i.e.

age, height and weight) are crucial for the online matching of gay men. Future interactions are predicated on a mutual appreciation of each other's appearance. 'No face no talk' is a common rule for interaction over gay-tailored social media. User profiles have been conceptualised as psychological promises (see Rousseau, 2001) between social media users looking for potential partners. Such promises presume that information is exchanged in a mutually agreed upon and equitable manner.

Orientation towards sex

Sex is central to intimate and romantic relationships. Web 2.0 resources offer relatively easy access to sexual activity (Hospers et al., 2005), and gay men often use specific social media to look for an eye candy or a casual sex partner nearby (Gudelunas, 2012). As Bull and McFarlane (2000) mention, online sexual partners may have a lower level of objectives, and people who seek sexual contacts online may therefore feel less inhibited to engage in sexual activity. Thus, demand for casual sex can be straightforward.

Multi-tasking

Seeing and connecting with new people is the core goal of most gay-tailored social media users. On online social networking platforms, one can 'shop around' and communicate with multiple potential partners at the same time. In a world where sexual identity is restrained and less directly observable, such functional innovation enlarges the possibility of meeting particular types of people. To most users, people met over social media platforms are strangers. Active engagement in gay-tailored social media always leaves individuals struggling to balance priorities (e.g. studying, working and socialising with friends and acquaintances) against engaging with a growing pool of new people.

Frequency and intensity

As communication platforms, gay-tailored social media are places through which users display and perform their sexual identity and look for people who are similar. Frequent logins and active interaction form the practice of intimacy seeking. A gay man may log in to gay-tailored social media platforms multiple times a day – when he wakes up, when he feels bored at work/school, when he moves from one location to another, before his bedtime and so forth. In addition to multi-tasking, frequent use is another strategy used to maximise one's chances of successfully achieving relational goals.

Crooks (2013) reflects that gay-tailored social media not only facilitate the search for partners but also foster learning about the gay community. One retains the culture of this community when relocating. The above media affordances of communication over gay-tailored social media are meaningful for understanding the changing relationship patterns between partners within a digital and networking context. The low cost of using social media has enabled massive adoption among the gay population. Furthermore, location proximity and immediate interaction have led the online interaction to parallel offline, non-virtual life. These social media platforms place a heavy emphasis on the construction of profiles and the removal of constraints when seeking sexual contact. To a certain degree, the design of such social media encourages frequent and intensive interactions with multiple potential partners. It is these features that continuously shape the way in which gay individuals manage their relationships over social media.

Collective but fluid intimacy

Mowlabocus (2010) sees mobile technologies as forms of both digital cruising and gay congregation. Gay-tailored social media create an overlaying space – a community for gay men that is superimposed on the actual physical place in which one is located (Brubaker, Ananny and Crawford, 2016). We argue that the status of staying connected with an individual or group of individuals relates directly with intimate feeling. Studies have provided empirical evidence that various computer-mediated communication (CMC) forms are useful for sexual minorities' search for belonging and exploration of stigmatised identities, both with and without anonymity. Social media platforms are the most outstanding forms of CMCs (Baams et al., 2011; Chong et al., 2015; Davison et al., 2000; McKenna and Bargh, 1998).

Facilitation of a hidden network or secret community is actually nothing new to sexual minorities. Gay-tailored social media echo the techniques that gay men have used to meet each other since the 1940s, including book and pen pal clubs and travel guides identifying gay-affirmative spaces (e.g. gay bars) (Meeker, 2006). Earlier studies have shown that, before the digital age, gay men used discreet communication channels and lived double lives to cope with a homophobic environment (Chauncey, 1994). It is noteworthy, however, that the adoption of social media has significantly enhanced the scale and scope of the gay community by extending physical experiences and providing a virtual space for gay socialising.

Social identity theory posits that membership to social groups provides important fuel for one's evaluation of a self-concept (Tajfel and Turner, 1979). Meyer (2003) states that being an LGBT person can be stressful and lead to adverse mental health outcomes. Community building via virtual platforms has unique meaning for non-heterosexual populations. Particularly in some Asian cultures, which may be more biased and less accepting of LGBT individuals than Western societies (Pew Research Center, 2013), social media serve as precious channels for LGBT individuals to foster resilience, support one another, combat discrimination/stigma and strengthen healthy development (Chong et al., 2015).

Nevertheless, the social embeddedness facilitated over gay-tailored social media is somehow fluid. One main reason for this is the ambiguity of online connections. Compared to heterosexual individuals, gay men may be quite likely to be exposed to many kinds of existing and potential relationships on social media at one time: friendships, casual sex partnerships, dubious relationships, long-term romantic relationships, ex-partnerships or a mix of these. Ties among gay-tailored social media users are dense, but the strength of these connections is usually fragile. From a structural perspective, the cohesion and connectedness of these virtual networks are loose and even random. Therefore, we critically argue that gay-tailored social media successfully provide gay individuals with an accessible channel for relationship interactions, and reduce feelings of helplessness in finding others. However, the objects of the sense of belonging are still vague. Finding a specific person or group of people who are able to provide reliable, comforting and even intimate feelings is still not a clear and stable process.

The intimate but emotionally fluctuated self

Empirical evidence reveals that loneliness can be attributed to differences in social embeddedness, which is determined by factors such as having a stable partner, having a supportive family, having frequent contact with friends and being welcomed by other people (Fokkema and Kuyper, 2009; Kuyper and Fokkema, 2010). Avoidance of loneliness is an internal force that makes people hope to feel intimacy with others. Driven by emotional and sexual needs, gay men continuously look for intimate relationships through the use of social media. Nevertheless, one's expected outcome may not occur after a certain period of social media usage. At times, emotional fluctuation is observed. It is argued that, although online engagement requires less responsibility, risks and emotional pain are not significantly reduced, especially for gay individuals.

One finding from a study in Hong Kong reveals that, unlike in the lesbian community, gay men's motivation for seeking intimacy is negatively correlated with the intensity of their social media use (Zhang and Chong, 2013). This suggests that failure or negative experiences in seeking intimacy might more or less discourage the use of gay-tailored social media. Baams and colleagues' (2011) research found that age also factors into the online communication of sexual minorities. That is, younger sexual minorities are more likely to use online communities for social support, while older individuals are more likely to use them to seek sexual partners. We argue that this is not simply because of maturity and generational differences but also because of individual experiences with social media use.

In an investigation of why gay men stop using Grindr (a gay dating app), Brubaker, Ananny and Crawford (2016) discovered three main reasons:

a) they see the app as a waste of time; b) they experience a disconnect between purpose and outcome; and c) they see the app as a medium that objectifies humans. It is noteworthy that certain negative emotional impacts brought on by gay-tailored social media are revealed in their qualitative interviews.

In relation to the complexity of communication patterns summarised above, the functional design of many gay-tailored social media sites often makes interaction with other gay men require a large amount of time and attention. Such intensive participation and investment is likely to be seen as a distraction from life and work that also interferes with other activities, such as learning, dining and even resting. The individual criteria required for a match are unpredictable, and the amount of time needed to screen people's profiles and be screened often leads to users' perception of the app's ineffectiveness.

More importantly, intimacy and long-term partnerships are never easy to achieve. The ambiguous purpose of social media adoption is another important reason for the significant gap between users' expectations and outcomes. Users screen hundreds of profiles in a fast and unthoughtful manner. Even when connections are established, interactive dynamics might not be ideal. It is thus understandable for users to feel frustrated and helpless about their inability to establish meaningful connections after repeated self-introductions (to new contacts).

Furthermore, reflection revealed that gay male culture tends to focus more on sex than on intimacy between partners; at least, it focuses on sex in a different way than in other relationships. Sexuality for gay men is complicated beyond fighting broad systems of oppression. There are ways in which that oppression – and especially isolation and rejection from families and society – can inspire fears of rejection and suffering (Aviance, 2014).

Social media help sexual minorities identify nearby others with the same sexual orientation. A conversation that begins with romantic intention may eventually turn into a one-night stand, after which the two men are likely to remain strangers. The fast change from strangers to sexually intimate partners and back to strangers is a typical process that gay men who use these social media platforms are likely to experience. Such experiences embody the contradictions between: a) matches and mismatches; b) embedding and disembedding in a relationship; and c) sexual excitement and emotional emptiness in a short amount of time. Whenever a gay man fails to find 'Mr Right', feelings of frustration and realisations of regret tend to emerge.

In short, gay-tailored social media provide new opportunities for locating and communicating with potential and current sexual and romantic partners, although the introduction of a new means for seeking intimacy has not yet remedied the frustration experienced with traditional, offline means of finding a mate (Stephure et al., 2009).

Previous CMC studies have situated the act of quitting social media within evolving user relationships and their sociotechnical contexts, and these studies have found quitting social media to be a fluid and unfixed phenomenon (Birnholtz, 2010; Mainwaring et al., 2004). People who choose to disconnect from social media rarely hold absolute opinions about infrastructure and instead value a 'selective and reversible disconnection' (Mainwaring et al., 2004, p. 425). Nevertheless, disconnecting means more than just logging out or deleting an app – it involves notifying others, anonymising one's profile and archiving conversations. More importantly, quitting can be a temporary act for many gay users. Some may switch to other social media platforms or re-adopt the initial one after a certain period of time. This pattern also hints at a very common and recursive struggle experienced by gay individuals: users enter (virtual networks) with expectations and exit with disappointment. Gay-tailored social media are imperfect, and emotional fluctuation always accompanies usage, but such platforms provide the most direct way of getting involved in the circle.

Conclusion

Gardner and David (2013, p. 7) note that, in today's mobile era, people think of the world as 'an ensemble of mobile apps, or perhaps, in many cases, a single, extended, cradle-to-grave app'. Norms of online interaction and communication gradually change. Diverse identities and various ways of life produce new and more complex patterns of relationships. Sociocultural contexts, available technologies and media use all influence romantic relationships, which involve intimacy. Due to the above theoretical basis and empirical observations, we believe that intimacy experienced by sexual minorities over social media is a meaningful research subject. Based on a review of current literature, we have attempted to highlight what is particular to homosexual experiences while also drawing parallel with changes in society as a whole. To conclude, seeking intimacy over social media is firstly a communicative process of exploring potential partners with the same identity in a mediated world. These social media platforms – and particularly gay-tailored dating apps – have cultural significance with respect to intimate relationships. Modernity and networked individualism contextualise intimacy among gay individuals, who rely heavily on mediated ways of achieving their relationship goals, fulfilling sexual needs and managing diverse relationships in a heterosexual society. Communication over gay-tailored social media is inexpensive, instant and frequent, and capable of multiple relational targets; it offers locational proximity and highly values appearance and sexual attraction. Although gay-tailored social media have successfully facilitated relationship interactions, the social embeddedness is still fluid, mainly because of the ambiguity of relationships online. Gay men often adopt media technologies and enter virtual networks with high expectations, while certain contradictions in the mediated intimacy-seeking process can be very discouraging.

References

Anderson, D. et al. (eds.) (1992). *The Loss of Virtue: Moral Confusion and Social Disorder in Britain and America*. Social Affairs Unit: A National Review Book.

Aviance, J.N. (2014). Sex, Intimacy, and Being Gay. The Huffington Post. Retrieved from www.huffingtonpost.com/j-nelson-aviance/sex-intimacy-and-being-ga_b_5693464.html (July 21, 2016).

Baams, L., Jonas, K., Utz, S., Bos, H. and van der Vuurst, L. (2011). Internet use and online social support among same sex attracted individuals of different ages. *Computers in Human Behavior*, 27(5), pp. 1820–1827.

Bargh, J. and McKenna, K. (2004). The Internet and social life. *Annual Review of Psychology*, 55, pp. 573–590.

Barraket, J. and Henry-Waring, M. (2006). Online dating and intimacy in a mobile world. In: V. Colic-Peisker, B. McNamara, and F. Tilbury, eds., *Sociology for a mobile world: proceedings of The Australian Sociological Association 2006 Conference*. The Australian Sociological Association (TASA), pp. 1–10.

Bauman, Z. (1993). *Post-Modern Ethics*. Cambridge: Polity Press.

Bauman, Z. (2000). *Liquid Modernity*. Cambridge: Polity Press.

Bauman, Z. (2003). *Liquid Love: On the Frailty of Human Bonds*. Cambridge: Polity Press.

Beck, U. (1992). *The Risk Society: Towards a New Modernity*. London: SAGE.

Beck, U. and Beck-Gernsheim, E. (1995). *The Normal Chaos of Love*. Cambridge: Polity Press.

Birnholtz, J. (2010). Adopt, adapt, abandon: Understanding why some young adults start, and then stop, using instant messaging. *Computers in Human Behavior*, 26(6), pp. 1427–1433.

Blackwell, C., Birnholtz, J. and Abbott, C. (2014). Seeing and being seen: Co-situation and impression formation using Grindr, a location-aware gay dating app. *New Media & Society*, 17(7), pp. 1117–1136.

Brubaker, J., Ananny, M. and Crawford, K. (2016). Departing glances: A sociotechnical account of 'leaving' Grindr. *New Media & Society*, 18(3), pp. 373–390.

Bull, S. and McFarlane, M. (2000). Soliciting sex on the Internet – What are the risks for sexually transmitted diseases and HIV? *Sexually Transmitted Diseases*, 27, pp. 545–550.

Castells, M. (2000). *The Information Age: Economy, Society and Culture. The Rise of Network Society* (vol. 1, 2nd ed.). Malden, MA: Blackwell.

Chan, L. and Lee, J. (2016). A preliminary exploration of networked intimacy: Gay Asian Americans' experiences of using dating apps. In: *International Communication Association Annual Conference*. Fukuoka.

Chauncey, G. (1994). *Gay New York: Gender, Urban Culture, and the Makings of the Gay Male World*. New York: Basic Books.

Chong, E., Zhang, Y., Mak, W. and Pang, I. (2015). Social media as social capital of LGB individuals in Hong Kong – Its relations with group membership, stigma, and mental well-being. *American Journal of Community Psychology*, 55, pp. 228–238.

Crooks, N.R. (2013). The rainbow flag and the green carnation: Grindr in the gay village. *First Monday*, 18(11). Retrieved from http://firstmonday.org/ojs/index.php/fm/article/view/4958/3790 (29 June 2016).

David, M., Hart, G., Bolding, G., Sherr, L. and Elford, J. (2006). E-dating, identity and HIV prevention: Theorising sexualities, risk and network society. *Sociology of Health & Illness*, 28(4), pp. 457–478.

Davison, K., Pennebaker, J. and Dickerson, S. (2000). Who talks? The social psychology of illness support groups. *American Psychology*, 55, pp. 205–217.

Fiore, A. and Donath, J. (2004) Online personals: An overview. In: *The Conference on Human Factors in Computing Systems*. New York: ACM, pp. 1395–1398.

Fokkema, T. and Kuyper, L. (2009). The relation between social embeddedness and loneliness among older lesbian, gay, and bisexual adults in the Netherlands. *Archives of Sexual Behavior,* 38, pp. 264–275.

Gardner, H. and David, K. (2013). *The App Generation: How Today's Youth Navigate Identity, Intimacy, and Imagination in a Digital World.* New Haven, CT: Yale University Press.

Giddens, A. (1991). *Modernity and Self-Identity: Self and Society in the Late Modern Age.* Stanford, CA: Stanford University Press.

Giddens, A. (1992). *The Transformation of Intimacy: Sexuality, Love & Eroticism in Modern Societies.* Stanford, CA: Stanford University Press.

Gudelunas, D. (2005). Online personal ads – Community and sex, virtually. *Journal of Homosexuality*, 49(1), pp. 1–33.

Gudelunas, D. (2012). There's an app for that: The uses and gratifications of online social networks for gay. *Sexuality & Culture*, 16(4), pp. 347–365.

Hardey, M. (2004). Mediated relationships. *Information, Communication & Society*, 7(2), pp. 207–222.

Heino, R., Ellison, N. and Gibbs, J. (2010). Relationshopping: Investigating the market metaphor in online dating. *Journal of Social and Personal Relationships*, 27(4), pp. 427–447.

Himmelfarb, G. (1999). *One Nation, Two Cultures.* New York: A. Knopf.

Hospers, H., Kok, G., Harterink, P. and De Zwart, O. (2005). A new meeting place: Chatting on the Internet, e-dating and sexual risk behaviour among Dutch men who have sex with men. *AIDS*, 19, pp. 1097–1101.

Joffe, H. (1997). Intimacy and love in modern conditions. In J. Ussher, ed., *Body Talk: The Material and Discursive Regulation of Sexuality, Madness and Reproduction.* London: Routledge.

Katz, E., Blumler, J. and Gurevitch, M. (1974). Utilization of mass communication by the individual. In: J. Blumler and E. Katz, eds., *The Uses of Mass Communications: Current Perspectives on Gratifications Research.* Beverly Hills, CA: SAGE, pp. 19–32.

Kuyper, L. and Fokkema, T. (2010). Loneliness among older lesbian, gay, and bisexual adults: The role of minority stress. *Archives of Sexual Behavior, 39*, pp. 1170–1180.

Luhmann, N. (1986). *Love as Passion.* Cambridge: Polity Press.

Mainwaring, S., Chang, M. and Anderson, K. (2004). Infrastructures and their discontents: Implications for Ubicomp. In: *UbiComp 2004: Ubiquitous Computing.* Berlin and Heidelberg: Springer, pp. 418–432.

McKenna, K. and Bargh, J. (1998). Coming out in the age of the Internet: Identity 'demarginalization' through virtual group participation. *Journal of Personality and Social Psychology*, 75(3), pp. 681–694.

Meeker, M. (2006) *Contacts Desired: Gay and Lesbian Communications and Community, 1940s–1970s.* Chicago, IL: University of Chicago Press.

Meyer, I. (2003). Prejudice, social stress, and mental health in lesbian, gay, and bisexual populations: Conceptual issues and research evidence. *Psychological Bulletin*, 129, pp. 674–697.
Mowlabocus, S. (2010). *Gaydar Culture: Gay Men, Technology and Embodiment in the Digital Age*. Farnham: Ashgate.
Pew Research Center (2013). The Global Divide on Homosexuality. Retrieved from www.pewglobal.org/files/2013/06/Pew-Global-Attitudes-Homosexuality-Report-FINAL-JUNE-4-2013.pdf. (2 October 2015).
Plummer, K. (2003). *Intimate Citizenship: Private Decisions and Public Dialogues*. Seattle, WA: University of Washington Press.
Rainie, L. and Wellman, B. (2012). *Networked: The New Social Operating System*. Cambridge, MA: MIT Press.
Rousseau, D. (2001). Schema, promise and mutuality: The building blocks of the psychological contract. *Journal of Occupational and Organizational Psychology*, 74(4), pp. 511–541.
Schwartz, R. (2011). Out of the grind? Grindr and teen queer identity work in rural US. In: *The American Anthropological Association (Invited Session)*. Montréal.
Stephure, R., Boon, S., Mackinnon, S. and Deveau, V. (2009). Internet initiated relationships: Associations between age and involvement in online dating. *Journal of Computer-Mediated Communication*, 14(3), pp. 658–681.
Sternberg, R.J. (1986). A triangular theory of love. *Psychological Review*, 93(2), pp. 119–135.
Tajfel, H. and Turner, J. (1979). An integrative theory of intergroup conflict. *The Social Psychology of Intergroup Relations*, 33, p. 47.
van Dijck, J. (1999). *The Network Society: Social Aspects of New Media*. London: SAGE.
van Dijck, J. (2013). *The Culture of Connectivity: A Critical History of Social Media*. New York: Oxford University Press.
Young, G. (2004). From broadcasting to narrowcasting to 'mycasting': A newfound celebrity in queer Internet communities. *Continuum: Journal of Media & Cultural Studies*, 18(1), pp. 43–62.
Zhang, Y. and Chong, E. (2011). Invisible Network, Hidden Identity, and Mitigation of Minority: Social Networking Service Usage Among Homosexual/Bisexual Individuals in Hong Kong. I · Care Program Report (Research Project No. R14-11), The Chinese University of Hong Kong.

Part III

Integrating and domesticating

11 Mediating intimacies through mobile communication

Chinese migrant mothers' digital 'bridge of magpies'

Yang Wang and Sun Sun Lim

Introduction

During the past two decades, China has witnessed a steady stream of school-aged children venturing overseas for education, accompanied by their mothers. Singapore is deemed one of the most popular destinations for this purpose, due to its cultural proximity to Chinese society, its bilingual education system and its incentive schemes for foreign students. The mothers involved in this endeavour are commonly referred to as *peidu mama* (literally 'study mothers'), who accompany their young children abroad while leaving their husbands behind in China. As de facto 'single mothers' in the host society, they must overcome acculturation challenges and pave the way for their children to quickly thrive in an alien environment and simultaneously maintain affective bonds with their family and friends back home. In this context, mobile communication is of crucial significance for their daily micro-coordinations and emotional exchanges with children and remote loved ones.

Similar to the romantic Chinese legend of the weaver girl and the cowherd who reunite only once a year on a bridge formed by magpies, transnational families who are separated by insurmountable geographical distance also 'meet' each other on the digital 'bridge of magpies' forged by information and communication technologies (ICTs). From delayed, asynchronous connections via tapes and telegrams to sporadic and costly conversations over landline telephones all the way to synchronous communication with internet-enabled mobile devices such as smartphones and tablet computers, the range of options for international migrants to maintain long-distance relationships has grown in line with the proliferation and development of ICTs (Thomas and Lim, 2011; Wilding, 2006). In technology-mediated spaces, transnational family members can remain involved in one another's mundane experiences and perform familial responsibilities from afar on a daily basis, thus reconstituting family intimacies across national borders (Madianou and Miller, 2011; Parreñas, 2005).

Building on prior research on the role of technologically mediated communication in the enactment of long-distance intimacy, this chapter features the narratives of three Chinese study mothers in Singapore, presenting detailed accounts of their transnational communication practices to demonstrate their use of mobile communication to manage their intimate relationships with children and left-behind families and friends. Particular focus is placed on the way in which contextual constraints shape their experiences of mediated intimacy, and how – in the face of these constraints – they maximise possibilities for mediated intimacy via all available resources. An innovative 'content-context diary' cum participant observation and the visualised technique of culturagram (Congress, 1994, 2005) were employed to map the topographies of the mothers' mediated relationships, both distant and proximate, and to identify the contextual constraints and dynamic strategies that were employed within quotidian routines of transnational communication.

Chinese 'study mothers' in Singapore

In contemporary Asian society, a 'cosmopolitan' educational background is increasingly perceived as an essential pathway to upward social mobility (Huang and Yeoh, 2005; Waters, 2006). The overseas education of adolescent children, therefore, has become a top priority for many middle- and upper middle-class families in Asia, and these families brave painstaking journeys to unfamiliar foreign lands and are prepared to weather the transnational split of their households for this purpose (Chee, 2003; Huang and Yeoh, 2005; Lee and Koo, 2006). In typical cases, the mothers uproot and resettle with their children abroad, while the fathers are 'left behind' in the home country to continue working and to provide financial support for the long-term transnational family situation. The phenomenon of the transnational household has been witnessed in several Asian societies, such as Hong Kong and Taiwan ('astronaut families') (e.g. Chee, 2003; Waters, 2006), South Korea (*kirogi* families) (e.g. Lee, 2010; Lee and Koo, 2006) and Mainland China (*peidu* families) (e.g. Huang and Yeoh, 2005, 2011).

According to previous studies, mothers in these transnational families usually pay the greatest price for the migratory journey, as they sacrifice opportunities for personal career development and often experience an overwhelming sense of loneliness, helplessness and insecurity due to a loss of financial independence and support networks of family and friends (Ho, 2002; Waters, 2006). Moreover, as de facto 'single mothers' in the host country, they tend to privilege 'motherhood' over 'wifehood' and 'selfhood', to the extent of sacrificing conjugal relations and individual aspirations in favour of maternal obligations (Chee, 2003; Huang and Yeoh, 2005).

During the past two decades, a considerable number of Chinese mothers have ventured overseas to accompany their children as they pursue education abroad. Singapore is one of the most popular destinations for Chinese families due to its incentive schemes for foreign students, its high standard of public safety, its cultural proximity to Chinese society, its bilingual education system and so forth (Huang and Yeoh, 2005, 2011). Chinese *peidu* families in Singapore range from wealthy and upper middle-class families to lower middle-class families (Huang and Yeoh, 2005). However, under the influence of the 'one-child policy' in China (Fong, 2004), the pursuit of overseas education is no longer exclusive to wealthy 'elite families'. In contrast, growing numbers of middle and lower middle-class parents are sending their children abroad, even at the cost of depleting their household savings (Huang and Yeoh, 2005).

Mediated intimacies of transnational families – A review of prior research

Over the past several decades, the increasing accessibility, affordability and rich functionality of advanced ICTs (especially mobile devices and the internet) have emancipated people from temporal and spatial constraints and brought unprecedented flexibility to social interaction and communication (Fortunati, 2002; Licoppe, 2004; Turkle, 2011). The enactment and reproduction of intimacies – be these at the level of the individual, community or even society – are increasingly shaped by this emerging media-rich environment (Hjorth, 2011; Hjorth and Lim 2012). Nonetheless, this intensely mediatised landscape introduces uncomfortable tensions and contradictions that individuals must negotiate. On the one hand, mediated communication offers new and effective approaches to expressing affection and building intimate relationships (Clark, 2012; Licoppe, 2004; Wajcman et al., 2008). On the other hand, the wealth of technological affordances may also cause emotional burdens and impair rather than nurture intimacies (Lim, 2014; Lim and Soon, 2009; Madianou and Miller, 2012; Turkle, 2011).

For transnationally separated households, mediated communication through ICTs assumes particular significance, as it is the only viable way for members to keep family bonds alive (Horst, 2006; Pham and Lim, 2016; Uy-Tioco, 2007). Extensive research has delved into mediated intimacies within transnational households, with a major strand of literature focusing on the renegotiation of parenthood – especially motherhood – in transnational families in which children have remained in the home country (e.g. Chib et al., 2014; Madianou and Miller, 2011; Uy-Tioco, 2007). Instead of forsaking parental responsibilities after physical separation, migrant mothers often seek to reconstitute or even strengthen their gender identity as 'ideal mothers' via virtual involvement in diverse facets of their children's daily routines (Madianou, 2012; Peng and Wong, 2013; Uy-Tioco, 2007). These mediated mothering practices often include quotidian elements of everyday life such as waking their children up and saying goodnight, reminding them to have meals, helping with their homework and providing comfort when they are depressed (Chib et al., 2014; Madianou, 2012; Peng and Wong, 2013; Uy-Tioco, 2007).

Another important thread in extant research sheds light on the way in which transnationally separated couples employ ICTs to reproduce conjugal intimacies across vast geographical distances (e.g. Cabanes and Acedera, 2012; King-O'Riain, 2015; Neustaedter and Greenberg, 2012). In particular, distant couples have been observed to 'hang out' in mediated spaces where they share mundane and bittersweet everyday occurrences, cooperate on family affairs and express affection to each other (King-O'Riain, 2015; Neustaedter and Greenberg, 2012). Mediated communication has been found to play a dual role, in that it can both enable new practices of cooperation between husbands and wives (Cabanes and Acedera, 2012; Kang, 2012) and thrust migrants back into their family lives, allowing them to hold on to their previous family roles (Cabanes and Acedera, 2012; Madianou, 2012; Uy-Tioco, 2007).

The majority of studies have noted the indispensable role of mediated communication as the 'social glue of transnationalism' (Vertovec, 2004: 219). ICTs – and especially webcam software such as Skype – allow separated family members to 'stream' each other's daily routines in a mediated space of co-presence that enables information and emotions to be reciprocated in a precise and ongoing manner as if the family were still together (King-O'Riain, 2015; Longhurst, 2013; Wilding, 2006). Some studies have also scrutinised the potentially burdensome implications of mediated communication. In particular, mediated interactions mean far less than the immediate company of loved ones. Sometimes it is precisely the simulated togetherness that reminds migrants and their families of the actual physical distance between them and accentuates feelings of guilt, anxiety and loneliness (Parreñas, 2005; Uy-Tioco, 2007; Wilding, 2006).

Although prior research has offered considerable insight into the multifarious roles of mediated communication in remote family intimacies, the range of transnational families that are studied is far from complete. Specifically, previous studies have paid exclusive attention to the use of ICT by 'mother-away' transnational households, in which women have migrated alone for financial benefits and left their children and husbands behind in their home countries (e.g. Chib et al., 2014; Madianou and Miller, 2011; Thomas and Lim, 2011; Uy-Tioco, 2007). However, despite the prevalence of education migration across Asia, 'mother-child resettlement' transnational households and the migrant mothers involved remain understudied in media and communication research.

Moreover, transnational families do not live in isolated environments but are located in and shaped by a series of social and geographical inequalities (Parreñas, 2005). Many sociocultural factors, such as gender, ethnicity, nationality and social class, may be foregrounded and bleed into their experiences of mediated intimacy (Anthias, 2002; Parreñas, 2005; Plüss, 2013). However, to date, research has only examined 'salient' influential factors such as gender (e.g. Hannaford, 2015; Kang, 2012), place of origin and destination (e.g. Cabanes and Acedera, 2012; Peng and Wong, 2013) and working conditions (e.g. Parreñas, 2005; Thomas and Lim, 2011), while many seemingly prosaic yet crucial factors, such as language proficiency, housing conditions and motivations for relocation, have been overlooked. In this context, this chapter proposes a closer investigation of the quotidian routines of mobile communication by Chinese study mothers and their families in their home country, with a particular focus on the contextual constraints that shape their transnational communication practices and, in turn, their proactive strategies of negotiating family intimacies in the face of such constraints.

Research method

For this study, an innovative 'content-context diary' cum participant observation was designed and conducted with ten Chinese study mothers of diverse sociocultural backgrounds. Each participant was shadowed by the same researcher for two days, one weekday and one weekend day; in this way, the research covered as many contexts of her daily life as possible within the limited research period. Each observation lasted for 8 to 12 hours, according to the schedule and convenience of the participant. During the observation, participants were told to behave naturally while the researcher accompanied them and observed their mobile communication practices. After completing the two-day observation process, each participant was given a shopping voucher as a token of appreciation. The detailed research protocol was approved by the National University of Singapore's Institutional Review Board.

Participants were recruited through a combination of convenience sampling and snowball sampling from multiple sources, including the researcher's personal networks, instant messaging groups that specifically catered to Chinese study mothers in Singapore and local churches with Chinese fellowship groups. Participants were selected in order to achieve diversity in demographic traits (e.g. age of child, years of relocation, type of employment, etc.). Thus, the final sample was representative of the social group.

A researcher-administered 'content-context diary' was employed during the observation to record both content- and context-related aspects of mobile communication. Specifically, the content-related aspects included the correspondent and platform of communication, details of the content exchanged, the mode of expression and so on; context-related aspects encompassed the temporal and spatial settings of communication, the attitudes and emotions involved, special behaviours and their meanings during mediated communication and so on. Since the participants primarily spoke Mandarin, diary entries were maintained in English, Chinese or a mixture of both during the fieldwork, and later transcribed into English. Informal interviews were also incorporated into the observation to gather background information and elicit the subjective opinions of participants when interesting issues emerged from the research process.

Qualitative data collected from participant observation was analysed through the visual technique of the culturagram (Congress, 1994, 2005). The culturagram is a multi-dimensional family assessment tool that is employed by social workers to understand and intervene in culturally diverse families, and it has proven to be particularly effective in identifying the impact of cultural values and practices on family functioning (Brownell, 1997; Congress, 2005). The prototype culturagram model embraces ten sociocultural dimensions of family life, including legal status, time in the community, family values and contact with cultural/religious institutions (as shown in Figure 11.1).

For this study, the culturagram model was adapted for the particular life situation of the Chinese study mothers in order to identify crucial factors in their transnational life that could affect their daily routines and strategies of mediated communication. The adapted model, the 'transnational culturagram', encompassed 18 dimensions of transnational life, including: demographic factors, such as residential status; subjective factors, such as motives for relocation; relational factors, such as social activities; and life transition factors, such as significant life events that preceded and/or accompanied the relocation (see Figure 11.2).

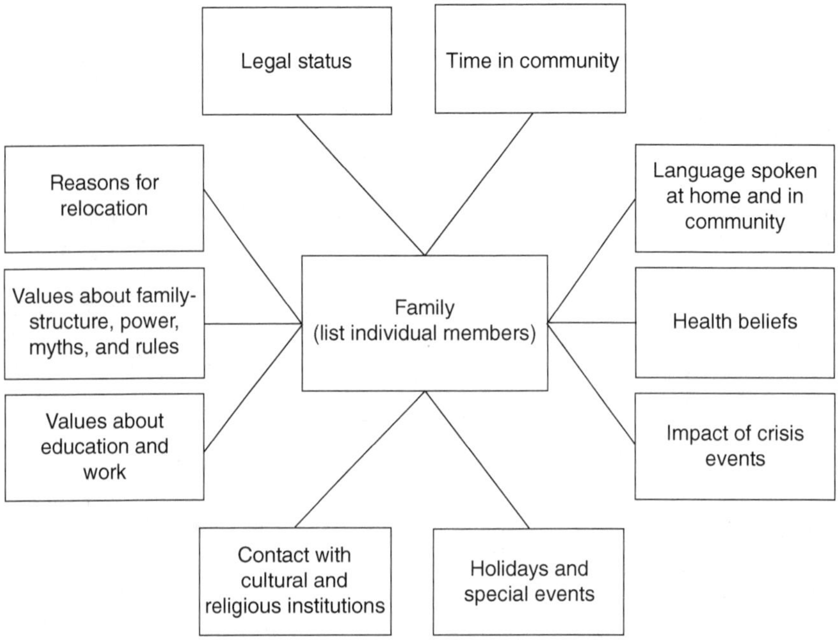

Figure 11.1 Culturagram (Congress, 2005).

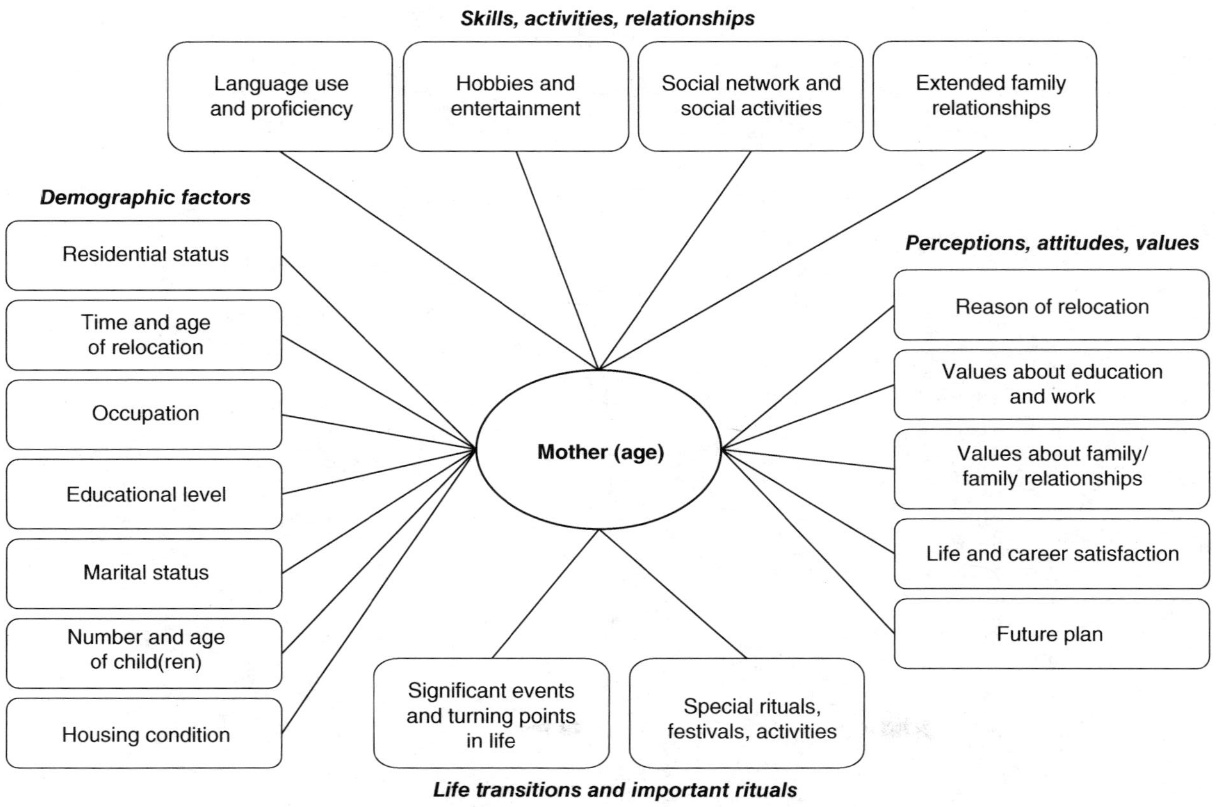
Skills, activities, relationships
Language use and proficiency
Hobbies and entertainment
Social network and social activities
Extended family relationships
Demographic factors
Residential status
Time and age of relocation
Occupation
Educational level
Marital status
Number and age of child(ren)
Housing condition
Mother (age)
Perceptions, attitudes, values
Reason of relocation
Values about education and work
Values about family/ family relationships
Life and career satisfaction
Future plan
Significant events and turning points in life
Special rituals, festivals, activities
Life transitions and important rituals

Figure 11.2 Transnational culturagram

Findings

In this chapter, we present the experiences of three of the ten mothers in our study, representing different socioeconomic profiles. We seek to demonstrate how transnational life situations posed significant constraints on the migrants' expression of intimacies, while also showing that the migrants could be highly creative in circumventing these contextual limitations.

Ms Zhang: Multi-sited householding by a 'digital immigrant'

Having relocated with her son in 2002, 49-year-old Ms Zhang was among the 'first-wave' Chinese study mothers in Singapore. As a lower middle-class family, the Zhangs had to drain their household savings and even borrow money from relatives to support the move. After relocating to Singapore, Ms Zhang managed to find employment in the service sector, which guaranteed her sufficient income to cover all of her expenses in the host country. Several years later, her husband quit his job in China and joined his wife and son in Singapore. However, the joy of the family reunion did not last long, as Ms Zhang soon discovered that her husband had become addicted to gambling and had squandered almost all of their hard-earned savings. Bitterly disappointed in her husband's impenitence, she moved out of their home and planned to get divorced after her son's graduation from college. A full snapshot of Ms Zhang's transnational life is shown in Figure 11.3.

Ms Zhang had two mobile phones: an old-fashioned cell phone that had been given to her by her employer for work purposes and a smartphone of her own. As a 'digital immigrant' with low proficiency in ICTs, she utilised only very limited functions of both devices, and showed a strong preference for more 'traditional' functions on the old-fashioned cell phone over 'new' platforms that were available on her smartphone for daily communication.

Due to her strained relationship with her husband, Ms Zhang seldom spoke to him, either in person or through technological mediation, even though they lived in the same city. At the time of the research, she was living separately from her son, yet remained updated on his daily routines and provided real-time help when necessary via mediated communication. For example, when she was preparing dinner for herself one evening, she remembered the shrimp and sausages she had bought for him several days prior and paused what she was doing to remind him, over WeChat, to cook the food without delay (see the excerpt from the content-context diary in Figure 11.4).

Such short and sporadic conversations characterised the mediated communication between Ms Zhang and her son. Her working conditions as a tea lady and in-home cleaner rendered it impossible for her to maintain continuous contact with him. Moreover, since she lived in a small maid's room and shared the apartment with several other tenants, she tended to avoid prolonged mediated conversations at home. In view of these obstacles,

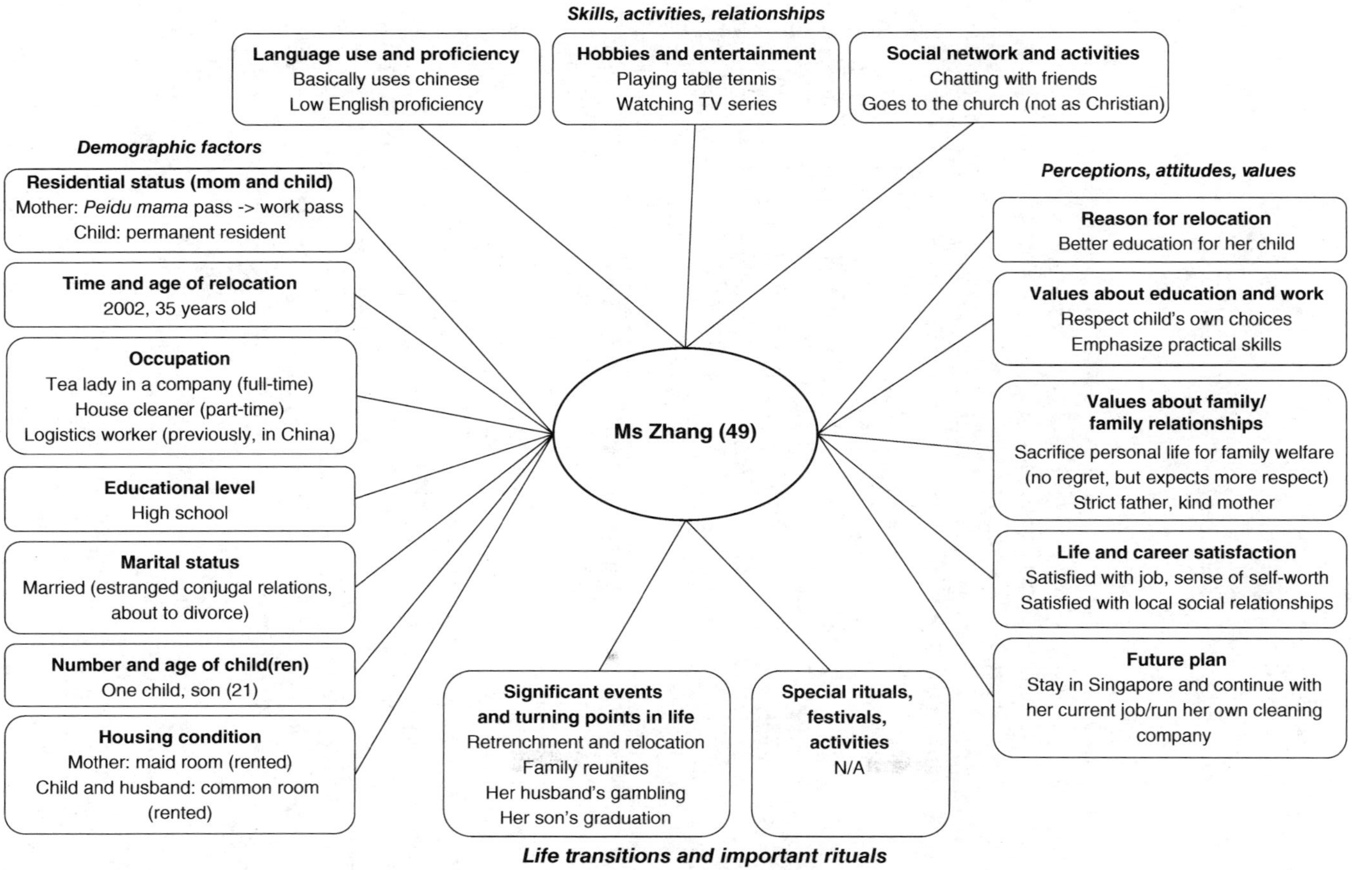
Skills, activities, relationships
Language use and proficiency
Basically uses chinese
Low English proficiency
Hobbies and entertainment
Playing table tennis
Watching TV series
Social network and activities
Chatting with friends
Goes to the church (not as Christian)
Demographic factors
Residential status (mom and child)
Mother: Peidu mama pass -> work pass
Child: permanent resident
Time and age of relocation
2002, 35 years old
Occupation
Tea lady in a company (full-time)
House cleaner (part-time)
Logistics worker (previously, in China)
Educational level
High school
Marital status
Married (estranged conjugal relations, about to divorce)
Number and age of child(ren)
One child, son (21)
Housing condition
Mother: maid room (rented)
Child and husband: common room (rented)
Ms Zhang (49)
Perceptions, attitudes, values
Reason for relocation
Better education for her child
Values about education and work
Respect child's own choices
Emphasize practical skills
Values about family/ family relationships
Sacrifice personal life for family welfare
(no regret, but expects more respect)
Strict father, kind mother
Life and career satisfaction
Satisfied with job, sense of self-worth
Satisfied with local social relationships
Future plan
Stay in Singapore and continue with her current job/run her own cleaning company
Significant events and turning points in life
Retrenchment and relocation
Family reunites
Her husband's gambling
Her son's graduation
Special rituals, festivals, activities
N/A
Life transitions and important rituals

Figure 11.3 Transnational culturagram of Ms Zhang

ITEM	CONTENT	CONTEXT
6:17pm–6:19pm	Sent voice message to her son Smartphone, WeChat Reminded him and his father to cook the shrimps and sausage she bought for them last weekend	About to cook dinner, standing in front of the refrigerator No one else in the living room or kitchen (public spaces of the apartment) Explained that she usually did not speak much with her son and husband during the weekdays unless there was something urgent

Figure 11.4 Diary excerpt: Ms Zhang's communication with her son

she relied more on regular face-to-face communication with her son to maintain their intimate relationship. Mobile communication played a supplementary role and was only utilised occasionally for coordinating schedules and spontaneously chatting.

Although Ms Zhang managed to maintain a close relationship with her son, she found it difficult to get emotional support from him after he became an independent adult. As the years went on, extended family members increasingly constituted her main source of emotional comfort. Mobile communication enabled her and her left-behind family to share personal experiences at length, and hence secured for her constant companionship and support during her 'tough days'. For example, after she discovered her husband's gambling addiction, she made many phone calls to her aunt in Shanghai to pour out her feelings and seek suggestions in dealing with this thorny issue:

> She [my aunt] is the only person who can fully understand me [...] I called her immediately [after I found out about my husband's gambling]. I cried and scolded him [my husband]. She talked to me for more than two hours, comforting me throughout. She also suggested that I talk to my husband calmly before making any hasty decisions [...] I really appreciated her. Without her, I might have done something irrational.

Besides strengthening long-distance intimacy with her family back home, mobile communication also nurtured Ms Zhang's intimate relationships in the host society. In particular, her regular sharing of useful information and mundane experiences with local friends and colleagues in the mediated space not only helped her to resolve everyday challenges but, more importantly, granted her a sense of 'being accompanied'.

Ms Yu: Negotiating a hectic schedule of work-life blending at home

Ms Yu was a 40-year-old mother of two boys, aged 13 and 2 at the time of research. In 2010, her entire family resettled in Singapore in pursuit of a better education for her elder son. One year later, her husband returned to China while she and her son remained in Singapore. Compared with Ms

Zhang, who had to work to make ends meet, Ms Yu was from an affluent middle-class family and received sufficient financial support from her husband. However, she decided to take on some part-time work, including a job as a direct seller of health products, in order to relieve the burden on her husband. As a Christian, she participated in many activities and made many good friends in church. A full snapshot of Ms Yu's transnational life is shown in Figure 11.5.

As a full-time 'single mother' and a part-time homeworker, Ms Yu was located in a situation of 'work-life blending' (Clark, 2000), wherein her already hectic family life was constantly punctuated by work-related demands. In this context, mobile communication assumed crucial significance in her daily juggling of work and family obligations. Through strategic deployment of her smartphone, she was able to maintain intimate relationships with family members back home, stay in contact with networks of local friends and colleagues and reach out to increasing numbers of customers without stepping out of her house.

Rather than comprising merely routine greetings or discussions of major domestic affairs, mediated communication between Ms Yu and her husband usually went deep into mundane daily activities and feelings, relating to dinner plans, anecdotes about their children, the weather and other topics. Considering her tight schedule, Ms Yu tended to use all available 'fragmented time' – such as during her younger son's afternoon nap and while cooking or waiting for the bus – to exchange messages with her husband. For example, when she browsed group chats on WeChat during cooking, she found a new reading group for Christians and recommended it to him immediately (see the diary excerpt in Figure 11.6).

Since Ms Yu's husband was also very busy with his job in China, the fragmentary yet continuous trickle of mediated communication was optimal for the spouses to reproduce long-distance family intimacy on a daily basis, while minimising interruptions to their regular schedules.

Beyond using mobile communication in the domestic sphere, Ms Yu also used mobile communication to seek various forms of social support from larger social networks in the host society. In particular, as a busy mother who spent most of her time at home, she relied heavily on a series of WeChat group chats with church friends for companionship and emotional comfort. Rather than discussing or solving practical problems, most conversations in these groups comprised daily greetings or affective expressions (see examples in Figure 11.7).

According to Ms Yu, the simple posts of 'Amen' and 'Christ be with you' built strong and intimate bonds between the group members and afforded her a strong sense of belonging and togetherness despite her relatively isolated life. In her own words, these virtual communities served as 'a second home' for her and her friends, where they could 'express their feelings freely, without reservations'.

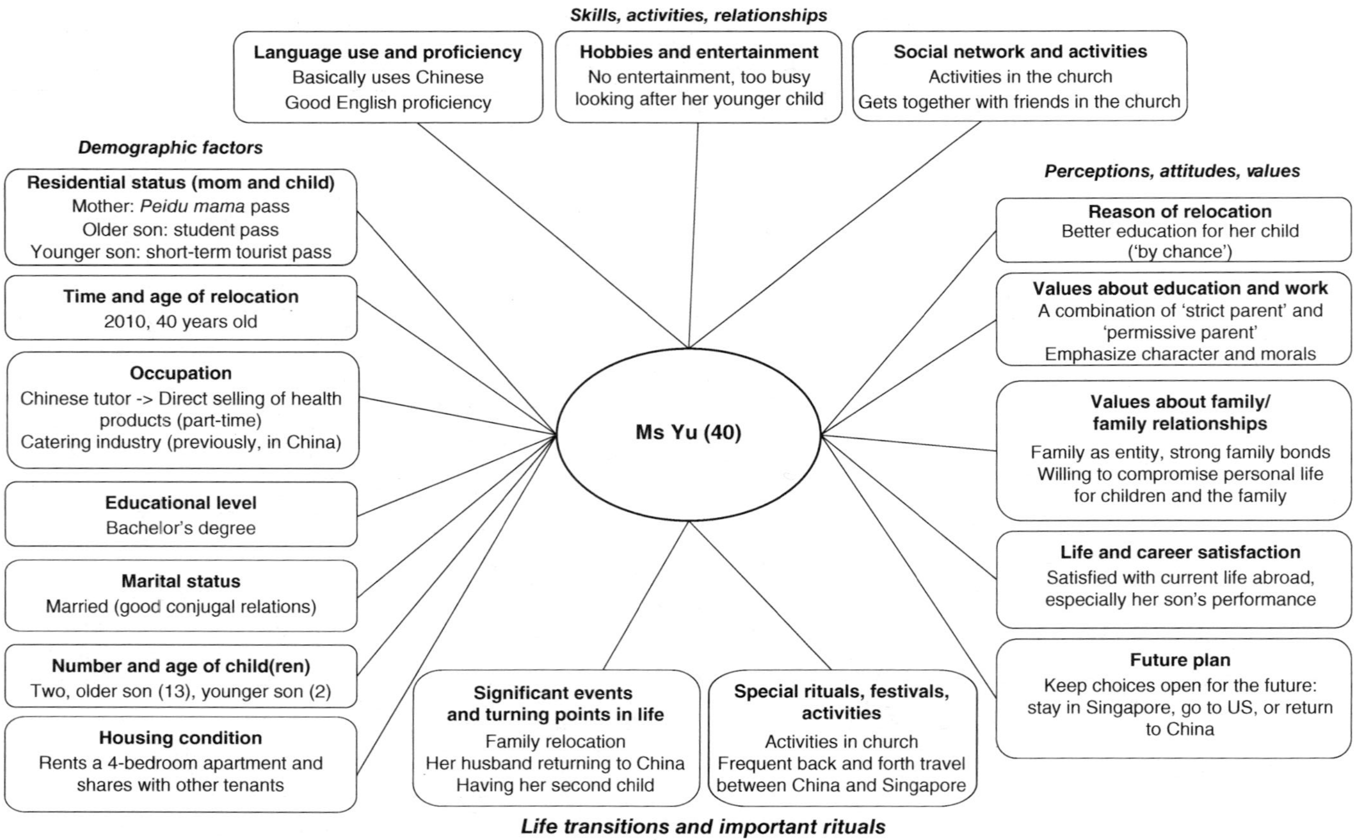
Skills, activities, relationships
Language use and proficiency
Basically uses Chinese
Good English proficiency
Hobbies and entertainment
No entertainment, too busy looking after her younger child
Social network and activities
Activities in the church
Gets together with friends in the church
Demographic factors
Residential status (mom and child)
Mother: Peidu mama pass
Older son: student pass
Younger son: short-term tourist pass
Time and age of relocation
2010, 40 years old
Occupation
Chinese tutor -> Direct selling of health products (part-time)
Catering industry (previously, in China)
Educational level
Bachelor's degree
Marital status
Married (good conjugal relations)
Number and age of child(ren)
Two, older son (13), younger son (2)
Housing condition
Rents a 4-bedroom apartment and shares with other tenants
Ms Yu (40)
Perceptions, attitudes, values
Reason of relocation
Better education for her child ('by chance')
Values about education and work
A combination of 'strict parent' and 'permissive parent'
Emphasize character and morals
Values about family/ family relationships
Family as entity, strong family bonds
Willing to compromise personal life for children and the family
Life and career satisfaction
Satisfied with current life abroad, especially her son's performance
Future plan
Keep choices open for the future: stay in Singapore, go to US, or return to China
Significant events and turning points in life
Family relocation
Her husband returning to China
Having her second child
Special rituals, festivals, activities
Activities in church
Frequent back and forth travel between China and Singapore
Life transitions and important rituals

Figure 11.5 Transnational culturagram of Ms Yu

ITEM	CONTENT	CONTEXT
5:49pm–5:50pm	Sent text messages to her husband Smartphone, WeChat Recommended that her husband join a reading group on WeChat (initiated by church friends)	Cooking dinner in the kitchen Her son was reading a picture book about vehicles in the living room (sometimes ran around the dining room and the kitchen) Explained that her husband was also a Christian, so she often recommended materials in her church groups to him

Figure 11.6 Diary excerpt: Ms Yu's communication with her husband

Figure 11.7 Ms Yu's group chats on WeChat

Ms Gu: Transnational companionship on the webcam

Ms Gu, a 42-year-old mother of a 13-year-old son, had been in Singapore for three years at the time of the research. As she came from an upper middle-class family, abundant financial support from her husband and other family members spared her the toil of taking on unsatisfactory jobs and allowed her to fully concentrate on child-minding while enjoying a rich social life in the host society. As a former high school English teacher in China, she had good English proficiency, and this facilitated her quick adaptation and creation of local networks in Singapore. A full snapshot of Ms Yu's transnational life is shown in Figure 11.8.

For Ms Gu and her husband, mutual virtual presence in each other's customary routines was their 'default state' of daily life after the relocation. Continuous mediated communication via the smartphone and iPad, especially on WeChat, bridged the physical gulf between them and allowed

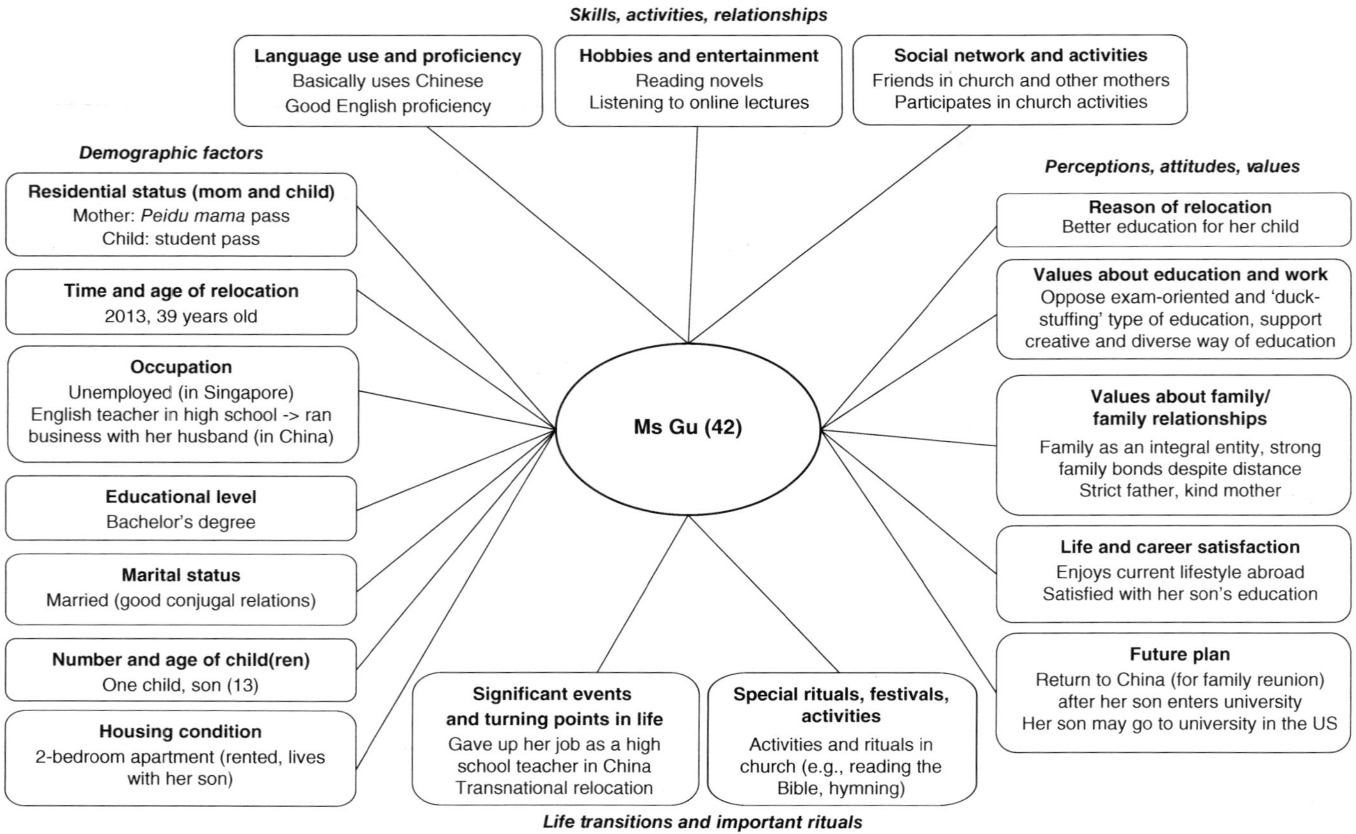
Skills, activities, relationships
Language use and proficiency
Basically uses Chinese
Good English proficiency
Hobbies and entertainment
Reading novels
Listening to online lectures
Social network and activities
Friends in church and other mothers
Participates in church activities
Demographic factors
Residential status (mom and child)
Mother: Peidu mama pass
Child: student pass
Time and age of relocation
2013, 39 years old
Occupation
Unemployed (in Singapore)
English teacher in high school -> ran business with her husband (in China)
Educational level
Bachelor's degree
Marital status
Married (good conjugal relations)
Number and age of child(ren)
One child, son (13)
Housing condition
2-bedroom apartment (rented, lives with her son)
Ms Gu (42)
Perceptions, attitudes, values
Reason of relocation
Better education for her child
Values about education and work
Oppose exam-oriented and 'duck-stuffing' type of education, support creative and diverse way of education
Values about family/ family relationships
Family as an integral entity, strong family bonds despite distance
Strict father, kind mother
Life and career satisfaction
Enjoys current lifestyle abroad
Satisfied with her son's education
Future plan
Return to China (for family reunion) after her son enters university
Her son may go to university in the US
Significant events and turning points in life
Gave up her job as a high school teacher in China
Transnational relocation
Special rituals, festivals, activities
Activities and rituals in church (e.g., reading the Bible, hymning)
Life transitions and important rituals

Figure 11.8 Transnational culturagram of Ms Gu

Figure 11.9 Ms Gu's WeChat conversations with her husband

them to enjoy family life as if they were still living under the same roof. Most of the time, their conversations – whether in the form of video, voice or text – were prosaic 'small talk' without any practical purpose. For example, every evening Ms Gu 'showed off' pictures of dinners she had cooked to her husband via WeChat (see examples in Figure 11.9). Over time, 'sharing dinner' became a habituated 'family ritual' between them, and often served as preludes to long mediated conversations over the webcam.

Compared to Ms Zhang and Ms Yu, whose daily routines largely hinged upon work-related demands, Ms Gu had generous space-time flexibility in her family life. Moreover, living in an apartment that was exclusive to her and her son, she also enjoyed a high degree of privacy and freedom in her mobile communication. In this context, she often left the webcam on for an extended period of time while engaging in domestic chores and personal activities, such as cooking, having dinner and reading. For both sides, mediated communication was more of a companionship that replicated an environment of 'togetherness' than a pragmatic tool for information exchange. This virtual companionship could take place almost anytime and anywhere. For example, when her husband was travelling late at night, Ms Gu stayed up until he arrived at his destination and talked to him via webcam as he settled down (see the diary excerpt in Figure 11.10).

Continuous mediated communication also allowed Ms Gu and her husband to coordinate domestic affairs such as decisions, online purchases and schedule confirmations in real time and in vivid detail, regardless of

ITEM	CONTENT	CONTEXT
0:40am	Video chat with her husband Smartphone, WeChat Asked whether he had arrived at the destination Her husband dialed video chat and talked with her for about 20 minutes	Lying in bed She had a headache, and got up to eat a painkiller Her husband was travelling that night, so she chatted with him after waking up

Figure 11.10 Diary excerpt: Ms Yu's communication with her husband

their physical separation. For example, Ms Gu described how they would 'sit together' to purchase airline tickets on a Chinese website:

> My Singapore phone number could not receive the verification code, so I changed the reception number to my husband's [and booked tickets again]. After he received the code, he forwarded it to me immediately, and I completed the purchase [...] It was very quick, less than two minutes in all. It was just like we were sitting together [to buy tickets].

Owing to her strong English proficiency and relatively ample free time, Ms Gu was among the most 'sociable' study mothers. She participated actively in various local activities – both online and offline – and sought to expand her social circles in the host society. Mobile communication, which afforded Ms Gu a diversity of mediated interaction, boosted her ability to foster local networks of both co-national and foreign friends. Hence, she could effectively maintain intensive communication with several groups of Chinese friends on WeChat and exchange information with them on many aspects of daily life, such as cooking, children's education, shopping and so on. At the same time, she also participated in a variety of WhatsApp groups and email lists to remain updated on the latest news about local activities, such as hiking trips, lectures and religious activities.

Discussion and conclusion

The three cases presented above show that mobile ICTs – particularly smartphones, which are assemblages of early ICTs (Madianou, 2014) – were woven deeply into the fabric of the Chinese study mothers' quotidian routines and constituted indispensable parts of their family and social lives. Specifically, mobile communication served as a digital 'bridge of magpies' for these mothers, linking them to both left-behind family and local communities, and thus facilitating the reconstitution of transnational family intimacies and the nurturance of new social networks in the host society. In the face of various contextual constraints, these mothers developed idiosyncratic strategies for mediated communication according to their unique life situations, in order to perform multiple gender roles (such as mother, wife, daughter and friend) and to properly negotiate the complexity of social relationships in line with each of these roles.

In accordance with previous research, mobile communication was found to assume crucial significance for the transnational families in recreating the warmth of domesticity and maintaining affective bonds despite vast geographical distances (e.g. Parreñas, 2005; Wilding, 2006). The trickle of 'emotional streaming' (King-O'Riain, 2015), although piecemeal and prosaic, allowed information and emotions to flow smoothly across national borders, and thus reproduced family intimacies on a daily basis. While there seemed to be a universal desire for maintaining long-distance intimacy, routines and outcomes of transnational communication varied according to economic and sociocultural backgrounds (see also Parreñas, 2005). In the transnational context, in particular, each individual or household has a unique social position from which a certain amount of human resources can be accessed, while structural constraints are imposed (Anthias, 2002; Plüss, 2013). These constraints, which derive from diverse axes such as gender, nationality and social class, both delimit the possibilities for transnational families to practise mediated communication and, at the same time, encourage them to develop novel strategies for articulating intimacy (Clark, 2012; Parreñas, 2005).

For the Chinese study mothers, in particular, the principal constraints of mobile communication did not lie in economic concerns – such as those relating to the availability and affordability of ICTs (see also Madianou, 2014; Madianou and Miller, 2012) – but rather in a series of contextual factors tied to their daily routines. In this research, we identified three main dimensions of constraints that created significant obstacles to mediated intimacy: spatial, temporal and social constraints. Spatial constraints emerged when access to and the convenience of using mobile ICTs were restricted by immediate spatial settings in which a person was embedded. As in Ms Zhang's case, her isolated work conditions and her shared apartment rendered it impossible for her to maintain constant and unconstrained contact with her loved ones. Temporal constraints became evident when the routines of mediated communication were in tension with or interrupted by other obligations. For example, in Ms Yu's case, her hectic schedule as a mother of two children and part-time seller left her very little time for daily communication. Social constraints were shaped by social norms, policies and household power relations. For most of the mothers in this study, their primary role as full-time mothers in Singapore and their difficulty in finding local employment confined them to the domestic sphere, and this narrowed their range of mediated relationships.

Nevertheless, although these study mothers were initially circumscribed by various contextual constraints, they did not remain so. Over time, they manifested strong agency and creativity that enabled them to circumvent the constraints that were imposed on them and developed strategies to maximise mediated intimacies with any available resource. For example, in the face of spatial constraints, Ms Zhang established regular communication routines with her son and sought to replace mediated interaction with face-to-face interaction. Similarly, Ms Yu made good use of fragmented time to maintain a thin yet steady trickle of conversations with her husband in light of temporal constraints. As for the social constraints derived from their isolated life experiences, most of the mothers chose to actively approach local networks of co-national friends online for instrumental and emotional support. Indeed, the seemingly marginalised and powerless positions of these mothers actually compelled and impelled them to explore more possibilities for nurturing diverse forms of mediated intimacies and, as a result, led them to perform their roles as mothers, wives, daughters and friends in the transnational context more successfully.

Through an in-depth qualitative research method and a comprehensive evaluation of the panoply of factors that influence the transnational migrant existence, this chapter has sought to shed light on an understudied transnational migrant population with very specific sociocultural and contextual constraints. Our study has further identified the complex of social-temporal-spatial constraints that significantly impinge on mediated communication practices and personalised strategies for circumventing these limitations in order to build and sustain intimacies.

References

Anthias, F. (2002). Where do I belong? Narrating collective identity and translocational positionality. *Ethnicities*, 2(4), pp. 491–514.

Brownell, P. (1997). The application of the culturagram in cross-cultural practice with elder abuse victims. *Journal of Elder Abuse & Neglect*, 9(2), pp. 19–33.

Cabanes, J.V.A. and Acedera, K.A.F. (2012). Of mobile phones and mother-fathers: Calls, text messages, and conjugal power relations in mother-away Filipino families. *New Media & Society*, 14(6), pp. 916–930.

Chee, M.W.L. (2003). Migrating for the children: Taiwanese American women in transnational families. In N. Piper and M. Roces, eds., *Wife or Worker? Asian Women and Migration*. Lanham: Rowman & Littlefield, pp. 137–156.

Chib, A., Malik, S. Aricat, R.G. & Kadir, S.Z. (2014). Migrant mothering and mobile phones: Negotiations of transnational identity. *Mobile Media & Communication*, 2(1), pp. 73–93.

Clark, L.S. (2012). *The Parent App: Understanding Families in the Digital Age*. Oxford: Oxford University Press.

Clark, S.C. (2000). Work/family border theory: A new theory of work/family balance. *Human Relations*, 53(6), pp. 747–770.

Congress, E.P. (2005). Cultural and ethical issues in working with culturally diverse patients and their families. *Social Work in Health Care*, 39(3-4), pp. 249–262.

Congress, E.P. (1994). The use of culturagrams to assess and empower culturally diverse families. *Families in Society*, 75(9), p. 531.

Fong, V.L. (2004). *Only Hope: Coming of Age Under China's One-Child Policy*. Stanford, CA: Stanford University Press.

Fortunati, L. (2002). The mobile phone: Towards new categories and social relations. *Information, Communication & Society*, 5 (January 2015), pp. 513–528.
Hannaford, D. (2015). Technologies of the spouse: Intimate surveillance in Senegalese transnational marriages. *Global Networks*, 15(1), pp. 43–59.
Hjorth, L. (2011 [1984]). Mobile specters of intimacy: A case study of women and mobile intimacy. In: *Mobile Communication: Bringing Us Together and Tearing Us Apart*, pp. 37–60.
Hjorth, L. and Lim, S.S. (2012). Mobile intimacy in an age of affective mobile media. *Feminist Media Studies,* 12(4), pp. 477–484.
Ho, E.S. (2002). Multi-local residence, transnational networks: Chinese 'astronaut' families in New Zealand. *Asian and Pacific Migration Journal*, 11(1), pp. 145–164.
Horst, H.A. (2006). The blessings and burdens of communication: Cell phones in Jamaican transnational social fields. *Global Networks*, 6(2), pp. 143–159.
Huang, S. and Yeoh, B.S.A. (2005). Transnational families and their children's education: China's 'study mothers' in Singapore. *Global Networks*, 5(4), pp. 379–400.
Huang, S. and Yeoh, B.S.A. (2011). Navigating the terrains of transnational education: Children of Chinese 'study mothers' in Singapore. *Geoforum*, 42(3), pp. 394–403.
Kang, T. (2012). Gendered media, changing intimacy: Internet-mediated transnational communication in the family sphere. *Media, Culture & Society*, 34(2), pp. 146–161.
King-O'Riain, R.C. (2015). Emotional streaming and transconnectivity: Skype and emotion practices in transnational families in Ireland. *Global Networks*, 15(2), pp. 256–273.
Lee, H. (2010). 'I am a Kirogi mother': Education exodus and life transformation among Korean transnational women. *Journal of Language, Identity & Education*, 9(4), pp. 250–264.
Lee, Y.J. and Koo, H. (2006). 'Wild geese fathers' and a globalised family strategy for education in Korea. *International Development Planning Review*, 28(4), pp. 533–553.
Licoppe, C. (2004). 'Connected' presence: The emergence of a new repertoire for managing social relationships in a changing communication technoscape. *Environment and Planning D: Society and Space*, 22(1), pp. 135–156.
Lim, S.S. (2014). Women, 'double work' and mobile media: The more things change, the more they stay the same. *Routledge Companion to Mobile Media*, pp. 356–364.
Lim, S.S. and Soon, C. (2010). The influence of social and cultural factors on mothers' domestication of household ICTs – Experiences of Chinese and Korean women. *Telematics and Informatics,* 27(3), pp. 205–216.
Longhurst, R. (2013). Using Skype to mother: Bodies, emotions, visuality, and screens. *Environment and Planning D: Society and Space*, 31(4), pp. 664–679.
Madianou, M. (2012). Migration and the accentuated ambivalence of transnational motherhood: New media in Filipino migrant families. *Global Networks*, 12(3), pp. 277–295.
Madianou, M. (2014). Smartphones as polymedia. *Journal of Computer-Mediated Communication*, 19(3), pp. 667–680.

Madianou, M. and Miller, D. (2011). Mobile phone parenting: Reconfiguring relationships between Filipina migrant mothers and their left-behind children. *New Media & Society*, 13(3), pp. 457–470.

Madianou, M. and Miller, D. (2012). Polymedia: Towards a new theory of digital media in interpersonal communication. *International Journal of Cultural Studies*, 16(2), pp. 169–187.

Neustaedter, C. and Greenberg, S. (2012). Intimacy in long-distance relationships over video chat. In: *Proceedings of the CHI (2012)*. Austin, TX, pp. 753–762.

Parreñas, R. (2005). Long distance intimacy: Gender and intergenerational relations in transnational families. *Global Networks*, 5(4), pp. 317–336.

Peng, Y. and Wong, O.M.H. (2013). Diversified transnational mothering via telecommunication: Intensive, collaborative, and passive. *Gender & Society*, 27(4), pp. 491–513.

Pham, B. and Lim, S.S. (2016). Empowering interactions, sustaining ties: Vietnamese migrant students' communication with left-behind family and friends. In: S.S. Lim, ed., *Mobile Communication and the Family – Asian Experiences in Technology Domestication*. Dordrecht: Springer, pp. 109–126.

Plüss, C. (2013). Chinese migrants in New York: Explaining inequalities with transnational positions and capital conversions in transnational spaces. *International Sociology*, 28(1), pp. 12–28.

Thomas, M. and Lim, S.S. (2011). On maids and mobile phones: ICT use by female migrant workers in Singapore and its policy implications. In: J.E. Katz, ed., *Mobile Communication: Dimensions of Social Policy*. New Brunswick, NJ: Transaction Publishers, pp. 175–190.

Turkle, S. (2011). *Alone Together: Why We Expect More from Technology and Less from Each Other*. New York: Basic Books.

Uy-Tioco, C. (2007). Overseas Filipino workers and text messaging: Reinventing transnational mothering. *Continuum*, 21(March 2015), pp. 253–265.

Vertovec, S. (2004). Cheap calls: The social glue of migrant transnationalism. *Global Networks*, 4(2), pp. 219–224.

Wajcman, J., Bittman, M. and Brown, J.E. (2008). Families without borders: Mobile phone connectedness and work-home divisions. *Sociology*, 42(4), pp. 635–652.

Waters, J.L. (2006). Geographies of cultural capital: International education, circular migration and family strategies between Canada and Hong Kong. *Transactions of the Institute of British Geographers*, 31(2), pp. 179–192.

Wilding, R. (2006). 'Virtual' intimacies? Families communicating across transnational contexts. *Global Networks*, 6(2), pp. 125–142.

12 Young children and digital media in the intimacy of the home

Perceptions and mediation

Rita Brito and Patrícia Dias

Introduction

The end of the twentieth century and the beginning of the twenty-first century have brought about fast changes in the economy, technology and society that have impacted on families and childhood. Contemporary society is profoundly shaped by the integration of digital technologies into our daily routines (Kucirkova, 2011). Children are being born into homes filled with computers, smartphones and tablets, and they are exposed to and engaging with digital media at an increasingly younger age (Marsh et al., 2005; Plowman, 2014). Even children under 1 year old are exposed to screens through access to tablets, smartphones, consoles and other internet-connected devices (Connell et al., 2015). These children are considered 'digitods' (Leathers et al., 2013), born after the launch of smartphones in the market (2007), and their parents are usually experienced digital users, themselves.

Our research focuses on this understudied age range (Plowman, 2014; Vatavu et al., 2014) and explores the engagement of digitods with digital technologies in the home. We consider two dynamics: a) between the child and the family; and b) between practices and perceptions. Thus, our study considers four research questions that result from the intersection of these axes. First, with respect to individual practice: How do children under the age of 8 engage appropriately with digital media? Second, with respect to parental mediation: How do parents manage their younger children's use of digital media? Third, with respect to shared practice, focusing on intimacy: How are digital media domesticated and what is their impact on family dynamics? And fourth, with respect to awareness of the benefits and risk of digital media: How are digital media perceived by young children and their parents?

Theoretical framework

The mediation of intimacy

Intimacy is a core feature of human interaction, connected to the classical needs identified by Maslow (1943) of belonging to a group and feeling loved by others. The proliferation of personal media since the 1990s and their integration in homes and daily routines has contributed to an increased mediation of intimacy (Robson and Maggie, 1998). Though this process has been studied abundantly, it continues to raise discussion and pose challenges (Vetere et al., 2005).

One of these challenges is methodological, as it is difficult for researchers to glimpse the dynamics of intimate relationships without imposing a bias or relying on self-reported data. Digital media can register use practices and content, and this may threaten privacy and raise ethical concerns; however, it may also provide deeper insight into mediated practices of intimacy (Harper, 2003).

Another challenge is the paradoxical mutually exclusive nature of mediation and intimacy. Turkle (2011) argues that users turn to digital media to fulfil their need for intimacy; thus, they engage in frequent and spontaneous communication. However, this mediated interaction is not as rich as face-to-face communication and it ultimately creates a sense of solitude by not fully fulfilling the needs that drive it. Haythornthwaite and Wellman (2002) and Ling (2008) add that, cumulatively, mediated interaction weakens social skills and social capital. In contrast, researchers working in the field of human-computer interaction (HCI) argue that digital technologies can support and even promote intimacy (Freeman et al., 2016; Vetere et al., 2005). Howard and colleagues (2004) define intimate acts as those entailing physical proximity, self-disclosure, the sharing of emotions, privacy, mutuality and reciprocity, which are often subtle and implied. They further argue that digital media support intimate acts by providing a sense of 'absent presence'.

In the same way that research on pioneering digital practices has focused on teenagers, studies of the mediation of intimacy usually address romantic relationships that are mediated by internet-based platforms (mainly social media and online dating platforms) (e.g. Donn and Sherman, 2002) or mobile devices (e.g. Taylor and Harper, 2003). Our chapter looks into the intimate relationship between parents and young children during a period when physical proximity is essential, in order to discuss the consequences of digital mediation (Hofmeer, 1999).

Technologies in the home

The domestication of digital media (Silverstone and Hirsch, 1992) has been discussed abundantly over the last decades, due to the personal nature and integration of digital media in homes (e.g. Berker et al., 2006; Haddon, 2011). The mobile phone stands out as the device that has become the most widespread, intensely used and fully integrated into daily life in the shortest span of time (Green and Haddon, 2009; Oksman and Rautianen, 2003; Silverstone and Haddon, 1996). Ito and colleagues (2006) highlight the device's personal and private character. Indeed, research has shown that the privacy afforded by the mobile phone was the main motivation for its initial adoption by teenagers (Katz and Aakhus, 2002). Lasen (2002) further stresses that the portability of the device, enabling permanent connectivity, enhances spontaneity and the instant sharing of emotions. Ling (2004) emphasises the mobile phone's symbolic dimension, representing both the self – identity, group belonging and status – and the constant company of others – 'perpetual contact' (Katz and Aakhus, 2002). Vincent (2005) adds that the mobile phone is an affective technology, as it mediates close relationships and its content (photos, messages) has important emotional and symbolic value to its users.

Rakow and Navarro (1993) were the first to report the mobile phone's role in the intimacy of the home, and particularly as a mediator of the relationship between parents and teenage children. They coined the term 'remote parenting' to refer to the importance of this device for working mothers, who can use it to keep in touch with their children during the day, to make sure they get home from school, to coordinate meals and homework and to get a sense of security from knowing their children are permanently reachable. Ling (2004) later described a double nature of this mediated parenting, as some children perceived their mobile phone as a 'teddy bear' – a comforting object that kept them connected to their parents; others characterised it as a 'leash', feeling that it caused them to be excessively controlled by their parents.

Nowadays, homes are even more digital and connected than in the late 1990s, and children have their own personal devices from an early age (Plowman, 2014). Thus, it is necessary to take a deeper look at the domestication of digital devices and how this has impacted and shaped the intimacy of families.

Digital practices of young children

Although scarce, the existing body of academic literature and industry reports (produced in different contexts and using diverse methodologies) agree that young children have access to digital media at a very young age, and are spending an increasing amount of time interacting with such media, at the expense of time spent with others.

Young children usually start by exploring their parents' smartphones and occasionally interacting with computers at home and in school. But their favourite digital device is the tablet (CommonSense Media, 2013; Lauricella et al., 2015; Teuwen et al., 2012). The percentage of young children who own a personal tablet is increasing (Kabali et al., 2015; OFCOM, 2014), and the time that children spend interacting with such devices is also increasing, often at the expense of time spent interacting with other media devices, such as televisions, consoles and computers (ChildWise, 2016). Their favourite activities with the tablet are playing games, watching online videos and listening to online music (CommonSense Media, 2013; Luscombe, 2015). However, these activities are strongly gendered: boys enjoy games related to races, sports, adventure and fighting, while girls like fantasy, story-making, dressing up and caring for pets; children's choice of apps tends to reflect gendered fictional universes of superheroes and princesses (Chaudron et al., 2015; OFCOM, 2014).

The important role played by parents in the domestication of digital media

Both academic literature and industry reports show that young children have facilitated access to digital technologies at home, and that parents are the main mediators of their digital experiences (Bittman et al., 2011; Livingstone, 2007; Kucirkova and Sakr, 2015), as they learn directly from their parents' help and support or by observation and imitation (Genc, 2014; Nathanson et al., 2002; Plowman et al., 2008). As a consequence, parental modelling is critical for promoting safe use of these devices (Lauricella et al., 2015; Livingstone and Bober, 2004).

The concept of parental mediation, which originally referred to the television, describes the role played by parents as mediators of young children's engagement with communication media, shaping their children's practices and perceptions. Livingstone (2007) applies this term to digital media, arguing that parents often draw on the authority afforded by family roles to negotiate media-related rules and practices. Proposals made by several authors on the role of parents in this context (e.g. Barkin et al., 2006; Eastin et al., 2006; Livingstone and Helsper, 2008; Valcke et al., 2010; Valkenburg et al., 1999) can be synthesised into two categories: a) parents who tend to 'support' and 'instruct' their children's digital practices, thus teaching them and helping them to overcome difficulties; or b) parents who tend to 'control' and 'restrict' their children's digital practices. Instructive mediation involves shared experiences and teaching, while restrictive mediation is based on the use of filters and other software and monitoring tools, rules that restrict online activity and active monitoring of children's digital practices (for example, checking online history and reading emails).

Parents tend to be generally permissive with the use of mobile devices in the home (Genc, 2014; Plowman et al., 2008), but there are some rules that are common to many homes, such as those that only allow mobile use after homework is finished and those that limit the extent or time (e.g. only just before bedtime) of mobile use. In fact, it is more common for parents to control the devices that children are allowed to use and the time at which they are allowed to use them than the content to which children are exposed (Duimel and de Haan, 2007; Wang et al., 2005).

Among the variables that shape parental mediation of digital media, parents' perceptions stand out (Kirwil, 2009; Valcke et al., 2010). Research shows that parents who are frequent and competent digital users have more positive attitudes towards technologies, are more comfortable co-using them with their children and teaching their children how to use them and create more opportunities for digital engagement that is shared by the whole family (Connell et al., 2015; Hollingsworth et al., 2011).

Parental mediation style, in turn, affects children's practices and perceptions. Valcke and colleagues (2010) report that children of permissive parents are more tech-savvy and active online, while children of authoritarian parents show lower levels of digital literacy. Also, mediation style may determine the degree to which digital media is harnessed for learning (Barron et al., 2009; Bittman et al., 2011; Eynon and Malmberg, 2012; Livingstone et al., 2015). Padilla-Walker and colleagues (2012) suggest that families that spend more time playing console games together have enhanced affective connectivity.

Empirical research

Methodology

This chapter presents national results of a cross-national study coordinated by the Joint Research Center of the European Commission, 'Young Children (0–8) and Digital Technologies', which followed a qualitative approach. In 2015, it included 180 qualitative interviews with families with children aged 6 or 7 years old.

In this chapter, we present and discuss results relating to the digital practices of young children in the home, parental mediation style and family dynamics and intimacy. Our sample includes ten families with children aged 6 or 7 years old, who were interviewed and participated in activities as part of the study. The interviews consisted of three parts – an icebreaker activity with the whole family (filling in a schedule of daily routines with stickers) and simultaneous but separate interviews with the parents and children. The researchers also used multiple activities to encourage the participation of the children: a) a card game about favourite activities, wherein the children were asked to classify online and offline activities, as presented on cards, with 'happy', 'indifferent' and 'unhappy' smiley faces; b) a grid for identifying apps, wherein children were asked to point to the apps they used and knew from a visual list; and c) a digital tour given by the children, in which they were asked to show the researchers their favourite devices, where these devices were used and their favourite activities, enabling the researchers to observe whether the setting of their activities was private or shared and provided greater insight into their interests, preferences and digital skills. The researchers took notes and photos of their observations.

A purposive sample was selected and varied on gender, family type, income and use of digital technologies (Lindlof and Taylor, 2002). Data was coded in a database according to a system of thematic categories and keywords, following the qualitative comparative analysis (QCA) method (Boyatzis, 1998; Braun and Clarke, 2006), then analysed and discussed. All of the families and their members were coded in order to ensure anonymity and confidentiality. The coding for each family member started with the initials of the country (in our case PT – Portugal) and a number from 1 to 25. This was followed by a letter to indicate family role ('f' for father, 'm' for mother, 'g' for girl, 'b' for boy) and the age.

Our findings must be considered in the context of the limitations of our study. First, we relied mostly on self-reported data, although we triangulated the information by comparing the discourses of parents and children with our observations. Second, we opted for a small sample, which was designed to afford diverse portrayals and narratives of the domestication of digital media and the mediation of intimacy. As a consequence, our findings are not representative and cannot be generalised. Finally, the exploratory nature of our study only allowed us to present a snapshot of this phenomenon.

Findings and discussion

Digital practices of young children

In this section, we briefly describe the main digital practices of the children in our sample. They enjoy using digital media, and their favourite device is the tablet, which is replacing the television and the console to some extent (cf. Kabali et al., 2015; Lauricella et al., 2015). Children's main activities on these devices are playing games and watching videos on YouTube, and their choices are extensions of their offline preferences, as they tend to choose games related to their favourite activities/sports and fictional characters/toys (cf. CommonSense Media, 2013; OFCOM, 2014). Their choices are also strongly gendered: boys like adventure and fighting games with superheroes, while girls like dress-up, nails and makeup, princesses and virtual pets.

Children know more about digital media than their parents think (cf. Kucirkova and Sakr, 2015; Luscombe, 2015; Plowman et al., 2008). Parents often use the tablet as a 'babysitter' or 'SOS' – something that will keep their children entertained when they are busy (cf. Dias and Brito, 2016; Kabali et al., 2015) – and leave their children to explore, experiment and learn by themselves.

Parental mediation style and perceptions about digital media

Our qualitative comparative analysis of the parental mediation styles in this sample, which follows the model of Valcke and colleagues (2010), shows that authoritative mediation is most common. This parenting style is characterised by low involvement (e.g. parents justifying the need to keep children entertained while they do chores or work from home) and high control. Some rules are common to most homes. Parents claim that these rules are the result of negotiation, but children often perceive them as imposed.

I: When do you play with the tablet?
PT6b: During the weekend.
I: During the week you are not allowed?
PT6b: No.
I: Why?
PT6b: Because they are school nights.
I: How do you feel about this rule of just playing in the weekend? Do you agree?
PT6b: Yes, because on the other days I have school and my mother cannot let me play because my father is still at work.
I: Would you like to play during the week if you could?
PT6b: Yes [...] Because if you play with the tablet it is not that aggressive and if you imitate it you have to be more aggressive.

Our findings reiterate a strong relationship between parents' perceptions towards digital media and the mediation style they adopt (cf. Kirwil, 2009; Valcke et al., 2010). Furthermore, parents often act based on misperceptions. For instance, they regard the tablet as a toy and overlook its pedagogical potential; they undervalue their children's digital skills and believe that their digital practices are more limited than they actually are; and they believe that their children are not exposed to dangers at an early age, when they in fact are. As a consequence, parents tend to monitor and set rules on the time spent playing and only occasionally monitor the game selection and online content that is watched. Parents are more concerned with the consequences of excessive use (e.g. stress, frustration, hyperactivity, fatigue, lack of social contact and lack of outdoor activities) than with risks associated with content (e.g. violent content, advertisements and sexual content).

Furthermore, parents do not promote learning activities or co-use digital devices for pedagogical purposes (cf. Nikken and Jansz, 2014); only a few parents report high involvement and seek to make the most of the tablet's pedagogical potential. For instance, PT9m likes to be present when her daughter plays with the tablet, so that she can help her and influence her in choosing more pedagogical apps.

PT9m: I prefer if she plays with me.
I: For instance, she watches videos on YouTube, or she doesn't do that yet?
PT9m: She knows there are videos ... [laughter]. But I don't allow her to be very autonomous with the videos because I want to be

> with her, so that she doesn't watch anything that comes on […] But she knows we can go online and search for movies or short videos. However, she knows she must always do it with me, she is not allowed to do it alone.

Most parents believe that, in light of online dangers, talking to their children and monitoring their online activity are more effective than prohibiting use of the internet, as they fear that forbidding the internet will make their children even more curious about it. For example, when PT10m noticed that her daughter had installed violent games, she explained to her that those games were inappropriate for her age, and the child stopped playing them. However, most parents have not yet felt the need to have similar conversations with their children. PT4g9 had asked her mother to create a Facebook profile, but her mother did not allow this and explained to her daughter that she could never know who was behind each profile 'asking for friendship'.

Family dynamics and intimacy

Digital media are used in the intimacy of the home, but they are not the *locus* of an intimate space shared by family members, mostly because young children do not use their personal digital devices (mostly tablets, as they do not yet own smartphones) for maintaining 'perpetual contact' (Katz and Aakhus, 2002) with other family members (cf. Ling, 2004; Rakow and Navarro, 1993). In the sample, there is one exception to this: PT5b7, who uses his tablet to communicate with his father via an instant messaging app, while living with his mother, as his parents are divorced and have shared custody.

We found that two main dimensions of the tablet are pivotal for family intimacy. On the one hand, the tablet often triggers intimate shared moments of co-use. On the other hand, it offers young children an intimate space, playing a similar role for them as the mobile phone plays for teenagers (cf. Lasen, 2002; Ling, 2004).

With respect to intimate family moments around digital media, the most common shared activity is game playing. Mothers often play dance and karaoke games in consoles and watch YouTube videos about baking and makeup with their daughters, while fathers are their sons' companions in action and adventure games. Furthermore, PlayStation is seen as the most difficult device to use, so parents often help children use it by playing with them. Most parents enjoy these activities and complain about not having more free time to dedicate to them.

> *I:* Do you usually play with them?
>
> *PT4m:* Yes! Me and also my husband. They call him: '[PT4f], come help me pass this level because I can't …' And in a bit we are all in the room playing PlayStation.

Although these activities promote the co-use of technologies, sometimes parents say they don't have as much time as they wish to dedicate to them.

I: Do you like playing games with him?
PT2f: I do, the problem is that I don't have a lot of time.

Schoolwork and sporadic searches for answers to questions also trigger the co-use of technology. PT2m conducts research with PT2b7 to answer questions about homework, and PT2f also helps her child conduct online research, following the suggestions of the school's activity book. Furthermore, they also use the web for casual research, when PT2b7 has questions.

PT2f: The other day we were searching with him because of his homework. The book itself said what the homework was and it was searching online. It was about animals or so.

Another common practice, particularly between mothers and daughters, is watching videos or listening to music on YouTube together. Both PT3m and PT9m report watching video clips and tutorials (relating to makeup, baking, etc.) with their daughters, with this activity sometimes replacing the traditional bedtime story. PT6m asks PT6b7 to search for music from a specific singer and they listen to the resulting tracks together. A second common activity is searching for and installing games on mobile devices. Parents help children who are not yet able to write and are learning how to read.

PT1m: We install, see if it's nice or not … go to Playstore …
I: Who goes to Playstore? You or him?
PT1m: I do.
I: He doesn't know who to access??
PT1m: No, no. I don't think so! We see the pictures and if we consider it appealing, we choose and download it.

Because of its portability, the tablet sometimes enables a shared sense of intimacy, even if parents and children do not engage in the same activity. For instance, PT6m tells us that on weekend mornings, when her son PT6b6 wakes up, she allows him to play with her smartphone in her bed while she sleeps in a bit longer. PT1b7 explains why he likes his tablet so much: it is portable and he can use it around the house instead of just playing in his room; he carries it to wherever his parents are, as he likes to be near them, even if they do not play with him. Instead of perceiving this as 'absent presence' (Ling, 2004) or being 'together alone' (Turkle, 2011), parents and children describe these moments as times of shared intimacy and relaxation, simply because the portable device facilitates physical proximity (cf. Howard and Vetere, 2004). PT10m also tells us that her daughter PT10g6 sometimes watches videos on YouTube in the living room while she cooks dinner in the nearby kitchen; they interact about which song to choose next, and sing and dance together. This practice reveals reciprocity and emotional sharing, which are indicators of intimacy (cf. Howard and Vetere, 2004).

Children are left alone with their tablet for quite some time. Thus, the device is more often a 'companion' to the children than a trigger of family interaction. Parents justify this by claiming to not have time to use the tablet with their children due to domestic chores or work.

> *PT8m:* I can't be always on top of everything, or I wouldn't do anything else.

PT9g7 even describes the tablet as her 'best friend', along the lines of Ling's (2004) 'teddy bear' metaphor and Vincent's (2005) conceptualisation of the mobile phone as an affective technology. In fact, the tablet is often the main *locus* of imaginary worlds and playfulness, which sometimes blend with physical space and toys. Children enjoy being able to manage their own device and decide which games to install and uninstall.

Concluding remarks

In this study, we concluded that the digital practices of children and parents are deeply interconnected. Our findings corroborated other studies that have found that the strongest factor in shaping mediation styles is parental perception of digital media (cf. Kirwil, 2009), adding that misperceptions are equally influential. One example of a parental perception is the view of digital devices – in particular tablets – as sources of entertainment or toys; in this view, educational activities are largely underexplored (cf. Fallon, 2013). Another example is the belief that young children are not exposed to online dangers, as their digital skills are insipid and they do not engage in social media. Naively, parents are more concerned about the negative effects of overuse, instead of content, and provide only scarce and discreet supervision.

Regarding intimacy, we concluded that digital media do not support mediated intimacy across physical distance in young children as they do in older children (cf. Freeman et al., 2016), but the media may trigger intimate moments of co-use and reinforce features of intimacy, such as emotion sharing and reciprocity. In addition, the tablet is becoming a personal, private and portable device for young children, as the mobile phone became for teenagers (cf. Katz and Aakhus, 2002; Ling, 2004; Vincent, 2005), fostering a space of personal intimacy, exploration and expression, freedom and entertainment that is now being offered to children from a very young age.

References

Aunola, K., Stattin, H.K. and Nurmi, J. (2000). Parenting styles and adolescents' achievement strategies. *Journal of Adolescence*, 23, pp. 205–222.

Barkin, S., Richardson, I. and Klinepeter, S. (2006). Parental media mediation styles for children aged 2 to 11 years. *Pediatrics Adolescents*, 160, pp. 395–401.

Berker, T., Hartmann, M., Punie, Y. and Ward, K. (2006). *Domestication of Media and Technology*. London: Open University Press.

Bittman, M., Rutherford, L., Brown, J. and Unsworth, L. (2011). Digital natives? New and old media and children's outcomes. *Australian Journal of Education*, 55(2), pp. 161–175.

Boyatzis, R.E. (1998). *Transforming Qualitative Information: Thematic Analysis and Code Development*. Thousand Oaks, London and New Delhi: SAGE.

Braun, V. and Clarke, V. (2006) Using thematic analysis in psychology. *Qualitative Research in Psychology*, 3(2), pp. 77–101. ISSN 1478-0887.

Chaudron, S., et al. (2015). *Young Children (0–8) and Digital Technology: A Qualitative Exploratory Study Across Seven Countries*. JRC 93239/EUR 27052.

Childwise (2016). The monitor report. Children's media use and purchasing. Retrieved from http://goo.gl/Vdb3b9.

CommonSense Media (2013). Zero to eight: Children's media use in America 2013. Retrieved from https://goo.gl/DbZTXw.

Connell, S.L., Lauricella, A.R. and Wartella, E. (2015). Parental co-use of media technology with their young children in the USA. *Journal of Children and Media*, 9(1), pp. 5–21. doi: 10.1080/17482798.2015.997440.

Dias, P. and Brito, R. (2016). *Crianças (0 a 8 Anos) e Tecnologias Digitais*. Lisboa: Centro de Estudos em Comunicação e Cultura, Universidade Católica Portuguesa. Retrieved from http://goo.gl/obFv4L.

Donn, J.E. and Sherman, R.C. (2002). Attitudes and practices regarding the formation of romantic relationships on the Internet. *CyberPsychology & Behavior*, 5(2), pp. 107–123.

Duimel, M. and de Haan, J. (2007). *Nieuwe links in het gezin*. [New links in the family]. Retrieved from www.scp.nl/publicaties/boeken/9789037702873/Nieuwe_links_in_het_gezin.pdf (17 October 2016).

Eastin, M.S., Greenberg, B.S. and Hofschire, L. (2006). Parenting the Internet. *Journal of Communication*, 56, pp. 486–504.

Eynon, R. and Malmberg, L.-E. (2012). Understanding the online information-seeking behaviours of young people: the role of networks of support. *Journal of Computer Assisted Learning*, 28, 514–529. doi:10.1111/j.1365-2729.2011.00460.x

Fallon, G. (2013). Young students using iPads: App design and content influences on their learning pathways. *Computers & Education*, 68, 505–521.

Freeman, G., Bardzell, J. and Bardzell, S. (2016). Revisiting computer-mediated intimacy: In-game marriage and dyadic gameplay in audition. In: *Proceedings of CHI – Conference on Human Factors in Computing Systems 2016 (May 7th to 12th)*. Santa Clara, CA, pp. 4325–4336.

Genc, Z. (2014). Parents' perceptions about the mobile technology use of preschool aged children. *Procedia – Social and Behavioral Sciences*, 146, pp. 55–60.

Green, N. and Haddon, L. (2009) *Mobile Communications. An Introduction to New Media*. Oxford: Berg Publishers.

Goh, W., Bay, S. and Chen, V. (2015). Young school children's use of digital devices and parental rules. *Telematics & Informatics*, 32, pp. 787–795.

Haddon, L. (2011). Domestication analysis, objects of study, and the centrality of technologies in everyday life. *Canadian Journal of Communication*, 36(2), pp. 311–323.

Harper, R. (ed.) (2003). *Inside the Smart Home*. London: Springer.

Haythornthwaite, C. and Wellman, B. (2002). *The Internet in Everyday Life*. London: Wiley-Blackwell.

Hofmeer, K. (1999). The digital hug: Keeping families together. *Interactions Special Issue*, 6(6).

Hollingsworth, S., Mansaray, A., Allen, K. and Rose, A. (2011). Parents' perspectives on technology and children's learning in the home: Social class and the role of the habitus. *Journal of Computer Assisted Learning*, 27, pp. 347–360.

Hourcade, J.P., Mascher, S.L., Wu, D. and Pantoja, L. (2015). Look, my baby is using an iPad! An analysis of YouTube videos of infants and toddlers using tablets. In: *Proceedings of the 33rd Annual ACM Conference on Human Factors in Computing Systems (CHI '15)*. New York: ACM, pp. 1915–1924.

Howard, S. and Vetere, F. (2004). Mediated intimacy: Digital kisses and cut and paste hugs. Presentation at the 18th British HCI Group Annual Conference, HCI 2004: Design for Life. London.

Ito, M., Okabe, D. and Matsuda, M. (2005). *Personal, Portable, Pedestrian: Mobile Phones in Japanese Life*. Cambridge: MIT Press.

Kabali, H., Irigoyen, M., Nunez-Davis, R., Budacki, J., Mohanty, S., Leister, K. and Bonner Jr., R. (2015). Exposure and use of mobile media devices by young children. *Pediatrics*, 136(6), pp. 1044–1050.

Katz, J. and Aakhus, M. (2002). *Perpetual Contact: Mobile Communication, Private Talk, Public Performance*. Cambridge: Cambridge University Press.

Kirwil, L. (2009) Parental mediation of children's Internet use in different European countries. *Journal of Children and Media*, 3(4), pp. 394–409. doi: 10.1080/17482790903233440.

Kucirkova, N. (2011). Digitalised early years – Where next? *New Voices*, 24(12), pp. 938–940.

Kucirkova, N. and Sakr, M. (2015). Child-father creative text-making at home with crayons, iPad collage and PC. *Thinking Skills and Creativity*, 17, pp. 59–63.

Lasen, S. (2002). The social shaping of fixed and mobile networks: A historical comparison. Retrieved from www.kiwanja.net/database/document/report_mobile_history.pdf.

Lauricella, A., Wartella, E. and Rideout, V. (2015). Young children's screen time: The complex role of parent and child factors. *Journal of Applied Developmental Psychology*, 36, pp. 11–17.

Leathers, H., Summers, S. and Desollar, A. (2013). *Toddlers on Technology: A Parents' Guide*. Chicago, IL: AuthorHouse.

Lindlof, T. and Taylor, B. (2002). *Qualitative Communication Research Methods*. London: SAGE.

Ling, R. (2004). *The Mobile Connection: The Cell Phone's Impact on Society*. EUA: Morgan Kauffman.

Ling, R. (2008). *New Tech, New Ties: How Mobile Communication is Reshaping Social Cohesion*. Cambridge, MA: MIT Press.

Livingstone, S. (2007). Strategies of parental regulation in the media-rich home. *Computers in Human Behavior*, 23, pp. 920–941.

Livingstone, S. and Bober, M. (2004). UK children go online: Surveying the experiences of young people and their parents. Retrieved from www.york.ac.uk/res/e-society/projects/1/UKCGOsurveyreport.pdf (19 March 2009).
Livingstone, S. and Helsper, E.J. (2008). Parental mediation of children Internet use. *Journal of Broadcast & Electronic Media*, 52, pp. 581–599.
Livingstone, S., Cagiltay, K. and Olafsson, K. (2015). EU Kids Online II dataset: A cross-national study of children's use of the Internet and its associated opportunities and risks. *British Journal of Educational Technology*, 46(5), pp. 988–992.
Luscombe, B. (2015). YouTube's view master. *Time*, 186(9/10), pp. 7–14.
Marsh, J., Brooks, G., Hughes, J., Ritchie, L., Roberts, S. and Wright, K. (2005). Digital beginnings: Young children's use of popular culture, media and new technologies. The University of Sheffield. Retrieved from www.digitalbeginnings.shef.ac.uk/DigitalBeginningsReport.pdf.
Maslow, A.H. (1943). A theory of human motivation. *Psychological Review*, 50(4), pp. 370–396.
Nathanson, A.I., Eveland, W.P., Park, H.S. and Paul, B. (2002). Perceived media influence and efficacy as predictors of caregivers' protective behaviors. *Journal of Broadcasting & Electronic Media*, 46, pp. 385–410.
Nikken, P. and Jansz, J. (2013). Developing scales to measure parental mediation of young children's Internet use. *Learning, Media and Technology*, 39, pp. 250–266. doi: 10.1080/17439884.2013.782038.
Nikken, P. and Jansz, J. (2014). Developing scales to measure parental mediation of young children's Internet use. *Learning, Media and Technology*, 39(2), pp. 250–266.
OFCOM (2014). Children and parents: Media use and attitudes report. Retrieved from http://goo.gl/7jx2BV.
Oksman, V. and Rautianen, P. (2003). 'Perhaps it is a body part': How the mobile phone became an organic part of the everyday lives of Finnish children and teenagers. In: J. Katz, ed., *Machines that Become Us: The Social Context of Personal Communication Technology*. Piscataway, NJ: Transaction Publishers, pp. 161–170.
Padilla-Walker, L.M. (2006). 'Peers I can monitor, it's media that really worries me!': Parental cognitions as predictors of proactive parental strategy choice. *Journal of Adolescent Research*, 21(1), pp. 56–82. Retrieved from http://dx.doi.org/10.1177/0743558405282723.
Padilla-Walker, L.M., Coyne, S.M. and Fraser, A.M. (2012). Getting a high-speed family connection: Associations between family media use and family connection. *Family Relations*, 61, pp. 426–440.
Palaiologou, I. (2014, print publication 2016). Children under five and digital technologies: Implication for early years pedagogy. *The European Early Childhood Research Journal*, 24(1). doi:10.1080/1350293X.2014.929876.
Plowman, L. (2014). Researching young children's everyday uses of technology in the family home. *Interacting with Computers*, 27(1), pp. 36–46.
Plowman, L., McPake, J. and Stephen, C. (2008). Just picking it up? Young children learning with technology at home. *Cambridge Journal of Education*, 38, pp. 303–319.
Rakow, L. and Navarro, V. (1993). Remote mothering and the parallel shift: Women meet the cellular telephone. *Critical Studies in Mass Communication*, 20(3), pp. 144–157.

Robson, D. and Maggie, R. (1998). Intimacy and computer communication. *British Journal of Guidance and Counselling*, 26(1), pp. 33–42.

Silverstone, R. and Haddon, L. (1996). Design and the domestication of information and communication technologies: Technical change and everyday life. In: R. Silverstone and R. Mansell, eds., *Communication by Design: The Politics of Information and Communication Technologies*. Oxford: Oxford University Press, pp. 44–74.

Silverstone, R. and Hirsch, E. (eds.) (1992). *Consuming Technologies: Media and Information in Domestic Spaces*. London and New York: Routledge.

Strauss, A. and Corbin, J. (1998). *Basics of Qualitative Research: Techniques and Procedures for Developing Grounded Theory* (2nd ed.). Thousand Oaks, CA: SAGE.

Taylor, A. and Harper, R. (2003). The gift of the gab?: A design oriented sociology of young people's use of mobiles. *Computer Supported Cooperative Work*, 12(3), pp. 267–296.

Teuwen, J., De Groff, D. and Zaman, B. (2012). Flemish preschoolers online: A mixed-method approach to explore online use, preferences and the role of parents and siblings. Presentation at Etmaal van de Communicatiewetenschap, Leuven, Belgium. Retrieved from https://lirias.kuleuven.be/bitstream/123456789/350708/1/Flemish+Preschoolers+Online_English+version.pdf.

Turkle, S. (2011). *Alone Together: Why We Expect More from Technology and Less from Each Other*. London: Basic Books.

Valcke, M., Bonte, S., Wener, B. and Rots, I. (2010). Internet parenting styles and the impact on Internet use of primary school children. *Computers & Education*, 55(2), pp. 454–464.

Valkenburg, P.M., Krcmar, M., Peeters, A.L. and Marseille, N.M. (1999). Developing a scale to assess three different styles of television mediation: 'Instructive mediation', 'restrictive mediation', and 'social coviewing'. *Journal of Broadcasting & Electronic Media*, 43, pp. 52–66.

Vatavu, R.D., Cramariuc, G. and Schipor, D.M. (2014). Touch interaction for children aged 3 to 6 years: Experimental findings and relationship to motor skills. *International Journal of Human-Computer Studies*, 74, pp. 54–76.

Vetere, F., Gibbs, M.R., Kjeldskov, J., Howard, S., Mueller, F., Pedell, S., Mecoles, K. and Bunyan, M. (2005). Mediating intimacy: Designing technologies to support strong-tie relationships. In: *Proceedings of CHI – Conference on Human Factors in Computing Systems 2005, April 2nd to 7th*. Portland, OR.

Vincent, J. (2005). Emotional attachment to mobile phones: An extraordinary relationship. In: L. Hamill and A. Lasen, eds., *Mobile World: Past, Present and Future*. London: Springer.

Walrave, M., Lenaerts, S. and De Moor, S. (2008). Cyberteens @ Risk: Tieners verknocht aan Internet, maar ook waakzaam voor risico's [Cyberteens @ risk: Teenagers addicted to the Internet but vigilant as to Internet risks]. Retrieved from www.e-privacy.be/SID-TIRO-PERSMAP-samenvatting-survey-UA-OSC120208.pdf (2 March 2009).

Wang, R., Bianchi, S.M. and Raley, S.B. (2005). Teenagers' Internet use and family rules: A research note. *Journal of Marriage and Family*, 67, pp. 1249–1258. doi:10.1111/j.1741-3737. 2005.00214.x.

Zevenbergen, R. and Logan, H. (2008) Computer use in preschool children: Rethinking practice as digital natives come to preschool. *Australian Journal of Early Childhood*, 33, pp. 2–44.

13 Connecting with the dead

Vernacular practices of mourning through photo-sharing on Facebook

Tobias Raun

Introduction

My mother died of lung cancer on a Tuesday morning at a hospice, leaving me traumatised from having experienced what felt like a short period of illness and a long death struggle. On my train ride home to Copenhagen the very same day, I posted on Facebook that I would never be the same, having seen someone I loved die right in front of my eyes. My urge to make that post was acute and overwhelming, and it started a line of posts in the days, weeks and months that followed. One of these included a more recent (17 September 2015) sharing of a photograph of her grave site: a triangular composition of the grave stone with her engraved name and my wife holding our then 1-month-old child, with the caption: 'Life and death are peculiar dimensions'.

Figure 13.1 Photograph of mother's grave site

I clearly remember taking that photograph. My wife knelt in order to make it easier for me to include her, our son and the engraved stone in the same image. It was our first time at the cemetery after the birth of our son, and I felt the urge to take a picture of them together: the people I loved. I remember the happiness I felt about fathering a child being followed by a melancholic sadness that my mother would never meet/see my child and would never build a relationship with him. Furthermore, my mother would not be there as a historical witness to my rite of passage – my transformation from being a child, myself, to having a child of my own. I felt that important knowledge of my own historical self died with her, making this information inaccessible and forever lost. Taking this picture was a way of joining together the family I had been born into and the one I had chosen and created for myself. I also wanted to instantiate a meeting and create a bond between my mother and my son, even though it had to take place symbolically, with the engraved stone (and the knowledge of her ashes beneath it) as a stand-in for her living, breathing, bodily self.

Sensitive digital ethnography – a methodological approach

My own experience of loss – and not least my immediate urge to post about it on Facebook – prompted a research project about new and mediatised practices of memory and mourning through social media, exploring the use of Facebook by a group of Danes to cope with the death of a close relative. This chapter zooms in on the practice of photographing the grave site and circulating it on Facebook – a practice that many of the Facebook users in this study engaged very actively in, and one that, in general, seems quite common on Facebook. I explore the practice of taking and sharing images of the grave site by investigating the visual expression of the images shared, the incentives for sharing them and the cultural meaning and significance that can be attached to them. My investigation takes its point of departure in the juxtaposition of the posted images with the Facebook users' motives, thoughts, feelings and experiences, as communicated to me in semi-structured interviews.

The users were recruited via a publicly visible request post on my wall, encouraging my vast network of Facebook friends to share the post on their own profile and in relevant groups. I interviewed eight Facebook users (none of whom I knew beforehand) in the age range of early 20s to mid-50s, from lower- to upper-middle-class. There was a clear predominance of women in the sample, but a diversity of lost kin (child, sibling, parent) and time of death (from one to ten years ago). I anonymised the interviewees by giving them different names (all chosen from among the 20 most common names in Denmark and somehow relating to their actual names) and not stating their exact profession or workplace.

The interviews were centred on the mourners' general use of digital media (in particular, their use of Facebook), their grieving over the lost relative, their Facebook posts relating to the lost relative and the responses these received and their experienced effects of using Facebook to share information on/feelings about their deceased relative. The interviews lasted approximately two hours and took place at a location chosen by the mourners, themselves; typically, this was their home, where they could talk extensively about their practice without being disturbed. The users were encouraged to bring or have a computer/tablet ready that they were familiar with using. This enabled the interviews to be conducted as media go-alongs, during which we looked at their Facebook profile, posts and online interactions together, while talking. The media go-along method allows the researcher and participant to navigate and talk about media while sharing sensorial access (Jørgensen, 2016, p. 39). By actively engaging with Facebook during the interview, the users' memory of posts – not least the motivations, feelings and experiences attached to these – were (re)activated. Likewise, being online together encouraged a dialogue about the significance and importance of specific posts and interactions on Facebook that might not have come up in an interview without the media at hand, and certainly not by simply mapping/analysing the posts.

I place this study within the interdisciplinary field of digital ethnography, wherein attention is paid to the status and meaning of digital media and technologies as part of, and hence inseparable from, the everyday. Of prime concern is how 'the digital has become part of the material, sensory and social worlds we inhabit' (Pink et al., 2015, p. 7). In line with autoethnography, I include my own online mourning practice as empirical material and actively use my own experience of loss as a prerequisite for building trust and enriching the dialogue with the interviewed Facebook users. In this chapter, I use and propose autoethnography as an analytical mode or sensitising device, affectively inscribed in and self- and meta-theoretically reflexive about what is at stake both individually and culturally when grave site images are shared. The overall purpose of autoethnography is, as noted by Stacy Holman Jones, Tony Adams and Carolyn Ellis, 'to show how the aspects of experience illuminate more general cultural phenomena' (2013, p. 23). One of my greatest inspirations in this regard is Roland Barthes – first and foremost his writing on (analog) photography in *Camera Lucida: Reflections on Photography*, which is a very personal account of the ontology and effect of photography following the death of his mother.

I also place this study within the growing field of online mourning, wherein pre-existing studies have often focused on online peer grief support groups, memorialised profiles and R.I.P. sites (see, e.g., Brubaker et al., 2013; Christensen and Sandvik, 2015; Church, 2013; DeGroot, 2014; Frost, 2014; Kern et al., 2013; Klastrup, 2014; Marwick and Ellison, 2012; Segerstad and Kasperowski, 2015). Content analysis of textual posts and interactions tend to dominate this field of study, and interviews with online media users are scarce (for exceptions, see Brubaker et al., 2013, Segerstad and Kasperowski, 2015). As Amanda Lagerkvist points out, there is 'scant understanding in media studies of what these new cultures of memory mean for people existentially' or their 'implication in people's lives' (Lagerkvist, 2013, p. 10). This chapter draws on – but also expands – the existing line of research by turning to this existential dimension and, not least, by attending to the online visual culture of mourning, which has not yet been subject to extensive study.

Sharing photographs of the grave site on Facebook

Five of the eight people in this study share images of their lost relative's grave site (Helle[1], Camilla[2], Christian[3], Birgitte[4] and Anna[5]), but Helle and Camilla, especially, frequently share such images. The shared images can tentatively be divided into three subcategories (although these may overlap):

1) The grave site as depicted as a small garden of its own, often with visible signs of commemoration. Such pictures are either taken at a longer distance – more or less gathering the site in its totality, making the grave site appear as a small garden of its own – or they are taken at a closer distance, focusing equally on the engraved stone and the objects that have been placed there in commemoration. The engraved stone and/or the surrounding vegetation (through the different seasons) are often emphasised. The images are often taken during spring or summer, with flowers or herbaceous perennials emerging/blooming and trees turning green. They are also often taken during wintertime, usually around Christmas, featuring snow and cut flowers, candles or other things placed at the grave site in seasonal commemoration.

2) The grave site as depicted through abstract beauty and the transformation of nature. Such images are close-ups of flowers or other kinds of vegetation that grow on the grave site, taken either in the early spring (when the first flowers appear) or in summer (when the trees/flowers are in bloom). Examples of this include Christian's photographs of snowdrops and hyacinths emerging, with the accompanying text: 'More spring [smiley emoticon]' (5 March 2014); and Helle's close-ups of crocuses (26 March 2009) and blooming roses (5 July 2014), the latter of which was also her cover photograph at one point. An uninformed/inattentive viewer might not make the immediate connection between the vegetation and the grave site, and might perceive the flowers only as signs of spring or beautiful nature and not see their additional metaphorical meaning, pointing to life and hope in the midst of grief and despair. Adding multiple symbolic layers to the meaning of the vegetation and thereby preventing one's posts from being read too explicitly allows the Facebook users to mourn in/through social media in an implicit, abstract way.

3) The grave site as depicted as a site of (re)union. Such photographs are taken at a longer distance and include living significant others placed at or next to the grave site. An example of this style is the photograph I shared of my wife and child in front of my mother's grave stone. Anna and Helene

also share similar photographs, but their images appear more as snapshots of everyday life lived in close proximity to the cemetery. Nonetheless, their photographs suggest another layer of meaning, manifesting a co-existence between dead and living relatives.

The grave site as a green garden

All of these subcategories tie into a particular construction and arrangement of death. As Anne Louise Sommer points out, the Danish cemetery of today appears as 'a garden of the dead'. This type of cemetery is a modern Western invention from around the nineteenth century, when the crowded and contagious cemeteries in the middle of the cities – which were primarily founded in the Middle Ages – were replaced by large cemeteries on the outskirts of the city in an attempt to domesticate death and keep it separate from everyday life (Sommer, 2003, pp. 14, 87). As industrialisation and secularisation increased, cemeteries turned more and more green, becoming aestheticised with inspiration from garden art, wherein 'death and the garden of the dead is disguised as a welcoming park, where the decay is staged and beautified, and nature takes over the reconciliating role of religion' (ibid., p. 15, my translation from Danish). The beauty of nature was the red thread, and infinity became tangible – materialised as a man-made paradise instead of a diffuse, transcendent place (Sommer, 2003, p. 94).

The reconciliation of death through the greenness of the cemetery is present in the photographs in both the first and second subcategory and the interviews with the Facebook mourners. In the interview with Christian, as well as in his posts, he consistently refers to his deceased daughter's grave site as 'a garden'/'the garden of [name of his daughter]'. Christian does not share photographs frequently, as he is more private about visual images than about expressing personal and emotional things in text, and he also has concerns about the (mis)use and circulation of shared images. He has only uploaded one photograph of his deceased daughter, but he has shared images of her grave site as a small garden of its own (cf. the first subcategory).

When we discuss why he shares images from her grave site, he says:

> I guess it is because of the ambiance ... well ... a desire to show that something new has happened, or that there is now flowers or a candle lit [...] well, uploading photographs from the past ... well, that is the past. Because basically I would want [her] to live on, so that is why the grave site or [name of daughter]'s garden with some snowdrops popping up ... well, there is life in that, whereas photographs from the past – well, they are photographs from the past.
>
> (Interview with Christian)[6]

As Christian notes, there is more 'life' in new images of his daughter's grave site – especially when these images show 'snowdrops popping up' – than in older photographs of her. Somehow, she is more present and alive to him in the small signs of living, growing nature than in actual photographs of her, which to him, exclusively connote the 'past'. According to Roland Barthes, one of the most noteworthy signifiers of (analog) photography is its indexical relation to the subject as a 'certificate of presence' (Barthes, 1981, p. 87), which, in effect, simultaneously immortalises and mortalises its subject. However, Barthes emphasises death as an essential part of the ontology of (analog) photography, especially in the depiction of people:

> In front of the photograph of my mother as a child, I tell myself: she is going to die: I shudder, like Winnicott's psychotic patient, over a catastrophe which has already occurred. Whether or not the subject is already dead, every photograph is this catastrophe [...] there is always a defeat of Time in them: that is dead and that is going to die.
>
> (Barthes, 1981, p. 96)

Photographs of our loved ones capture a moment in time that has already passed; hence, they remind us of their (and our own) mortality. Not just Barthes, but various photography theorists have pointed out that death is an almost inseparable part of the history of photography. As Geoffrey Batchen notes, 'photography has been associated with death since the beginning' (Batchen, 2000, p. 10). On the one hand, early photographs – daguerreotypes, which were introduced in 1839 – were produced from such lengthy exposure time that models had to be placed in a restraining device to ensure a still posture: 'photography insisted, that if one wanted to appear lifelike in a photograph, one first has to act as if dead' (ibid., p. 11). On the other hand, post-mortem photographs were common in American and European culture in the nineteenth and early twentieth centuries. Many persons had a picture taken of their dead relative after he/she was placed in the coffin; scenery would be arranged to suggest the relative was sleeping or still alive, surrounded by family members (Meinwald, 1993, p. 5). In the early history of photography, this was often the only photograph a family would have of the deceased: 'a preservation of the body for the gaze of the observer' (ibid., pp. 6, 4).

In line with Barthes, Christian seems to connect the images of his daughter to death, pointing to a past and a body that has been, but no longer is. The photographs evoke a number of feelings and act as 'a wound' or a 'mark made by a pointed instrument' that 'bruises me' (Barthes, 1981, pp. 26–27). Hence, they become too painful to share. But sharing images of the grave site is different, not least when it is surrounded by growing vegetation, which seems to suggest life, hope and continuity to Christian. If the images of his daughter become a painful reminder of her death – mortalising her yet again – the images of her grave site seem to immortalise the relationship, the affects and the feeling of missing her.

Figure 13.2 Photograph of Helle's son's grave site

Contrary to Christian, Helle shares many photographs, and has done so since her son's death. Accessible on her profile are photographs of her son that were uploaded around the time of his birth, as well as photographs of him dying in her arms and of him dead and in a coffin. She felt compelled to share the images of him dying/dead because she had recently shared images of him alive and wanted to let people know what was happening. But she was very uncertain of how she should mourn her son and what role Facebook could or should play in this – and whether posting these images was 'overstepping the boundaries'; still, she felt a need to have 'all of his story gathered here [on Facebook]' (interview with Helle). Helle has shared numerous photographs of her son's grave site, from its foundation to its development into a garden-like place. Most of her photographs focus on the ever-evolving, growing and blooming vegetation (cf. subcategories one and two), not least the butterfly bush that is placed just behind the engraved stone. She captions one of these images: 'The butterfly bush has never been bigger. It reminds me of how big [name of son] should have been. Almost first grade, almost 7 years old. Our big wonderful boy' (5 July 2014).

To Helle, continually sharing photographs of the grave site mimics the sharing of images of him that she could/would have done had he been alive:

> Well, this is what is happening with him. This is the place there is. I cannot take photographs of him, who [...] and somehow it's also about the physical aspect of things changing, or [...] In April, he died in

> October, we bought and planted one of these butterfly-bushes and now it's a huge tree. It's the physical aspect of it [...] it reminds me that it's been ... that time passes by.
>
> (Interview with Helle)

Like Christian, Helle connects the vegetation at the grave site to growth and life; hence, the vegetation becomes a stand-in or an ersatz body (Belting, 2011, p. 168) for the growth of the infant, whose life terminated almost before it really started. It becomes an ongoing documentation of her son – a way of keeping him present, even in dispersed material form, while also reminding her of her years lived with and transformed by grief.

In Anna's interview, she also highlights how taking and sharing photographs of the grave site is a way of keeping her deceased daughter present, not least through the continued intensity of mourning:

> It is like sharing a photograph of one's cute child at Shrovetide. This is all I've got – this is my cute child. And then I've got a lot of Facebook friends with dead children – and they also post photographs of the grave site, and then we say 'Ohhh that is nice', well like when the rest of you post photographs of your living children [...] It highlights that it is not limited to the day she was buried or cremated – it is still going on [...] we need to tell that it is not over [...] they keep on living inside of us, and one of the things you can do is to take care of a grave site, create new memories.
>
> (Interview with Anna)

Sharing the images serves to manifest Anna's deceased daughter's continued presence and significance in her life.

Intimacy as mediated acts and sharings

In the interview with Helle it becomes apparent that her mourning is a mediatised doing. As she notes, the combination of physically being at the grave site, taking the picture and sharing it on Facebook 'creates some kind of intimacy'; hence, collectively, these acts become 'a way to be close to him [her deceased son]' (interview with Helle). Intimacy is described by Lauren Berlant as affective 'attachments' (Berlant, 1998, p. 283) that are not just there, but rather evoked and constituted through certain acts and mediations. The supposed inwardness of intimacy is animated through an expressive publicness (ibid., p. 281). As every aspect of our everyday life is saturated with media to a degree that has never before been seen (Hepp, Hjarvard and Lundby, 2015, p. 319), a continued intimate relationship (whether to a dead or living person) is not only lived through offline physical meetings, but is also supported – or even made possible – through online claims of attachment that assist in strengthening personal ties. Although there tends to be public anxiety and moral panic surrounding social media, in that it is often blamed for a decrease in close, genuine bonds, social media has become important for cultivating personal relationships and forging new ways of being intimate and 'doing intimacy' (Chambers, 2013, pp. 2–3). This is not least the case for mourning social media users, as pointed out by Dorthe Refslund Christensen and Kjetil Sandvik in their study of Danish mourners' use of the site Mindet.dk (*mindet* means memory in Danish) – a site that enables users to create memory profiles for their lost loved ones, and contains a light-a-candle function and a forum for debate:

> By enrolling themselves in this 'editable' community, the bereaved commit themselves to an ongoing communication with the person they lost and with other people in the same situation as themselves. And this continued dialogical practice accentuates the feeling of still being in close contact with the deceased.
>
> (Christensen and Sandvik, 2015, p. 59)

Mourning and connecting with one's lost relative through a personal profile on Facebook is, however, slightly different, as the forum is not exclusively used for such purposes. A Facebook profile is not a segregated, designated space such as Mindet.dk, where mourners can legitimately preoccupy themselves with their loss in an 'immersed and focused' setting (Christensen and Sandvik, 2015, p. 62). On the contrary, a personal Facebook profile serves more as a site for self-presentation, where many kinds of thoughts, feelings, experiences and actions can be shared as they unfold. Mourning through a personal Facebook profile therefore involves a larger degree of 'emotional self-management', as mourning Facebook users must negotiate expressions of grief in relation to their self-presentation through other posts/interactions, as well as to ever-changing norms of what is unwanted or considered too much or overly self-exposing information; this makes posting on death and mourning a difficult balancing act.

However, mourning through one's personal Facebook profile enables mourners to let the deceased relative and mourning become part of their ongoing, everyday digital life. As approximately 3.5 million Danes (out of a total population of 5.7 million) have a Facebook account, and 62 per cent of account holders check Facebook daily (Danielsen, 2016), the platform is an active and integrated part of everyday life. Helle's sharing of images of her son's grave site on Facebook therefore embeds her deceased son in her life and makes him visible to a broader sociality. As she states:

> By holding on to the place where he is [the grave site] I am showing the world, and I get to live with the fact, that I have a fourth child [...] and I am able to insist, in relation to family and friends, that it [his existence and her grief] is still part of our life and history.
>
> (Interview with Helle)

Helle's need to show the world – and not least her family and friends – that her son is still a part of her life and that she still grieves him arises from her feeling that he could easily 'disappear from the family picture'. Taking and sharing the photographs compels herself and others to acknowledge 'that he is there and that he will not be forgotten' (interview with Helle).

See me showing you the grave site

Camilla often shares photographs of her mother's and sister's grave site (cf. the first subcategory). Usually, these photographs focus on the engraved stone and things that are left, in commemoration, next to it: cut flowers, flower arrangements (depending on the season) and lit candles.

When I ask her why she shares these images she emphasises her need for other people to see 'how neat and fine it is' and 'that I am thinking of them', not least during the high seasons, and that 'they are still with me' (interview with Camilla). The photographs witness and become part of a ritualisation of mourning: the practice of leaving or doing the same things at the grave site and sharing the same kinds of images again and again. Camilla seems to feel the need to not only do certain things, but also to have other people see her doing them. The importance of presenting the grave site as neat and fine seems to be both a declaration of love to the people lost and a way of showing herself and others that she remains a good and thoughtful daughter and sister, and is hence continuing that relationship. The photographs thereby highlight 'a desire to continuously display care' (cf. Segerstad and Kasperowski, 2015, p. 29). They become pointers – an antiphon of 'Look', 'See', 'Here it is' (Barthes, 1981, p. 5). As pointers, the photographs have a performative function, calling attention to something, which becomes even more pronounced when circulated on Facebook. Sharing the images thereby points to the loved ones' existence/memory and the mark their lives have made on Camilla, while also showing Camilla doing grief. Digital photography (taken with an always available mobile phone) involves several layers of performance: choreographing, taking, selecting and uploading photographs. As Susan Sontag pointed out already in the 1970s – and which seems even more true now – 'having an experience becomes identical with taking a photograph of it' (Sontag, 1977, p. 24). One might also argue that experience, to a certain extent, has become inseparable from mediation, which manifests and intensifies experience.

Although Camilla visits the grave site often to mourn her lost relatives, it is not the place where she feels her sister's presence the most. She explains to me that she considers the cemetery the place where 'her shell' is, whereas Facebook is 'where she is' – 'it is her'. When Camilla scrolls through her sister's Facebook profile, she 'feels close to her'; and when she writes posts to her sister (which she always does, addressing her as 'you'), she feels as if she 'is in contact with her' and that her sister 'sees' and 'hears' her words (interview with Camilla). In other words, the cemetery houses her sister's physical remains, but Facebook houses her soul/essence. Thus, Facebook is a kind of telepathic, metaphysical channel where she can maintain close contact with her.

Continuous bond and care

Over the last 15 years, grave sites have become simultaneously more intimate and more anonymous, with grave stones no longer containing the full name of the deceased and their date of birth and death, but instead listing their first name, their nickname and their kinship status (e.g. mother, father, etc.). As Sommer argues, the intimate space is expanding and taking over the grave site; hence, the public space of the grave site is becoming increasingly individualised and made homely with toys, letters and other personalised items that have been made or bought especially for the deceased (Sommer, 2003, p. 268). The photographs that are taken and shared by Anna (18 December 2008) are exemplary of these trends, as they show a regular stone (not the traditional large, decorated or sandblasted stone) with what looks like a handmade inscription of her deceased daughter's first name in red (and not her full name in the traditional black, grey or white).

The stone is placed in garden-like surroundings, flanked by two large lanterns with burning candles, cut flowers and a flower arrangement in a vase with a Winnie the Pooh motif. All around are Christmas decorations: small elves, crafted red and white mushrooms and red hearths hanging from

Figure 13.3 Photograph of Anna's daughter's grave site

a tree. The photographs depict the grave site as a small, intimate garden (cf. subcategory one), which has been personally designed and decorated in order to have a homely look and feel. The images of the site, with all the objects placed near it, might comfort Anna in her mourning, giving her the impression that her daughter is safely placed in a warm home of her own, and not at a public cemetery. Likewise, the photographs also document mourning as a doing, emphasising decorating as an act of commemoration. These images might showcase to Anna as well as to others that she is mourning in a loving and caring way. Looking at these images, I am reminded of something Helle said in the interview: 'Just as you want to be a good mother to your living child I also wanted to be a good mother to my dead child' (interview with Helle). Helle raises the issue of 'how to mourn properly', which she explains is a point of wonder and investigation to her, because she does not feel it is immediately evident how one should display care in relation to a dead child. As argued by Dorthe Refslund Christensen and Kjetil Sandvik, grieving parents on Mindet.dk not only commemorate the life that once was, but also establish, maintain and reclaim themselves as parents through online grief work. When a child dies, parents are no longer needed as parents; hence, the loss of a child is also the loss of a constitutive role as a parent. When a mother lights a candle or writes on the site to say 'goodnight', she is 'claiming the right to motherhood and performing herself as a (good) mother' (Christensen and Sandvik, 2015, p. 63). The mourners transform past into a time 'they live with as opposed to the past being a time they live in. The dead child is transformed from the child we lost to the dead child we have' (ibid., p. 60). Likewise, sharing images of a grave site with visible signs of commemoration can be seen as a way of keeping the relative present and continuing a relationship with them (considering them the dead relative one *has*), while also reconstituting and reclaiming one's role as a mother, a father, a sister or a daughter.

Exit: To live with the dead as an integrated part of one's ongoing life

As I have argued in this chapter, sharing images of a grave site can be interpreted as a semi-public practice that serves to keep a loved one present in one's ongoing, everyday life. Facebook seems to be a particularly suitable channel for this, as it is a familiar setting (Marwick and Ellison, 2012, p. 395) that allows 'mourning and memorializing to take place more easily within the mundane' (Ebert, 2014, p. 27). When images are shared on Facebook they become part of and integrated into a broader social domain; they become subjects of ongoing conversations and acknowledgement. However, sharing the images on Facebook also entails archiving or manifesting a life worth noticing and a continued relationship.

Shared images of the grave site often focus on the vegetation around the grave stone, which becomes a stand-in or ersatz body for the deceased loved one. Such images represent attempts to keep the deceased relative among the living, although in dispersed material form. The images assure and remind the mourner and others of the continued presence of the loved one, and enfold the deceased relative's existence in an ongoing, everyday mediated life. The past becomes something the mourners live with in the present. Death does not end the loved one's existence and the mourners' relationship to them, but becomes an integrated part of the deceased's ongoing life.

Photography serves as a connecting force that can help instantiate and create relational proximity by either gathering loved ones within the same picture frame or continuously pointing to the deceased loved one. A continued relationship is constituted and claimed, not least through the performance of grief. By visiting, photographing and uploading images of the grave site, mourners engage in continued relationship-making and thereby constitute themselves as good and proper mourners and reconstitute themselves as loving and caring mothers, fathers, sisters and daughters. Image sharing is therefore first and foremost about relationality – about the significance of the deceased and the imprint they have made on other people's lives, which mourners will not or cannot leave behind. Openly maintaining a relationship with the dead is often discouraged, and may even be pathologised as a sign of failed, unresolved or unhealthy grief (Segerstad and Kasperowski, 2015, p. 28). Sharing images of the grave site becomes a way of insisting on a continued relationship, and an important ingredient in maintaining this relationality is sharing the relation (semi-)publicly.

Notes

1 Helle is in her 40s and has lost her infant. At the time of the interview her son had been dead for nine years. She works at an institution of higher education. The interview was conducted on 31 March 2015.
2 Camilla is in her 30s and has lost her mother and sister. At the time of the interview her mother had been dead for three years and her sister for one year. She works as a sale assistant. The interview was conducted on 26 March 2015.
3 Christian is in his 50s and has lost a daughter. At the time of the interview she had been dead for ten years. He works in coaching. The interview was conducted on 3 March 2015.
4 Birgitte is in her 50s and has lost her partner. At the time of the interview he had been dead for 18 months. She works with socially marginalised people, in a communications role. The interview was conducted on 27 March 2015.
5 Anna is in her 30s and has lost an infant. At the time of the interview her daughter had been dead for nine years. She works as a teacher. The interview was conducted on 6 March 2015.
6 All of the quotes that appear in this chapter are my own translations from the original Danish.

References

Barthes, R. (1981). *Camera Lucida. Reflections on Photography*. New York: Hill and Wang.

Batchen, G. (2000). Ectoplasm: Photography in the digital age. In: *Over Exposed: Essays on Contemporary Photography*. New York: WW Norton & Co, pp. 9–23.
Belting, H. (2011). *An anthropology of images: Picture, medium, body*. Princeton, NJ: Princeton University Press.
Berlant, L. (1998). Intimacy: A special issue. *Critical Inquiry*, 24(2), pp. 281–288.
Brubaker, J.R., Hayes, G.R. and Dourish, P. (2013). Beyond the grave: Facebook as a site for the expansion of death and mourning. *The Information Society*, 29(3), pp. 152–163.
Chambers, D. (2013). *Social Media and Personal Relationships: Online Intimacies and Networked Friendship*. New York: Palgrave Macmillan.
Christensen, D.R. and Sandvik, K. (2015). Death ends a life not a relationship: Timework and ritualizations at Mindet.dk. *New Review of Hypermedia and Multimedia*, 21(1-2), pp. 57–71.
Church, S.H. (2013). Digital gravescapes: Digital memorializing on Facebook. *The Information Society*, 29(3), pp. 184–189.
Danielsen, M. (2016): Sociale medier 2016 i Danmark [Social media 2016 in Denmark]. Socialemedier.dk. Retrieved from www.socialemedier.dk/sociale-medier-2016-i-danmark/ (7 September 2016).
DeGroot, J.M. (2014). 'For whom the bell tolls': Emotional rubbernecking in facebook memorial groups. *Death Studies*, 38(2), pp. 79–84.
Ebert, H. (2014). Profiles of the dead: Mourning and memorial on Facebook. In: Moreman and Lewis, eds., *Digital Death. Mortality and Beyond in the Online Age*. Santa Barbara, CA: Praeger, pp. 23–42.
Frost, M. (2014). The grief grapevine: Facebook memorial pages and adolescent bereavement. *Australian Journal of Guidance and Counselling*, 24(02), pp. 256–265.
Hepp, A., Hjarvard, S. and Lundby, K. (2015). Mediatization: Theorizing the interplay between media, culture and society. *Media, Culture & Society*, pp. 1–11.
Jones, S., Adams, T. and Ellis, C. (2013). Introduction: Coming to know autoethnography as more than a method. In: *Handbook of Autoethnography*. London: Routledge.
Jørgensen, K.M. (2016). The media go-along. Researching mobilities with media at hand. *MedieKultur*, 32(60), pp. 32–49.
Kern, R., Forman, A.E. and Gil-Egui, G. (2013). RIP: Remain in perpetuity. Facebook memorial pages. *Telematics and Informatics*, 30(1), pp. 2–10.
Klastrup, L. (2014). 'I didn't know her, but…': Parasocial mourning of mediated deaths on Facebook RIP pages. *New Review of Hypermedia and Multimedia*, pp. 1–19.
Lagerkvist, A. (2013). New memory cultures and death: Existential security in the digital memory ecology. *Thanatos*, 2(2), pp. 1–17.
Marwick, A. and Ellison, N.B. (2012). 'There isn't wifi in heaven!' Negotiating visibility on Facebook memorial pages. *Journal of Broadcasting & Electronic Media*, 56(3), pp. 378–400.
Meinwald, D. (1993). Memento mori: Death and photography in nineteenth century America. *CMP Bulletin*, 9(4), pp. 1–33.
Pink, S., et al. (2015). *Digital Ethnography: Principles and Practice*. SAGE.
Prosser, J. (2005). *Light in the Dark Room: Photography and Loss*. Minneapolis, MN: University of Minnesota Press.

Segerstad, Y. and Kasperowski, D. (2015). A community for grieving: Affordances of social media for support of bereaved parents. *New Review of Hypermedia and Multimedia*, pp. 1–17.
Sommer, A.L. (2003). *De dødes haver: Den moderne storbykirkegård.* Odense: Syddansk universitetsforlag.
Sontag, S. (1977). *On Photography*. London: Macmillan.

14 Bleeding boundaries

Domesticating gay hook-up apps

Kristian Møller and Michael Nebeling Petersen

> I personally don't wanna walk into the local gay bar and everyone in have just been sharing my Scruff profile that might say that I just drunk a gallon of piss.
>
> (Interview with James, 2014)

Introduction

Hook-up apps such as Grindr and Scruff have become important sites for the negotiation of sex between men, in that they shape the ways intimacy cultures are practised and become visible (Mowlabocus, 2010; Race, 2014; Duguay et al., 2016). While such apps enable different intimacy cultures, they also come paired with anxieties. In the epigraph the interview participant James[1] expresses concerns about the how the hook-up app Scruff might restructure the boundaries of privacy and make him vulnerable to exposure. Such technological ambivalence is central to domestication theory, which focuses on the processes through which media are *controlled*. As Berker et al. (2005) argue: 'These "strange" and "wild" technologies have to be "house-trained"; they have to be integrated into the structures, daily routines and values of users and their environments' (p. 2).

The previous quotes mark the understanding of 'home' as a concept around which normative and material boundary work is done. Despite this normative sensibility, domestication theory has typically responded to the introduction of media technologies into homes that more or less align with heteronormative configurations of feelings, gender, sex and family. Silverstone points out that the home is the privileged site of the production of safety and peace, and its normative power becomes apparent when attention is turned to those without a home: 'To characterise someone as homeless is to imply some kind of moral lack or weakness' (Silverstone, 1994, p. 26). These views can be read as a response to societal and academic anxiety about the power of television to disrupt the workings of the home. Such anxieties around media's potential destabilisation of family life might explain why the domestication approach has given little attention to gay lives and homes, for such lives have historically been considered outside the institutions, spaces and norms that delineate traditional conceptualisations of 'the home'. From a straight perspective, gay lives and intimacies seem homeless, or 'beyond reach' (Silverstone, 2006, p. 243). Although domestication theory points to the normative workings of the home, in practice, it has not adequately addressed gay home-making practices. This makes it difficult to imagine domestication as something that occurs across non-normative, built and media spaces, or between two or more partners engaging in sex with others. However, it is exactly these mobile and non-normative lives that are the focus of this chapter.

To expand domestication to include non-normative lives and intimacies, we turn to the home-making practice of James. In his 30s, James lives with his two male partners in a 'throuple' – a polyamorous and non-monogamous relationship. James uses hook-up apps to find gay sex without his partners, which in turn makes him visible to everyone nearby who also uses the app. To James, the app's blocking function, which enables him to become invisible to selected other users, is central. Staying invisible to his partners online is crucial for maintaining his sexual independence. James worries that online visibility between his partners and him could produce what he calls a 'bleeding boundary' between his long-term partners and his potential extradyadic sexual partners. Thus, the app's blocking function allows him to manage the borders between his intimate partners and others, allowing him to not only become invisible to his long-term partners, but also to alleviate normative pressures from non-partners:

> the thing that's playing out for me most at the moment, is encountering people I know, in my neighbourhood, who are on Scruff [gay dating app], who message me or leave me tracks, who I feel have some level of opinion or judgment about me being sexually active outside of my relationships […] So I now block pretty much everybody I know.
>
> (James)

As James is in a non-normative, non-monogamous relationship, he experiences the actualisation of normative pressures as a side effect of his online visibility. As a response, he uses the blocking function to domesticate the standard visibility of the hook-up app and become what we term 'strategically (in)visible': he remains visible to a sexual public of strangers while becoming invisible to his partners and to people he knows in his neighbourhood. James tames his intimate media technologies and maintains a sense of 'ontological security' by controlling the normative pressures that come with the 'wild' visibilities the hook-up apps introduce. His story lends urgency to the call to reconfigure and apply domestication theory to the roles that digital and mobile media play in (non-normative) intimacies. Analytically, to expand the scope of domestication theory to include non-normative media homes, this chapter considers the way in which media-strategic visibilities and invisibilities play into the construction and maintenance of the home sphere.

The proliferation of hook-up apps opens up new ways of organising sexual encounters and intimacies, while simultaneously disrupting (old) distinctions of private and public. As the introductory quote makes clear, the apps risk making visible what users might prefer to stay invisible. Like other new technologies, the apps require users to 'tame' perceived potential dangers in order to benefit the most from their use.

In this chapter, we interrogate the process of domesticating '"strange" and "wild" technologies' (Berker et al., 2005, p. 2) in non-monogamous gay male relationships. Drawing on interviews, we examine the way in which hook-up apps are 'house-trained'. In focusing on people in non-monogamous relationships that inherently operate across different social, sexual and intimate scenes, we shed light on the domestication of new media technologies and the way in which they interweave with intimacy. Approaching the relationship between medium and practice as a dynamic intersection acknowledges both the *moulding* force of the medium (Hepp, 2013) and – equally important – the way in which people *mould* the medium to fit their cultural setting (Jansson, 2015a). We combine this mediatisation perspective with an understanding of intimacy as a kind of affective action that produces boundaries between public and private. Thus, in this chapter we ask: How are hook-up apps domesticated in the context of sexually non-monogamous, gay relationships?

Hook-up apps, mediatisation of intimacy and theories of domestication

In this chapter, we draw on domestication analysis of media's 'double articulation' (Silverstone et al., 1996) and its relation to 'the home'. In defining 'home' and the way in which media are domesticated in relation to the home, the chapter continues Peil and Röser's work, which 'sheds light on the entanglement of different domestic practices, mediated and non-mediated, and links them back to discourses and changes in society' (2014, p. 235).

The apps in focus belong to the category of 'online hook-up devices': services that build on network connectivity and 'make use of these capacities to facilitate sexual and social encounters between men' (Race, 2014, p. 254). These capabilities draw on standard repertoires of mobile social media but extend them by making relative user proximity the organising principle by which certain user profiles are made visible (see Figure 14.1). In order to reflect this chapter's focus on smartphone-based services, we use the term 'hook-up apps' to describe them.

Technologies are domestic objects 'mediating in their aesthetic the tension between the familiar and the strange, desire and unease, which all new technologies respectively embody and stimulate' (Silverstone et al., 1996, p. 48). The act of domesticating technologies into the home thus does not do away with the strange; rather, in this act, technologies are appropriated to

Figure 14.1 Screenshots of 'hook-up' apps

incorporate the strange and familiar, the inside and outside, the private and the public into the home. Here, we suggest that the production and consumption of such distinctions can be understood through Berlant's work on intimacy (2000): Berlant argues that scripts of intimacy – of performing domesticity, coupledom and identity – are widely circulated in 'the public' through television shows, novels, institutions and ideologies; further, they 'migrate' to 'the private', creating hegemonic forms of intimacy (Berlant, 2000, pp. 3–4). Intimacy allows a subject to feel a sense of emotional belonging – to find a 'home'. Following this depersonalised understanding of intimacy, we understand the 'home' as an *experience of belonging*. Thus, the 'home' in this chapter is operationalised as the production of an affective domain of intimate belonging.

Further, drawing on Sixsmith and Sixsmith (1990), we understand 'home' as variously unfolding in different experiential domains. This allows us to extend the concept of home to include life that does not conform to heteronormativity, and to also extend its meaning along several dimensions, including but not limited to that of materiality. Following this, we focus on the way in which hook-up apps are domesticated in relation to the specific moral economy of a gay, non-monogamous household. 'Home' is thus a product of *affective work* that produces *intimate belonging* (Berlant, 2000) that is 'technologically enhanced as well as technologically disrupted' (Silverstone, 2006, p. 243).

Intimacy is commonly understood to describe practices and feelings of proximity, love, familiarity, specialness to someone and so forth (Jamieson, 2005, p. 1). As suggested by Jamieson, it involves creating 'protective' boundaries that encapsulate intimates and it 'keeps non-intimates out' (ibid.). In this chapter, we combine Jamieson's conceptualisation of intimacy as boundary work with Berlant's conceptualisation of intimacy as a script. Thus, we do not understand intimacy as a (natural) feeling that emerges *from* the private through love or closeness; rather, we understand intimacy as the practices and work done to produce affective domains that *constitute* the private and the sense of home. These practices and work are characterised by the creation of boundaries that mimic hegemonic and subcultural scripts of intimacy. Thus, we draw on feminist work that deconstructs 'the public' and 'the private', and we understand these spheres as the product of affective and discursive work.

The domestication of hook-up apps, then, is the production of 'public' and 'private' through material and affective boundary work that responds to the mediatised visibilities and presence of hook-up apps. Our reading strategy is informed by an understanding of media as doubly articulated: 'they are part of household's private as well as the public sphere; they are material artefacts and bearers of meaning in more than one sense' (Berker et al., 2005, p. 4). Thus, we read for both materiality and meaning-making related to hook-up apps. These distinctions are epistemological rather than ontological; media materialities and meanings are only conceptually separated in order to faciliate an analysis of the way in which they are interwoven.

Case material and analytical strategy

The case material draws from a larger corpus of interviews performed in London and Brighton (UK), as well as Copenhagen (Denmark). These interviews were conducted face-to-face in the period of early 2013 through 2014. All of the interview participants signed consent forms. Transcriptions of the 30- to 90-minute long interviews and media go-along situations (Jørgensen, 2016) were coded and accumulated in Atlas.TI. Most participant recruitment was conducted via a personal profile on Scruff, which is an app directed at 'gay, bi, and curious guys'.[2] In the following, hook-up app use in gay, non-monogamous relationships is represented through three cases (i.e. three relationships), which derived from four interviews with five men living in the UK. All participants in the sample are men in gay, non-monogamous relationships; all are white and cis-gendered men.

The first case is that of the London-based French couple Sebastien and Julien. Sebastien works long hours in the banking industry, while Julien is currently the 'stay-at-home dad' for their young son. Both in their early 30s, they use hook-up apps individually, but, as we will see, interactions between the partners do occur. The second case is of Tim and George, who live on the outskirts of Brighton. They are in their early 60s and have been partners for eight years. Tim has lived in Brighton for most of his life. He has long been using computers to connect with other gay men across the world, since the days of the computer chat application ICQ. Tim is the main operator of the dating and hook-up apps, and his partner George mostly steps in whenever a connection has been made. Finally, there is James, who is in his 30s. James lives in East London with his two male partners in a 'throuple' – a polyamourous relationship. He uses hook-up apps to find gay sex with men who are not his partners.

The interview transcripts are analysed through poststructuralist reading strategies (Søndergaard, 2002). Rather than understanding sexual encounters, intimacy and types of relationships as things that depart from subjects, we understand them as phenomena that emerge socially and relationally 'through and within discursive power' (ibid., p. 189). Further, we understand hook-up apps as discursive regulatory devices, wherein the affordances and technologies of the apps co-create possibilities and frames for organising privacy, intimacy and relationships. In order to analyse the use of hook-up apps as a double articulation, we interrogate the affective and discursive production of intimacy (and subjectivity) that is formed by and within discursive power, as well as the materiality of the app.

As suggested by Søndergaard, we look for 'inclusive and exclusive discursive processes' (ibid., p. 189) as ways of making boundaries and thus creating a sense of intimacy. This means that we read the material and look for the way in which intimacy is spoken into existence through the creation of boundaries and categories of intimacy and desire. We do this by asking how the empirical material organises desire and emotions into appropriate and inappropriate forms; organises different forms of (virtual and physical, visible and invisible) proximity to create intimacy and intimate belonging; categorises, hierarchises and valorises different forms of encounters and relationships; and creates, maintains and valorises different affective domains in relation to each other.

In order to analyse affective domains, we draw on the work of Sara Ahmed (2004) and Mary Douglas (1966): From Ahmed, we deploy an analytical perspective that sees emotions not as subject-emergent, but as relational and social phenomena. Thus, we analyse not what emotions *are*, but what emotions *do* to create a sense of intimacy. We combine this perspective with that of Mary Douglas' work on purity (1966), wherein dirt is understood not as an ontological phenomenon but as a disorder – a matter that is out of place. To understand the way in which 'intimacy builds worlds' (Berlant, 2000, p. 2) – how the interviewees make order and organise emotions to produce boundaries between the 'public' and 'private' – we combine Ahmed and Douglas' perspectives to develop the analytical construct of *emotions out of place*. This functions as a reading strategy to understand the way in which affective work is performed by placing emotions in different (proper) affective domains and thereby creating a sense of intimacy.

Intimacies at work

The apps fundamentally disturb clear distinctions between 'private' and 'public', demanding users to work affectively to distinguish these domains. The disturbance is felt as troublesome, disorderly or a 'bleeding of boundaries'. These disturbances occur when different categories of social relations are conflated through the use of hook-up apps; for example, when James meets his long-term partners on Scruff, when a colleague from work accidentally sends him naked pictures or when his students appear on his grid of nearby users on Grindr. The bleeding of boundaries shows how hook-up apps destabilise the social categories of relations, making colleagues and students potential sex partners and anonymous one-night stands part of social life. As the analyses will show, the users manage the bleeding boundaries both by doing affective work to demarcate private and intimate arenas and by controlling the affordances of the apps.

We analyse the way in which the users discursively and affectively create distinct affective domains by placing emotions in their proper places, which are defined by scripts of intimacy. We identify two intimacy scripts at work – 'monogamous intimacy' and 'non-monogamous intimacy' – and trace their logical locuses to ideologies of kinship and relationship-making.

Monogamous intimacy

Sebastien has been in a long-term relationship with his partner Julien since he was a teenager. When they met, Julien was in a relationship with a girl, and Sebastien explains that this formed the basis of their non-exclusive relationship: 'I knew from the beginning that I couldn't expect him to be monogamous, and he certainly wasn't going to be right in the beginning when he still had a girlfriend.' Even though they and their relationship have 'matured' and 'gone through phases' over the years, the couple remain non-exclusive.

Although Sebastien describes the relationship as non-monogamous, we argue that Sebastien articulates a *monogamous intimacy*, wherein intimacy is kept inside the relationship. In psychological studies of gay men's non-exclusive relationships, emotional exclusivity has been identified as central to the production of partner intimacy and conceptualised as 'monogamy of the heart' (LaSala, 2004) and 'emotional monogamy' (Bonello and Cross, 2010). In contrast to these studies, we suggest that the relationship between intimate monogamy and the potential for extradyadic sex is not casually achieved; rather, it is governed by ongoing reaffirmations and applications of certain scripts of intimacy. The script at play corresponds with what David Eng calls 'Queer Liberalism' (2010), which includes the domestication of gay lifestyles into monogamy and marriage (Nebeling Petersen, 2012). This monogamous intimacy is a neoliberal and 'homonormative' (Duggan, 2004) script of intimacy, elevating coupledom and reframing extradyadic relations as commodities of choice for purchase and consumption.

Sebastien creates two distinct affective domains, wherein emotions are kept in their proper places according to the intimacy script of monogamous intimacy. The first affective domain is the sphere of the devoted relationship between Sebastien and his partner. Sebastien states that he and his partner met online and talked for a long time on the chat service IRC:

> Just from the conversation even talking to him online, that's actually when I decided I wanted to have him as my boyfriend [...]. It's romantic [...]. I decided I wanted to be with him for the rest of my life during that chat.
>
> (Sebastien)

In this articulation, the dyadic relationship is staged as romantic, within homonormative assumptions: it is 'meant to be' and lifelong, and its value is measured in terms of devotion. Later on, Sebastien explains that he and his partner do not hide their extradyadic sexual relations from one another; rather, they have a rule that each must tell the other if they have had sexual encounters. Though the other often 'doesn't care and doesn't want to know' (Sebastien), the rule mimics intimacy in Anthony Giddens' late-modern sense of the word, in which concepts of mutuality, openness and equality form the 'pure relationship' (Giddens, 1992).

The second affective domain that Sebastien creates is related to the individual extradyadic relations. When he and Julien had a child, Sebastien stayed home and had what he calls his 'slutty year as a housewife'. He explains that, during that year, he learned that he could 'just show up at somebody's house. Screw around and leave and that's fine'. Though Sebastien doesn't use the apps very frequently anymore, he still uses them as 'jerk-off material' and he characterises his meetings with other men as: 'It's a new body, new face, new attraction and then you're done and you walk away and it's – that's it. That was your interaction with him.' Sebastien uses consumerist logic, 'consuming' bodies and faces and rendering them unthreatening to his monogamous intimacy with Julien, which, in contrast, is staged as romantic and not consumerist. By way of derogatory descriptions such as 'slutty', 'sleazy' and 'filthy', Sebastien marks these encounters as out of place: it isn't the acts themselves that are 'sleazy', but the displacement of desire outside the intimate affective domain.

In these ways, Sebastien constructs and maintains two affective domains, wherein a homonormative script of intimacy functions as the demarcating structure: The first domain is characterised as 'pure' intimacy, which emphasises openness, mutuality and devotion as not only valuable but characteristics that are strongly associated with coupledom. The other affective domain is characterised by non-intimate emotions and metaphors such as 'sluttyness', commodified exchange, crime, aggression and coldness. Even though the couple are non-exclusive, they affectively devalorise extradyadic relations by placing intimate emotions in their proper places. In other words, a careful management of emotions aims to ensure that the boundaries that contain them do not bleed.

The management of the extradyadic domain is not only a matter of discursive and affective devalorisation, but is also highly contingent on embedded norms of self-presentation. In a hook-up app, such norms are expressed in affordances of self-categorisation and community standards (e.g. explicit pictures), as well as the typical ways that users present themselves. Within hook-up apps that target gay men, there is great variety in these norms. Sebastien explains in much detail about the different ways in which users can display pictures on the apps. For instance, unlike Grindr, Manhunt allows explicit pictures but also enables a private gallery feature, allowing users to hide specific pictures from the general public. He continues: 'This is the difference. Grindr has my face but nothing explicit. Manhunt is very explicit but doesn't have my face. It's maybe splitting my personas a little bit.' Sebastien's personal profile is visible to both his partner and the wider app community, and must be regulated accordingly. Taming Grindr and Manhunt to make them support the separation of intimacy while allowing extradyadic sex thus requires different strategies. As Grindr serves double duty as both a social and a sexual space, it potentially troubles the intimacy work more than Manhunt. This is why Sebastien carefully presents himself as 'proper' and 'whole' on Grindr, while he can be more 'sleazy' on Manhunt.

As Grindr makes the user visible to several publics, the need for the user to perform boundary work is intensified. The user becomes visible by way of the *online status indicator* (see Figure 14.1). This little 'green light' on the user profile allows for at least two different but simultaneous visibilities: that between one partner and potential intimate others, and that between partners, forming the basis of partner surveillance. This double visibility complicates the work of putting emotions in their proper places. Sebastien explains this as follows:

> On Grindr we [Sebastien and Julien] know each other. Usually when I look at it randomly and I'll see he's signed on an hour ago or something. 'So where have you been? I didn't see you around' [...] It feels funny [...] It gives me something to tease him with [...] I come to the office quite often in the weekend to work but then I'll go out to smoke [...] and I'll check Grindr [...] And then he'll [Julien] send me a message like, 'Shouldn't you be working? What are you doing on this app?'
>
> (Sebastien)

Logging on with the intention of looking 'randomly' represents a use that looks towards potential intimate others outside the couple. The described encounter establishes the partners as persons who are looking both outwards and inwards, being neither fully inside nor outside the home. Sebastien uses a domestication strategy of playfully shaming Julien ('something to tease him with') to counter the effect of double visibility. This takes outward gazes and redirects them to produce couple intimacy out of a situation that could potentially break the public/private distinction established by monogamous intimacy. This redirection of affect can be understood as a form of 'interveillance' (Jansson, 2015b), in that the visibility is consumed as a way of generously recognising the partners' individual sexual agency by reinscribing it into the fabric of the intimate domain. Interveillance addresses the 'social deficit of recognition that characterizes highly individualized societies' (ibid., p. 81). In material terms, Sebastien and Julien's mostly individual use of hook-up apps produces opportunities, but also a deficit that is addressed by discursively and affectively creating mutual recognition and acceptance of extradyadic desires. Their interveillance enables feelings of intimacy to flow through the potentiality of an intimate other to its proper place; that is, in the first domain – inside the relationship. Thus, the online, locational visuality of their individual embeddedness in – and orientation towards – a gay public sex culture is playfully domesticated into the dyadic, affective domain.

To this public sex culture belongs a certain language and modes of self-presentation, which can be adopted into private sexual encounters. This can be observed in the following articulation by Sebastien about a hook-up app interaction between Julien and himself:

> here's my boyfriend, us telling each other, 'Hey, sexy', 'Hey sexy, looking good' and then sending each other dirty pictures [...] I think I was actually in the bedroom downstairs and then sent it to him upstairs.
>
> (Sebastien)

The extradyadic desires associated with hook-up apps are domesticated through the reappropriation of 'hook-up app talk' and the representational style and culture of 'dick pics' that are characteristic of online sex culture. The style of cruising is playfully eroticised into Sebastien and Julien's intimate domain and becomes a part of their intimate language. The culture cited plays an active role in their individual sexual practices and personal biographies, and the depersonalised sex role playing both acknowledges and eroticises the limits of their intimacy. Hook-up app visibilities give rise to new forms of interveillance, which trouble the distinctions between 'private' and 'public', allowing registers of public sex culture to be integrated into the private domain.

From the monogamous intimacy of Sebastien and Julien, we now turn to Tim and George. Tim and George also have extradyadic sex, but govern this according to what we call a *non-monogamous* intimacy script.

Non-monogamous intimacy

For Tim and George, extradyadic sex is not problematised in their relationship. They have sexual relations with other men together, not separately. When asked about using the hook-up apps, Tim explains that he does not like people who 'have that three-letter word in the back of their head all the time. Sex.' Rather, to Tim, friendship is important:

> I always say that we are looking for good friends. If fun comes along, that's always a bonus, but friendship has to be the number one thing. It has to be. Because you can't go through life just looking for that three-letter word all the time. You need to try and make good friends.
>
> (Tim)

Interestingly, to Tim, friendship, long-term relationships and sexual encounters seem to coincide. Quite different from Sebastien, Julien and James, who govern the emotional distinctions between sexual encounters, friends and long-term relationships in separate affective domains, to Tim, these social categories and practices occur within the same affective domain. The most important thing to Tim is friendship, and within friendship, sexual relations are welcomed and not problematised. Furthermore, Tim talks about friends he has had sex with and friends he has not had sex with in the same vein, emphasising the devotion, closeness and intimacy they share. In this way, sexual encounters are construed as intimate in the form of friendship, emotional closeness and devotion.

Here, the script of intimacy is quite different from that of Sebastien and Julien. Tim doesn't valorise coupledom, nor does he frame extradyadic relations with consumerism or characterise it as 'filth'. We argue that Tim uses another script of intimacy, one that is rooted in 1980s and 1990s gay and lesbian culture. According to Kath Weston (1997), during this period, gay and lesbians formed 'chosen families' consisting of lovers, friends, ex-lovers and other significant others. These families were not organised by the structure of the traditional nuclear family: the chosen family was based on choice, devotion and shared experiences, not genetic relatedness or birth bonds. These kinship forms occurred in response to the homophobic climate and the AIDS epidemic, which often led to the exclusion or marginalisation of gay people from their 'blood families'.

This structure of kinship – or, as we argue, script of intimacy – is no longer prevalent within gay culture. As we have mentioned in the case of Sebastien and Julien, today, such a culture is a gay liberalism, valorising individuality, homonormativity (same-sex marriage or coupledom) and consumerism. Tim registers this change in gay culture, leaving him with a feeling of loss. Gay culture has, to Tim, eroded from one of intimacy, mutuality and honesty to one of insincerity, lies and the commodification of sex.

To Tim, the domain of non-monogamous intimacy is that of a chosen family of sincere friends; the alternative to this is characterised by 'insincere others' – faceless persons who are only looking for sex or who have 'alternative motives'. As Tim says: 'Some people are very upfront and come out and say, "Nice talking to you but you're not my type." And I said, "What? Friendship has a type?" And to me, friendship doesn't have no type.' Thus, to Tim and George, the hook-up apps are not domesticated to separate dyadic relations from extradyadic sexual encounters. Rather, Tim and George use the apps to support domestic intimacy *across* such a distinction. This is apparent in Tim's spatial expansion of the home. The geolocative function of apps such as Grindr and Scruff makes Tim feel close to people living nearby: 'I have friends who I talk to on here and it's just talking, these people who are the closest here, live the closest.' This has led Tim to develop a close friendship with another gay man in his neighborhood:

> I've been talking to him for well over a year. We've never met face to face [...] But we have conversations most days. He will send me messages and I will reply to him, etc [...] if he's in the country, because he works for an airline. So he's home today. He flew in this morning.
>
> (Tim)

The app's geolocative function makes Tim's friend visible to him, and vice versa. This allows Tim to keep track of his friends' everyday rhythms, routines and workflows. In this way, Tim uses the locationally afforded visibilities to gain a sense of closeness to his friends, and this turns into an emotional investment that is nurtured in the distance-agnostic, computer-mediated communication network.

The network of friends and lovers who are connected through the apps is a family to Tim and George, wherein the shared experience of being gay, combined with everyday devotion and intimacy, form a kinship and sense of belonging. The geolocationality of the apps enables interveillance not solely between Tim and George, but between a selected group of confidentials. Whereas Sebastien and Julien use interveillance to counter the destabilising effect of online visibility and to keep emotions in their proper places, Tim and George interveil others in order to reinforce a sense of proximity and intimacy in their chosen family.

Strikingly, even though Tim operates in an intimate sphere that incorporates extradyadic relations and sex, he still articulates a second affective domain that must be contained. To Tim, 'chosen families', friendships or shared affective positions as gay men become a script of intimacy that works to keep emotions in their proper places. The distinction between public and private is not created for and by intimate monogamy, as in the case of Sebastien and Julien; rather, the distinction serves to demarcate sincere from insincere others who only want to have 'cold' sex. This creates a public affective domain characterised by consumerist behaviour devoid of intimate potential. To Sebastien, Julien and James, extradyadic sex belongs *outside* the intimate domain; conversely, for Tim and George, extradyadic sex is placed *within* it. To all, the private sphere constructed by intimacy is construed in contrast to consumerist logic.

While the affective and discursive work enables a demarcation between the private and the public, the hook-up apps continuously trouble and break this distinction. Thus, the domestication of hook-up apps also tames their material and designed functionalities and enables partners to demarcate the private from the public in accordance with their ideals.

Conclusion

Though gay hook-up apps allow extradyadic sex to be had and felt, relationship partners must perform a great deal of work to make themselves available for such encounters while retaining a sense of intimacy with their partner. Using the theoretical framework of domestication, we have shown how the possibilities of new app technologies destabilise 'old' scripts of intimacy: the visibilities that hook-up apps afford disturb distinctions between 'private' and 'public' in new ways. Thus, the apps produce 'bleeding boundaries'; that is, unwanted visibilities to partners or persons in their surroundings. We find that the potential of 'bleeding' in sexually non-monogamous relationships must be contained through domestication processes that adhere to monogamous or non-monogamous intimacy scripts, respectively.

New app visibilities not only disturb, but also serve as resources for intimate practices. The visibility of location and online activity places partners within a gay, public sex culture. This culture's sexual discursive and representational registers are reappropriated into a monogamous intimacy practice. Thus, playful communicative acts simultaneously contain and reappropriate the felt risk. In a non-monogamous intimacy practice, hook-up app visibilities allow for networked interveillance among not only partners, but also a larger circle of confidentials; this, in turn, produces a sense of recognition and mutuality.

We have argued that, in the context of sexually non-monogamous, gay relationships, hook-up apps are domesticated in accordance with either monogamous or non-monogamous scripts of intimacy. Partners work to reconstitute private and public affective domains in line with either homonormative or chosen family scripts of intimacy. Homonormative monogamous intimacy and the non-monogamous intimacy of chosen families maintain separate affective domains – one of intimacy and one of commodified, 'cold' encounters. For partners enacting monogamous intimacy, emotions are kept in their proper places through the discursive devalorisation of extradyadic relations and the placement of these relations outside the intimate, affective domain. Conversely, for partners enacting non-monogamous intimacy, extradyadic relations mark an extended population that is included *within* the intimate domain. We suggest that the demarcation of domains is governed by affective work that operates according to affective economies (in the form of intimacy scripts) to keep emotions in place. We have shown how new technologies are 'housetrained' by being affectively, discursively and technologically moulded into old (dominant and subcultural) scripts of intimacy and belonging. We suggest that the scripts do not emerge from the subject, but are discursive regulatory regimes of intimacy that enable subjects to feel a sense of belonging and home. Thus, we conclude that the moulding forces of new technologies do not necessarily disturb intimate relations; rather, the technologies are moulded into existing intimacies – intimacies that, themselves, are products of societal and public scripts.

Most analyses of media domestication processes presume the home as a given in the setting of the (heterosexual) family. Combining an expanded conception of 'home' with Berlant's understanding of intimacy as a sense of belonging, we have shown that home-making should be understood as a spatial, material and psychological construct. Through the presentation of three cases, we have demonstrated that this construct is a product of continuous affective work to demarcate a private sense of belonging from the public domain. Rather than understanding these affective processes as emerging from the subject, such processes must be understood as producing the very limits of subjectivity.

Notes

1 Real participant names and other identifying features have been redacted.
2 Scruff Facebook page (2016). Retrieved from https://www.facebook.com/scruff/info.

References

Ahmed, S. (2004). *The Cultural Politics of Emotions*. Edinburgh: Edinburgh University Press.

Berker, T., Hartmann, M., Punie, Y. and Ward, K. (2005). Introduction. In: T. Berker, M. Hartmann, Y. Punie and K. Ward, eds., *Domestication of Media and Technology*. Maidenshead: Open University Press, pp. 2–17.

Berlant, L. (2000). *Intimacy* (Critical Inquiry Book). Chicago, IL: University of Chicago Press.

Bonello, K. and Cross, M. (2010): Gay monogamy: I love you but I can't have sex with only you. *Journal of Homosexuality*, 57(1), pp. 117–139.

Douglas, M. (1966). *Purity and Danger: An Analysis of the Concepts of Pollution and Taboo*. London: Ark Paperbacks.

Duggan, L. (2004). *The Twilight of Equality – Neoliberalism, Cultural Politics and the Attack on Democracy*. Boston, MA: Beacon Press.

Duguay, S., Burgess, J. and Light, B. (2016). Mobile Dating and Hookup App Culture. In P. Messaris and L. Humphreys (Eds.), *Digital Media: Transformations in Human Communication*.

Eng, D.L. (2010). The feeling of kinship. Queer liberalism and the racialization of intimacy. Durham, NC: Duke University Press.

Giddens, A. (1992). *The Transformation of Intimacy: Sexuality, Love and Eroticism in Modern Societies*. Oxford: Polity.

Hepp, A. (2013). The communicative figurations of mediatized worlds: Mediatization research in times of the 'mediation of everything'. *European Journal of Communication*, 28(6), pp. 615–629.

Hirsch, E. and Silverstone, R. (eds.) (1992). *Consuming Technologies: Media and Information in Domestic Spaces*. London and New York: Routledge.

Jamieson, L. (2005). Boundaries of intimacy. In S. Cunningham-Burley, ed., *Families in Society. Boundaries and Relationships*. Bristol: Policy Press, pp. 189–205.

Jansson, A. (2015a). The molding of mediatization: The stratified indispensability of media in close relationships. *Communications*, 40(4), pp. 379–401.

Jansson, A. (2015b). Interveillance: A new culture of recognition and mediatization. *Media and Communication*, 3(3), pp. 81–90.

Jørgensen, K.M. (2016). The media go-along: Researching mobilities with media at hand. *MedieKultur. Journal of Media and Communication Research*, 32(60), pp. 32–49.

LaSala, M.C. (2004). Monogamy of the heart. Extradyadic sex and gay male couples. *Journal of Gay & Lesbian Social Services*, 17(3), pp. 1–24.

Mowlabocus, S. (2010). *Gaydar Culture. Gay Men, Technology and Embodiment in the Digital Age*. Farnham: Ashgate.

Nebeling Petersen, M. (2012). *Somewhere, Over the Rainbow. Biopolitiske rekonfigurationer af den homoseksuelle figur*. PhD dissertation. University of Copenhagen.

Peil, C. and Röser, J. (2014). The meaning of home in the context of digitization, mobilization and mediatization. In: A. Hepp and F. Krotz, eds., *Mediatized Worlds*. New York: Palgrave McMillan.

Race, K. (2014). 'Party 'n' Play': Online hook-up devices and the emergence of PNP practices among gay men. *Sexualities*, 18(3), pp. 253–275.

Silverstone, R. (1994). *Television and Everyday Life*. London: Routledge.

Silverstone, R. (2006). Domesticating domestication. Reflections on the life of a concept. In: T. Berker, M. Hartmann, Y. Punie and K. Ward, eds., *Domestication of Media and Technology*. Maidenhead: Open University Press, pp. 229–248.

Silverstone, R. and Haddon, L. (1996). Design and the domestication of ICTs: Technical change and everyday life. In: R. Silverstone and R. Mansell, eds., *Communication by Design: The Politics of Information and Communication Technologies*. Oxford: Oxford University Press.

Sixsmith, J. and Sixsmith, A. (1990). Place in transition: The impact of life events on the experience of home. In: T. Putnam and C. Newton, eds., *Household Choices*. London: Futures Publications.

Søndergaard, D.M. (2002). Poststructuralist approaches to empirical analysis. *International Journal of Qualitative Studies in Education*, 15(2), pp. 187–204.

Weston, K. (1997). *Families We Choose: Lesbians, Gays, Kinship*. New York: Columbia University Press.

Part IV

Becoming and performing

15 Teen boys on YouTube

Representations of gender and intimacy

Claire Balleys

Videos about me, by me – introductory remarks

Every day around the world, thousands of teenagers post YouTube videos about themselves. Boys and girls get in front of their cameras, at home, and address internet audiences, sharing confidences, indulging in self-derision, offering advice and telling their stories. YouTube, the top file-sharing site on the planet, provides a brave new world for expressing, experimenting with and negotiating adolescence (Caron, 2014; Lange, 2014; Saul, 2010).

Make no mistake, these videos do not attest to a lack of intimacy or the demise of any notion of privacy among teens (Balleys and Coll, 2016). Instead, they reveal an extremely nuanced appropriation of what intimacy entails and represents today, in terms of a subjective relationship with one's individuality, body and feelings. The self-presentation offered in these amateur videos is altogether different from what we see in spontaneous, unmanaged clips, such as ones parents post online of their children awkwardly blowing out their first candle. By making themselves the subject and expressing themselves publicly, teenagers are conducting an exercise in social and identity positioning, leveraging intimacy to tell their stories and triggering recognition and identification in their online audience.

In this chapter, we will analyse the gender performances (Butler, 2007) and gender display (Goffman, 1979) conveyed on YouTube by boys aged 12 to 17, who author videos to problematise their relationship with physical or relational intimacy. As Judith Butler puts it, 'gender is always a doing' (2007, p. 34), and this activity 'is performatively produced and compelled by the regulatory practices of gender coherence' (ibid.). Our research objectively examines the modalities of self-presentation (Goffman, 1959) as a boy on YouTube. The starting point of our investigation is the statement of gender membership, and we focus our research on content in which adolescent boys specifically problematise their masculinity by using expressions such as 'us guys' and by staging a type of intimacy: corporeal, relational or subjective.

When teenagers stage themselves as boys and talk about masculine intimacy on the public platform of YouTube, what modalities of the 'gender display' (Goffman, 1979) do they submit for their audience's evaluation? Erving Goffman describes 'gender display' as having a 'dialogic character of a statement-reply kind', and 'conventionalized portrayals' of gender (1979, p. 1). The interactive aspect that is articulated in the notion of gender display is very useful for the problematisation of our subject, because amateur video practices involve an eminently dialogic, relational (Lange, 2007, 2014; Marwick, 2016) and participatory (Caron et al., 2017; Jenkins, 2009) dynamic. These videographers enter into a relationship with an imagined audience (boyd, 2008), who – like any audience – have the capacity for 'collective meaning-making' (Liebes and Katz, 1990), mainly through the comment space attached to each video. Indeed, the young YouTubers in our corpus constantly reference the agency of their audience, using ritualised solicitations for participation: 'If you like this video, give me a thumbs-up – it's always appreciated' and 'Don't forget to subscribe to my channel.'

A YouTuber's presumed quality is closely correlated to the audience feedback generated by his or her videos (Beuscart and Mellet, 2015). There are three measures of popularity on YouTube: number of views for each video, number of 'likes' generated by each video and number of subscribers to the author's channel(s). The YouTubers in our corpus constantly manage their 'micro-celebrity' (Marwick, 2016; Senft, 2012) by employing strategies to increase their online popularity.

Traditionally, discussions of intimacy are associated with feminine socialisation (Giddens, 1992); but on YouTube, themes related to puberty, sexuality, body experience and relationships are very popular among boys, and are typically approached through the genre of humour. Humour seems to be one possible vector of male confidences – perhaps the only one that is compatible with standards of virility (Duret, 1999). The figure of the male hero who is shrewd, rather than Herculean, and who has the gift of being able to make his peers laugh and wriggle out of the most ludicrous situations, was not invented by YouTube videographers. Many studies have documented the way in which boys play with irony and humour to talk about their feelings (Allen, 2007, 2014; Korobov and Thorne, 2006, 2007).

Teen videos offer a key to understanding the gender and sexuality socialisation process that is played out, in part, through the vector of the internet. The fact that the videos are written, produced and edited does not undermine the scope or originality of the content. Caricature is an excellent tool for understanding components of social awareness. We want to clarify, however, that these videocasts stem from an appropriation of existing cultural standards and do not offer true access to the intimate adolescent experience. The performance context follows a tradition of subjective male speech, modelled in particular by professional comedians (Quemener, 2014) and comedic characters on television series (Pasquier, 1999).

Methods

The results presented here are drawn from two fields. The first is an online ethnographic study conducted on YouTube between February 2014 and November 2015. Every day, we viewed dozens of teen videos, navigating from channel to channel by following the comment threads posted by viewers. The objective was to sidestep the YouTube suggestions in order to amass an amateur corpus that closely reflected the activities of a small group of minor YouTubers. Teens who are active on YouTube are often both the producers and viewers of these videos. Thanks to the comments posted by YouTube 'juniors' – either among themselves or to professional YouTubers – we were able to build a corpus that accounted for and, to some extent, circumvented the algorithmic logic of the YouTube platform. This ethnographic observation allowed us to hone in on the visual and discursive language of this cultural genre, as well as the prevailing rules and codes for amateur YouTubers. The multiple cultural references employed by the teens – particularly those references that had been borrowed from the video gaming world – demanded a lengthy decoding effort.

This initial ethnographic fieldwork allowed us to identify the dominant video format boys use to declare their gender identity and stage a form of intimacy: the humour category. YouTube 'provides its users with accessible categories of different content' (Simonsen, 2011, p. 75), which the author selects before posting a video. One of the results revealed by our initial ethnographic fieldwork was the prevalence of videos in which the author declares membership to the masculine gender, problematises a form of intimacy and affiliates the video with the humour category on YouTube.

From the results of this ethnographic fieldwork, we were able to build and stabilise a corpus of 60 comedic videocasts that were created and posted on YouTube by 30 boys aged 12 to 17 (according to the information they provided on the website) living in France, French-speaking Switzerland, Belgium and Québec.[1] The term 'videocast' is used here to mean that the videos are available on channels, similar to podcast sound files. The videos on these videocast channels were selected on the basis of three criteria, in addition to the age and sex of the videographer. First, since we were interested in amateur practices, we limited the maximum number of views for each video to 100,000. Accordingly, views of the videocasts we analysed ranged from 167 to 91,964. The publication date of the video was also taken into account; we correlated this with the number of subscribers to the author's channel, in order to avoid looking at a video with 60,000 views that had been posted the day before by a professional YouTuber. The second criterion was videos designated as comedic by the author; that is, videos that were associated with the humour category on YouTube. The third criterion was a focus on relational intimacy (i.e. relating to feelings, friendship or romantic relationships) or physical intimacy (i.e. relating to puberty, virility or sexuality). We searched for videos on these themes by subscribing to 140 channels administered by boys. As this was a study of available online content and did not involve direct contact with the authors, the teens' social background was not known; however, videocasting practices involve technical and expressive learning and know-how that depend on multiple social and family resources (Lange, 2014). Each video was downloaded in order to be analysed offline and transcribed in order to enable us to reconstruct the discursive, visual and audio content. Gestures, tones, looks, sighs, laughter and winks were included in the content analysis, as were editing effects, changes of frame and setting, textual inserts into the image, music and background noise.

Ethical considerations also directed the construction of the corpus. While all of the YouTube videos are publicly accessible, we took precautions to ensure that the chosen content had been designed and constructed as a cultural product destined for wide broadcast. First, we focused our attention on videos with a studied, stylised format. A number of indicators revealed the level of writing and production effort that went into a video; for example, a variety of shots, a range of backgrounds and visual inserts (images and/or text) suggested high production effort. The authors, themselves, frequently mentioned the time they had spent writing their scripts and sometimes showed themselves at their writing desk or mentioned it in the comment space. This methodological choice allowed us to eliminate any content that was not the result of in-depth reflection and a desire to make the content publicly available. Videos that appeared to be filmed spontaneously in the 'vlogging' style, for example, were not taken into consideration. Second, we only selected videos with content that was explicitly and purposefully public; that is, videos in which the authors mentioned their desire to see the video viewed as widely as possible. At the end of each video in our corpus, the author asks his audience to like the video, to subscribe to his channel and to share it on social media. Thus, the content is clearly intended for mass consumption.

As the authors of these videos are minors, we changed their names and the nicknames of their channels, along with any other clues that might enable them to be recognised. Posting a video on YouTube is not the same as giving consent as a research subject. Accordingly, we felt that the anonymisation of the profiles and content was a necessary precaution.

Results

Male adolescence and socialisation among peers

Anthropologically, becoming a man is a process that involves male self-segregation (Godelier, 1982). Since the inception of the concept of adolescence in the Western world and its related status (Thiercé, 1999), pubescent boys have been subjected to the evaluation of their male peers with respect to the acceptance of sexual independence and demonstration of virility (Fine, 1987; Kehily, 2001; Pascoe, 2007; Richardson, 2010). From a somewhat vertical transmission process, masculine socialisation has become more horizontal. A teen's capacity to engage in the process of 'becoming a man' is evaluated mainly by his male comrades and friends. Girls are also stakeholders in the assessment, but largely as a yardstick of the boy's capacity to seduce them. It is the boys who are in charge of deciding who among them meets the standards of masculinity, which imply: heterosexuality – a standard that is still very meaningful today (Clair, 2012; Pascoe, 2007); sexual agency (Bourdieu, 1998; Goffman, 1977); emotional control (Allen, 2003; Eder et al., 1995); and love of competition (Ayard, 2011).

The ritual of losing one's virginity, for example – a classic virility ritual – is subject to validation by male peers: 'Actually, for a lot of boys, the "first time" is to prove his virility and its corollary, heterosexuality, not so much to girls but to his peers. They are the ones who validate the first sexual experience' (Revenin, 2015, p. 230; our translation). The notion of virility in adolescence is therefore subject to relational dynamics among peers (Balleys, 2015) and recognition by peers (Duret, 1999).

The masculine intimacy that is explored and performed by teenagers on YouTube is dialogic and relational in nature. It relies on ways of subjectivising the self, the body and maturation that seek the validation of peers, who are embodied in the web audience. In their YouTube performances, the boys largely address other boys, using expressions such as, 'You know what I mean, right, guys?' and 'Hey, guys, we're not going to lie to each other, right?' and 'You've got to admit it's the worst thing that can happen to us, yo, dude, I'm talking to you, yeah, you!' The teen videocasters' quest for recognition of their work, their individuality and their masculinity is omnipresent in the content they offer.

As we will see, the performance of masculine intimacy is closely articulated through the performance of 'growing up' and 'becoming a man'. The physiological and psychological transformations that are triggered by puberty are especially crucial in male teen performances on YouTube. As Antoine (15) says: 'Adolescence is really a change in the life of a man. With a capital M.' This 'change' is featured in most of the intimacy videos and reveals the authors' pride at leaving the world of children. Talking about their private lives is the same as talking about their masculinity and therefore adopting the stance of a man-in-the-making. The authors are no longer 'kids' who dare not tackle intimate issues head-on, and who are scared or ashamed. By proclaiming an unabashed body and adopting uninhibited discourse with humour and self-assurance, these young videographers prove both their virility and their maturity and establish a position as individuals who are different from girls and children. In particular, the systematic references to their sexual organ, sexuality and sexual agency constitute important proof of their virile self-affirmation. As Cyril (14) tells us: 'Yeah, puberty is a kind of metamorphosis, into something way better! And that's it, you get bigger, more mature, like my dic–[gestures with both hands toward his penis]–tionary … hey, what did you think I was going to say!?'

These videos give us access to masculine discourse on the experience of male adolescence, in the context of negotiating identity and status, that aims to create male complicity and a sense of closeness. In each video in our corpus, the author expresses himself explicitly as a member of the male teen group, in particular by referring to himself and his audience as 'us guys'. For example, Jules (14) says: 'Us guys get hard-ons, but not just for any old reason!' By playing the role of spokespersons for masculinity – even parodically – and addressing themselves explicitly to their peers, the young YouTubers position themselves as leaders (Balleys, 2015), capable of speaking on behalf of the group. 'So I'm sending out a message to all the men in the world,' declares Ben (16), as if he were addressing the universal male.

Desiring means becoming a man

It has been demonstrated that female comedy videos on YouTube are received and commented on more harshly than male comedy videos (Wotanis and McMillan, 2014). The reactions of web users (through comments) refer more frequently to the bodies and personalities of girl YouTubers, while boy YouTubers are critiqued for their content. Our results show that the subject sexuality, as explored through humour, is still considered by teenagers a male territory (Goffman, 1977). For example, referring to and even mimicking masturbation is an often-used comedic ploy and is always presented as a specifically masculine practice: 'To start with, in puberty, there's masturbation. Yes! One day, man discovered his penis!' (Jack, 15).

Boys playfully explore the effects of puberty on their physiology, and sexuality is a very present theme in their videos: body hair (especially pelvic), voice change, erections, penis size, sexual desire and masturbation are recurring themes. These physical manifestations are considered in the discourse to be 'natural' phenomena in boys – 'simple' and 'normal' – that are integral to their masculinity.

Masturbation is also associated with pornographic videos and the presence of paper towels or facial tissues in the bedroom. A boy who masturbates and ejaculates is, indeed, a pubescent boy, set apart from 'little boys' who cannot yet do so. Male sexual desire is also a recurring theme. Thinking about sex constitutes a form of masculine normality in the boys' self-presentation. Sometimes figures or statistics (from unnamed sources) are used to support their statements, as demonstrated by Antoine (15), who explains, wearing a doctor's lab coat and brand-name glasses: 'Did you know? A man thinks about sex 18 times a day.' These male sexual impulses are often related to female physiological changes. Thus, female puberty is broached from the angle of the male desire that is provoked by their new appearance, as shown in this excerpt by Cyril (14):

> What's great about puberty in girls, is that their butt – brains get bigger. They become smarter. [Change to close medium shot] Big tits! [Change

to close-up facing camera] Riper! [Change to close medium shot] Big tits! [Wide movement with arms] No, really, I'm only interested in tits!

While these words do not authentically or exhaustively reveal what the boys who author the videos think or feel any more than they reveal the intimate experiences of the thousands of teens who watch them, they nevertheless allow us to grasp the standards of self-presentation as a boy and particularly, a boy becoming a man. They also throw into relief what is silenced or at least not acknowledged or problematised: female sexual desire. Boys talk about female puberty, but solely in reference to the effects that feminised bodies have on their own libidos or in reference to menstruation and the mood changes that are supposedly associated with it. The male videocasts give us a window into the ways in which boys define sexuality and its urges as something eminently masculine.

It is interesting to note that the teen videos about masculine intimacy do not, in any way, dissociate the experience of the body from the experience of the mind. The authors appear to be comfortable recognising sexual desire and its manifestations – naming them, talking about them and accepting them as part of the self, part of masculinity and part of 'growing up'. Their words show that what is happening in the boys' heads lines up with what is happening in their bodies. Justin (15), for example, explains that in adolescence, 'it's not just the body that changes, it's also the soul! [...] what I mean is that you think a little more – just a little – about the opposite sex.' The changes in the 'body' and the 'soul' are presented as correlated and consistent. The rhetoric of change is very present in these videocasts, problematising the passage from childhood to adolescence and linking it to 'becoming a man'. As Antoine (15) explains: 'But adolescence, especially for a guy, is, uh, [leans into the camera] a mental change! Yeah, it's in our heads, dude! Yeah, because sometimes, our ideas can be kind of screwed up, right?' The upheavals experienced in the body are echoed in the 'head' and confirm a budding masculinity – 'especially for a guy', as Antoine specifies.

Presenting the relationship: Personal success (or failure)

Male teens are confronted with a two-part contradictory injunction: they must demonstrate some measure of relationship expertise to show they are not 'little' any more and to demonstrate their interest in the opposite sex; at the same time, they must show distance from and dismissiveness with regard to emotions and related issues. For example, Antoine (15), who tells us that 'men think about sex 18 times a day', acts out a young boy who 'thinks about *Call of Duty* [a first-person shooter game] 18 times a day'. Antoine gives this boy all the characteristics of a child, lisping and jumping up and down, yelling '*Call of Duty*! *Call of Duty*! *Call of Duty*!' This figure also embodies the 'geek' who is not (yet) capable of having an intimate relationship. He wears big glasses and a headset that allows him to communicate when he is playing online with others. The term 'teen geek' is shown in the video image when Antoine jumps around in his bedroom with the video game in his hands. When Antoine becomes 'himself' once more and returns to the role of narrator, facing the camera, he wears a cap and speaks in a much lower, calmer voice.

A mature boy is therefore supposed to be interested in emotional relationships and seducing girls. In many of the videocasts devoted to relationships, Valentine's Day or hitting on girls, the love relationship is problematised as a conquest and personal success, associated with a certain level of pride. In fact, it is not so much emotion that is the focus of the discourse but prestigious, enviable social status: being in a relationship. Marc (15) expresses his desire to be in a relationship in these terms:

> When you become an adolescent, you just have one idea in mind. Getting a girlfriend! Because for a man, it's always good to show you are with a woman. It's better than being single. Otherwise you're like an old bachelor. The school loser. And besides, there's no harm in getting a few more notches on your belt. Male pride!

This discourse, although intentionally caricatured, expresses a point of view shared by all of the videocasts about relational intimacy: 'dating a chick' provides proof – for oneself and for others – of a particular personal skill. As Jonathan (12) says: 'If you have succeeded in finding a girl and you're in a relationship' – or Alexandre (15): 'The guys who are really good at hitting on girls and manage to get a girlfriend' – the couple relationship is not a given; rather, it is the result of a specifically masculine challenge. Succeeding in this challenge is presented as a victory. Many boys begin their videos on the theme of relationships by declaring 'I'm in a relationship!' or 'I did it! I got a girl!' raising their arms and dancing to a musical soundtrack as if it were a sports victory. Arno (17) shares this moment of euphoria with a friend before putting him firmly in his place: 'You're a piece of shit. You're just a piece of shit: you don't have a girlfriend. Get out of my video if you don't have a girlfriend!' In this way, he demonstrates that this status is a matter of prestige, even though it is handled as a joke.

It is interesting to note that narratives of rejection and other relationship failures hold an important place in this category of videocasts about relational intimacy. Teen boys use the figure of the 'lovable loser' (Korobov, 2009) to stage their first emotional experiences. The girl's role, in these narratives, is reduced to total passivity. All she controls is access to her body: what she authorises and to whom. In Mo's video (17), he parodies the girl he is in love with, who is dating another boy and explains to him on the phone: 'Yeah, you know, the guy took me, he turned me over, and he took me like a bitch, and you can't, you see, because you're too ugly, that's it. I have to say that you're [...] you're a piece of shit! So you'll never do to me what he did to me. Bye now!'

We are given to understand that this lack of ability to 'hook up with chicks' does not fundamentally cast doubt on the authors' virility. On the contrary. Through narratives of failures, they add proof to their compliance with standards of masculinity, thereby confirming: a) their heterosexuality; b) their sexual desire and, by extension, their agency; c) their desire to be in a relationship – ergo, their maturity; and d) their capacity to accept the male rivalry inherent in accessing the female body.

The boys' narrations of relationships on YouTube therefore focus more on their capacity to become sexually desirous and agentic than on their feelings. This is not to claim that feelings are absent from the discourse, but they seem to be subject to the imperative of masculine sexualisation. The boys problematise feelings through the prism of sexual desire. We must insist, again, on the fact that our point is not to say that boys are less sentimental or less emotionally engaged than girls, which is also refuted in the literature (Giordano, Longmore and Manning, 2006). What we want to describe here are representations of relational intimacy, as expressed on YouTube by minors. In this sense, we now examine the representations of girls offered by the young YouTubers in our corpus.

Representations of the feminine and male cross-dressing

Twenty-five of the 30 boys cross-dress in at least one of the videos in our corpus. Sometimes the cross-dressing is minimal, going no further than a boy putting a scarf on his head, and sometimes it is very elaborate, involving wigs, makeup and girls' clothes. The authors use all the standards of cross-dressing offered in the comedic world: speaking with a drawling, nasal voice and using affected gestures and inane facial expressions. The cross-dressing allows the authors to show dialogues between themselves and female characters, who usually represent persons they want to seduce or are dating.

The first characteristic attributed to teenage girls is jealousy. Female jealousy is more problematised by the boys than male jealousy. Many of the boys talk about the feeling of being endlessly 'controlled' by their girlfriends, particularly through their cell phones. This situation is exaggerated for comic effect, with scenes in which the girls appear armed, dangerous and even enraged. Nicolas (17), after expressing his pride at having a girlfriend, enacts his fear in response to the constant control his omnipresent girlfriend has over him:

> Message to all guys: erase all your messages! [He looks all around, as if petrified] Messages, Facebook, everything, Instagram, Snapchat, erase it all! Everything! They're everywhere, they control everything: your phone, everything, your computer, everything! They're everywhere! [He turns his head all around] So if you value your life, really, guys, erase it all. [He jumps and cries out] [...] and if by some misfortune you sent a heart to another girl – or several – just get the hell out of there. In any

> case, you're dead. So just get the hell out. Girls don't mess around. [Frightened voice and eyes wide open] They don't mess around.

Girls' behaviour is described as 'worse than customs' or 'worse than the FBI' in their desire to control their partner's relationships with other girls. The boys show themselves in a position of weakness – even submission – within the couple relationship. Dylan (17) films himself with his hands tied behind his back, blood on his torn T-shirt, sitting on a chair in the middle of an empty room, as if he has just undergone an intense interrogation. He explains in a voice-over that this is reprisal for having forgotten Valentine's Day: 'And you better not forget to wish your girlfriend Happy Valentine's Day or even get her a present because otherwise, I can assure you, dude, you will regret it!'

While girls are shown to be controlling and even harassing with regard to the relational and emotional availability they demand from their partner, they are simultaneously depicted as frightened – if not disgusted by – sexuality. When Ben (16) produces a videocast about sexuality, he writes a girl into his script who interrupts him with an offended tone and expression:

> We'll all have sex some day. Or perhaps you already have [...] [small, knowing smile; cut to Ben playing a girl with a scarf on his head, who reacts with a disgusted expression]: Oh, you're really a pig, aren't you!

Male sexual excitement is presented as potentially dangerous for girls. The figure of the sexual pervert is often parodied through a fixed stare and drooling mouth. While boys distance themselves from this character, it is exclusively attributed to the male sex and embodies a threat to girls. The boys represent themselves as ready for a sexual relationship before girls are. Félix (15) problematises the question of his virginity and asks how he can lose it as quickly as possible. One of his first missions is to succeed in convincing the girl he likes to have sex with him. He imagines several scenarios in which she always ends up telling him she is not 'ready', to his great disappointment.

These excerpts show that the boys do not paint themselves as all-powerful heroes in the imagined scenes. On the contrary, they seem subject to the control and goodwill of their female partners. And yet what we notice is how consistently sexuality is presented as an exclusively masculine domain. The naturalisation of differences in gender and sex, which is present in all the videos in our corpus, points to a common premise: sexuality is naturally masculine and masculinity is naturally sexual. Feminine sexuality is reduced to provisions made to acquiesce to or avoid masculine impulses, as summarised so well by Jules (14): 'But anyway, erections are natural. So if you guys have ever had one while eating a kebab, or if you girls are going to run away the next time you see a guy with his hands in his pockets ...'

Conclusion

The problematisation by teenage boys of physical and relational intimacy on YouTube is, in fact, a problematisation of gender and sexuality. Parody and caricature are the means of constructing and presenting binary masculine and feminine intimacies. At this moment of adolescent socialisation, there is no subversive proposition concerning gender norms. Boys are subject to the emotional impulses of girls and girls are subject to the sexual impulses of boys. 'There is no gender identity behind the expressions of gender,' writes Judith Butler (2007, p. 34), 'that identity is performatively constituted by the very "expressions" that are said to be its results' (ibid.). Although YouTube offers a brand new platform for expressing gender identity in adolescence, there is no doubt that the masculinity performed there is deeply imprinted with a traditional form of heteronormativity. The 'gender displays' (Goffman, 1979) and 'expressive behaviour' (p. 3) present a 'naturally' hetereosexual masculinity that is obsessed with sex and considers girls as beings who are 'naturally' frightened or even disgusted by sex.

While sexual agency is continually mobilised in the discourses the boys present about themselves as boys, they portray themselves as completely passive in social situations related to being in a couple: sexuality is depicted as potentially dangerous for girls and masculine desire is depicted as something that is likely to represent a threat to girls' physical integrity. The romantic relationship is presented as potentially dangerous for the boys, because of the controlling power girls have over them.

An analysis of the performances of masculinity through the staging of intimacy by boys on YouTube reveals the dual effect of cultural standardisation and the 'hyper-ritualization' of gender (Goffman, 1979, p. 84). The forms of self-presentation performed by boys on YouTube result from the standardisation and caricature of masculinity as experienced at the moment of puberty.

There are YouTube videocasts created by young adults, men and women alike that question and shake up sexual roles, but we posit that teens, who are still in the process of being socialised to gender and sexuality, are not inclined to distance themselves from the social and identity characteristics that they are only just acquiring. However, this does not, in our opinion, mean that amateur video does not permit the expression and adoption of subversion.

The next question would be: What about the socialisation of girls in this situation? Can we imagine a 15-year-old girl talking about the configuration of her vulva on YouTube? About masturbation? Vaginal lubrication? A corpus of videos made by teenage girls, currently under analysis, allows us to respond in the negative. Socialisation to gender and sexuality is still very divided. The boys we followed on YouTube voluntarily show their naked torsos in their videos and sometimes even film themselves in briefs in the shower, and it neither shocks nor upsets the viewers. By comparison, when a 13-year-old girl we will call Chloe shows herself in short shorts in one of her videos, she receives dozens of comments from viewers playing the roles of do-gooder and moral entrepreneur (Becker, 1963): 'your level of sluttishness is impressive'; 'OMG where is your mother to let you dress like that?'; and 'little slut, you are setting a bad example'.

Note

1 The video excerpts presented in this chapter were translated into English from the original French.

References

Allen, L. (2003). Girls want sex, boys want love: Resisting dominant discourses of (hetero)sexuality. *Sexualities*, 6(2), pp. 215–236.

Allen, L. (2007). Sensitive and real macho all at the same time: Young heterosexual men and romance. *Men and Masculinities*, 10, pp. 137–152.

Allen, L. (2014). Don't forget, Thursday is test[icle] time! The use of humour in sexuality education. *Sex Education*, 14(4), pp. 387–399. doi: 10.1080/14681811.2014.918539.

Ayard, S. (2011). *La fabrique des garçons: sanctions et genre au college*. Paris: PUF.

Balleys, C. (2015). *Grandir entre adolescents: à l'école et sur Internet*. Lausanne: PPUR.

Balleys, C. and Coll, S. (2016). Being publicly intimate: Teenagers managing online privacy. *Media, Culture & Society*. doi:10.1177/0163443716679033.

Becker, H. (1963). *Outsiders: Studies in the Sociology of Deviance*. New York: The Free Press.

Beuscart, J.S. and Mellet, K. (2015). La conversion de la notoriété en ligne: une étude des trajectoires de vidéastes pro-am. *Terrains et Travaux*, 26(1), pp. 83–104.

Bourdieu, P. (1998). *La domination masculine*. Paris: Seuil.

boyd, d. (2008). *Taken Out of Context. American Teen Sociality in Networked Publics*. PhD dissertation. University of California. Retrieved from www.danah.org/papers/TakenOutOfContext.pdf.

Butler, J. (2007). *Gender Trouble*. New York: Routledge.

Caron, C. (2014). Les jeunes et l'expérience participative en ligne. *Lien Social et Politiques*, 71, pp. 13–30.

Caron, C., Raby, R., Mitchell, C., Théwissen-LeBlanc, S. and Prioletta, J. (2017). From concept to data: sleuthing social change-oriented youth voices on YouTube, *Journal of Youth Studies*, 20:1, 47–62, doi: 10.1080/13676261.2016.1184242

Clair, I. (2012). Le pédé, la pute et l'ordre hétérosexuel. *Agora Débat Jeunesse*, 1(60), pp. 67–78.

Duret, P. (1999). *Les jeunes et l'identité masculine*. Paris: PUF.

Eder, D., Colleen Evan, C. and Parker, S. (1995). *School Talk: Gender and Adolescent Culture*. New Brunswick, NJ: Rutgers University Press.

Fine, G.A. (1987). *With the Boys: Little League Baseball and Preadolescent Culture*. Chicago and London: University of Chicago Press.

Giddens, A. (1992). *The Transformation of Intimacy: Sexuality, Love and Eroticism in Modern Societies*. Cambridge: Polity.

Giordano, P., Longmore, M.A. and Manning, W.D. (2006). Gender and the meaning of adolescent romantic relationships: A focus on boys. *American Sociological Review*, 71(2), pp. 260–287.

Glevarec, H. (2014). L'attachement aux univers fictionnels et déplacement du champ du dicible et du pensable: la sériphilie des jeunes adultes. In: J. Lachance et al., eds., *Séries cultes et culte de la série chez les jeunes*. Laval: PUL.

Godelier, M. (1982). *La Production des Grands-Hommes*. Paris: Fayard.

Goffman, E. (1959). *The Presentation of Self in Everyday Life*. New York: Anchor Books.

Goffman, E. (1977). The arrangements between the sexes. *Theory and Society*, 4(3), pp. 301–331.

Goffman, E. (1979). *Gender Advertisements*. New York: Harper and Row Publishers.

Jenkins, H. (2009). *Confronting the Challenges of Participatory Culture: Media Education for the 21st Century*, MacArthur Foundation, Chicago. Retrieved from www.macfound.org/media/article_pdfs/JENKINS_WHITE_PAPER.PDF.

Kehily, M. (2001). Bodies in school: Young men, embodiment, and heterosexual masculinities. *Men and Masculinities*, 4(2), pp. 173–185.

Korobov, N. and Thorne, A. (2006). Intimacy and Distancing: Young Men's Conversations About Romantic Relationships, *Journal of Adolescent Research*, Vol. 21 No. 1, 27-55 DOI: 10.1177/0743558405284035.

Korobov, N. and Thorne, A. (2007). How late adolescent friends share stories about relationships: The importance of mitigating the seriousness of romantic problems. *Journal of Social and Personal Relationships*, 27, 971–992.

Korobov, N. (2009). Expanding hegemonic masculinity: The use of irony in young men's stories about romantic experiences. *American Journal of Men's Health*, 3:4, 286–299, DOI: 10.1177/1557988308319952.

Lange, P. (2014). *Kids on YouTube: Technical Identities and Digital Literacies*. Walnut Creek: Left Coast Press.

Liebes, T. and Katz, E. (1990). *The Export of Meaning. Cross-Cultural Readings of Dallas*. New York and Oxford: Oxford University Press.

Marwick, A. (2016). You may know me from YouTube: (Micro)-celebrity in social media. In: D. Marshall and S. Redmond, eds., *Companion to Celebrity Studies*. Malen, MA: Wiley-Blackwell.

Pascoe, C.J. (2007). *'Dude You're a Fag': Masculinity and Sexuality in High School*. Berkeley, CA: University of California Press.

Pasquier, D. (1999). *La culture des sentiments*. Paris: Editions de la Maison des Sciences de l'Homme.

Quemener, N. (2014). *Le pouvoir de l'humour*. Paris: Armand Colin.

Revenin, R. (2015). *Une histoire des garçons et des filles: Amour, genre et sexualité dans la France d'après-guerre*. Paris: Vendémiaire.

Richardson, D. (2010). Youth masculinities: Compelling male heterosexuality. *The British Journal of Sociology*, 61(4), pp. 738–756.

Saul, R. (2010). KevJumba and the adolescence of YouTube. *Educational Studies*, 46, pp. 457–477.

Senft, T. (2012). Microcelebrity and the branded self. In: J. Burgess and A. Bruns, eds., *Blackwell Companion to New Media Dynamics*. Chichester: Blackwell.

Simonsen, T.M. (2011). Categorising YouTube. *MedieKultur: Journal of Media and Communication Research*, 27(51), pp. 72–93.

Thiercé, A. (1999). *Histoire de l'adolescence (1850–1914)*. Paris: Belin.

Tolman, D. (2005). *Dilemmas of Desire: Teenage Girls Talk About Sexuality*. Cambridge, MA and London: Harvard University Press.

Wotanis, L. and McMillan, L. (2014). Performing gender on YouTube: How Jenna Marbles negotiates a hostile online environment. *Feminist Media Studies,* 14(6), pp. 912–928.

16 Technical intimacies and Otherkin becomings

Eva Zekany

Non-human intimacies – introductory remarks

Networked technologies, with the internet at their apex, have long provided opportunities for experimenting, self-fashioning and transgressing the categorical boundaries that order social existence and physical embodiment. In the early stages of networked connectivity, the telegraph enabled its users to engage in gender play amidst a 'quasi-physical connection across the obstacles of time and space' (Peters, 1999, p. 5). The telegraphic code was germane to gender 'troubles': in a nineteenth century short story, we encounter the already familiar (in contemporary times) case of two people falling in love over the telegraph lines, only to discover that they are each the opposite gender of what they have presented. Fast forward almost a century, and Allucquere Rosanne Stone writes about the early days of CompuServe chat lines – a ground rife with what she describes as tangles of nested assumptions and a loss of innocence, raising questions about our understanding of the body (Stone, 1995, p. 65). The story is simple and – again – familiar: a person uses networked media to create an alternate, differently gendered and differently abled person, and forms intimate connections with other users through this persona. In more recent times, net users have taken to practices of gender-switching in online games and on social media (Martey et al., 2014). In some cases, this is done to avoid online harassment; in other cases, it is done simply for the pleasure and possibilities offered by non-normative identity performance (Huh and Williams, 2010). But gender is but one identity nexus that can be destabilised through a user's interactions with connected media. Online communities provide ample opportunities for users to explore and reorganise the possibilities and constraints of bodily norms, embodied experience, species identity or the assumed certainty of human nature grounded in organic reality.

One community that consistently tests the limits of networked communication is the Otherkin community. In their concise history on the topic, Orion Scribner, a member of the community, describes the Otherkin as 'kin to the Other'; as 'people who [...] look human, but identify as supernatural entities ordinarily thought of as legendary or mythological, most commonly elves, Fae, and dragons, but many other kinds of creatures are represented as well' (Scribner, 2012, p. 5). Otherkin identify as partially or entirely non-human; they believe that their true, transcendental self – their embodied subjectivity – is outside of the human spectrum. For Otherkin, the transcendence of species identity is not limited to the choices offered by material and organic boundaries: alongside the often-encountered 'kintypes' such as wolfkin, foxkin or catkin,[1] many kintypes can be traced back to fiction, mythology or folklore: angelkin, elfkin, dragonkin and so on. One's kintype is to some extent predicated on a spiritual belief in metempsychosis, which has led some scholars to classify Otherkin as a religious movement – a community based on metaphysical questioning (Cusack, 2013; Kirby, 2014) or an 'alternative *nomos* – a socially constructed worldview – that sustains alternate ontologies' (Laycock, 2012, p. 65). However, Otherkin have no established common metaphysics or rules of deportment. As Pedro Feijó notes, Otherkin enact a 'postidentitarian dynamics' that does not search for a community based on truth; rather, they search for a collective identity that:

> has less to do with medical disclosure or realist claims, and more with what Foucault called parrhesia – to talk openly and sincerely, in a mode in which truth is not equivalent to undeniability or evidential necessity, but to honesty even when it means taking a risk (of being segregated or ridicularized [*sic*], for example).
>
> (Feijó, 2016, p. 8)

However, the alternate ontology of the Otherkin is still structured by a precise and generally internally accepted vocabulary and set of conventions. Otherkin identify as such as a result of a process of 'Awakening' – a cathartic event that allows them to discover and accept both the spiritual side of their identity – their 'True-Self' – and its bodily aspect – their 'True-Form'. The sematic field of Otherkin experience encompasses various linguistic tools that express this process of becoming in its various stages: 'seeming' – passing as human; 'transforming' – being in touch with one's True-Form or physically appearing as one's True-Form; and 'sleeping' – existing in an unawakened state.[2] But for every agreed convention within the Otherkin community there are countless opposing views on the boundaries of Otherkin identity. Fictionkin are a particular point of contention among Otherkin. These Otherkin identify as fictional (often human) characters from video games, animations, comics, books or movies, often drawn from Japanese pop culture; this has led to Fictionkin to be accused of 'taking things too far' and 'being copycats'.[3] However, despite the different states of being and identifications of different kintypes, Otherkin generally accept that there is a disconnect between their physical body and their inner self. They mostly accept that their bodies are entirely human (although many report experiencing phantom limbs such as tails, ears or wings) and see their experiences as consistent with a spiritual system, a psychological condition, a belief in reincarnation and the multiverse or a coping mechanism for trauma (Justanotherkin, 2013).

Otherkin comprise a loosely affiliated, non-hierarchical community without clear rules or social structures, whose defining trait is its primarily mediated existence. What Laycock calls the alternative *nomos* of Otherkin is intertwined and sustained by networked connectivity. Since the advent of the internet in the 1990s, Otherkin communities have shaped and been shaped by media platforms that have helped to sustain their existence. In particular, contemporary Otherkin are associated with blogging and social media platforms such as Tumblr and Reddit. The label of Otherkin is nearly synonymous with the 'weird world of Tumblr identity politics' (Read, 2012) and it describes both an affective relationality with non-human life and a form of intimacy with the technics of the internet. Otherkin Tumblr blogs are highly personal spaces that operate as loci of self-discovery and self-construction. This is not to suggest that Otherkin create so-called virtual digital personas that are distinct from their 'real' selves. Rather, their blogs are incorporated into their ongoing process of subject formation.

Rather than a fixed identity, Otherkin is perhaps more accurately understood as a Deleuzian becoming: a dynamic process of transformation, affirming the dynamic and generative difference potentials of the connections and lines of flight that arise between the self and others (Deleuze and Guattari, 1995). Otherkin can be seen to embody a particular way of relating to their self, to others and to milieu based on affinity, positive difference and creativeness. The embodied process of becoming Otherkin seems firmly rooted in the medium and technology of the internet, in the sense of an originary technicity rooted in an implicit and inseparable articulation between the individual and technics (Stiegler, 1998). In Bernard Stiegler's understanding of the relationship between technics and humanity, technics is understood as the constitutive drive that allows humanity to emerge as a category; some of the technologies of the internet, such as the connectivities of social media and the Otherkin, are fused into a similarly co-originary relationality. While technics is integral to the human in all its forms, I argue that originary technicity and technical connectivity are particularly highlighted in communities such as that of the Otherkin, wherein the technical medium cannot be dismissed as a mere platform for networking, but must be acknowledged as part of the process of becoming.

This chapter focuses on the technical aspect of Otherkin becoming – the way in which the encounter with technicity, understood as the medium of the internet, allows the emergence of forms of intimacy both *with* and *within* media that translate into alternative ontologies. Instead of adhering to the popular conception of Otherkin and related communities as fantasies that are strictly limited to online performance and divested from 'real' life (Roberts, 2015), we might productively frame Otherkin as embodying a form of media intimacy based on the transcorporeal relation between user and media technics. In this sense, Otherkin point not only towards the potentiality of an alternative, mediated *nomos* and mode of affectivity, but also towards the need to radically reconceive the ontology of the media user. Otherkin identity is performed on a variety of affective levels: first, through flows and intensities of the technical medium, itself; second, within the affinity-based communities that are constructed through online platforms; and third, as an intimate encounter between the user and a machine that empowers a particular kind of embodied performance – one that is post-human not through its denial of humanity, but through the continuous mutual construction of humanity and technics. Thus, it can be productive to approach the Otherkin phenomenon through the lens of media ontology – particularly Bernard Stiegler's theory of originary technicity and N. Katherine Hayles' exploration of technogenesis in the context of digital culture.

Technogenesis and the non-human user – theoretical approaches

Otherkin can be seen to be firmly rooted in a tradition of personal and metaphysical questioning (Laycock, 2012). But the medium of the internet is crucial for the emergence and consolidation of the Otherkin community (Kirby, 2014, 286). This is not to say that the experience of Otherkin becoming is exclusively predicated upon interaction with the connected medium or to dismiss the experience of Otherkin who experience a metaphysical awakening independent of internet use; nor does it claim that Otherkin experience (if not necessarily identity) was non-existent before the advent of the internet. However, the questioning of humanness that is enacted through the process of Otherkin becoming incorporates an intensely technical aspect – one that is axiomatic for the community and, as such, not brought up for examination. On the contrary, for detractors of Otherkin, the technical aspect is crucial and proof that participation in the Otherkin community is merely a fad that has resulted from Tumblr and LiveJournal's propensity for creating 'minority identities' through the language and tropes of social justice discourse (Mawer, 2014).

The ontological destabilisation at the core of Otherkin identity has already been analysed by Jay Johnston, who argues that Otherkin subjectivity is based on the 'demise of the "human" and "animal" as ontologically distinct categories' (Johnston, 2013, p. 297). Elsewhere, Johnston notes that Otherkin and associated subcultures such as lycanthropes and vampires, transgress and inhabit 'boundaries between matter and spirit; between the human and the animal and the human and non-human species, with "species" taken as it can be most broadly conceived' (2015, p. 412). For Johnson, the concept of the animal other is crucial for conceptualising Otherkin identity. She argues that although Otherkin can be accused of relying on an unproblematised and universal concept of the animal that does not take into account the radical differences that are inherent in the concept (as per Derrida and Kelly Oliver), Otherkin also question normative identity categories that dominate discourses on the human. Thus, Johnston considers Otherkin identity an ethical and political project that entails a 'complex, creative and respectful approach to the subject of identity' (Johnston, 2013, p. 305).

There is another level on which Otherkin perform an act of boundary crossing and destabilisation: that of the relationship between humanness and technics. Otherkin discourse – stemming from either members of the community or those who ridicule or question them – is implicitly articulated upon the technical medium that (currently) sustains it. Animal hybridity is tied to another form of hybrid subjecthood: one that results from the interaction between the subject and technics. The media object – whether we consider this to be the internet in general, specific social media platforms or a material technical configuration such as a computer or smartphone – is an integral component of Otherkin becoming and its destabilisation of the category of human. In this sense, Otherkin embodiment and identification emerge through the conjunction of the body and technics. The Otherkin community, as well as other communities that have emerged mainly in online spaces, does not comprise 'real' fleshly bodies enacting a form of virtual performativity. By considering the interrelation between media and users we avoid the reductive dualism of online/offline, real/virtual altogether. Instead, we arrive at an understanding of humanity through the lens of technicity, which forces us to reconsider the ontological status of the media user.

Theorists such as Bernard Stiegler and N. Katherine Hayles argue that technics is and has always been embroiled in shifting epistemologies of human as a category. Hayles notes that 'we think through, with and alongside media' (Hayles, 2012, p. 1), and that this coexistence requires a radical rethinking of the relationship between humans and media. For Hayles, media interaction is embodied and has bodily effects on a psychic and physical level. At the same time, media are also embodied, though their embodiments demand a non-human frame of reference. In Hayles' conception, media and their users are caught up in a mutually dependent relationality – an intimacy that leads to a temporary fixity of our abstract concepts of media and humanity. Otherkin are one node in a vast network of human-media intimacies that spans the entire non-linear history of humanity. Indeed, they can be seen as a pinnacle of user-media interrelation, in which the intimacy between the media object and the user and technics melds human and technics, dissolving them both in the process. Not being human (or being less than 100 per cent human) is at the core of Otherkin metaphysics. Tumblr user Justanotherkin, who identifies as a dragonkin, notes that the non-human identification of Otherkin does not automatically lead to the abandonment of a human frame of reference. According to this Otherkin: 'Personally I would describe Otherkin as any person who believes that they are, in some way, other than their kin (kin being humans), and kin to the other (the other being non-terrestrial/mythical/religious/etc. entities)' (Justanotherkin, 2013). Otherkin seems to describe an embodied kinship or intimacy with otherness, but does not entail a complete rejection of a human frame of reference. As

Justanotherkin further writes, 'being human is a core aspect to identifying as an otherkin, as the term exists as a human construction [...] most otherkin acknowledge that, first an [*sic*] foremost, they are human' (ibid.). The Otherkin goes on to mention that while the Otherkin community is most certainly not a 'Tumblr fad', the community emerged through the means of online sources such as the Elfinkind Digest mailing list in 1990, which claims to have coined the term 'Otherkin' (Johnson, 2013). However, the human-technics intimacy that is showcased by the Otherkin phenomenon cannot simply be reduced to virtual performance, as argued above. Rather, it offers a practical entry point into an ongoing debate in the spheres of media theory and philosophy, relating to the co-emergence of humans and technics.

Stiegler and Hayles, two of the chief contemporary proponents of this line of thought, propose general frameworks to explain contemporary media discourse and ontology. These frameworks can have particular bearing on the way in which internet-based phenomena such as Otherkin are viewed. Simply put, both Stiegler and Hayles dismantle the notion that a pure humanity – one that is radically different and separate from anything non-human – can exist. Stiegler does not accept the possibility of an ahistorical 'natural man' who emerged before technics, culture or 'deferred nature', untouched by anything that did not properly belong to humanness and only humanness (Stiegler, 1998, p. 143). The fantasy of a human who emerges fully formed but untainted by culture is a false one: even the use of the hand constitutes a 'distancing, manipulation as a new form of mobilization, exteriorization' (ibid., 144). For Stiegler, this can only mean one thing: the 'natural' human has no origin and, furthermore, does not exist. Once we acknowledge that existence is only possible through technics – via the 'pursuit of life through means other than life' – we must also accept that speaking of the human requires a rejection of the very idea of the human. Of course, Stiegler's implied definition of technics is extremely broad and resonates with both Heidegger's notion of technology as an 'exteriorization of Being' (1977) and Marshall McLuhan's idea that media technologies (and here he does not distinguish between media and technologies) are an extension of man. In this framework, technics can just as accurately describe the evolution of bipedal walking to the invention of the wheel as it can to what we today call digital technologies.

For Stiegler, technics is a curious thing that demands its own explanatory framework. Neither biology nor science nor anthropology is adequate for this task on its own, but, taken together, they can lead towards the hypothesis that:

> between the inorganic beings of the physical sciences and the organized beings of biology, there does indeed exist a third genre of 'being': 'inorganic organized beings,' or technical objects. These nonorganic organizations of matter have their own dynamic when compared with

> that of either physical or biological beings, a dynamic, moreover, that cannot be reduced to the 'aggregate' or 'product' of these beings.
>
> (Stiegler, 1998, p. 17)

Technics, then, has its own internal logic that cannot be grasped through a traditional anthropocentric perspective on technology. More importantly, Stiegler brings the human and technics into a co-constructing assemblage that shares a mutual becoming. Interestingly, in this passage, Stiegler does not refer to the human but to the difference between two vast categories: living beings and technics. Herein lies one of the caveats that must be kept in mind when thinking of the human-technics relationship through the lens of originary technicity: the anthropocentric implications of originary technicity. According to Tracy Colony, Stiegler fails to account for the fact that both humans and non-humans are 'aporetic and constituted in terms of its relatedness to exteriority' (Colony, 2011, p. 75). Colony makes a compelling argument in stating that, in Stiegler's work, non-human life comes across as 'pure', and he does not account for the way in which technics can be seen as a given in the non-human sphere, as well. While Colony might be right, the assumption that non-human life presupposes a certain purity and consistency is most certainly in harmony with Otherkin's yearning for a hybridisation with non-human possibilities. The appeal of kinship and intimacy with the non-human consists precisely in its distance and assumed difference from the human sphere.

While Stiegler looks at technics from an ahistorical point of view, allowing it to encompass everything from the act of walking on two feet to fire, the wheel, pottery and complex technical systems such as communication networks, Hayles is more concerned with the nuances of contemporary networked technologies. Stiegler's technics is mundane, unobtrusive and often ignores technology that form the substrate of human (as well as much non-human) existence. Hayles, on the other hand, is explicitly concerned with the way in which the joint genesis of technics and humanity plays out in the context of digital media. For Hayles, speaking about contemporary culture, it is imperative to consider how:

> The capacity of networked and programmable machines to carry out sophisticated cognitive tasks [...] [how] embodiment then takes the form of extended cognition, in which human agency and thought are enmeshed within larger networks that extend beyond the desktop computer into the environment.
>
> (2012, p. 3)

Otherkin agency extends beyond the confines of online platforms while still preserving a connection to the medium that structures and shapes the implicit rules of the community. Mailing lists such as the early Elfinkind Digest and the Elf Queen's Daughters provided an avenue for early community-making among people who already felt that they were not fully human. At present, Otherkin-centred blogs also function to enable awakening as an Otherkin, providing practical advice and psychological support. In answering a Reddit thread asking whether Otherkin are products of the internet, several self-identified Otherkin responded that while their non-human identity had been crystallised before their participation in the community, the medium was crucial for forming their Otherkin identity. In the words of Redditor alynnafoxie:

> I knew I was something before the internet, but it was always kind of nebulous, I didn't really have the context to know what I was, even if I knew I was quite different from human. The internet gave me some context, a place to research, but most of all showed me I wasn't the only one. I will say I was out as a multitailed fox before I even knew what a kitsune was. The term kitsune was introduced to me in the upper 90's [*sic*].
>
> (alynnafoxie, 2015)

While many Otherkin confess to having begun the process of identifying as non-human before finding the community, others claim that forging an Otherkin identity through the medium does not affect the validity of their experience. As Redditor luigi_L comments in the same thread: 'I do also believe that many didn't consider themselves as another animal before, but began seeing themselves as one after discovering there was something like otherkin because it had always been a desire of theirs. That does however not make them less otherkin' (luigi_L, 2015). While older community members read their own experiences as a priori to joining the community, several Otherkin guides and primers insist on the centrality of the technical medium for Otherkin becoming. In an article published in the French magazine *Le Monde*, Olivier Clarouin concludes that all testimonies agree that for Otherkin and Therians, the internet plays an essential role by allowing them to contact people who have experienced similar feelings and by labelling these feelings (Clarouin, 2014).

While the community offers a space and resources for newly awakened Otherkin to explore their identity through the help of online connectedness, some Otherkin websites lend themselves more literally to a technogenetic interpretation. Rialian, a dragonkin, uses the technical medium as a tool for inducing awakening. By clicking the links provided by Rialian, prospective Otherkin access a page that was 'energetically charged this page to awaken the dragon within you (if you have it), and/or bring out more of those energies in you' (Rialian, 2016). The website functions as a conduit for Otherkin to become; its very code is meant to elicit the experience of not-quite-humanity – of queering normative identity categories through interaction with the medium. The medium, itself, becomes imbued with an other-than-human agency that shapes and moulds the user.

The problem with theorising human-media relationships, for Hayles, rests partly on the necessity of treating technologies not as 'static entities that, once created, remain the same throughout time', but 'as constantly changing assemblages in which inequalities and inefficiencies in their operations drive them towards breakdown, disruption, innovation and change' (Hayles, 2012, p. 13). In this view, technologies are more accurately referred to as technical individuals (Gilbert Simondon's term), whose agencies are acknowledged and seen as enmeshed in various social, economic and political networks. Their embodiments matter, and, as Hayles argues, it would be no exaggeration to say that they have an umwelt 'in the sense that they perceive the world, draw conclusions based on their perceptions, and act on those perceptions' (2012, p. 17). The technical medium of the internet and the various social media platforms it offers can be seen, in Hayles' framework, not as a mere incidental tool for solidifying online Otherkin communities, but as a full and active participant in the affective and relational process of Otherkin becoming.

Intimate connectivities

The intimate connectivities among Otherkin take shape both *through* the medium of the internet and *with* the internet. As in Hayles' understanding, the medium becomes possessed of agentic capabilities that allow it to directly participate in the other's subjectivation. The intimate connectivities that occur in the context of the Otherkin phenomenon are, on a primary level, those that emerge at the intersection of ontological categories, as argued by Laycock and Kirby; but on another level, they are also situated between the electronic medium and the user. In many ways, such intimacy becomes necessary for entering the Otherkin community. For many web users, the ability to use media technology is a lingua franca, functioning as a prerequisite for belonging to an online community in the first place. The intricacies of Otherkins' preferred media platforms are also crucial aspects of their participation: the 'language' of LiveJournal codes, command lines and clients; the rules and vernacular of Tumblr; the codes of WordPress; and the intricate pathways of Reddit. When technology breaks down, the fandom is disrupted: when the laptops of major figures in any given community are in the repair shop, there can be minor upheavals among followers; similarly, an unannounced update to the Tumblr interface can leave users struggling to readjust. To be a member of the online Otherkin community is to be unavoidably entangled with media technologies.

Although Otherkin are becoming part of the common parlance of the internet, mostly due to a number of articles that have endeavoured to shed light on a community that is treated as an object of ridicule or fascination (Mawer, 2014; Read, 2012; Roberts, 2015), part of these sometimes curious and often cautionary discourses on the internet's potential for 'weirdness' is rooted in a broader set of ideas surrounding the way in which media technologies should be used. The chief manifestation of contemporary anxiety over the potentially pathological nature of media use is formalised under the labels of internet addiction, gaming addiction or social media addiction, but they are nonetheless connected to countless satellite discourses manifesting the same type of concern, expressed in different vocabularies. Sherry Turkle aptly articulates these concerns in *Alone Together*, her exploration of the changing landscape of intimacy, authenticity and human relationships in the age of networked media: 'Technology reshapes the landscape of our emotional lives, but is it offering us the lives we want to live? [...] Are these propositions psychologically, socially and ethically acceptable propositions? What are our responsibilities here?' (Turkle, 2011, p. 17). For others, the moral angle is often rooted in neuroscience. According to Nicholas Carr (2010), attention must be paid to the effects of media use on the nervous system. It is not even the content of media that we should be concerned with, but their mere permeation of human lives: 'Media work their magic, or their mischief, on the nervous system itself. Our focus on the medium can blind us to these deep effects' (2010, p. 15). For Turkle as well as for Carr, media technologies are not seamlessly integrated into the fabric of daily existence; they are put into the spotlight not because they might deliver information that could harm the audience,[4] but because their existence renders them abnormal in some sense.

Media are involved in changing our understanding of sociality, intimacy and anatomical function, for Turkle, Carr and many others. These scholars and social commentators are searching for answers to powerful questions: What do media do? What do their users become? These questions are legitimate insofar as the management of life is concerned: they are biopolitical in nature, involved not only in disciplining individual bodies and their media habits but in managing entire populations. If for some users media erode traditional modes of social and political engagement or even put them outside the normal limits of health, then what should be done? However, such lines of questioning ignore the creative, ethical and even political potential that is inherent in Otherkin becomings, and the way in which their intimate connectivities with and through media allow them to inhabit a space that poses relevant questions regarding the nature of humanity and the usefulness of the concept in the contemporary socius.

The creative and liberating potential of human-media couplings is highlighted in the work of theorists such as Sarah Kember and Joanna Zylinska, who, similar to an increasing number of media theorists, speak the language of new materialism, assemblage theories and deconstruction. This new parlance of media theory is attentive to the ontologies, layers and interconnections of media history, and situates digital media users in a context that is much vaster than the contemporary digital economy. What is unique about the 'new' media theory is that it fully acknowledges media technologies as active agents on an equal footing with human users and seeks to undo the categories that separate them, similar to Stiegler's and

Hayles' media theoretical projects. Kember and Zylinska argue that categories are 'reductive and therefore unhelpful; it also has serious political and ethical consequences for our understanding of the world, its dynamics, and its power relations' (Kember and Zylinska, 2011, p. 2). Otherkin, similar to other denizens of the digital age whose becomings are closely linked to media use, are, through this lens, no longer seen as pathologised human agents who use media to fuel their delusions, but as examples of the way in which media technologies push the limits of the human, as both an abstract category and a lived experience.

Kember and Zylinska brilliantly illustrate how understanding media in terms of processes lends itself productively to the media objects of the digital age, when it is extremely difficult to distinguish where one medium ends and the other begins. Phones, digital cameras, film recordings, the internet, Bluetooth technologies, satellites, tablets and digital microscopes are all media based on a common language (that of binary codes and protocols), and are all on the verge of being absorbed either by Mark Weiser's tangle of ubiquitous computing or by the 'cloud' – that amorphous enterprise that is quickly becoming the paradigm of today's information infrastructure.[5] Kember and Zylinska insist on the interconnectedness of the biological and technological processes entailed by media, and argue that acknowledging this interconnectedness can lead to an ethical dissolution of the subject/object binary.

Kember and Zylinska's work is exemplary of a new wave of media studies that is heavily influenced by new materialisms and their focus on escaping the subject/object dualism, while also recognising the agency of non-human actors. This type of media work makes an important contribution to the ontology of media through addressing media's conditions of possibility and their radical inseparability from notions of life.[6] However, mediation might not always be able to account for the way in which people experience media and narrate their experiences to themselves within the strata of power in which they situate themselves. That is, it can easily sideline the phenomenology of media use. How do media users make sense of their mediated lives? What kinds of discourses construct the meaning of media as part of lived experience, and what sort of discourses do media construct in turn? In other words, how do we construct knowledge about media, through what means and for what purposes? If we take disordered media use as an example, the discourses presented in the previous chapter suggest that there is a variety of biopolitical techniques that function on the premise of a radical separation between media and humanity. Media users, who also live in a technicised environment, are still responsible for maintaining a modicum of biological purity. Interconnectedness or hybridity is accepted only insofar as it does not truly trouble any subject/object boundaries; that is, insofar as it is still possible to distinguish where the media end and the human begins. To date, there has been scarce research – academic or otherwise – on the relationships that Otherkin and similar communities maintain with the media that sustain their communities to a large extent.

Concluding remarks – Are media users ever human?

Scholarly work on the spiritual aspect of Otherkin becoming, and framing the Otherkin community as a decentred non-normative religious experience based on a quest to establish a metaphysics, allows us to see the online Otherkin community as a means of affirming and embracing species difference and ontological reconfiguration. At the same time, the technological mediation that allows the emergence and structure of online communities of Otherkin and other subcultures is a significant articulation of the identity and its project of questioning the meaning of humanity. Otherkin becomings can be seen through the lens of philosophies of technology that bring to the fore the indelible and originary relationship between the categories of human and technics, and which posit that the human inhabits a ontological space that, at its core, is *non-human*. For Stiegler, Hayles and others, the human – unstable and shifting as the concept might be – emerges in conjunction with technics. This conjunction is made more visible through the work of digital technologies, which allow communities such as that of the Otherkin to revel, reveal and formulate their non-human state of being. As Kirby argues, the notion of the animal other is central to the understanding of Otherkin processes of being. The non-humanity of Otherkin is essentially an embrace of the other in its animalistic and mythopoetic forms. Yet popular media's sporadic criticism of Otherkin relies on the assumption that technical intimacy – or non-human intimacy mediated through digital media – proves that Otherkin metaphysics is invalid at its core. By putting the Otherkin in the context of originary technicity and acknowledging the ways in which technicity is integrated into the very notion of humanity, itself, we can view Otherkin not as an exception to 'normal' technical intimacies but as an exemplary phenomenon that highlights the way in which digital media and the ongoing destabilisation of humanness are connected. Otherkin becomings can be approached as modes of intimacy between technics and humans – as becomings that queer not sex and gender (although these axes are also part and parcel of Otherkin identity) but bodies and species. Otherkin showcase digital media's potential for the creation of new ethical and political possibilities through their sustained attack on accepted notions of what it means to be human.

Notes

1 Kin who identify with non-human life forms that factually exist are often collectively referred to as 'Therianthropes' or 'Therians'.

2 otherkin.peperonity.com.

3 Otherkin Wikia. Retrieved from http://otherkin.wikia.com/wiki/Fictionkin.

4 As, for example, discourse around inappropriate violence and sexual content in media that are accessible to children, which are thought to potentially affect children's later stage psychological development (Earles et al., 2002).

5 Cloud computing is a mode of information processing wherein information is not locally stored on a personal device's hard drive but, rather, on the internet. The cloud is a metaphor for the internet and refers to the fact that the resources needed by a device are not stored *on* the device, but on shared remote servers. Google Docs and Google Drive are two examples of popular cloud services.

6 One of the main claims of Kember and Zylinska's book is that mediation is an all-encompassing process that affects every aspect of lived experience. For this reason, one cannot speak of any subject independent of mediation. For the authors, mediation is a 'theory of life' through which 'mediation becomes a key trope for understanding and articulating our being in, and becoming with, the technological world, our emergence and ways of intra-acting with it, as well as the acts and processes of temporarily stabilizing the world into media, agents, relations, and networks' (Kember and Zylinska, 2011, p. xv).

References

Alynnafoxie (2015). Re: I am not an Otherkin, but did were any of you 'Otherkin' before reading about it on the Internet or is this a product of the Internet? Reddit. Retrieved from https://www.reddit.com/r/otherkin/comments/2r9m4f/i_am_not_an_otherkin_but_did_were_any_of_you.

Calvert, S.L, Jordan, A.B. and Cocking, R.R. (2002). Identity construction on the Internet. *Childhood: A Global Journal of Child Research*, 13(1), pp. 57–70. doi:10.1177/0907568206058610.

Carr, N. (2010). *The Shallows: What the Internet is Doing to Our Brains*. New York: W.W. Norton & Co.

Clarouin, O. (2014). Pas complètement humains: La vie en ligne des thérians et Otherkins. Le Monde. Retrieved from www.lemonde.fr/cultures-web/article/2014/05/20/pas-completement-humains-la-vie-en-ligne-des-therians-et-otherkins_4410306_4409029.html?xtmc=otherkin&xtcr=1.

Colony, T. (2011). Epimetheus bound: Stiegler on Derrida, life, and the technological condition. *Research in Phenomenology*, 41(1), 72–89.

Cusack, C.M. (2013). Fantasy and belief: Alternative religions, popular narratives and digital cultures. *Culture and Religion*, 14(4), pp. 498–499. doi:10.1080/14755610.2013.840137.

Deleuze, G. and Guattari, F. (1995). A thousand plateaus. *SubStance*, 20. doi:10.2307/3684887.

Derrida, J. and Mallet, M.-L. (2008). *The Animal that Therefore I Am*. New York: Fordham University Press.

Feijó, P. (2016). Doctor Herding Cats: The Misadventures of Modern Medicine and Psychology with NonHuman Identities. Retrieved from www.academia.edu/24718674/Doctors_Herding_Cats_The_Misadventures_of_Modern_Medicine_and_Psychology_with_NonHuman_Identities

Gunkel, D.J. and Gunkel, A.H. (1997). Virtual geographies: The new worlds of cyberspace. *Critical Studies in Mass Communication*. doi:10.1080/15295039709367003.

Hayles, N.K. (2012). *How We Think: Digital Media and Contemporary Technogenesis*. Chicago, IL: University of Chicago Press.

Hayles, N.K. (2007). Hyper and deep attention: The generational divide in cognitive modes. *Profession*, 2007(2007), pp. 187–199. doi:10.1632/prof.2007.2007.1.187.

Heidegger, M. (1977). *The Question Concerning Technology and Other Essays. Technology and Values: Essential Readings*. doi:10.1007/BF01252376.

Huh, S. and Williams, D. (2010). Dude looks like a lady: Gender swapping in an online game. *Online Worlds: Convergence of the Real and the Virtual*, pp. 161–174. doi:10.1007/978-1-84882-825-4.

Johnson, K. (2013). The elfkind digest. Murkworks. Retrieved from www.murkworks.net/~elflist.

Johnston, J. (2013). On having a furry soul: Transpecies identity and ontological indeterminacy in otherkin subcultures. In: J. Johnston and F. Probyn-Rapsey, eds., *Animal Death*. Sydney: Sydney University Press, pp. 293–306.

Johnston, J. (2015). Vampirism, lycanthropy, and Otherkin. In: C. Patridge, ed., *The Occult World*. Abingdon: Routledge, pp. 412–423.

Justanotherkin. (2013). An FAQ on Otherkin for the perplexed observer. Just Anotherkin. Retrieved from http://justanotherkin.tumblr.com/post/58429596952/an-faq-on-otherkin-for-the-perplexed-observer.

Kember, S. and Zylinska, J. (2012). *Life After New Media: Mediation as a Vital Process*. Cambridge, MA: MIT Press.

Kirby, D. (2012). Alternative worlds: Metaphysical questing and virtual community amongst the Otherkin. In: A. Possamai, ed., *Handbook of Hyper-Real Religions*. Leiden and Boston: Brill, pp. 129–140.

Kirby, D. (2014). *Fantasy and Belief: Alternative Religions, Popular Narratives, and Digital Cultures*. New York: Routledge.

Laycock, J.P. (2012). 'We are spirits of another sort': Ontological rebellion and religious dimensions of the Otherkin community. *Nova Religio: The Journal of Alternative and Emergent Religions*, 15(3), pp. 65–90. doi:10.1525/nr.2012.15.3.65.65.

luigi_L (2015). Re: I am not an Otherkin, but did were any of you 'Otherkin' before reading about it on the Internet or is this a product of the Internet? Reddit. Retrieved from https://www.reddit.com/r/otherkin/comments/2r9m4f/i_am_not_an_otherkin_but_did_were_any_of_you.

Martey, R.M., Stromer-Galley, J., Banks, J., Wu, J. and Consalvo, M. (2014). The strategic female: Gender-switching and player behavior in online games. *Information, Communication & Society*, 17(3), pp. 286–300.

Mawer, K. (2014). Tumblr's strange trend of creating minority identities. Thought Catalog. Retrieved from http://thoughtcatalog.com/keisha-mawer/2014/09/tumblrs-strange-trend-of-creating-minority-identities.

Oliver, K. (2009). *Animal Lessons: How They Teach Us to Be Human*. New York: Columbia University Press.

Peters, J.D. (1999). *Speaking into the Air: A History of the Idea of Communication*. Chicago, IL: Chicago University Press.

Read, M. (2012). From Otherkin to transethnicity: Your field guide to the weird world of Tumblr identity politics. Gawker. Retrieved from http://gawker.com/5940947/from-otherkin-to-transethnicity-your-field-guide-to-the-weird-world-of-tumblr-identity-politics.

Rialian (n.d.). The awakening page. Rialian. Retrieved from www.rialian.com/eyovah1/awaken.html.

Roberts, A. (2015). Otherkin are people too; they just identify as nonhuman. Vice. Retrieved from www.vice.com/read/from-dragons-to-foxes-the-otherkin-community-believes-you-can-be-whatever-you-want-to-be.

Scribner, O. (2012). Otherkin timeline: The recent history of elfin, fae, and animal people, v. 2.0. Retrieved from http://orion.kitsunet.net/time.pdf.

Stiegler, B. (1998). *Technics and Time 1*. Stanford, CA: Stanford University Press.

Stone, A.R. (1995). *The War of Desire and Technology at the Close of the Mechanical Age*. Cambridge, MA: MIT Press.

Turkle, S. (1996). Virtuality and its discontents: Searching for community in cyberspace. *The American Prospect*, 24, pp. 50–57.

Turkle, S. (1999). Tinysex and gender trouble [Internet World]. *IEEE Technology and Society Magazine*, 18(4), pp. 8–12. doi:10.1109/44.808843.

Turkle, S. (2011). *Alone Together: Why We Expect More from Technology and Less from Each Other*. London: Basic Books.

17 Broadcasting the bedroom

Intimate musical practices and collapsing contexts on YouTube

Maarten Michielse

Introduction

In an era of social media and online participation, uploading a personal video to a platform such as YouTube appears to be an easy and natural activity for large groups of users.[1] Various discourses on online narcissism and exhibitionism (Balance, 2012; Keen, 2007, 2012; Twenge and Campbell, 2010) give the impression that current generations have become extremely comfortable (perhaps even too comfortable) with the online possibilities of self-exposure and self-representation (Mallan, 2009). As I will argue in this chapter, however, this is largely a misrepresentation of the everyday struggles and experiences of online participants. For many, posting a video on YouTube is a rather ambivalent activity: joyful and fun at times, but also scary and accompanied by feelings of insecurity, especially when the content is relatively delicate.

This shows itself perhaps most clearly in a particular genre of online videos: the 'musical bedroom performance'. On YouTube, this genre has become a popular trope in the last couple of years. In these videos, a person sings and/or plays a musical instrument in front of the camera from the private sphere of the home. As Jean Burgess (2008) argues, the musical bedroom performance 'draws on the long traditions of vernacular creativity articulated to "privatised" media use' (p. 107).[2] Historically, the bedroom has functioned as a crucial site for cultural expression and experimentation. This is especially true for teenagers and young adults, for whom the bedroom is, as Sian Lincoln (2005) writes, a domain 'in which they are able to exert some control, be creative and make that space their own' (p. 400). In the case of music, particularly, the bedroom is also a major site of informal learning. As many researchers in the field of popular music have argued, (beginner) musicians often pick up skills and techniques by playing along with records, rather than attending formal music classes (Bennett, 1980; Finnegan, 1989; Green, 2001; Miller, 2012; Toynbee, 2000). In such practice, the private sphere of the home also functions as a key site for people to explore their musical talents in a controlled and safe environment – one that is occasionally intimately shared with family or close friends.

With the rise of webcams and social media websites, however, such domestic forms of musical learning and play have become increasingly public. Through the help of platforms such as YouTube, any small-scale bedroom video can be distributed to a wide group of viewers, extending its impact far beyond the domestic sphere. The result is what in academic circles is often called a 'context collapse'; that is, a clash between multiple performance situations in which different (and often opposite) norms, expectations and conventions play a role (boyd, 2008, 2011, 2014; Wesch, 2009). As I will illustrate in this chapter, the concept of a context collapse can be an important tool in understanding the daily worries and struggles of bedroom musicians on a platform such as YouTube. However, while previous research has mainly theorised the concept in relation to issues of privacy (see, e.g., boyd, 2014; Lincoln and Robards, 2014; Marwick and boyd, 2010, 2014; Vitak, 2012), I argue that it can be extended to other aspects of online interaction, as well. Indeed, bedroom videos not only blur the lines between the private and the public; they also complicate the boundaries between the domains of practising and rehearsing, as well as product and process. Moreover, while it is sometimes suggested that participants are not aware of such complexities (see, e.g., Regan, FitzGerald and Balint, 2013), my argument underscores that the opposite is the case. Participants on YouTube are quite conscious of their situation. They view their online musical practices as important opportunities to establish intimate connections with audiences and peers around the world. But they are also very aware of the potential problems that come with trying to explore such intimacies on an open and popular platform such as YouTube.

Indeed, if we understand intimacy as being centred on aspects such as self-disclosure, reciprocity and mutual understanding (Chambers, 2013; Farci et al., 2016; Mashek and Aron, 2004), musical bedroom videos on YouTube both enhance and problematise issues of intimacy. While YouTube provides bedroom musicians with the opportunity to disclose their personal and otherwise hidden musical practices in new collective and shared ways, the rise of context collapses on this platform also means that these practices (and their underlying intentions and goals) are often misinterpreted and misunderstood by everyday users and social critics, alike. For this reason, bedroom musicians on YouTube are forced to continuously negotiate their activities. In fact, as I will show, participants often develop specific tactics in order to openly share their musical activities while simultaneously preventing the clashing of contexts from getting out of hand.

Drawing on 18 months of ethnographic research within a community of online bedroom musicians, this chapter investigates how users deal with the opportunities and challenges that come with practising their musical activities online. By zooming in on the concept of 'context collapse', this chapter puts claims of alleged exhibitionism and narcissism into perspective and aims at contributing to a better understanding of the more contemplative and vulnerable aspects of online participation.

Theory: Collapsing contexts and YouTube

In recent years, the notion of 'context collapse' has gained quite some attention in academic studies on online participation and self-representation (boyd, 2008, 2011, 2014; Hodkinson, 2015; Lincoln and Robards, 2014; Marwick and boyd, 2010, 2014; Vitak, 2012; Wesch, 2009). The way the concept is used in these studies draws heavily on Erving Goffman's (1967, 1990 [1959]) theories on social interaction. In his work, Goffman understands all social interactions as 'performances' that are ideally addressed to (and fit to) specific contexts and audiences. For Goffman, it does not matter whether such interaction involves an employer conducting a job interview, a professor giving a lecture or a stage performer doing a routine for a paying audience. In all cases, people try to adjust their performances to fit certain conventions and expectations. This is a process that Goffman calls 'impression management' (1990 [1959]). Managing such impressions, however, can be difficult in contexts where there is a relatively unknown audience or where different social relations and cultural conventions overlap and blend (the so-called 'context collapse'). In such contexts, participants may feel vulnerable and misunderstandings between a performer and an audience can easily arise.

Although context collapses can occur in any social situation (mediated or unmediated, online or offline), they are often thought to be particularly apparent in today's online networked spaces and social media environments (boyd 2008, 2011, 2014; Hodkinson, 2015; Lincoln and Robards, 2014; Vitak, 2012).[3] According to boyd, context collapses should even be understood as one of the defining aspects of the current social media landscape (boyd, 2014). This has primarily to do with the fact that social media bring a wide variety of practices and participants together in a single (virtual) environment. Most social media platforms operate on a global basis, turning every discussion (at least potentially) into a worldwide conversation, far exceeding the context in which the message was originally sent. Moreover, participants often have the opportunity to communicate under pseudonyms or to be present in a fully covert way (through a process called 'lurking'). This can make it difficult to demarcate separate social groups.

In the case of YouTube, in particular, context collapses are bound to occur because of the complex forms of transmission the platform allows. YouTube has become famous for its slogan 'Broadcast Yourself'. As other media scholars have pointed out, however, one can question the extent to which 'broadcasting' is the correct term for the types of transmission made on this platform (Kant, 2014; Kim, 2012; van Dijck, 2008).[4] On YouTube, different media logics blend and interact. Some content is produced by professional media companies and/or taken directly from mass media outlets such as television and film, while other content is fully user-generated. Some videos are directed at a global audience, while others are targeted at specific subcommunities, or even just family and friends. Moreover, we increasingly see small-scale productions going viral (either purposefully or accidentally), gaining huge global audiences. As such, the practices on YouTube navigate constantly between forms of broadcasting and 'narrow casting' (Kant, 2014; Kim, 2012) – a type of transmission directed towards highly segmented audiences and specific communities.

To make things more complex, many practices on YouTube (such as those of bedroom musicians) are grounded explicitly in the private sphere of the home. As such, they pertain to a category that José van Dijck (2008) calls 'homecasting'. In her definition, homecasting distinguishes itself from both broadcasting and narrow casting, not only due to the role of the domestic sphere, but also due to the manner in which this particular form of media production lowers the threshold of participation and interaction. As she writes: 'Homecasting accommodates the individual in the private sphere who feels the urge to make his or her opinions, insights and experiences available to everyone out there' (van Dijck, 2008, p. 7). Conceptually, homecasting has strong ties with so-called 'home-mode' forms of cultural production, which were part of the cultural landscape long before the rise of social media (Chalfen, 1987; see also Lange, 2009, 2014). However, if home-mode forms of cultural production were traditionally consumed within fairly small and intimate circles of individuals (Lange, 2009, 2014), in the current media landscape, such practices tend to move freely between 'relatively private and more public practices' (Lange, 2014, p. 17; see also Buckingham, Willett and Pini, 2011), thus complicating issues of privacy and intimacy. Indeed, if we understand the private as that which is relatively personal and secluded and the public as that which is relatively open and revealed (Weintraub, 1997), many homecasting practices on YouTube are positioned precisely in-between these realms (Lange, 2007), and can best be described as 'privately public' or 'publicly private' (Lange, 2007).

While current generations of media users may seem unaware of such complexities, recent ethnographic research suggests otherwise. According to boyd, for example, online participants actively negotiate the lines between the private and the public in their social media practices (boyd, 2014). In a similar way, in her work on teenage bedroom cultures, Sian Lincoln (2005, 2014) describes a process she calls 'zoning', whereby participants tactically navigate the ways in which they open (and close) their private lives to the outside world. Such zoning practices can involve the strategic use of 'tags' or privacy settings in order to ensure certain messages or performances stay within a particular context. By creating such zones, participants are able to influence when, how and with whom they establish intimate connections online, and can minimise the negative consequences of potential context collapses.

During my own empirical research, I found that bedroom musicians actively negotiate context collapses, as well. For them, however, these contextual issues are not solely related to the issue of private versus public. Their daily activities also involve other balancing acts, which are closely tied to aspects relating to music, collaboration and learning. Looking into these aspects in more detail, as I do below, can give us more insight into the different ways in which context collapses occur online.

Investigating a community of bedroom musicians

As part of a larger research project on online musical participation (Michielse, 2015), I conducted virtual ethnographic fieldwork (Hine, 2000) in a community of bedroom musicians on YouTube. This fieldwork took place mainly between December 2012 and May 2014, although some of the contact with participants continued until 2015. The community I investigated was formed around the 'Gregory Brothers' – a musical band that was particularly popular and influential around that time. In their videos, the Gregory Brothers performed so-called 'songified' versions of famous internet videos. They took existing, non-musical content from YouTube and turned it into a song, complete with elaborate musical arrangements, backing vocals and a beat. At the end of their videos, they explicitly invited viewers to upload their own versions of the songs. Often, such invitations would lead to dozens of uploaded musical reinterpretations from people all around the world. Most of these videos would be recorded in or near a bedroom, although occasionally they would be performed in other parts of the house, such as a kitchen, attic or basement. Some participants would perform the song with their voice, while others would play along with the tracks on guitar, piano or drums.

I chose to focus on the Gregory Brothers' 'songify' projects because these were some of the most popular participatory musical events on YouTube at the time. As such, they enabled me to come into contact with a large number of participants. Moreover, by using the 'songify' projects as a starting point for my investigation, I also got the chance to explore other types of musical performances that did not immediately pertain to the Gregory Brothers' work. Some of the people I met, for example, did performances of songs from bands such as Maroon 5 or Daft Punk, as well; others performed musical interpretations of film scores or soundtracks from popular computer games. By looking into these different practices, I was able to get a better idea of the wide variety of musical activities that bedroom musicians engage in on YouTube.

During my fieldwork I watched relevant videos, read comments, monitored new uploads and asked questions via email or private messages. Furthermore, I conducted longer qualitative interviews via Skype with 20 participants.[5] These interviews lasted between 50 and 150 minutes (sometimes spread over multiple sessions). The male and female participants in these interviews were between the ages of 18 and 40 and were based in countries around the world, including Australia, Brazil, Belgium, Sweden, the United States and the United Kingdom. During the interviews, I asked them about their motivations, experiences and struggles, as well as about particular activities or interactions I had seen during my fieldwork. All participants gave me permission to use their quotes and usernames in my research.[6] They also gave me permission to discuss their experiences and examples in my work.

Apart from the issue of private versus public, two other examples of collapsing contexts seemed key to the everyday experiences and struggles of the bedroom musicians. First, their practices tended to waver between rehearsing and performing. As I show below, this balancing act was not always understood or appreciated outside the community of practitioners. Second, the bedroom videos often straddled (individual) products and (collective) processes, which could give rise to worries and misunderstandings. While both examples are, of course, intertwined with the issue of private versus public, they also point at other struggles and negotiations that, to date, have rarely been explored and discussed from a scholarly angle.

Between rehearsing and performing

The bedroom has historically functioned as an important space for musical experimentation and learning (Lincoln, 2005), and the YouTube videos I studied clearly show traces of this, although in a new way. During the fieldwork, it became clear that it is quite common for bedroom musicians on YouTube to 'play along' with recorded songs, rather than to reperform a song from scratch (see also Miller, 2012). Some participants wear earplugs or headphones, while others have the original track (or an instrumental version) playing on a laptop or stereo set. In these videos, they try to keep up with the pace of the original track when playing their instrument or singing. While some participants look into the camera, others turn inwards, concentrating on their musical instrument or their voice. Often, little mistakes are audible and occasionally a performer has to start over. Indeed, as became clear during the interviews, many of these videos are recorded early on, in what Bennett (1980) calls the 'song-getting' process; that is, the process by which musicians familiarise themselves with the melody, chords and sound of a particular song. While participants usually go over the song a couple of times before they film, it normally does not take long before they press the record button. As a result, their performance is often far from polished when it is uploaded online. In fact, the video presented online may be seen as an integrated part of the song-getting practice.

By uploading such semi-rehearsals to an open platform such as YouTube, the producers challenge what Goffman (1990 [1959]) calls the 'front region' and 'back region' of performance (or the frontstage and backstage). If rehearsing is traditionally a backstage affair – an activity through which performers prepare for and strategically plan the way they will present themselves to the outside world – these bedroom videos explicitly open up such backstage practices and turn them into a shared activity. As my fieldwork revealed, bedroom musicians do this purposefully. Few of the participants I met are interested in (or striving for) perfectionism in their work, as they associate it with a sense of distance and a lack of personal contact between the performer and viewers. Instead, they consider their bedroom videos opportunities for them to disclose relatively vulnerable moments of the song-getting process and to create a sense of intimacy by letting viewers in on their musical struggles and explorations.[7] Moreover, many bedroom musicians see their practices as opportunities for learning. They use their videos to train particular musical skills, to experiment or to get feedback from fellow music enthusiasts. Thus, they explicitly allow room for more undeveloped aspects of musical performance in their videos.

However, combining such practices of performing and rehearsing on an open platform such as YouTube is not an easy task. Participants sometimes receive critical remarks about the way in which they present themselves in front of the camera. For example, one of the interviewees, JTehAnonymous, told me: 'People watch like if you're smiling, or if you're like totally into your music or, you know? [...] Sometimes they don't even comment on the music, they are just like "You look really sad when you play, you should smile", you know?' (30 March 2013). While such remarks may seem rather innocent, they are sometimes accompanied by harsher criticisms, especially from viewers who are outside the community of bedroom musicians. During my fieldwork, it became clear that participants sometimes get fiercely attacked for their lack of skill ('You suck'; 'This sucks hardcore') or lack of musical originality ('Stupid meaningless copying'; 'Stupid copy'; 'Welcome to the world of copying an already successful song').[8]

While comments and critiques are often sought after and welcomed by bedroom musicians, they can also be demotivating and hurtful, especially when they are grounded in adverse expectations. Even in more professional social-critical commentaries (Keen, 2007, 2012; Carr, 2016), online participatory practices are sometimes dismissed for their lack of quality, side-stepping the fact that many of these activities are meant as forms of learning and experimentation. During the interviews, participants were actually quite humble about their performance skills. As Guilherme (username zzzzzzzwakeup) phrased it: 'I'm not a stage artist. I am just a guy who likes music as a language and as a communication tool' (3 April 2013). During our conversation, he described his bedroom video to be 'more akin to singing in the shower' than to any professional musical production. On a platform such as YouTube, however, where bedroom videos appear alongside content from more established musicians and bands, such differences in artistic standards and motivations can easily be mixed up by the audience.

In order to minimise misunderstandings, some participants include small warning signs or disclaimers in and around their videos. Participants state phrases such as: 'I was in a rush making this'; '[E]xcuse the struggle'; or '[It is] not flawless but what is?'[9] Such disclaimers can be either phrased verbally in the video or articulated in the video's title, description or comment section. For relative outsiders, warning messages and disclaimers might perhaps point at a false sense of modesty. During the fieldwork, however, I found that these functioned as an important tactic to temper expectations and avoid reaching the 'wrong' audience with a video. Thus, such disclaimers should be regarded as a good example of what Lincoln calls 'zoning practices' (Lincoln, 2005, 2014). By adding phrases about the still underdeveloped nature of their performances, the bedroom musicians explicitly try to shield their videos from contexts and expectations with which they are incompatible. Thus, this is an important way for them to reduce the negative consequences of the context collapse surrounding these practices.

Between (individual) product and (collective) process

While bedroom musicians sometimes feel misunderstood in their practice, this is not only because their work is judged according to the 'wrong' standards, but also because their videos are evaluated as individual products rather than parts of larger, collective *processes*. Though bedroom videos are usually produced and uploaded in relative isolation, they are ultimately meant to function in larger networks of other performances and interactions. These networks give the individual videos meaning and purpose. On YouTube, bedroom musicians sometimes strategically select songs that have already been covered by their peers. Moreover, participants explicitly link their own work to that of others. They write comments on work made by peers, upload video responses and take part in online collaborations. In this way, they actively and purposefully engage in 'pooling' practices through which they embed their work in larger networks of participants.

While such 'pooling' practices are sometimes regarded as a simple tactic for generating traffic and views (DeMers, 2015; Lastufka and Dean, 2009), they actually serve important other purposes. First, they make it possible for participants to socialise and to create a sense of reciprocity (see also Lange, 2009). As one of the interviewees, Vincent J. Wicker, explained: 'Views just means that someone saw it, it doesn't mean that someone engaged in it [...] I am looking for people to interact with, I'm looking for people to comment on my stuff, to tell me what they like or what they didn't like' (30 May 2013). During the interviews, participants continuously stressed how they enjoy being part of a 'group' or a 'circle' of peers, highlighting the social and intimate aspects of their practice as much as the musical aspects. Besides this, many of the bedroom videos are, as I have shown above, explicitly based on practices of learning and experimentation. These activities do not take place in isolation, but are supported by larger networks of peers. A good example of this is the production and exchange of so-called 'tutorial videos'. In these videos, participants explain to each other how to approach a given song on a particular musical instrument (see also Miller, 2012). These tutorial videos are often purposefully interlinked with, and circulated amongst, existing bedroom videos. By creating and sharing such educational videos, bedroom musicians purposefully embed themselves in larger communities of practice (Lave and Wenger, 1991) in which different forms of peer-directed learning can take place.

Even when there is no explicit tutorial available, the sheer fact that YouTube makes it possible to navigate from one video to another is crucial for some participants. Many of the interviewees described, for example, how they value the ability to watch all the different iterations of a particular song that have been uploaded to YouTube, in order to see what other bedroom musicians have done with it. By comparing slight changes in the iterations of these songs – called 'small creative acts' in other research (Michielse and Partti, 2015; Toynbee, 2000, 2001) – bedroom musicians are able learn a lot about processes of musical variation and interpretation. Moreover, they can gain a better understanding of the possibilities of different musical tools and instruments. Thus, the pooling practices of these bedroom musicians function not only as a way for them to gain a sense of reciprocity, but also as an important opportunity for them to improve their skills by mutually comparing personal approaches and struggles.

Seen from this perspective, an individual bedroom video (taken as an isolated product) is much less important to the participants than the collective processes, experiences and relations that such a video allows. It is for this reason that participants sometimes feel hesitant and anxious about leaving their videos online for longer periods of time. Especially in an era of viral media, the interest in particular artists or songs can rise quickly, but also disappear rapidly. This implies that the musical communities around a particular artist or song may swiftly dissolve. For bedroom musicians, such a situation poses a risk as it means that their videos will stop being part of a collective endeavour and start functioning again as individual, isolated events. In order to avoid such a situation, many participants choose to update their video libraries regularly. This may involve adding, removing or 'privatising' particular videos. Indeed, many of the participants I followed have taken down one or more of their videos from their YouTube channels simply because they felt the videos were no longer relevant or because interest around a certain song had died down. Such practices can also be seen as important strategies of 'zoning', as they are meant to 'shield' the musical practices from misunderstanding and reduce the chance that the videos will be consumed out of context.

Conclusion

On YouTube, bedroom musicians find new possibilities to disclose their otherwise private musical practices and establish new connections with people all around the world. At the same time, their activities are met with criticism and misunderstanding, especially from relative outsiders to the community of practitioners. In this chapter, I have explored this double-sided situation with the help of the concept of context collapse. As I have shown, bedroom performances not only blur the boundaries between the private and the public, but also complicate the distinction between rehearsing and performing, and product and process. By zooming in on these blurry boundaries, my argument reveals the precarious situation of bedroom musicians and their occasional struggle to produce or maintain meaningful and intimate connections with other viewers and peers on YouTube. At the same time, my discussion highlights some of the tactics and strategies used by participants to negotiate this position and turn their online practices into meaningful and valuable shared activities.

As the fieldwork for this study reveals, bedroom musicians are hardly oblivious to the tensions surrounding their daily activities. If participants, despite these tensions, decide to upload their work to YouTube, it is not because they believe themselves to possess a special set of skills or because they are exhibitionists or narcissists. Rather, it is because they see important possibilities and advantages in doing so. As I have shown, posting bedroom covers on YouTube can form the basis of different forms of musical experimentation and learning. In addition, the sharing of videos has important social functions. YouTube gives musical performers the ability to connect with others and share musical activities between one bedroom and another, anywhere in the world. This opportunity is historically unique. As authors such as Bennett (1980) and Green (2001, 2008) have shown, informal processes of musical learning and experimentation have long remained hidden in the privacy of the home. Before the rise of social media platforms, domestic learning practices were rarely discussed or shared amongst (beginner) musicians, making it difficult for them to learn from peers or to establish personal contacts. Today, however, such processes are increasingly revealed and opened up. While this is something both performers and audiences may still need to get used to, it also brings important new possibilities for current and future generations of music enthusiasts.

Notes

1 Parts of this chapter are based on my PhD dissertation (Michielse, 2015).
2 Burgess uses the term 'virtuosic bedroom performance' in her work (2008, p. 107). In this chapter, I use the more neutral term 'musical bedroom performance', as part of my argument is that many of these videos are actually quite modest in their showcasing of technical and musical skills.
3 It is for this reason that Goffman's theories (which were originally largely grounded in non-mediated encounters) have been widely adopted in new media studies.
4 This slogan is no longer used by the platform (see also Burgess, 2015).
5 Most of the interviewees clearly fit the label of 'bedroom musician'. A few of them, however, also experimented with different variations on the bedroom performance. They would record their videos, for example, in other domestic places, such as the attic, basement, kitchen or living room. A couple of the interviewees even experimented with moving their performance outside the home, in some of their videos. While the study of such variations was highly relevant to my larger research project on online musical practices (Michielse, 2015), in this

chapter I focus mainly on the participants, performances and experiences that related explicitly to the bedroom.

6 Usernames are not completely anonymous, as they may carry traces of the user's offline life. As such, the use of these names in research requires careful handling by the researcher. At the same time, however, as authors such as Bruckman (2002) and Bakardjieva and Feenberg (2000) have argued, working with usernames can be an important way to pay respect to online participants and their creative practices. This is especially true for amateur performers, who might feel alienated from their creative labour when their work, experiences and practices are not properly credited. In this chapter I refer to usernames, where possible, but refrain from mentioning such specifics when discussing particularly sensitive examples or issues.

7 One of the performers, JTehAnonymous, explained that he imagines his viewers to be literally positioned close to the screen, potentially with headphones on, when watching his videos.

8 These examples come directly from my field notes, taken between December 2012 and May 2014.

9 These examples also come directly from my field notes, taken between December 2012 and May 2014.

References

Balance, C.B. (2012). How it feels to be viral me: Affective labor and Asian American YouTube performance. *Women's Study Quarterly*, 40(1–2), pp. 138–152.

Bakardjieva, M. and Feenberg, A. (2000). Involving the virtual subject. *Ethics and Information Technology*, 2, pp. 233–240.

Bennett, H.S. (1980). *On Becoming a Rock Musician*. Amherst, MA: University of Massachusetts Press.

boyd, d. (2008). *Taken Out of Context. American Teen Sociality in Networked Publics*. PhD dissertation. University of California. Retrieved from www.danah.org/papers/TakenOutOfContext.pdf.

boyd, d. (2011). Social network sites as networked publics. Affordances, dynamics, and implications. In: Z. Papacharissi, ed., *A Networked Self. Identity, Community, and Culture on Social Network Sites*. New York: Routledge, pp. 39–58.

boyd, d. (2014). *It's Complicated. The Social Lives of Networked Teens*. New Haven, CT: Yale University Press.

Bruckman, A. (2002). Studying the amateur artist: A perspective on disguising data collected in human subject research on the Internet. *Ethics and Information Technology*, 4(3), pp. 217–231.

Buckingham, D., Willett, R. and Pini, M. (2011). *Home Truths? Video Production and Domestic Life*. Ann Arbor, MI: University of Michigan Press.

Burgess, J. (2008). 'All your chocolate rain are belong to us?' Viral video, YouTube and the dynamics of participatory culture. In: G. Lovink and S. Niederer, eds., *Video Vortex Reader: Responses to YouTube*. Amsterdam: Institute of Network Cultures, pp. 101–109. Retrieved from http://networkcultures.org/wp-content/uploads/2008/10/vv_reader_small.pdf.

Burgess, J. (2015). From 'broadcast yourself' to 'follow your interests': Making over social media. *International Journal of Cultural Studies*, 18(3), pp. 281–285.

Carr, N. (2016). *Utopia is Creepy: And Other Provocations*. New York: W.W. Norton.

Chalfen, R. (1987). *Snapshot Versions of Life*. Bowling Green, OH: Bowling Green State University Press.

Chambers, D. (2013). *Social Media and Personal Relationships. Online Intimacies and Networked Friendship*. Houndmills: Palgrave.

DeMers, J. (2015). 50 Free Ways to Grow Your YouTube Channel Subscribers and Views. Forbes. Retrieved from www.forbes.com/sites/jaysondemers/2015/06/25/50-free-ways-to-grow-your-youtube-channel-subscribers-and-views/3/#b82b8c85f183.

Farci, M., Rossi, L., Artieri, G.B. and Giglietto, F. (2016). Networked intimacy. Intimacy and friendship among Italian Facebook users. *Information, Communication & Society*, June, pp. 1–18. Retrieved from www.tandfonline.com/doi/full/10.1080/1369118X.2016.1203970.

Finnegan, R. (1989). *The Hidden Musicians. Music-Making in an English Town*. Cambridge: Cambridge University Press.

Goffman, E. (1967). *Interaction Ritual. Essays on Face-To-Face Behaviour*. Harmondsworth: Penguin.

Goffman, E. (1990 [1959]). *The Presentation of Self in Everyday Life*. London: Penguin.

Green, L. (2001). *How Popular Musicians Learn. A Way Ahead for Music Education*. Aldershot: Ashgate.

Green, L. (2008). *Music, Informal Learning and the School: A New Classroom Pedagogy*. Aldershot: Ashgate.

Hine, C. (2000). *Virtual Ethnography*. London: SAGE.

Hodkinson, P. (2015). Bedrooms and beyond: Youth, identity and privacy on social network sites. *New Media & Society*, 22 September, pp. 1–17.

Kant, T. (2014). Giving the 'viewser' a voice? Situating the individual in relation to personalization, narrowcasting, and public service broadcasting. *Journal of Broadcasting & Electronic Media*, 58(3), pp. 381–399.

Keen, A. (2007). *The Cult of the Amateur. How Blogs, MySpace, YouTube and the Rest of Today's User-Generated Media are Destroying our Economy, our Culture, and our Values*. London: Nicholas Brealey Publishing.

Keen, A. (2012). *Digital Vertigo. How Today's Online Social Revolution is Dividing, Diminishing, and Disorienting Us*. London: Constable.

Kim, J. (2012). The institutionalization of YouTube: From user-generated content to professionally generated content. *Media, Culture & Society*, 34(1), pp. 53–67.

Lange, P.G. (2007). Publicly private and privately public: Social networking on YouTube. *Journal of Computer-Mediated Communication*, 13(1).

Lange, P.G. (2009). Videos of affinity on YouTube. In: P. Snickars and P. Vonderau, eds., *The YouTube Reader*, pp. 70–88. Retrieved from http://pellesnickars.se/index.php?s=file_download&id=30.

Lange, P.G. (2014). *Kids on YouTube. Technical Identities and Digital Literacies*. Walnut Creek, CA: Left Coast Press.

Lastufka, A. and Dean M.W. (2009). *YouTube: An Insider's Guide to Climbing the Charts*. Sebastopol: O'Reilly Media.

Lave, J. and Wenger, E. (1991). *Situated Learning. Legitimate Peripheral Participation*. Cambridge: Cambridge University Press.

Lincoln, S. (2005). Feeling the noise: Teenagers, bedrooms and music. *Leisure Studies*, 24(4), pp. 399–414.

Lincoln, S. (2014). Young people and mediated private space. In: A. Bennett and B. Robards, eds., *Mediated Youth Cultures. The Internet, Belonging and New Cultural Configurations*. Basingstoke: Palgrave, pp. 42–58.
Lincoln, S. and Robards, B. (2014). Being strategic and taking control: Bedrooms, social network sites and the narratives of growing up. *New Media & Society*, 18(6), pp. 927–943.
Mallan, K. (2009). Look at me! Look at me! Self-representation and self-exposure through online networks. *Digital Culture & Education*, online publication April 22. Retrieved from www.digitalcultureandeducation.com/uncategorized/mallan-2009-html.
Marwick, A.E. and boyd, d. (2010). I Tweet honestly, I Tweet passionately: Twitter users, context collapse, and the imagined audience. *New Media & Society*, 13(1), pp. 114–133.
Marwick, A.E. and boyd, d. (2014). Networked privacy: How teenagers negotiate context in social media. *New Media & Society*, 16(7), pp. 1051–1067.
Mashek, D.J. and Aron, A. (2004). Introduction. In: D.J. Mashek and A. Aron, eds., *Handbook of Closeness and Intimacy*. Mahwah, NJ: Lawrence Erlbaum, pp. 1–6.
Michielse, M. (2015). *Remix, Cover, Mash. Remediating Phonographic-Oral Practice Online*. PhD dissertation. Maastricht University.
Michielse, M. and Partti, H. (2015). Producing a meaningful difference: The significance of small creative acts in composing within online participatory remix practices. *International Journal of Community Music*, 8(1), pp. 27–40.
Miller, K. (2012). *Playing Along. Digital Games, YouTube, and Virtual Performance*. Oxford: Oxford University Press.
Regan, P.M., FitzGerald, G. and Balint, P. (2013). Generational views on information privacy? *Innovation: The European Journal of Social Science Research*, 26(1–2), pp. 81–99.
Toynbee, J. (2000). *Making Popular Music. Musicians, Creativity and Institutions*. London: Arnold.
Toynbee, J. (2001). Creating problems: Social authorship, copyright and the production of culture. In: *Pavis Papers No. 3*. Milton Keynes: Pavis Centre for Social and Cultural Research, The Open University.
Twenge, J.M. and Campbell, W.K. (2010). *The Narcissism Epidemic. Living in the Age of Entitlement*. New York: Free Press.
van Dijck, J. (2008). Television 2.0: YouTube and the Emergence of Homecasting. Retrieved from http://web.mit.edu/comm-forum/mit5/papers/vanDijck_Television2.0.article.MiT5.pdf.
Vitak, J. (2012). The impact of context collapse and privacy on social network site disclosures. *Journal of Broadcasting & Electronic Media*, 56(4), pp. 451–470.
Wesch, M. (2009). YouTube and you. Experience of self-awareness in the context collapse of the recording webcam. *Explorations in Media Ecology*, 8(2), pp. 19–34.
Weintraub, J. (1997). The theory and politics of the public/private distinction. In: J. Weintraub and K. Kumar, eds., *Public and Private in Thought and Practice*. Chicago, IL: University of Chicago Press, pp. 1–43.

18 Fashion blogging as a technology of bodily becoming

The fluidity and firmness of digital bodies

Louise Yung Nielsen

Introduction

As Marshall McLuhan (1964) famously declared, media are extensions of man. Every time users encounter a new type of media, their bodily experiences change. This chapter explores the way in which the body is performed on one of the oldest forms of so-called social media, the blog – particularly the fashion blog. I analyse the way in which two bloggers use a fitness regime, clothing and plastic surgery as bodily technologies to produce new forms of embodiment, while also producing intimacy. Further, the study takes the digital medium of the blog and digital imagery into account and explores how these devices can be thought of as bodily technologies of becoming. By doing so, the chapter highlights the intertwined relation between bodies and media and examines how this intimate relation is performed on the personal fashion blog.

In what follows, I analyse bodily performance, drawing on feminist theory concerning the body. First, I discuss the relation between the body and media and examine how the body is performed through its entanglement with exercise, clothing and plastic surgery. I then argue that the images and blogs are technologies of bodily becoming, and that intimacy is present in very different manners on the two blogs analysed here.

I focus on two (Danish) blogs: Sidsel and Lasse and Gina Jaqueline. Gina Jaqueline is now inactive, while Sidsel and Lasse remains active. Both blogs are or have been quite successful, and have been operated professionally, cooperating with companies to create sponsored content; in this way, they have performed what could be categorised as 'affective labour' (Hardt, 1999), producing affect and becoming subjects as a form of labour. Following this, the concept of the 'microcelebrity' (Marwick and boyd, 2011; Senft, 2008) is relevant, because it emphasises the fashion bloggers' resemblance to more conventional celebrities and their commodification.[1]

Bodies and blogs that matter – Theoretical framework and methodology

The theoretical basis of this study is Judith Butler's account of how bodies materialise through a process of performativity (Butler, 1999 [1993]) and, subsequently, Karen Barad's development of Butler's concept into posthumanistic performativity (Barad, 2003, 2007). For both thinkers, bodies (and materiality) are performative; in other words, they are in a constant process of becoming. However, I do not advocate a fluent and limitless state of bodily becoming, but rather a *material-discursive* bodily becoming.

During the 1990s, fascination was with all things cyber and the body was widely regarded as obsolete. But as Katherine N. Hayles argues, information also has a body (Hayles, 1999), and Donna Haraway's cyborg (Haraway, 1991) provides one example of the merger of body and technology. Thus, 'we have always been mediated', as Sarah Kember and Joanna Zylinska argue (2012, p. 194): we have always been part of a complex and intra-active relationship with technology and non-human agents.

There have been many attempts at defining a 'blog'. One such definition is provided by Jill Walker Rettberg: 'a frequently updated Web site consisting of dated entries arranged in reverse chronological order so the most recent post appears first' (Rettberg, 2008, p. 19). Moreover, several researchers have approached the blog as a personal performance. danah boyd writes that the blog 'becomes part of the blogger' (boyd, 2006, p. 18), drawing on Jenny Sundén's claim – from her study of text-based communities – that users 'write themselves into being' (Sundén, 2003, p. 3). Adam Reed suggests that 'my blog is me' (2005) and Joanna Zylinska calls the personal blog a 'performative space' (2009, p. 82).

Several studies of fashion blogs have focused on notions of identity (Chittenden, 2010) and the negotiation of authenticity in a commercialised space (Marwick, 2013); others have focused on immediacy and honesty (Rocamora, 2011) or taken a more critical approach, examining the gendered and racialised body (Pham, 2011) or female voices (Rocamora, 2012). In contrast, in this chapter I examine the fashion blog as a producer of both new bodies and new ways of experiencing and performing bodies. At least two studies (Pham, 2011; Rocamora, 2012) have addressed the body in relation to fashion blogs, but the ambitions of these studies differ from that of this chapter.

As almost all domains of consumer culture are somehow linked to the body, the fashion blog is an obvious site for an exploration of digital media and consumption. The two fashion blogs that form the basis of this study focus on fashion, exercise, plastic surgery and other matters that can be linked to the body. In the context of this article, fashion, exercise and plastic surgery are considered not only lifestyle components, but also 'technologies of the self' (Kember and Zylinska, 2012, p. 133). They shape the body through a never-ending cycle of consumption – a bodily becoming.

Drawing upon critical approaches to visual analysis incorporating the body (Coleman, 2009; Ferreday, 2003), I approach the fashion blogs through their use of images, taking a dual methodological approach. While I am interested in articulations and representations of the body in a traditional sense, I am also interested in the way in which images (and hence the blogs) are used as body performances. Thus, I perform both traditional content analysis, focused on bodily discourses, and an analysis focused on the interplay between the body and the medium (i.e. the images and the blogs).

The two very personal fashion blogs I am focusing on – Sidsel and Lasse, and Gina Jaqueline – are very different. Sidsel and Lasse is a professional blog that produces much commercial content, but it also performs privacy and intimacy in a controlled and courteous manner, displaying a sensitivity to personal boundaries. Gina Jaqueline, on the other hand, showcases a much more flamboyant mixture of high fashion, deeply personal issues and extreme party life. The conventional boundaries of the self are challenged and, at times, even broken down. Furthermore, the blogs represent two very different takes on fashion and the body. The analysis presented in this chapter reflects these differences, which contrast a fairly conventional body with one that is more fluid and experimental. The difference of these blogs provides insight into both a dominant and homogenous approach to consumption, body and the self and a more marginalised and experimental approach. Nonetheless, there are plenty of similarities between the blogs. Both channel a combination of lifestyle, consumer culture and body culture and both stage the bloggers' bodies in and through the blog. Furthermore, they can both be categorised as 'personal fashion blogs' (Rocamora, 2012) or as 'narcissus', as Engholm and Hansen-Hansen describe fashion blogs projecting a personal narrative (2014).

The body, as performed through the before-and-after image

In addition to being blogging partners, Sidsel and Lasse (www.sidseloglasse.com) are also romantic partners. Fashion and consumer lifestyle content occupies most of their blog posts, but the partners also regularly blog about their education and employment. Lasse has an MA in Media Studies and Sidsel has an MA in Experience Economy, both having had part-time jobs in retail and later on full-time jobs; Lasse working with marketing in the fashion industry and Sidsel as a digital consultant at a bureau. Most noticeably they blog about their romantic relationship. Posts about their relationship are both delivered as everyday musings, but also as more serious posts about their temporary breakup while Sidsel was attending an exchange programme in Australia. The couple reunited later on. The rhythm of their blog is steady: new content is posted every day and sometimes even twice a day.

Lasse exhibits a metrosexual masculinity, as he cultivates his look through outfits and, as we will see in the following, fitness. In autumn 2014, Lasse posts two posts on the blog in which he discusses his recent experience with the discipline of CrossFit. He explains that he did CrossFit as a 'challenge' posed by a local CrossFit centre.

> Part of the challenge is that I will post a before-and-after shot. And here's the before shot. I think it is a little taboo breaking for me to post

> such an image, but here it is. Go easy on me! [...] I won't be changing my diet drastically during the weeks of crossfit, but try to drink fewer beers and cut back on the carbs. Let's see what happens :).
>
> (23 October 2014)

Lasse speaks from within a performance culture in which the evaluation and assessment of bodies is a normal practice (Featherstone, 2010). 'Go easy on me,' he says, while exposing his body. The parallel between the before-and-after image and reality television's makeover genre is obvious. First, reality television's makeover genre almost always uses before-and-after images to illustrate a positive change or transformation, whether the subject of the transformation is a home, a business, a body or a household economy. Second, Lasse's post is built on the expectation of positive change. After all, a makeover is only considered a success if the result is positive (Featherstone, 2010, p. 203). Thus, the makeover genre and general arguments for a makeover's positive change celebrate a neoliberal ideal in which individuals are responsible for their own personal growth, success, beauty and body through the 'right' kind of consumption (CrossFit) and the 'right' kind of effort. Diet and exercise are commodities in a growing market for healthy bodies – a market regulated by strict and normative bodily discourses promoting a certain consumption.

20-11-14 LASSE
CROSSFIT CPH - EVALUERING
Før/efter. Ikke den store forandring udenpå ud over længere hår og et, om muligt, endnu mere akavet ansigtsudtryk. Men indeni kan det mærkes!

Figure 18.1 Screenshot from Sidsel and Lasse, from post dated 20 November 2014

In the above quote, Lasse makes it clear that he does not subscribe to an extreme celebration of bodily improvement but rather to a moderate or even bourgeois improvement, wherein the body is disciplined through slow body technologies such as diet and exercise. However, this is not an average bodily performance, but one of gender and class. Lasse performs a specific type of middle-class masculinity in which the body is shaped through the 'natural' and 'functional' movements of CrossFit. CrossFit is a relatively new type of exercise that is often practiced in urban closed industrial spaces, and appeals to young urban creatives. It is recognised for its focus on 'natural' and 'functional' body movement and its downplay of bodily aesthetics. While the thinking of Butler is suitable for the more general observations of bodily and gendered performances, Mike Featherstone is more specifically commenting on the use of body images in popular culture. Also, Butler's main errand is onto-epistemological. She is interested in the nature of the body, the status of matter; while Featherstone is criticising a specific cultural phenomenon and his thoughts on the improvement of bodies in reality shows can thus contribute to a critical framework for the two fashion bloggers' bodily performances.

Featherstone comments on the reality celebrity's life as something that 'constantly swings between successes and failures, between a beautiful healthy body and an abandoned ill-disciplined body that bears the marks of constant excesses' (Featherstone, 2010, p. 202). While Lasse is not a reality star, his position as a successful fashion blogger resembles the position of the reality star; he produces himself as the core commodity of his entrepreneurship. In this case, Lasse refuses to submit to the logic of the bodily extremities that Featherstone mentions and will not 'change his diet during the weeks of crossfit', thus advocating a 'sensible' and 'balanced' bodily regime in which enjoyment and pleasure are important components.

This example emphasises the intimacy of the relation between Lasse's body, his blogging practice and his blog. Lasse might never have received the offer of a CrossFit introduction course had it not been for his association with a successful blog. Furthermore, his investment in the course was most likely accelerated by the fact that he was obliged to post before-and-after shots of his body. Lasse's body, his blogging practice and the images on the blog cannot be said to be separate entities; rather, they are defined by their proximity and intimate connections. They are entangled.

Performing the media as insignificant

In Lasse's construction of the CrossFit narrative, it is remarkable how small a role the medium, itself, plays. In his narrative, his body is shaped by technologies that are 'outside' the medium, such as diet and exercise. But in fact, the medium – the before-and-after image – contributes significantly to his bodily performance. When Lasse puts his body on display, as he does in these posts, he uses the blog as a surveillance technology. The blog documents his body and he shares it with his readers so that they, too, can monitor his body's progress. In the context of Lasse's narrative, the images are given the status of documentation. They document Lasse's 'real' body and prioritise the real body over the imagery.

Before-and-after images rely on an underlying assumption that images carry the truth – that they do not lie. Hence, images are used here to determine the truth-value of Lasse's bodily improvement. Much as in a 'find five errors' game, blog readers are tasked with identifying improvements or a lack thereof: Are his abs more defined? Are his biceps more toned? Has he got rid of the small roll of fat on his stomach? Readers can judge for themselves, and this is exactly what they do. 'Clear visible difference!' comments one reader; 'your chest has grown bigger, congrats!' writes another. Thus, the use of the before-and-after image encourages the formation of a positive and affirmative community based on naive pseudo-positivistic assumptions about the truth of images.

Instead of subscribing to the old dichotomies such as body-mind and unmediated-mediated, I prefer to read this as a bodily performance in which the before-and-after image (as well as the blog, itself) is the medium through which the body becomes. When reading Lasse's bodily performance, it becomes obvious that the body is performative in Butler's sense (Butler, 1999); but in this case, the *medium* (the before-and-after image) is also performative, emphasising Barad's posthumanistic performativity (Barad, 2003). Thus, agency is not being distributed through anthropocentric principles, as Barad puts it (Barad, 2003, p. 828). Rather, it becomes obvious how the medium (the image) conquers agency and is able to put on a performance on its own. Through the relatable articulation of his approach to the CrossFit course, Lasse initially comes across as if he is in control of the narrative of his bodily improvement. Furthermore, the images allow him the material-discursive rendering of his body as a body 'outside' the image – 'outside' the blog; thus, he performs the image as a *documentary* his body. But at the same time, Lasse *loses* control. The before-and-after image *does* something to him and his body and does not leave him unaffected; rather, it forces him to come into being *through* the image.

Through this approach to the use of images as well as to blogging, Lasse attempts to distance himself from the medium, refusing to engage in an intimate interplay with the blog. Through his performance of body, the relation between his body and the medium becomes less intimate. He subscribes to a traditional understanding of the blog and images as things that separate humans from technology, and thus refuses to acknowledge that we are in fact 'becoming with the technological world' (Kember and Zylinska, 2012, p. xv).

Authenticity and the firm body

Lasse performs his body according to a late modern notion of the body as a self-project (Giddens, 1991), seeing it as plastic and mouldable according to specific codes of culture. However, for Lasse, the medium, itself, is not part of the equation. Hence, the blog and the image are neglected in his articulation, and performed as insignificant (though, of course, they are not). Lasse indirectly addresses blogging as a reflexive practice by emphasising that sharing pictures of his body is 'taboo-breaking'. He openly reflects on his motivations for beginning the CrossFit course, pointing towards the performance of 'backstage' access and giving his readers a sense that they are sharing an intimate or private space with him. This also points to authenticity as a confessional space, highlighting the blog's history as a digital diary (Rettberg, 2008, p. 12). Returning to the notion of intimacy, it becomes apparent that Lasse performs another type of intimacy relating to a more traditional understanding, in which proximity and intimacy are achieved not through the entanglement of the medium and the body, but through the confessional space of the blog, in which authenticity and intimacy are inextricably linked.

Lasse's bodily performance privileges the 'real' physical body over the digital body. The digital medium is 'just' a representation of reality and is not 'real', in itself. The body outside the digital realm is the producer of all things authentic, and authenticity is highly valued on many blogs. This example shows how the physical and coherent body is tested. When navigating between the digital and the non-digital, Lasse meticulously documents the small changes in his body through the use of 'objective' photos. He thus copes with the entanglement of body and media by working against it. When working with and within the performative space of the digital medium, Lasse seeks the safe and coherent body of the physical world.

The plastic and digital body

The second case of this study is that of Gina Jaqueline – a blog run by the blogger Gina Jaqueline. Gina blogged from 2009 to 2014, about fashion and everyday life. However, her approach seems to divert from that of most other Danish fashion bloggers. As opposed to Lasse's readers, hers are almost never used as a source of income, and the manner in which she leads her life (on the blog) is often controversial. During her most active years of blogging, Gina partied quite hard. On her blog, this is usually depicted through lengthy series of images portraying the previous night's party, often in blurry photographs that provide an artistic account of exhilaration and intoxication. Fashion-wise, Gina favours a less accessible style, combining vintage clothing with inexpensive high street and expensive luxury brands. I now take a look at the manner in which she wears her clothes on the blog.

When looking at Gina's 'outfit of the day' images, it quickly becomes clear that her body willingly changes its posture depending on the type of outfit she is wearing. In one image, she poses in skinny fit stonewashed jeans, a white Levi's T-shirt that is tied in a knot on her stomach and white Converse trainers. She sucks in her stomach to appear thinner, and pushes

Figure 18.2 Four 'outfit of the day' shots of Gina Jaqueline from June to July 2010

her breasts forward and her shoulders back, drawing attention to certain features of her body. She is portrayed from the side, which highlights her sucked in waist. In another image, she is wearing her boyfriend's band T-shirt with a suspender belt, stockings and a designer bag. The T-shirt seems oversized on her tiny body and hangs lazily on her frame, almost hiding it. In this image, her posture is completely different. She faces the camera with her shoulders relaxed; her face wears no expression and her eyes are hidden behind sunglasses. Barad argues that 'matter is not little bits of nature, or a blank slate, surface, or site passively awaiting signification' (Barad, 2003, p. 821). This becomes obvious when looking at the bodily performance on Gina's blog. Her body can be characterised as shapeable and almost fluent, willingly submitting to the aesthetic codes of her outfits. The different fashionable outfits dictate the design of her body, her posture and her pose. They are more like costumes than conventional clothing: she performs her outfit, and the way her body takes different shapes resembles an actor stepping into character. Her body is plastic and its potential for change is seemingly never-ending. The becoming of her body is conditioned by aesthetics, with her body entangled with the textiles of the clothing.

Here it becomes apparent that Gina embraces the performative dimension of blogging to another degree than Lasse. And it is not only Butler's version of performativity at play here. While Butler's notion of performativity allows me to analyse the bodily performance(s) of Gina, the breakdown of the distinction between subject and objects invites to an analytical attention to the entanglement of body and media. In a third photo, Gina poses in a park with a Baroque castle in the background. She is wearing a jumpsuit, looking sophisticated and mature. The park and the majestic character of the castle are props in Gina's performance of her body. And in the fourth photo, in which Gina sits backwards on a staircase, she wears a short dress covered in a batik print, stockings and trainers. The clothing and her posture on the staircase connote 'small' and 'infantile', as opposed to 'big' and 'adult'. The photo is taken from a downwards angle, making Gina look smaller. Thus, it is not just the fashion that enters into dialogue with the body, but also the surroundings, which become part of the bodily performance. Again, we must remember what is so easily forgotten: the medium, itself – the image. As Rebecca Coleman writes: 'bodies and images, then, are not separate but rather bodies are known, understood and experienced through images' (Coleman, 2009, p. 19) or we are 'becoming with the technological world' (Kember and Zylinska, 2012, p. xv). For Gina performativity becomes an endless space of possibilities; the images, the clothing, the blog are all used as technologies that shape and reshape self and body. She embraces the performance, enjoys the playfulness of it all. Here it becomes apparent just how different Gina's and Lasse's bodily performances are. While Gina embraces the change, Lasse rejects the 'becoming with media' preferring to stay in control of his own becoming.

The nature of fashion

Gina displays a playful approach to fashion that allows her to experiment with identity, costumes and corporealities. But what at first appears to be an emancipatory practice of fashion, setting the body free and allowing the fluidity and digitality of the medium to work for her, is in fact a well-known high fashion practice – as is remixing and referencing styles from fashion history. Georg Simmel and Walter Benjamin are both thinkers of modernity and both perceive fashion to be a defining trait of modernity, emphasising the individual's desire to stand out (Benjamin, 1973; Simmel, 1998 [1911]). Fashion is a means of obtaining uniqueness as well as signalling status and belonging to a certain socioeconomic group.

Their reflections on the nature of fashion are relevant to this day and are still widely used in the study of sociology of fashion (e.g. Barnard, 2007). Thus, Gina's bodily performance should not be understood as a unique ability to act independent of cultural and aesthetic conventions, but should emphasise the paradox of fashion that materialises dream images while at the same time corresponding with notions of social status and cultural capital.

The images on Gina Jaqueline are of a much higher quality than the photos on Sidsel and Lasse. It is obvious that colour, setting and composition are taken into account before the photographs are taken. Knowledge of established genres within fashion photography is required to produce these photos. Thus, Gina recirculates and recycles well-known aesthetic fashion discourses. The visual language is used as a language of the self, creating Gina, over and over, through the images. In this way, the personal fashion blog can be said to be a highly intimate technology of the self, conveying dreams and desires. Benjamin's depiction of the passages of nineteenth century Paris link the display of fashion with the production of desire, seduction and dream images (Benjamin, 1973). Through the same logic, conventional fashion photography can be understood to sell one thing: clothing and accessories. But in the context of the fashion blog and the logic of the economy of social media, Gina Jaqueline sells something else: herself. This is a major difference that confirms the intimacy between the blog and the blogger. The blog becomes the blogger, and vice versa. Thus, this analysis has shown that technologies at all levels of blog production become indispensable for bodily performance through the blog. The medium – be it clothing or image – enters into an intimate connection with the body. In fact, the body of Gina Jaqueline is not possible without it.

Lip enhancement

A radical approach to the plastic body is found in the performance of clothing on Gina's blog. But this approach to the body is articulated even further in a blog post in which she announces that she is 'having her lips done' (18 March 2010) – meaning that she is planning to have them enhanced by means of injection. This 'invasion' of the body suggests an even more intimate relationship between the body and technologies, wherein the blog, surgery and the body are bound together through a blogging practice of intimacy. Gina presents her new lips on the blog by sharing images and reporting from her visit to the clinic. When sharing her enhanced lips, she shows two images along with a bit of text. One image is a close-up of her face in semi-profile (not shown); the other is a waist shot. Her body faces the camera but her head is turned away, with her bob hiding most of her face except for her lips. She writes:

> I am just home from brunch with people from the party last night. Here's a quick today's – but the picture doesn't do my lip-enhancement justice because of my naked face, but I will share some proper images later tonight.
>
> (26 March 2010)

Figure 18.3 Screenshot from Gina Jaqueline, from post dated 26 March 2010

Gina apologises that the photo 'doesn't do her lips justice' because of her 'naked' face. Her declaration that her face is 'naked' is quite interesting. Usually, a face with no make-up is described as a 'natural' face, but 'naked' suggests that the point of departure for Gina is her made-up face – her face, performing. Her enhanced lips are part of an outfit; they need to be performed, much as the rest of her outfits do.

Still, it seems that there are small openings towards a more conventional understanding of the body. The 'natural' becomes an issue once again when Gina describes the amount of Restylane she has had injected: 'I've had 0,6 ml in my upper lip and 0,4 in my lower lip, so that it fits my lip's natural size' (27 March 2010). According to Butler, the 'natural' body is just as discursive as the technologically modified body, because our only access to the materiality of the body is through discourse (Butler, 1999 [1993], p. 38). But despite embracing the bodily technology of plastic surgery, Gina's discourse about 'naturalness' is strong and the natural is constantly up for negotiation in the becoming of Gina's lips. In this quote, 'naturalness' is understood as a potential that demands work and improvement through, for example, plastic surgery. This shows us that Gina is very aware of the stigma of plastic surgery and makes sure to distance her lip enhancement from grotesque or monstrous versions of the procedure. Not surprisingly, 'naturalness' is a concept that plays a considerable role in the becoming of her lips; it is seemingly not an intrinsic value of the lips, but a performed 'naturalness'. Thus, performativity becomes a *potential* for Gina letting her stay in control of her own bodily narrative. While 'naturalness' is not a stable entity of originality, Gina *performs* 'naturalness' as a flexible and mouldable entity that has the potential to repeatedly change and transform.

Lasse's use of the before-and-after photo testifies to an attempt to isolate the body and to view bodily improvement through a 'neutral' or 'objective' lens. His before-and-after photos could almost be seen as a substitute for a mirror, as they enable Lasse to reflect himself in his readers' gaze. Through the readers' acknowledging and assessing gaze, the image becomes a fetish; it is meticulously scrutinised in the smallest detail and celebrated as a source of objectivity. In contrast, the photo of Gina's enhanced lips is of a completely different character. In the second photo, Gina lets her lips take part in an overall styling of her body. Mike Featherstone argues that the common mode for plastic surgery advertisement 'entails a particular view of the body, as bounded and compartmentalised into separate domains, each of which can be renovated or upgraded' (Featherstone, 2010, p. 205), but Gina refuses to submit to this logic of improvement. Her lips are shown in the context of the rest of her body, and she only shares an 'after' shot, omitting the 'before' image entirely. When Gina breaks the news to her readers that she is planning to get her lips enhanced, she does not explain her motivations. Rather, she declares that lip enhancement through injection will happen in the near future. Thus, she refuses to let any causality and temporality define her body.

The lips 'kick back'

Through this reading of how the body is shaped by clothing and plastic surgery, I have observed how two very different technologies intra-act with the materiality of the body. The shape and materiality of Gina's body allows her to perform both body and clothing in a desirable manner; the clothes intra-act with the body in an almost non-committal and playful fashion. Her body is performed through images and it looks a certain way. A pair of stilettos can be uncomfortable and certain clothing items can be too light to wear during winter, but none of these potential material consequences is quite the same as the needle's penetration of the flesh of the lips. On the one hand, the injection demands a professional operation involving a clinic, a needle and trained staff. On the other hand, clothing enters into dialogue with the body by covering its surface – almost as an extra skin – and use of clothing does not require formal education or training (though a trained sense of style or trends provides an advantage). When describing her visit to the clinic, Gina writes on her blog:

> The restylane injection has been a really positive experience. They give local anesthesia at the clinic, so I didn't feel much pain even though I felt it pinch a bit. Ii went rather quick though, so it's manageable.
>
> (27 March 2010)

These words are a testimony to the body's resistance to the surgery. Intra-acting with the clothing, the body is willingly shaped by the aesthetic codes of the clothing. But intra-acting with the needle, or the gel, the body is in pain. Maybe just a 'pinch' she says, but the voice of the body is nevertheless much more distinct, much louder. As Karen Barad would say: matter kicks back (Barad, 2007).

There are small cracks in Gina's performance of the fluid digital body. These cracks suggest that she slides in and out of different and conflicting understandings of the body – in and out of gravity and play. Images are often the favoured form of communicating this playfulness, while words communicate more traditional bodily discourses. These cracks further suggest that 'the becoming with media' has its limits and is inadequate for portraying certain bodily becomings.

Conclusion

Intimacy, it seems, is present on the blogs in different ways. The intimacy on Lasse's blog is created by the truth-telling narrative, in which the before-and-after image plays a prominent role, allowing his readers to access the personal and intimate space of his body. Furthermore, he shows a willingness to allow his readers 'backstage' and explains his motivation and apprehensiveness to share images of his undressed torso.

But Lasse insists on establishing and reaffirming his body *outside* the medium, while Gina becomes one with it. Resembling Bodil Marie Stavning Thomsen's distinction between 'the sign' and 'the signaletic' (2012), Lasse and Gina represent different modes of bodily performance. The stable 'sign' while the 'signaletic' continuously transmit. While Lasse is much less willing to intra-act with the digital, Gina is more than willing to engage with the medium and establish intimacy in the relation between her body, herself and the medium.

Disunity and diffraction are unattractive to Lasse. Like the modern subject, he longs for unity and his bodily performances can almost be designated nostalgic in the way he insists on the utopia of the individual; that which cannot be divided. His performance seems to belong to an analog era and not a digital time. He seems to operate in the altmodisch mode of print media, while Gina operates in the digital mode, taking full advantage of digital potential. She multiplies (images of) herself, shapes and reshapes her body and self and intimately connects with the media. Lasse's bodily performance is included in a set of values. The CrossFit experience highlights a bourgeois morality: hard work pays off. In contrast, Gina's lip enhancement could be perceived as a tacky and tasteless shortcut. Gina is fluid, mouldable and flexible, representing a potential that can be fulfilled through various bodily technologies. Both clothing and plastic surgery – but especially the digital medium, itself – are used unapologetically. She flickers, she is unstable and she is chameleon-like in her performance, wearing costumes instead of displaying a core identity.

Note

1 This chapter builds on my PhD dissertation (2016), *Indfoldede og udfoldede kroppe – En undersøgelse af kropslig performance på modebloggen*. Centre for Youth Research, Aalborg University, Denmark.

References

Barad, K. (2003). Posthumanist performativity: How matter comes to matter. *Signs*.

Barad, K. (2007). *Meeting the Universe Halfway: Quantum Physics and the Entanglement of Matter and Meaning*. Durham, NC: Duke University Press.

Barnard, Malcolm (ed.) (2007). *Fashion Theory. A reader*. New York: Routledge

Benjamin, W. (1973). Paris, det 19. århundredes hovedstad. *Kulturindustri*. København: Rhodos.

boyd, d. (2006). A blogger's blog: Exploring the definition of a medium. *Reconstruction*, 6(4).

Butler, J. (1999 [1993]). *Bodies that Matter*. New York: Routledge.

Chittenden, T. (2010). Digital dressing up: Modelling female teen identity in the discursive spaces of the fashion blogosphere. *Journal of Youth Studies*, 13(4), pp. 505–520.

Coleman, R. (2009). *The Becoming of Bodies. Girls, Images, Experience*. Manchester: Manchester University Press.

Engholm, I. and Hansen-Hansen, E. (2014). The fashion blog as a genre – Between user-driven bricolage design and the reproduction of established fashion system. *Digital Creativity*, 25(2), pp. 140–154.

Featherstone, M. (2010). Body, image and affect in consumer culture. *Body & Society*, 16(1), pp. 193–221.

Ferreday, D. (2003). Unspeakable Bodies: Erasure, Embodiment and the Pro-ana Community. *International Journal of Cultural Studies*, vol 6, no. 3, pp. 277–295.

Giddens, A. (1991). *Modernity and Self-Identity*. Oxford: Polity Press.

Haraway, D. (1991). A cyborg manifesto: Science, technology, and socialist-feminism in the late twentieth century. In: *Simians, Cyborgs and Women: The Reinvention of Nature*. New York: Routledge, pp. 149–181.

Hardt, M. (1999). Affective labor. *Boundary*, 26(2).

Hayles, N.K. (1999). *How We Became Posthuman: Virtual Bodies in Cybernetics, Literature and Informatics*. Chicago and London: University of Chicago Press.

Kember, S. and Zylinska, J. (2012). *Life after New Media. Mediation as a Vital Process*. Cambridge, MA: MIT Press.

Marwick, A. and boyd, d. (2011). To see and be seen: Celebrity practice on Twitter. *Convergence*, 17(2), pp. 139–158.

Marwick, A. (2013). Conspicuous and authentic: Fashion blogs, style, and consumption. Retrieved from www.tiara.org/papers.html (April 2013).

McLuhan, M. (1964). *Understanding Media. Extensions of Man*. New York: Routledge.

Pham, M.T. (2011). Blog ambition: Fashion, feelings, and the political economy of the digital raced body. *Camera Obscura,* 26(1 76), pp. 1–37.

Reed, A. (2005). 'My blog is me': Texts and persons in UK online journal culture (and anthropology). *Ethnos: Journal of Anthropology*, 70(2), pp. 220–242.

Rettberg, J.W. (2008). *Blogging*. Cambridge: Polity Press.

Rocamora, A. (2011). Personal fashion blogs: Screens and mirrors in digital self-portraits. *Fashion Theory,* 15(4), pp. 407–424.

Rocamora, A. (2012). Hypertextuality and remediation in the fashion media. *Journalism Practice*, 6(1), pp. 92–106.

Senft, T.M. (2008). *Camgirls: Celebrity and Community in the Age of Social Networks*. New York: Peter Lang.

Simmel, G. (1998 [1911]). Moden. *Hvordan er Samfundet Muligt*. København: Gyldendal.

Sundén, J. (2003). *Material Virtualities*. New York: Peter Lang.

Thomsen, B.M.S. (2012). Signaletic, haptic and real-time material. *Journal of Aesthetics and Culture*, 4.

Zylinska, J. (2009). *Bioethics. In the Age of New Media*. Cambridge and London: MIT Press.

19 'My Friend Bubz'

Building intimacy on YouTube's beauty community

Florencia García-Rapp

Introduction

The relevance of establishing feelings of connection and intimacy with an audience for cinema, television and online celebrities has been extensively researched. It has been argued that, for television personalities, familiarity and regularity foster authenticity and renew viewers' interest (e.g. Dyer, 1998; Holmes, 2004; Marshall, 2014). This is similar for internet celebrities, for whom it is particularly important to remain 'ordinary' in order to foster a sense of 'realness' and authenticity (e.g. García-Rapp and Roca-Cuberes, 2017; Tolson, 2010).

For online celebrities, there is a strong expectancy of authenticity, due to social media's implicit values of immediacy and spontaneity, as well as the inherent image of grassroots, amateur and DIY culture (Banet-Weiser, 2012; Burgess and Green, 2009; García-Rapp, 2018) that the platform of YouTube started with and seeks to maintain. Successful online celebrity practice implies building intimacy through disclosure and connection-seeking. This legitimises celebrity practitioners' positions and reputations as renowned personalities (García-Rapp, 2016; Marwick and boyd, 2011; Smith 2014). As Cohen argues, self-disclosure is 'the engine that drives new relationships' (2001, p. 46; also Baym, 2010) and 'disclosing intimacy acts as a marker that defines authentic friendship' (p. 47).

To date, practices at play within YouTube's beauty community are still under-researched. The platform's beauty ecosystem is not only highly active and dynamic, but it also represents a large market that is steadily growing. The number of views for these videos grew by 50 per cent between January 2014 and April 2015 (Pixability, 2015). Moreover, the 1.7 billion beauty-related videos that populate YouTube have generated a total of 45.3 billion historical views and more than 123 million subscriptions (Pixability, 2015).

To understand the dynamics of YouTube's beauty community, it can be particularly fruitful to explore not only the celebrification processes of beauty gurus as *regular-users-turned-celebrities*, but, more specifically, to examine how they forge closeness and intimacy with their audiences. When compared to the '15 minutes of fame' of other popular content such as viral videos, the *sustained* popularity of these beauty channels (often over several years), in such a competitive and dynamic environment, is a relevant aspect to consider. To locate this 'new public intimacy' (Marshall, 2014, p. xii), one must explore affective and discursive practices, as well as the particular 'bonds of intimacy afforded by interaction' (Usher, 2015, p. 313). In this vein, it is relevant to look at how self-disclosure through uploaded content further sustains the celebrity position of popular beauty gurus. Here, I explain how the renowned guru Bubz addresses her viewers through her channel, Bubzbeauty.

This chapter contributes to the scholarly dialogue focused on current digital culture practices at the intersection of digital fandom and celebrity culture (Kanai, 2015; Marwick and boyd, 2011; Smith, 2014; Usher, 2015). I examine the way in which content fosters different modes of address and promotes various types of connection with viewers. In addition, I describe how viewers consume Bubz's different types of content, and often reciprocate by engaging in self-disclosing narratives through comments. Like Lange, I see intimate YouTube videos or videos disclosing intimate and personal moments as 'videos of affinity' (2009, p. 73) that strengthen feelings of closeness and connection between viewers and content creators.

I do not aim at discovering whether Bubz's performance of intimacy is 'sincere' or part of her self-brand; rather, my focus is on the affordances of her content for sustaining and legitimising her position, and what viewers *do* with this – how they consume and respond to her videos. I leave aside the often simplistic considerations of 'true' versus 'false' for two reasons. First, any evaluation of truth claims would not influence the phenomenon of her popularity. In other words, independent of any moral dualism, Bubz owns a very successful channel, and I present the way she seems to connect with her followers. As Abidin writes, in reference to Singaporean lifestyle bloggers: 'the intimacies negotiated are felt by followers as opposed to whether or not these intimacies are actually "authentic" or "genuine"' (2015, p. 6). What is more, in many cases, viewers are aware of Bubz's restraints in self-presentation as a popular personality, and they know that producing videos and engaging with her audience is her occupation. My perspective is close to that established by Lange, who acknowledges that intimate videos may well have 'varying degrees of sincerity' (2009, p. 83). However, rather than using this as a major point of discovery or interpretation, I focus on the affordances of content and users' responses to it.

Second, and most importantly, Bubz's interactions likely blend her acknowledgement of community-based rules, attention building strategies and genuine, 'sincere' self-expression. This is probably also true for the interactions of most online and mass media celebrities, who are also social (and human) beings. What is more, many of Bubz's 'everyday performances' that focus on 'impression management' are practices that we all engage in, as shown by the works of Goffman (1959) and Garfinkel (1967) on the relevance of dramaturgical action as social action in everyday human interaction and the notion of behaviour as ruled-governed, respectively.

Methods

This chapter draws on a broader ethnographic examination of YouTube, specifically its beauty community, between 2013 and 2015. The data collection and analysis are based on 22 months of immersed fieldwork, which involved systematic online observation and interpretation of 313 videos and more than 10,000 comments. For this chapter, I considered a purposeful sample of 20 videos, which were transcribed and interpreted in light of their qualities of building and strengthening feelings of connection and intimacy with viewers. Correspondingly, I analysed 3,000 user comments by manually coding them according to descriptive, verbatim and emotional codes (Saldaña, 2013) in order to assess the extent to which viewers reciprocated, responding to Bubz with their own self-disclosing narratives.

In crafting an ethnography, we look to achieve a 'theoretical description of the cultural patterns that cross-cut different domains of social activity' (Ardévol and Gómez-Cruz, 2014, p. 2), considering the meaning people give to their experiences and actions. My research follows ethnographic fieldwork techniques (Boellstorf, 2008; Kozinets, 2010; Wolcott, 1995, 2010) and aims at immersive observation, description and interpretation to uncover meanings that lead to practices and dynamics (Baym, 2010; Strangelove, 2010). In this vein, the project is structured as a data-driven, explorative study following an inductive rationale. I use qualitative data analysis to perform a contextual, open-ended examination (Creswell, 2013; Merriam, 2009; Saldaña, 2013). I not only consider the inherent intimacy of the content, as determined by the personal and private nature of the topics and Bubz's disclosure practices, but also take into account Bubz's audience´s responses in the form of textual comments.

From content-oriented to motivational videos: A scale of intimacy

The focus of my study is a very popular British Chinese girl, Bubz, who has been uploading video tutorials on beauty and lifestyle to YouTube since 2008. She is known as a beauty guru: a person who creates video tutorials demonstrating looks and offering advice on make-up, hairstyling techniques and cosmetics. Make-up tutorials are widespread on YouTube and constitute an essential part of its beauty community (García-Rapp, 2016; see also Spyer, 2011). Since 2010, Bubz has been one of the most viewed and subscribed YouTubers in the world. She is the sixth most viewed beauty guru in terms of historical views, which total more than 350 million (Pixability, 2015). Additionally, she has almost 3 million subscribers. Worldwide, only 30 other how-to channels – mainly beauty channels – have achieved such a high number of followers (Socialblade, 2016). The longevity of her channel and her influential role, together with viewers' sustained interest in her content, is rendered even more relevant considering the highly dynamic, competitive and ever-changing environment of YouTube.

Bubz's more than 300 videos can be grouped into four categories, which I term 'content-oriented', 'market-oriented', 'relational' and 'motivational' (García-Rapp, 2017). Content-oriented uploads are tutorials in which she demonstrates make-up and hairstyling techniques. Market-oriented videos are essentially product reviews of one or a set of products. Relational uploads are 'vlogs' (video blogs) that display her daily activities and depict her everyday interactions at home in Hong Kong, sometimes involving her husband and dogs. These videos also feature self-reflections on life and her role on YouTube, viewing it as both a platform and a community. Her content is often highly emotional and intimate, since she also discloses her own life experiences. Through her motivational videos, she offers advice and thoughts on relationships and career and personal development. In these self-help guides, she usually sits in her living room and talks to the camera in a frontal perspective, addressing her audience directly.

I argue that her videos can be arranged on a scale of increasing intimacy, with her subjective views and opinions progressing to personal, emotional narratives. I locate her videos on what I term a 'scale of intimacy', and propose this case study analysis because it can aid in the understanding of the creation of affective bonds online (Baym, 2010; Lange, 2007, 2009, 2014). Bubz's content ranges in intimacy, and her viewers' responses imply reciprocal feelings of connection and engagement, in line with the intimacy of her content. In other words, intimacy develops in a bifold sense: parting from the video content and finding its counterpart in the viewers' comments.

Bubz's content-oriented video tutorials can be positioned at the beginning of the scale, due to their focus on rather objective and straightforward steps to achieving a certain make-up or hairstyling look. These videos are simply structured, with an introduction and ending showcasing Bubz posing with the finished look and a voice-over throughout, explaining the steps she demonstrates. A greater sense of connection develops with her product reviews (market-oriented videos), which involve more subjective opinions and her personal experiences with the cosmetics. In these videos, as well as in her vlogs, Bubz addresses her audience directly, looking into the camera. Online intimacy continues to build through her personal vlogs (relational uploads), through which she shares her daily life and discloses life stories, dreams and even problems. Intimacy reaches its highest point in what I describe as motivational videos, in which she talks and advises her viewers

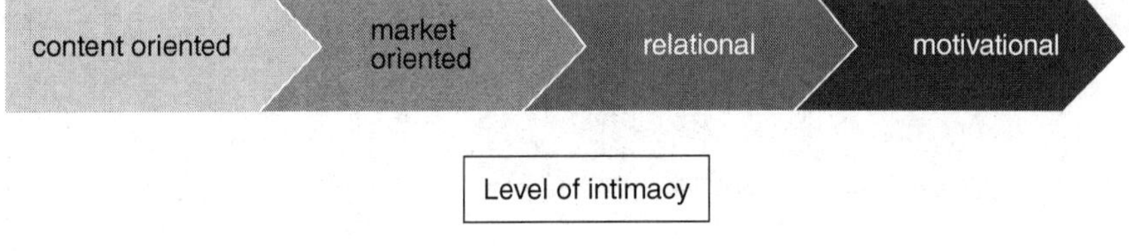

Figure 19.1 Scale of intimacy

with an implicit sense of trust and closeness, much as a friend would do. In this analysis, her content-oriented video tutorials and her motivational videos are on opposing sides of the scale, denoting the full range of intimacy and personal engagement.

Bubz's relational and motivational videos show the most explicit sense of intimacy, as evidenced by her personal disclosure and the feedback left in the comments. Her relational vlogs highlight subjective and personal topics, such as life stories, opinions and aspirations. Some of the titles of her vlogs are: 'A day in my life', 'Q&A with Bubz', 'Journey to Japan' and 'Meet my best friend'. In one of her vlogs, Bubz shares the experience of being bullied during high school in Northern Ireland because of her Chinese ethnicity. In some of the videos she cries and in others she laughs, and – according to the analysed comments – her viewers share these emotions and physical reactions with her.

This dynamic shows the extension of viewer engagement beyond beauty topics, which is a general thematic interest of the community. As Lange writes about YouTube vlogs: they 'give viewers the feeling of being connected not to a video, but to a person' (2009, p. 83). I suggest that, in this case, Bubz's viewers' feelings of closeness towards her are a prerequisite for their interest in watching and listening to her highly personal and subjective views on various life topics. Here, her know-how, centred on beauty and embodied by her tutorials, is relegated to the background by the increased relevance of her supportive and guiding role in broader life areas, including work and relationships. Bubz's vlogs motivate her viewers – through affective and communicative disclosure (Cohen, 2001) – to identify and engage with her and her content by commenting, sharing and discussing. As Abidin and Thompson argue, regarding fashion bloggers, the 'portrayal of their online persona is crafted through the narrative accounts of their everyday life' (2012, p. 472). These 'videos of affinity' (Lange, 2009, p. 73) can be seen as attempts at establishing closeness and a sense of familiarity (also Marshall, 2010).

Bubz can thus be seen as contributing to viewers' 'feeling of sharing a particular moment, large or small, or certain state of affairs in the creator's life' (Lange, 2009, p. 74). For instance, during the video 'Draw my life', she narrates the story of her life pre-YouTube. Some fragments are emotional – for example the fragment when she talks about her grandfather passing away:

> When I was 12 years old, my grandad was suddenly submitted into the hospital, he had gotten really sick and it really broke my heart because when I went to visit him, he couldn't even recognise who I was from all the medication. And he was only in the hospital for 2 weeks before he passed away. So, I didn't even get to say goodbye to my grandad and I miss him so much. I would go to his bedroom and crawl underneath his cover and just cry because I missed him so much and I would even get helium balloons and write messages on it and release it from his bedroom

> window. And I hoped that he would receive my message and just know how much I love and miss him.

To this 'private revelation for public consumption' (Marshall, 2014, p. xiii), viewers respond through comments that relate to her story and identify with her. This can be seen, for example, in the following comments:

> A tear went down my face about the grandpa part :/
>
> It is really sad about your granddad. but the balloon thing is kinda adorable
>
> Bubz on the hope you read this, you honestly made me cry. Because I can relate to you so much with your grandpa. It's so hard at the moment. Thanks for everything. Sam xx
>
> Omg the granddad part mad me cry T_T you inspire me! ^_^

During motivational videos – such as, for example, the video 'Finding happiness' – Bubz motivates her viewers to 'dream' and to 'try':

> If you try, it doesn't always mean you will win, but the only way that you could really lose is by not trying and I am willing to try. So if you have a dream, don't let it go! Hold it close to your heart and run with it! It's your dream and no one can really take it away from you. I believe that when you truly want something, you can actually achieve it. Whatever a mind can conceive, it can achieve but you have to make it happen and you have to believe.

In these videos, the topics do not pertain strictly to make-up or hairstyling; rather, they are oriented around themes such as friendship, career and relationships. Titles include 'Thinking about your future' and 'How to escape the friend zone'.

Additionally, and although they are located at opposing sides of the intimacy scale, the motivational videos are as pedagogical as her step-by-step tutorials (García-Rapp, 2017). The educational videos make more literal the traditional value incarnated by celebrities as 'pedagogical tools' (Marshall, 2010, p. 42) in their audience's lives. While the tutorials aim more literally at teaching make-up and hairstyling techniques, the vlogs focus on promoting self-help and positive messages as motivation for self-improvement – fitting today's 'therapeutical' society (Furedi, 2004, cited by Aslama and Pantti, 2006, p. 167). In her motivational videos, Bubz teaches and guides, much as she does in her tutorials, but rather than conveying a structured, step-by-step process, she advises her viewers through friendly, personal talk. She acts as a trusted friend and a guide/guru in the broader sense of the word, superseding her position as a 'mere' beauty expert. For example, during the video 'No pain, no gain', she says:

> Now a lot of people are miserable, and they complain about being unhappy, and they want to be happy. But then you would hear them just talking bad stuff about other people; they are always judging others and that's, like, no wonder you are miserable! And just, like, with weight loss, I think people should instead of focusing on 'Oh I can't do this and can't do that', I think what people should really focus on is just 'I'm going to lead a healthy lifestyle, I'm going to eat healthier, I'm going to be better for my body'. And, you know, when you do all of that, eventually your weight loss just follows behind.

Bubz's relational and motivational uploads create loyal subscribers, while her more content-oriented uploads receive more views (García-Rapp, 2017). According to her channel metrics, the proposed scale of intimacy matches the like, comment and share figures achieved by her content. Additionally, her relational and motivational videos generate the most subscriptions, implying not only interest but the intention of sustained engagement from viewers. This is why I argue that this type of video constitutes a major tool in building intimacy and creating a sense of connection with viewers. Viewers' comments advance from short, positive pieces of feedback such as 'great video, keep on doing this' that are posted in response to her tutorials, to self-disclosing life experiences in response to her vlog stories (García-Rapp, 2017). Furthermore, viewers thank her for helping them introduce changes into their lives and for contributing to them thinking differently about life and problems. We see, through the comments, how viewers express their appreciation to Bubz and underline their closeness:

> You are one of the biggest sweet hearts ever. You really make me feel better about things to come and I feel like even though you have no idea who I am, that we are close. Thank you so much. (:

Many viewers consider Bubz a positive influence in their lives – a 'role model' – and express admiration towards her. In line with the notion that 'celebrity taught generations how to engage and use consumer culture to "make" oneself' (Marshall, 2010, p. 36), Bubz's role in the lives of her fans is coupled with a sense of identification that fosters 'identity work' (also Marwick, 2013). This will be further explained in the following section:

> Maybe you will or will not read this, but you are our IDOL. I have watched all videos ...
>
> Good Job Bubz! You are amazing! I watch ur videos everyday and you inspire me in EVERY video. U a seriously our favorite youtuber in the ENTIRE universe! I wish I was u. Ur our role model.
>
> I have lots of photos hanging in my room and one of them is a picture of you. :) When someone asks me 'who is that?' I tell them 'she is my role model' :3 Love you bubz!! never stop making videos!

The proposed scale of intimacy should not be seen as a linear development, since viewers may choose to focus on one or other type of video and not engage with the others. However, in line with the scale, the content grows in subjectivity, emotionality and, as a result, intimacy. I argue that this development pre-defines certain viewers' affinity, growing from contextual (i.e. beauty-related) to a focus on Bubz as a person. While market-oriented and content-oriented tutorials focus on beauty, the other two categories of videos focus on Bubz and her advice (García-Rapp, 2017); this is why her role as a trusted friend and advisor is rendered more relevant through these videos. As Lange argues about vlogs: 'they typically interest delineated groups of people who wish to participate and remain connected social in some way' (2009, p. 73).

Thanks to Bubz I am 'a better version' of myself

In the previous section I explained how the development of topics in Bubz's videos progresses from content-based videos to guru-centred uploads that are increasingly subjective and personal. Through advice (e.g. motivational) videos, Bubz motivates her viewers to change aspects of their lives and improve themselves. These videos serve as self-development guidelines for 'being happier' and 'growing as a person'. As Lange writes, based on her ethnographic examination of online vlogging practices in 2007: '[bloggers] use intimacy to create reactions in viewers that encourage reconsideration of the blogger's own and viewers' ideas' (p. 1).

It is worth noting that I understand media, and particularly audience research, from the perspective of people actively using media to satisfy specific needs (Blumler and Katz, 1974; Rosengren, 1985; Ruggiero, 2000). This is why I leave aside perspectives focusing on 'audience manipulation', wherein the agency and understanding of viewers is not recognised or is overly simplified, automatically assuming symbolic inequalities and positioning the audience as 'disempowered fans [...] as a flattened mass or sameness of consumers' (Hills, 2006, p. 116). Instead, I draw from the research of scholars who acknowledge viewers' active and differing roles in processes of (new) media reception and consumption (e.g. Burgess and Green, 2009; Lange, 2009, 2014; Meyers, 2009; Smith, 2014; Strangelove, 2010). It is fruitful to consider how viewers use the content that this beauty guru makes available.

In line with this, we can see (through comments) how viewers follow Bubz's advice and actively adapt and 'update' their identities with the aim of being 'transformed to "better" versions of themselves' (Marwick, 2013, p. 356). In particular, Bubz's motivational videos play an important role in guiding and 'inspiring' her viewers to act (García-Rapp, 2017). The following comments help illustrate these points:

> i luv ya bubz! ur life may not be perfect but u definitely have made my life a step closer to where i want it to be

> This is amazing! Thanks Bubz for being such as inspiration and pushing us to leave our comfort zone and do new things …
>
> Bubz, you are amazing. Your videos are an inspiration to me and many others to go and live life beautifully.

People receive, through media and consumer goods – including celebrities and renowned personalities – 'exemplary models' (Marshall, 2014, p. 187) or, in the words of Thompson, 'mediated symbolic materials' (1995, p. 207) to choose from to actively construct an identity. According to the analysed comments, Bubz's videos aid viewers in building and transforming their 'narrative[s] of self-identity' (Thompson, 1995, p. 210). Marwick notes how identities are constructed 'through a bricolage of consumer goods, media, fashion, and styles' (2013, p. 358), facilitated by media and technology. This is reflected in 'the necessity of lining one's own identities into some sort of pattern, from Twitter to Facebook, from YouTube and Flickr to Myspace, from blogs to Digg' (Marshall, 2010, p. 42).

Drawing on the work of sociologists such as Giddens (1991) and Thompson (1995), parallels can be traced between viewers' comments and the notion of active engagement with one's identity as an ongoing 'project' (see also Cohen, 2001; Hills, 2002). Viewers let themselves be guided by Bubz and imitate not only her make-up and hairstyle, but also her general attitude towards life. As a viewer puts it in the following comment, Bubz seems to offer 'much more than just make-up', since 'it isn't just for looks':

> You always seem so happy and bubbly (even if you really aren't) and you have encouraged me to do the same and build my own life how I want it. Your beauty channel isn't just for looks, it's for personality too. Thank you for doing what you're doing. Never stop.

In her motivational videos, Bubz advises her viewers to be thankful for what they are given, but without forgetting their own achievements. She reminds her fans that the key to happiness rests in themselves and their way of seeing life. She moves her audience to appreciate the little things in life and to be patient and understanding with others, but also with themselves.

> You have great beauty videos also great advice videos! PLEASE uploads many more. You've made me more of a happy person! Happiness is so contagious!!
>
> I just want to say, watching your videos brightens my day and makes me smile. You are so beautiful inside and out!

To conclude this section, I would like to build on Redmond's observation of two types of intimacy (2014). I argue that Bubz's viewers experience a *private* intimacy between the guru and themselves when watching her videos, but enact a '*public* intimacy' (2014, p. 111, italics mine) when commenting, praising and thanking her for her disclosure, her trust and the role she plays in their lives. Viewers feel her joy, sadness, highs and lows; they share her stories, hopes and thoughts and reciprocate by sharing the same. Redmond's parallel between public and private intimacy is similar to Thompson's conceptualisation of 'lived experience' (unmediated) and 'mediated experience' (1995, p. 230). People draw components from both sources to creatively and reflexively integrate into their 'evolving life-project[s]' (p. 230). From the feelings of connection and identification arise not abstract, but very concrete uses and benefits for viewers.

Conclusions: Public, private and productive intimacy at play

With this study, I sought to contribute to the understanding of current digital culture practices through an examination of the dynamics of the YouTube beauty community. Drawing from findings of my ethnographic examination of the platform, I analysed and interpreted the data corpus of videos and comments in light of what I term a 'scale of intimacy'. Aided by the content typology of four categories (García-Rapp, 2017), I emphasised the relevance of Bubz's connection-seeking uploads for community building. Findings suggest that Bubz's development of closeness and intimacy with her audience can be seen as a progression that begins with tutorials (content-oriented videos), which usually catch the attention of random viewers through title keywords. Product reviews, in which Bubz addresses her audience in a more direct way and offers her opinion on products (market-oriented videos), are slightly more intimate. Intimacy then advances to her personal vlogs (relational videos), which generate stronger connections and maintain audience attention by showcasing her private life and activities. The highest degree of intimacy is found in Bubz's motivational uploads.

Considering the high number of shares, subscriptions and comments received by these two latter categories of videos, it is relevant to note how 'people may find a video personally meaningful in ways that merit attention despite its seeming lack of normatively valued "content"' (Lange, 2009, p. 70). I argued that Bubz's relational and motivational videos foreground her efforts to achieve a close connection with her audience, not least in order to sustain her popularity as a renowned beauty guru (also García-Rapp, 2017). Moreover, I suggested that the ties with viewers must be strong enough, a priori, for them to be interested in her experiences and highly subjective opinions about life and self-growth. In other words, viewing and commenting imply an interest in the person behind the channel – the guru, herself. Bubz turns from a stranger to a skilled guru who teaches useful beauty techniques, to a friend who shares her daily life and stories. At the same time, viewers turn from random viewers to loyal subscribers and fans (2016b).

All things considered, I believe it can be fruitful to not always see performers through 'the lenses of commodification', but to also recognise them as 'social and creative beings' (Baym, 2010, p. 294) who are not always 'selling us intimacy' (e.g. Littler, 2004, p. 4) or persuading us, but (and maybe even simultaneously) experiencing connections themselves and receiving personal rewards from the affective intimacies that are established. Rewards can be in the form of emotional support and feedback (Baym, 2010; Abidin, 2015), as Bubz herself discusses. Thanks to this approach, we can see how 'intimacy is not just something fans project onto artists, it can be something artists experience when they interact with their audiences' (2012, p. 312). Therefore, I locate viewers 'somewhere between unequal "fans" and equal "friends"' (p. 289), since celebrity/fan forms of connection are not only platform-based or community dependent, but often negotiated and experienced on an individual basis.

In conclusion, it is relevant to revisit Redmond's distinction between public, private (2014, p. 111) and 'productive intimacy' (2006, p. 35). In the case of Bubz and her viewers, three main practices are at play. As explained above, a *private* intimacy is represented by an individual viewer's experience of watching and eventually feeling connected to the content creator. Further, *public* intimacy is visible through viewers' engagement with the guru. Bubz's content fosters identification and promotes viewer engagement in the form of viewing, liking, subscribing, sharing links of her videos and leaving written comments on her channel. Lastly, a *productive* intimacy emerges from the feelings of closeness and identification, fuelling self-reflexivity and often even self-development. Besides being useful in pragmatic terms (by, e.g., helping viewers achieve a particular hairstyle), Bubz's relational and motivational videos are helpful as tools for motivating personal change and positive habits.

I argued that Bubz provides viewers with information-rich tutorials; personal, humorous and entertaining vlogs; and motivational self-help videos (García-Rapp, 2017) that her audience enjoy, discuss, criticise, reflect on in relation to their own lives and emulate, modify and find inspiration in. This is up to them. Moreover, viewers' reception practices are not meaningful because they are 'active' and 'productive' in this way, or because the videos are supposed to be empowering. Rather, the practices are meaningful because they reflect what viewers choose to do with their time at that moment. Some viewers claim that Bubz's content is helpful and useful in both practical and deep, personal ways. But I argue that other viewers may (also) 'just consume' the content as a 'mere' pastime to forget daily issues and overcome stress. This should not necessarily be understood as disempowering, nor should it reflect the often cynical academic view of the 'bad' side of fandom: 'the fan as consumer', as Hills aptly argues (2002, p. 30).

Acknowledgements

I am indebted to Alice Marwick for her valuable feedback on earlier versions of this chapter.

References

Abidin, C. (2015). Communicative intimacies: Influencers and perceived interconnectedness. *Ada: A Journal of Gender, New Media, and Technology*, 8.

Abidin, C. and Thompson, E. (2012). Buymylife.com: Cyber-femininities and commercial intimacy in blogshops. *Women's Studies International Forum*, 35(6), pp. 467–477.

Ardévol, E. and Gómez-Cruz, E. (2013). Digital ethnography and media practices. In: *The International Encyclopedia of Media Studies*, pp. 498–518.

Aslama, M. and Pantti, M. (2006). Talking alone: Reality TV, emotions and authenticity. *European Journal of Cultural Studies*, 9(2), pp. 167–184.

Banet-Weiser, S. (2012). *Authentic TM*. New York: New York University Press.

Baym, N. (2010). *Personal Connections in the Digital Age*. Cambridge: Polity.

Blumler, J. and Katz, E. (1974). *The Uses of Mass Communications*. Beverly Hills, CA: SAGE.

Boellstorff, T. (2008). *Coming of Age in Second Life*. Princeton, NJ: Princeton University Press.

Burgess, J.E. and Green, J.B. (2009). *YouTube*. Cambridge: Polity.

Cohen, J. (2001). Defining identification: A theoretical look at the identification of audiences with media characters. *Mass Communication and Society*, 4(3), pp. 245–264.

Creswell, J.W. (2013). *Qualitative Inquiry & Research Design: Choosing Among Five Approaches* (3rd ed.). Los Angeles, CA: SAGE.

Dyer, R. (1998). *Stars*. London: British Film Institute.

García-Rapp, F. (2016). The digital media phenomenon of YouTube beauty gurus: The case of Bubzbeauty. *International Journal of Web-Based Communities*, 12(4), pp. 360–375. DOI: 10.1504/IJWBC.2016.080810

García-Rapp, F. (2017). Popularity markers on YouTube's attention economy: The Case of Bubzbeauty, *Celebrity Studies*. 8 (2) pp. 228–245. DOI: 10.1080/19392397.2016.1242430

García-Rapp, F. (forthcoming, 2018) 'Come join and let's BOND': Authenticity and Legitimacy Building on YouTube's Beauty community, *Journal of Media Practice*.

García-Rapp, F. and Roca-Cuberes, C. (2017) 'Being an online celebrity – Norms and expectations of YouTube's beauty community', *First Monday*, 22 (7), July Issue 2017. http://dx.doi.org/10.5210/fm.v22i17.7788

Garfinkel, H. (1967). *Studies in Ethnomethodology*. Englewood Cliffs, NJ: Prentice-Hall.

Giddens, A. (1991). *Modernity and Self-Identity*. Stanford, CA: Stanford University Press.

Goffman, E. (1959). *The Presentation of Self in Everyday Life*. New York: Anchor Book.

Hartley, J., Burgess, J. and Bruns, A. (eds.) (2013). *A Companion to New Media Dynamics*. Oxford: Wiley-Blackwell.

Hills, M. (2002). *Fan Cultures*. London: Routledge.

Hills M. (2006). Not just another powerless elite?: When media fans become subcultural celebrities. In: S. Holmes and S. Redmond, eds., *Framing Celebrity*. London: Routledge, pp. 101–118.

Holmes, S. (2004). 'All you've got to worry about is the task, having a cup of tea, and what you're going to eat for dinner': Approaching celebrity in *Big Brother*.

In: S. Holmes and D. Jermyn, *Understanding Reality Television*. London: Routledge.

Holmes, S. and Jermyn, D. (2004). *Understanding Reality Television*. London: Routledge.

Holmes, S. and Redmond, S. (2006). *Framing Celebrity*. London: Routledge.

Kanai, A. (2015). Jennifer Lawrence, remixed: Approaching celebrity through DIY culture. *Celebrity Studies*, 6(3), pp. 322–340.

Kozinets, R. (2010). *Netnography*. Los Angeles, CA: SAGE.

Lange, P. (2007). The vulnerable video blogger: Promoting social change through intimacy. *The Scholar and Feminist Online*, 5(2).

Lange, P. (2009). Videos of affinity on YouTube. In: P. Snickars and P. Vonderau, eds., *The YouTube Reader*. Stockholm: National Library of Sweden, pp. 70–88.

Lange, P. (2014). *Kids on YouTube. Technical Identities and Digital Literacies*. Walnut Creek, CA: Left Coast Press.

Littler, J. (2004). Making fame ordinary: Intimacy, reflexivity, and 'keeping it real'. *Mediactive: Ideas/Knowledge/Culture*, 2, pp. 8–25.

Marshall, P.D. (2010). The promotion and presentation of the self: Celebrity as marker of presentational media. *Celebrity Studies*, 1(1), pp. 35–48.

Marshall, P.D. (2014). *Celebrity and Power. Fame in Contemporary Culture*. Minneapolis, MN: University of Minnesota Press.

Marwick, A.E. (2013). Online identity. In: J. Hartley, J. Burgess and A. Bruns, eds., *A Companion to New Media Dynamics*. Oxford: Wiley-Blackwell, pp. 355–364.

Marwick, A. and boyd, d. (2011). To see and be seen: Celebrity practice on Twitter. *Convergence: The International Journal of Research into New Media Technologies*, 17(2), pp. 139–158.

Merriam, S.B. (2009). *Qualitative Research*. San Francisco, CA: Jossey-Bass.

Meyers, E. (2009). 'Can you handle my truth?': Authenticity and the celebrity star image. *The Journal of Popular Culture*, 45(5), pp. 890–905.

Pixability (2015). *Report Beauty on YouTube*. Pixability.

Redmond, S. (2006). Intimate fame everywhere. In: S. Holmes and S. Redmond, eds., *Framing Celebrity*. London: Routledge, pp. 27–43.

Redmond, S. (2014). *Celebrity and the Media*. Basingstoke: Palgrave Macmillan.

Rosengren, K. (1985). *Media Gratifications Research*. Beverly Hills, CA: SAGE.

Ruggiero, T.E. (2000). Uses and gratifications theory in the 21st century. *Mass Communication & Society*, 3(1), pp. 3–37.

Saldaña, J. (2013). *The Coding Manual for Qualitative Researchers*. Los Angeles, CA: SAGE.

Senft, T.M. (2013). Microcelebrity and the branded self. In: J. Hartley, J. Burgess and A. Bruns, eds., *A Companion to New Media Dynamics*. Oxford: Wiley-Blackwell, pp. 346–354.

Smith, Daniel. 2014. Charlie is so 'English-like': nationality and the branded celebrity in the age of YouTube. *Celebrity Studies* 5(3): 256--274.

Snickars, P. and Vonderau, P. (eds.) (2009). *The YouTube Reader*. Stockholm: National Library of Sweden.

Socialblade (2016). Top 500 YouTubers How-to channels. Retrieved from http://socialblade.com/youtube/top/category/howto/mostsubscribed.

Spyer, J. (2011). *Making up Art, Videos and Fame. The Creation of Social Order in the Informal Realm of YouTube Beauty Gurus*. MSc thesis. University College London, University of London.

Strangelove, M. (2010). *Watching YouTube: Extraordinary Videos by Ordinary People*. Toronto: University of Toronto Press.

Thompson, J. (1995). *The Media and Modernity*. Cambridge: Polity Press.

Tolson, A. (2010). A new authenticity? Communicative Practices on YouTube. *Critical Discourse Studies*, 7(4), pp. 277–289.

Usher, B. (2015). Twitter and the celebrity interview. *Celebrity Studies*, 6(3), pp. 322–340.

Wolcott, H.F. (1995). *The Art of Fieldwork*. Walnut Creek, CA: AltaMira Press.

Wolcott, H.F. (2010). *Ethnography Lessons: A Prime*. Walnut Creek, CA: Left Coast Press.

Index

Locators in *italic* refer to figures
Notes are denoted by suffix n followed by note number